D0078164

ACTIVIST UNIONISM

STUDIES IN INSTITUTIONAL ECONOMICS

GARDINER C. MEANS
INSTITUTIONALIST AND POST KEYNESIAN
Warren J. Samuels and Steven G. Medema

THE HETERODOX ECONOMICS OF GARDINER C. MEANS
A COLLECTION
Frederic S. Lee and Warren J. Samuels, editors

UNDERGROUND ECONOMICS
A DECADE OF INSTITUTIONALIST DISSENT
William M. Dugger

THE STRATIFIED STATE
RADICAL INSTITUTIONALIST THEORIES OF
PARTICIPATION AND DUALITY
William M. Dugger and William T. Waller, Jr., editors

A VEBLEN TREASURY
FROM LEISURE CLASS TO WAR,
PEACE, AND CAPITALISM
Rick Tilman, editor

ACTIVIST UNIONISM
THE INSTITUTIONAL ECONOMICS OF SOLOMON BARKIN
Donald R. Stabile

ACTIVIST UNIONISM

The Institutional Economics of Solomon Barkin

Donald R. Stabile

M.E. Sharpe
Armonk, New York
London, England

Library of Congress Cataloging-in-Publication Data

Stabile, Donald
Activist unionism: the institutional economics of Solomon Barkin
Donald R. Stabile
p. cm.—(Institutional economics)
Includes bibliographical references and index.
ISBN 1–56324–292–3 (cloth).—ISBN 1–56324–293–1 (pbk.)
1. Industrial relations—United States—History—20th century.
2. Trade unions—United States—History—20th century.
3. Working class—United States—History—20th century.
4. Barkin, Solomon, 1907– .
I. Title.
II. Series: Studies in institutional economics.
HD8072.5.S73 1993
331.88′177′0092—dc20
[B]
93–23795
CIP

Printed in the United States of America

The paper used in this publication meets the minimum requirements of
American National Standard for Information Sciences—
Permanence of Paper for Printed Library Materials,
ANSI Z 39.48–1984

BM (c) 10 9 8 7 6 5 4 3 2 1
BM (p) 10 9 8 7 6 5 4 3 2 1

Contents

Foreword

I. Sol Barkin's Several Lives

Sol Barkin has been and is many things, as this broadly oriented intellectual history by Donald R. Stabile describes.

Sol has been a multiple-marginal man in the sense that he has been on the margins between and among workers and trade union leaders, unions and management, segments of the private economy and the government, and men of action and intellectuals. He has thus been in a position to learn and understand a great deal about many aspects of American society in the twentieth century. Few have ever been in a similar, advantaged position to see so much and to think about it so actively. Many observers have only a one-dimensional view on their attachment to their personal experiences and interests; some add an additional perspective from their point of view also as citizens; few, however, have had the multidimensional vantage point of Sol Barkin, which gives him a third, fourth, and fifth focus on the multiplicity of reality, as the chapters that follow so well show.

Sol also has been, however, and contrary as it may seem, a highly centered person, even in the midst of so many pulls and pushes. He has always known who he is and what he thinks, with little change during more than sixty years of active professional life. He is centered on the welfare of the working man, whether Sol is identified as a New Dealer or a Social Democrat or a Social Unionist, and on the ways the working man is best served by a pluralistic industrialism that keeps strong unions, strong enterprises, and strong government working together. Thus, as a trade union representative, for example, he has always supported high productivity in industry as the basis for higher wages for the workers. He is also centered on the pragmatic—what works best in practice.

Sol is a person with many skills: a protagonist at the bargaining table, a lobbyist in the corridors of power, a policymaker in the offices of influence, an ambassador to the intellectuals, and an analyst in the learned journals and the conferences of experts—always with his own point of view, boldly stated, and with well-assembled facts and logical arguments.

Sol has also been one of the great innovators in the field of industrial relations. He pioneered in the introduction of industrial engineering and cost analysis. He also developed the most advanced analytical approach to collective bargaining—start out by defining the problems and breaking them into their separate component parts, then devising alternative solutions, and then analyzing the costs and benefits of each—thus demonstrating logic in an area often devoted to passion. He advanced the strategic versus the usual tactical role of the intellectual who advises the responsible decision maker by drawing attention to potential changes in long-run policies and not alone providing factual information to support existing positions. He always knew and respected the difference between giving good advice and taking responsibility for decisions, and he sought to educate decision makers over the longer run and not merely advise them in emergencies—so also union members. He thought about what he was doing, and new ways of doing emerged.

Sol is also one of the last of an endangered species—the professional economic expert in an advancing labor movement. The labor movement is no longer advancing, and lawyers are taking over from economists, partly as economists become more narrowly trained technicians. I have known Sol to represent the Textile Workers Union of America, serve on government advisory bodies, originate public policy in the Organization for Economic Cooperation and Development, lead the Industrial Relations Research Association, and teach in an American university. Who is there taking his place now?

I once wrote (as quoted in the author's introduction) that Sol Barkin "belonged to two worlds." I should have written that he has "led several lives" and that few have led and still fewer will lead so many lives and in the particular combination he put together. We are what we do, and Sol Barkin has played many roles and played them all well.

Clark Kerr
Berkeley, California
September 1991

II. Sol Barkin—The Unionist

Sol Barkin was never an elected official in the trade union movement, but for twenty-six years, from 1937 until he retired in 1963, he played a unique role in the Textile Workers Union of America. He was invited by Sidney Hillman to become research director of the Textile Workers Organizing Committee (TWOC) following their close association in the National Industrial Recovery

Administration. When I first met Barkin in 1937, he was at the seat of leadership of the TWOC in New York, functioning both as research director and as assistant to Sidney Hillman, chairman of the TWOC.

In the spring of 1937, before the CIO textile workers' organizing drive was launched, I was assigned to be an organizer in West Warwick, Rhode Island, by the Federation of Dyers, Finishers and Bleachers, a division of the United Textile Workers Union, AFL. I sent a request to Sidney Hillman, asking to be transferred to the New Jersey region. That request was handled by Sol Barkin, acting as Hillman's assistant. I still have in my possession Barkin's letter to me of June 14, 1937, acceding to my request for a transfer to New Jersey. The request was approved on condition "that your devotion and unquestioned loyalty to the T.W.O.C. will remain unsullied." I am pleased to say that over the intervening half-century, this condition has not been violated.

In his twenty-six years with the Textile Workers Union, Sol left a marked imprint on textile workers and many others inside and outside the labor movement by way of his deep identification with unionism, his great knowledge as an economist, and his skills as an industrial engineer.

In May 1939, at the First Constitutional Convention in Philadelphia, the TWOC and the United Textile Workers of America (UTWA) were merged to form the Textile Workers Union of America (TWUA), and Emil Rieve was elected president. He had served as president of the American Federation of Hosiery Workers, a division of the UTWA. He brought with him the philosophy and techniques of the hosiery workers, who predicated their operations on a belief in arbitration, research, engineering, education, and public relations. In such an atmosphere, Sol Barkin's talents were utilized by Emil Rieve.

Between 1937 and 1947, TWUA membership grew rapidly from less than 100,000 to 375,000, representing one third of the work force in that industry. With the enactment of the Taft-Hartley Act, characterized by John L. Lewis as a slave labor act, a steady decline began. In time it also affected the general trade union movement, which shrank in coverage from 33 to 17 percent. Unionism was particularly fiercely resisted by Southern textile employers. In the Northern areas, mill closings and the shrinkage of employment were abetted by tax loopholes, mergers, and technological changes. The result was a drastic reduction of employment in the industry, dropping from 1,250,000 to 750,000, and with it, union membership also declined.

During that period, mill managements pressed strongly on applying current engineering techniques to reduce labor costs but bringing in their train a rising volume of workers' grievances and widespread unrest. Barkin and his Research and Engineering Department played a major role in restraining abuse and working out rational settlements to ensure maximum protection and benefits to the membership. When it was necessary, the department assisted in negotiations on the technical sections of agreements and handled arbitration cases on those issues. To advance the capabilities of the local leadership and membership to deal with these issues, training seminars were organized using the manuals developed by the department.

During the war period of intense government regulation, Barkin and his staff were particularly helpful in guiding local officials and their membership in the handling of the wide variety of petitions to and arguments before official labor agencies in order to secure approval for agreements negotiated by those locals.

Barkin was a prolific writer, a keen analyst and observer of economic trends. In the union's planning of the organization of targets, his research and analysis were highly respected by all the union's strata. His research and writings played a major role in unfolding to the membership, the public, and the government bodies the needy, repressed, and subservient character of Southern textile workers and the active employers' conspiracy to resist and combat unionism and workers' civil liberties and rights. His efforts and writings also gained the respect of employers in the industry for his knowledge, competence, honesty, and integrity. He was consulted by the CIO and, later, the AFL-CIO research departments for his contributions on economic issues. He promoted studies by nonprofit and government bodies of both the New England and Southern regions to advance their economic development and an understanding of their social issues.

President Rieve permitted the TWUA department heads a wide latitude so that Barkin was often considered a union spokesman reflecting the union's progressive policies in fields ranging from international trade, tariff, minimum wage, area redevelopment, industrial engineering, and insurance.

Thirty years ago, Sol Barkin wrote a seventy-four-page report for the Center for the Study of Democratic Institutions of Santa Barbara, California, titled *The Decline of the Labor Movement and What Can Be Done About It.* I recently reread the report and found it to be currently relevant. It is still a provocative, useful guide for analysis and debate at all levels of the union movement. Ahead of his time in 1961, Barkin's presentation remains a present challenge.

Sol Stetin
Past President,
Textile Workers Union of America;
Executive Vice President Emeritus,
Amalgamated Clothing and Textile Workers Union;
and President of the American Labor Museum, Haledon, New Jersey

Preface and Acknowledgments

This project began in a conversation with the late Allan Gruchy about the desirability of a series of articles, perhaps in book form, concerning the work of unsung contributors to the theory and practice of institutional economics. I concluded that historians of that school (including Gruchy and myself) had given excessive attention only to its giants—Thorstein Veblen, John R. Commons, and John K. Galbraith, for example—creating the impression that the school was very small in size and production. Gruchy agreed and encouraged me to follow up on the plan, suggesting several names as potential candidates. Solomon Barkin's name was among them.

On a subsequent trip to Amherst, Massachusetts, I found further encouragement from former mentors in the Economics Department of the University of Massachusetts. Of greater importance, Bruce Laurie, labor historian at the university, related to me that Barkin was interested in having his story told and that it was indeed one worth telling. After conversations with Barkin and a glimpse at his collected papers, it became apparent that his story would require more than a single article or chapter in a book. Thus the volume you hold in your hands.

The effort had a great deal of help and collaboration. At the University of Massachusetts, Bruce Laurie read several drafts and made many helpful suggestions, paying through hard work for his part in initiating the project. He also arranged for two of his former students, William Hartford and Elizabeth Fones-Wolf, to share with me their research on labor and the textile industry in New England. Hartford's manuscript on the deindustrialization of the New England textile industry provided additional information about Barkin from outside Barkin's papers; Hartford also read several drafts with great insight and offered numerous helpful hints. The staff in the archives at the university library were very kind in their efforts to assist me in copying the papers necessary for the work.

At St. Mary's College, James Nickel, as acting provost, arranged for a timely course release. Professor Andrew Kozak read a draft and made many enthusiastic and useful comments. Maura Keenan and Cory McCarthy, two exceptional students, prepared the bibliography, including an arduous collation of all of Barkin's writings.

Elsewhere, Franklin Gerry Bishop's kind incentive plan pulled me through a waning period of work, and his recollections filled in gaps. More than anyone else, obviously, Barkin strengthened the work. He read every draft, pointed out errors in fact, theory, and interpretation, directed me to additional material from his own work and that of others, challenged many of my ideas and misconceptions about unions, and corrected my grammar—doing so with extraordinary grace and tactfulness. We often disagreed, and I always had the last word as author, but we never argued. The extent of my gratitude will be found in the pages herein.

Additional appreciation is owed to my father, Jerome Stabile, who housed and fed me while I was on sabbatical during the early stages of the work.

Elaine Barkin inspired confidence in the project and furnished many tasty meals during my long meetings with her husband.

One of the lessons to be learned from a study of work and unions is that all labor is cooperative, meaning that efforts to identify and reward individual merit are ultimately futile. Nevertheless, as is always the case with intellectual output, responsibility for the final product is mine, even though that tradition violates many of the principles presented in the following pages.

St. Mary's City, Maryland
June 1992

ACTIVIST UNIONISM

The Institutional Economics of Solomon Barkin

Introduction

Intellectuals have not fared well in the house of labor. At best they have been invited guests or hired servants, but seldom have they been members of the family and worthy of trust. One reason for such strained relations is that when they serve the union it is as an appointed rather than an elected official. More important, however, is the age-old conflict between thinkers and doers. An intellectual's stock-in-trade is the ability to think clearly, creatively, and broadly about problems and to define alternative proposals indicating the advantages and disadvantages of them from the union point of view, whereas the union leader's calling is doing something about those problems. Rarely are the two traits found in one person. The subject of this book, Solomon (Sol) Barkin, is such a rare case, because for more than twenty-five years he worked in the labor movement as both a thinker and a doer.

Few intellectuals have had as many opportunities to translate their ideas into real-world applications as has Solomon Barkin. In a career spanning sixty years, he served as a consultant and writer of commission reports for state government on issues concerning old age assistance and older workers, as an analyst and administrator in the National Recovery Administration of the New Deal, as chief research officer of the Textile Workers Union of America (TWUA), and as secretary of research on manpower and social affairs in the Organization for Economic Cooperation and Development before finishing his career as professor of economics at the University of Massachusetts at Amherst. Although his experiences are diverse, they are bound together by Barkin's interest both in understanding and assisting the masses or working persons who constitute the main factor of production in our economy and in thinking about the "labor problem" and doing something about it. Clark Kerr once described Barkin as follows: "He has belonged to two worlds: the world of the trade union movement as an analyst and advocate for an important national union; and the world of the American intellectual as speaker and author interpreting American social currents."[1]

The emphasis of this book is on Barkin's ideas relating to labor unions and their development during his years of working in the union movement, with some attention given to his work in larger arenas after leaving the union movement; the area in which he did most of his work and on which this book concentrates is economic policy. During his years with the TWUA as well as in his later career, Barkin was both an activist and an academic. He functioned in all the phases of operation of the union. He took part in organizing drives and contract negotiations that handled major technical grievances, and he devised plans for improving technical operations in unionized mills. He was an arbitrator and representative of the union before federal and state legislative and executive branches and acted as spokesman for the union before groups of employers and public groups such as college students and the media. He served as an adjunct professor at Columbia University, participating in its graduate labor seminar, and at the New School for Social Research. He has published numerous articles in academic and other journals; in 1972, the *Journal of Political Economy* selected him for its award called Lifetime Achievement in Economics—Special Subfield of Labor Economics.[2]

In many writings, Barkin described what he had learned from his experiences, but those writings were specifically related to the problem he was currently facing. It is the purpose of this book to weave that written work into a coherent whole. The overall theme of the book can be simply stated: Barkin claims that work carries with it social costs that are not taken into account by market-determined wages, and the best way to ensure that those social costs of work are covered is to have a system of labor-management cooperation backed by strong union representation and sanctioned by government assistance when necessary. This view places Barkin clearly in the camp of those who used to be called proponents of industrial democracy, but who are now designated as proponents of social democracy.

Barkin's life and work have significance for three main reasons. The first relates to his position as TWUA chief of research, a union post that has been neglected in labor studies. Although there have been other pioneering researchers connected with unions, for example, Jett Lauck with the United Mine Workers and Leo Wolman with the Amalgamated Clothing Workers, their stories have not been told. Nor were their research efforts as vast and prolific as Barkin's. At the time Barkin started to work for the TWUA, the union research job was not clearly developed. Through his efforts to come to grips with the many problems facing industrial unions, Barkin delineated the tasks of the union researcher and was a trailblazer in the field of union studies. As part of his effort, he always sought to establish union research as an intellectual discipline and wanted university-run labor research centers to be organized as teaching and research establishments that would be comparable to collegiate schools of business. The ideas expressed in this book detail the type of course work and research that would be undertaken at such a labor research center.

Second, as will be described more fully later, Barkin was greatly influenced by the institutional school of economic thought. Although members of that school professed interest in the study of institutions, they usually did so from the outside. Barkin's work exemplified active application of the institutional approach to problems of the world by someone who faced them directly. As did other members of the school, Barkin too saw the economy as an ongoing process in constant need of adjustment. In the 1930s, leading members of the school, especially Rexford Tugwell, conceived of the New Deal as a means of establishing an adjustment mechanism for the economy. Barkin was part of that perception. When the New Deal ended, institutionalism declined as a school as the followers of Keynes replaced institutionalism's leaders in government and academic circles. Because he had worked in a union, Barkin retained a position that gave him the independence to develop his ideas further. Those ideas serve as an indicator of what the economy might have been like had the New Deal continued.

Third, among institutionalists, Barkin recognized that unions could also provide a way of attaining balance in the economy. He formed many of his ideas during an era when unions were central to American life and had made a deep impression on intellectuals. During the Cold War period of Red-baiting, amid probes of union racketeering, many intellectuals abandoned unions and their ideals, but Barkin remained committed to unions as a vehicle for social adjustment, continuing to propose policies that would promote the union perspective. He wanted unions to be as active as he was in seeking to aid workers; his policies sought an activist unionism in contrast with the pure and simple unionism or business unionism often found in the United States. Although these policies reflect Barkin's personal convictions and are broad in scope, they provide insight into the direction to which the U.S. economy might have evolved had unions not declined in strength, especially in the area of industrial government.

As will become obvious, this study is sympathetic toward Barkin and his ideas. I make no apologies for this sympathy, but perhaps an explanation will establish my own slant on economics and form the basis for that sympathy. My first full-fledged contact with Barkin occurred when I signed up for a course in institutional economics that he offered during my graduate school career. I had had a long-standing interest in institutional economics and was writing a doctoral dissertation dealing with the ideas of Thorstein Veblen, one of the founders of that school. I was leery of Barkin, however, for he had a reputation of being tough to work with, demanding, and combative—in short, he was considered by faculty and graduate students to be a really difficult person. In my casual contacts with him, I found him to discursive in thought and conversation.

The course went well and we maintained a lasting working relationship after. Barkin can indeed be difficult to work with because of his mission to push the union point of view and his aversion to high levels of abstract theorizing. He does not suffer gladly those who attack unions, especially on predominantly theoretical grounds, and his obstinacy and pride come from his sense of the importance of his mission. Disavowal of high theory is an attitude we share. We did not share a common perspective on unions, however. My understanding of unions was mainly theoretical and derived from a Marxian analysis, supplemented by small personal practice. My membership in a union—the New York Newspaper Guild, AFL-CIO—had not been an impressive experience. Still, I had some feeling of support for unions without really knowing why.

Work on this book, which required my reading much that Barkin and others had written in support of unions, helped me to appreciate what unions do for their members. I am sympathetic toward Barkin's ideas because I have learned much from writing about them and discussing them with him; any study of a thinker must be sympathetic if it aims at illumination. For those who have the patience to stay with him, he is an excellent though demanding teacher, which leads to another explanation for the sympathetic tone of the book. In many cases, the material presented here relies heavily on Barkin and his work, and it has been supplemented by the works of other labor experts, as can be seen by reading what follows. At times, however, no alternative sources of information were available, because what Barkin said about a topic was unique, no one else having ever considered it. Additional material might have been derived from a more detailed history of the textile industry and the TWUA, but that was not possible given the constraints of time and resources. Other scholars are now at work in those areas.[3]

Even more important, Barkin's ideas are enough for one person to cope with. Barkin's penchant for discursive conversation, mentioned earlier, can be recognized on closer examination as the workings of a very active mind, wherein one idea quickly leads to another, but all are eventually explained. From just such a far-ranging mind came a wide variety of ideas on many topics, and this book reflects that diversity of thought. Efforts to trace the development of Barkin's ideas in chronological order proved impossible. There are just too many of them to place in a meaningful sequence. Instead, the emphasis is on topics within general areas.

The overall approach of the study follows the institutional method. In the broadest usage of the term, institutions represent ways of controlling human behavior, what Veblen called "habits of thought." They are the rules of life both in written law and in social convention. In intellectual life, Veblen was concerned with a thinker's preconceptions or rules of thought. He found a relationship between the rules of thought and the rules of life, such that when institutions change, as they always do, the preconceptions of intellectuals are challenged. Some meet the challenge by clinging tightly to their old ways. Others shift their ideas to reflect the transfigured times. The New Deal brought a period of transformation in institutions, especially with regard to unions. Written law regarding unions broke new ground with passage of the Wagner Act, and social attitudes toward unions became positive with formation of the CIO. Barkin's ideas reflected that period and provided his own preconceptions. This book endeavors to elaborate on them. It also shows how Barkin altered his ideas under the impact of fluctuations in institutions, even as his philosophy of union and government action remained intact.

Because of his active mind and wide-ranging interests, Barkin was never able to set down his overall philosophy into a lengthy tome on unions. That failure to produce a systematic treatise can readily be explained. With his active mind, it is doubtful he could have concentrated long enough on one project to bring all the strands of his thought together into a coherent whole. This book is an attempt to do so, to produce the book on unions that Barkin never did. That attempt is the final explanation for the supportive partiality that follows. It would have been impossible to understand, appreciate, and present the worth of Barkin's ideas without becoming interested in them and influenced by them.

Notes

1. Clark Kerr, Foreword to Solomon Barkin, *The Decline of the Labor Movement and What Can Be Done About It* (Santa Barbara, CA: Center for the Study of Democratic Institutions, 1961).

2. *Journal of Political Economy* (April 1972). The award was based on the number of articles published in English-language refereed journals, with Barkin ranked seventh on the list for labor economics.

3. Professor Cletis Daniels is currently working on a history of the TWUA, and William Hartford has started work on an excellent draft manuscript, cited throughout this book, studying the deindustrialization of the New England textile industry.

1

The Two Worlds of Solomon Barkin

Don't trust intellectuals.

—*Solomon Barkin*

Solomon Barkin was born on December 2, 1907, in New York City.[1] His parents were Jewish émigrés from Russia, where his father had been trained as a carpenter and cabinetmaker and had become a committed socialist (bundist). In his early years in the United States, the elder Barkin worked in the housing alteration business, because like most Jews at that time, he was barred from membership in the trade unions that controlled the carpenters' trade, particularly on new construction; eventually, he began building homes on his own and operated a small construction company. He retained his interest in socialism, however, and discussions of the subject permeated the Barkin household. While attending high school, Solomon also went to a Yiddish school sponsored by a group called the Workmen's Circle (Arbeiter Ring), where he was party to further discussions of socialism.[2]

After high school from 1924 to 1928, Barkin attended City College of New York (CCNY), majoring in history. At the same time, he began teaching at the Yiddish high school on both the history of utopias and the labor movement at home and abroad. As a result, in addition to his formal training in history and economics, he received a heady dose of Marxian thinking, an appreciation for the trade union movement, and an understanding of the cultural values of Judaism, especially the stress on the life, outlook, and rights of the underdog.

During the 1920s, the version of Marxism that was in vogue in socialist circles relied heavily on economic determinism. Advocates of that brand of Marxism believed that the economic organization of society determined all other features of life and that as the economy industrialized further, it was inevitable that socialism would come about to handle the more complex economic organization that would result. The only split between socialists was over how long the process of achieving socialism would take, with a left-wing faction believing a revolution would soon take place and a right-wing group feeling that the revolution was a long way off but could be hastened through social reform.

As chairman of the History Club at CCNY, Barkin was once called upon to present a discussion on the issue of economic determinism, titled "Pitfalls of the Marxian Deterministic Theory of History." By that time, in his junior year, he had taken a course in statistics and probability, which led him to dissent from economic determinism and Marxism. For him, life and society are too filled with random events for there to be any unifying determinism in them. Still, he remained sympathetic with the right-wing socialists in seeking a middle way to resolve economic problems through reform. (These issues were hotly contested; Barkin carries a scar from a cut due to being hit by a thrown chair during a meeting of socialists in 1926.) He also began reading and immersing himself in the works of the British Fabian Socialists, especially Beatrice and Sidney Webb, and the Guild Socialists, represented by G. D. H. Cole.

The Guild Socialists placed heavy emphasis on the evolution of socialism brought about by government intervention in the economy under the leadership of enlightened civil servants. In the 1920s, they believed industry could be developed into guilds—loose associations of production wherein labor and government would interact to build a better society. In the United States, a similar set of ideas was conceived by a group of reformers and industrial experts who wanted to combine efficiency methods and worker participation into a system called industrial democracy. Thinkers such as Henry Louis Gantt, Morris L. Cooke, and, for a time, Herbert Hoover sought to use government support for programs of labor-management cooperation so as to bring about such industrial democracy.[3] In labor studies, the idea of labor-management cooperation was being advocated by such professionals as William Leiserson, who have come to be known as advocates of industrial pluralism, because they believed that conflicts between management and labor could be managed by collective bargaining in a pluralistic society.[4]

The idea that in a pluralistic society, government and labor could act as a counterforce to business through collective bargaining would follow Barkin throughout his life and work. Barkin's wide reading on socialism prevented him from taking a doctrinaire approach to the labor movement; he never joined the Socialist Party, nor was he ever a part of any faction of the Communist movement, as were many idealist intellectuals during the 1930s.[5] But his exposure to those progressive social ideas, when combined with his interest in practical affairs, constituted the ideal background for a career that would be both academic and active.

The Academic and the Activist

Barkin earned a bachelor of social science degree in history at CCNY (he felt the Economics Department was weak), then began graduate study in economics at Columbia University. Although his thinking about economics had been set by his own reading, he was able to learn from the faculty at Columbia, which was then an enclave of the institutional school of thought. Professor J. M. Clark, for example, who was noted for his synthesis of institutionalism with the traditional economics of his father, John Bates Clark, had recently completed his monumental *Studies in the Economics of Overhead Costs* (of which more is discussed in Chapter Two). Barkin took Clark's course on overhead costs and was greatly impressed by the concept, especially as it applied to labor. He also attended Wesley Clair Mitchell's courses on business cycles and on the history of economic thought, in which he was introduced to the ideas of Thorstein Veblen.

In 1929, while working on his Ph.D., Barkin was hired as a researcher for the New York State Commission on Old Age Security. The director of the commission, Luther Gulick, who was responsible for hiring him, was professor of political science and director of the Institute of Public Administration and a well-known scholar in public administration. The commission existed from 1929 to 1933; its active work took place in 1929–30 and resulted in a proposal for an old age assistance program that was adopted by the New York legislature in 1930. The proposal was bolstered by a study of old age security, to which Barkin contributed a substantial portion. He investigated the issue of whether workers could save for their old age retirement, and after reviewing savings accounts at the Bowery Savings Bank, he concluded that they could not. He also summarized the report in a talk before the National Association of Old Age Security, which also appeared in the *Old Age Security Herald* (November 1930).

After completion of its legislative program, the commission extended into the Continuation Committee of the New York State Commission on Old Age Security. That commission studied the problems of older workers in industry, which had worsened during the 1927 recession. It produced a report, *The Older Worker in Industry*, on which Barkin did all of the research and writing. In preparing the report, he had to master the fledgling art of coding computer cards (of which there were 350,000). To gather the data, he surveyed employee records from many New York industries and convinced Metropolitan Life Insurance Company to provide the service of tabulating the results for free. Barkin's work with the commission lasted until 1933 and when it ran out of funds later in the year, Barkin continued the work with support from a Columbia University fellowship. The report on older workers was printed as a state document. Barkin submitted it as his doctoral dissertation, but it was not accepted because one of his dissertation committee members wanted a supplemental section giving a theoretical version of the topic. By that time, Barkin had gotten too caught up in events around him to ever return to the task of completing his dissertation. The lack of a doctorate, however, did not prevent him from having a successful career.

On completion of the study of older workers, Barkin began looking for another job. In July 1933, he traveled to Washington to do so. He sought suggestions from his dissertation chairman, Leo Wolman, a noted labor economist who was on leave from Columbia to work as chairman of the Labor Advisory Board of the National Recovery Administration (NRA). Wolman offered Barkin a job with the NRA, which he held for several years through numerous changes in the organizational structure. He began as a staff member and eventually became assistant director of the Labor Advisory Board, with direct responsibility for supervising a professional staff that comprised as many as fifteen members.

The National Industrial Recovery Act (NIRA) was passed by Congress in 1933 to devise a set of industry codes for firm behavior in order to eliminate from the U.S. economy the ruinous effects of competition among business by putting a limit on price cutting. The labor provisions of the NIRA codes were considered especially useful for unions and for stabilizing the labor standards. Section 7a of the code strengthened the right of workers to organize unions and has been noted by historians as very important in terms of giving a needed boost to the union movement. Less noted by historians but of great importance to Barkin was Section 7b, which aimed at stopping ruinous wage-cutting. The Temporary Reemployment Program had established basic labor standards, which were later followed in the labor sections of the individual industry codes. The codes contained provisions establishing minimum wages, maximum hours (usually 40 hours per week), prohibitions on child labor, and worker safety and health programs. The labor codes allowed for variation by industry and location; in the case of the minimum wage, forty cents per hour was most common, but differentials were permitted, especially in the South, that allowed a minimum of as low as thirty cents or even lower in a few cases.

Interpretations of the NIRA have found it a failure, with the possible exception of the modest gains made by unions under Section 7a.[6] The problem may have been that although the NIRA was intended to be an equal sharing of power by business, labor, and government, in most cases it was business that dominated the codes[7] or simply ignored them, as in the case of Henry Ford. Business was able to use the industry provisions of the code to set industry-wide price guidelines by acting as a cartel. The wage provisions of the labor codes were not as effective. Although a few firms may have lost their blue eagles for not conforming to the codes, the Labor Advisory Board had no enforcement powers. The NRA staff with those powers contributed a modest effort to enforce the codes, and there were too many breaches for the staff of the Labor Advisory Board to monitor.[8]

Barkin's experiences of working with Section 7b, however, were an exception to this perception of a dismal performance by the NIRA and its administrative agency, the NRA, in working with the labor codes. He would remind historians of the NRA that its labor codes did make the 40-hour week standard and nearly eliminated child labor and that section 7b helped extend union standards to unorganized parts of some industries.

Industry code boards might have both business and labor representatives, but there was no legal requirement that labor representatives be on the board or that the labor members come from unions; the industry code itself established board membership. In some rare cases, labor representatives were made a part of the industry code, and when that happened, they were usually union members. The function of the Labor Advisory Board was to advise the NRA administrator on the content of the labor codes. In practice, Barkin and other staff members had to bargain with business and the administrator on the terms of the individual codes, acting on behalf of labor. That effort was needed, because management influenced the codes significantly more than labor did, and the NRA administration had a bias toward business. Management secured exceptions from the proposed standards, but unions, despite the boost given them by Section 7a, were not sufficiently organized or powerful to act on their own. The staff members who represented the Labor Advisory Board in the development of labor codes had great latitude in their negotiations.

When he became assistant director of the board, Barkin instituted a regular publication that presented board standards to serve as a guideline for staff members. Staff members were also instructed to keep in touch with union representatives for the industry, if any such representatives existed. Using the leverage attained from their policymaking responsibilities and from an appeal to the precedents of earlier practices, the staff of the Labor Advisory Board was able to attain modest gains in fighting against exceptionally low wage minima and other concessions to business.

Barkin's battle in establishing a code for the building construction trades demonstrated how the process of negotiations worked. Businessmen and General Hugh S. Johnson, administrator of the NRA, wanted a 48-hour week; Barkin and the unions sought 40 hours. The issue was eventually decided at a meeting with President Roosevelt, made especially ticklish because one of the business representatives was Jacob Raskob, an executive with DuPont and General Motors and treasurer of the Democratic Party. Barkin and the unions made this cause easier by planting several stories in the *New York Times* through its labor reporter, Louis Stark, that threatened a national strike. The strategy worked and the number of hours of work in the construction trade was reduced to 40 a week.

Barkin felt that the experience of setting the construction code was both exemplary and unique. As he later described it, "The experience in the negotiations of the construction codes differed radically from that prevailing for the run of industrie in NRA. In the construction industry organized labor furnished articulate spokesmen who were versed in the manners of the contractors, steeped in the problem of industrial relations, [and] acquainted with . . . the techniques of governmental control."[9] It was the efforts of union leaders in speaking out that helped carry the tide in getting a code fair to labor.

As noted previously, Barkin's efforts also played a part in getting the code accepted. Indeed, he felt that his own efforts should be spent on advising labor on codes in industries in which unions were weakest, so he could do the most good for them.[10] He recognized that when no one represented the interests of labor, such interests were not given adequate consideration.

After the Supreme Court declared the NIRA unconstitutional in 1935, parts of the organization were retained to study the experiences of the NRA. Barkin served as part of that organization, as head of the NRA Division of Review, Labor Studies, and prepared reports on child labor; policies on hours, wages, safety, and health; and industrial relations. The reports served as a basis for the final study of the President's Committee on Industrial Analysis. Barkin served as labor consultant for the committee and prepared drafts of its documents. In those reports, there are indications of lessons that Barkin would carry into his later work.

For example, in making his efforts to help labor under the NIRA, Barkin was guided by the words of President Roosevelt, which he quoted in his summation of the accomplishments of the NRA: "No business which depends for existence on paying less than living wages to its workers has any right to continue in this country."[11] As is discussed in later chapters, that belief formed a constant theme in Barkin's works through his use of the concept of the social cost of labor.

Another guideline for his later work that Barkin learned from his NRA days concerned the need for cooperative action in industry. He wrote, "NRA's experience indicates that industrial stability can be founded only on mutual understanding between employers and employees. Each must be fully organized to deal with the other collectively." Moreover, it was important that that collective action by business and labor be "affirmed by the government in the interest of the public."[12]

A final lesson Barkin drew from the NIRA was that not all of the elements for this industry/labor/government cooperation were in place. With regard to the government, he lamented, "the Administration [of the NRA] was not manned with a personnel dedicated to those conclusions with the devotion and fearlessness as had motivated the original passing of the bill. These persons were cautious and still respected the old gods of industry. They still spoke in terms of immediate profit rather than the welfare of the workers."[13] As a countervailing power to make up for the lack of sympathy for labor among government officials, labor was lacking as well. As Barkin suggested, labor needed personnel "equipped to defend labor's cases before government agencies in language, form and argument which the latter understand. The acts of administrative agencies need to be watched constantly so that governmental decrees issued as administrative orders or otherwise do not undo the achievements of labor over decades."[14] In his work with the NRA, Barkin tried to serve as a government agent sympathetic to labor, trying to make up for the defects of the union movement by preparing many statements that union officials would present before the NRA.[15] When the NRA was ended, he switched sides to become a labor union spokesman, presenting labor's case before government agencies.

While at the NRA, Barkin had met and worked with Sidney Hillman, head of the Amalgamated Clothing Workers Union, who was a member of the NRA Labor Advisory Board. He had several disputes with Hillman on NRA matters, feeling that Hillman took positions that served his union but had to be altered to fit the interests of workers as a whole. After completion of his reports for the NRA study, Barkin stopped in New York to visit Hillman. Hillman's secretary asked if Barkin had received a letter from Hillman. When he replied that he had not, he was told to see Hillman, who immediately offered him a job with the Textile Workers Organizing Committee (TWOC), which Hillman was just forming, on March 7, 1937, to mount an organizing drive among textile workers for the Committee of Industrial Organizations (CIO).

Barkin was never sure why Hillman wanted him to work for the TWOC, except that he had stood up to Hillman at meetings of the Labor Advisory Board. From his own view, Barkin believed that among CIO leaders, Hillman had the personal discipline and the discipline in his own union to succeed in instituting and implementing the TWOC. Still, it took a chance meeting to begin Barkin's long career with the Textile Workers Union of America (TWUA), confirming his view about the lack of determinism in life. This was such an opportunity that Barkin has said he would have worked for nothing. He began work on March 1, 1937, as the committee's research director. His first task was to set up a national staff while Hillman brought in organizers.

At the time Barkin joined the TWOC, the labor movement had been experiencing what Irving Bernstein has called "turbulent years." Spurred on by a new legal climate created by Section 7a of the NRA, and after its repeal by the Wagner Act, the unionists had begun a campaign of organizing the previously unorganized industrial workers in mass production industries. With successful organizing drives in coal behind him, John L. Lewis began looking for other areas of labor unrest.[16]

When the NIRA was declared unconstitutional by the Supreme Court in the *Schecter* decision in May 1935, the labor sections were deemed too important to be permanently voided. They were quickly replaced and expanded in July 1935 by the National Labor Relations Act (NLRA), often referred to as the Wagner Act. The Wagner Act set up specific procedures for recognition elections and established penalties for firms that did not follow those procedures or that committed stipulated unfair labor practices. It also set up the National Labor Relations Board (NLRB) to oversee the procedures and take legal action when they were not followed. These procedures were tilted toward industrial labor. As Steve Fraser notes, the NLRB "was conceived and administered to promote industrial unionism and at the national level was populated by sympathizers" to the CIO.[17] To take advantage of the upsurge in worker interest in unions that took place at the time of the passage of the NLRA, Lewis, Hillman, and others formed the CIO in 1935. By 1937, the CIO had taken advantage of the NLRA to win organizing drives in the steel, automobile, rubber, and other industries, including large and small units.

These victories were owed to much more than a change in the legal climate. Leaders and organizers of the CIO had to fight front-line battles against management, especially in management's use of company unions, using new techniques such as the sit-down strike. They also had to fight in rearguard action against the leaders and unions of the American Federation of Labor (AFL), who neither wanted to organize the industrial work force nor wanted to see the development of a dual union movement. In January 1938, the AFL rescinded the charters of CIO unions; in response, in November 1938, the CIO became the Congress of Industrial Organizations.

Besides their dissimilar attitudes toward organizing industrial workers, the CIO and AFL also disagreed on the role government should take in labor relations. Since the days of Samuel Gompers, the AFL had been wary of having the government intervene in its behalf on the premise that what the government granted, it could take away. For example, as Christopher Tomlins has argued, when the Wagner Act gave the NLRB the authority to determine bargaining units for the purpose of elections, it upset the whole set of jurisdictional rules that the AFL had developed in a plant. While it sanctioned labor's right to bargain collectively, the NLRB also brought collective bargaining under government regulation.[18] Scholars have questioned whether the CIO would have been successful without the NLRB's sanctioning of its representation claims. Although the argument here is plainly speculative, it is doubtful the CIO would have got very far without the NLRB, for without that help, the CIO would not have been able to wrest portions of the labor movement from the cautious hands of the AFL.

Against such AFL caution must be placed a picture of many industrial workers who were already organizing themselves. During its initial four and a half years, the NLRB held 2,500 elections with 1.2 million votes cast. Workers wanted unions and had awaited only a group of union leaders ready to take advantage of the opportunity being made available to them by the NLRA. As Walter Galenson has written, "What was needed above all was dynamic leadership, willing to run great risks on the assault on the citadels of the open shop. The AFL leadership did not see the opportunity, and it remained for John L. Lewis, perhaps the greatest entrepreneur of American labor organization, to step into the breach."[19]

If Lewis is to be accorded honor as the greatest labor entrepreneur, Sidney Hillman cannot be ranked far behind. Even though Lewis's reputation remains that of charismatic leader, Hillman was the one who got things done. Steve Fraser, for one, has accorded him the accolade as "the country's first and, to date, its only labor statesman."[20] And even Lewis maintained, "Sidney Hillman was after all the driving force behind many of the measures attributed to the New Deal."[21] His ability to work hard, often behind the scenes, at achieving results and his record of quiet, steady accomplishment surely rank him with the more bumptious Lewis as a legend of labor.

Born in 1887 in a Lithuanian village to a middle-class family, Hillman studied traditional Jewish subjects formally, but his association with socialists introduced him to the classics of Western liberalism and radicalism, from John Stuart Mill to Karl Marx. After several arrests in Russia for socialist activities, he came to the United States in 1907 as a self-educated young man and began work in the clothing industry in Chicago, learning the trade of cutter.

Hillman's educational background had made him a "half-intellectual," capable of moving in the world of ideas and able to translate the ideas of intellectuals into a form understandable by workers. He remained a practical doer and organizer, but one with a healthy respect for knowledge and reason. On his abilities as an organizer and negotiator, he rose rapidly to leadership in the Amalgamated Clothing Workers Union and was elected its president in 1914. A keen analyst himself, he had respect for intellectuals and progressive reformers, associating himself with the likes of Jane Addams, Clarence Darrow, Louis Brandeis, and Felix Frankfurter. He was also a part of the industrial democracy movement championed by industrial experts such as Morris L. Cooke.[22] In the 1920s, he had hired the labor economist Leo Wolman as the Amalgamated's research director.

While he always sought practical results, Hillman believed in the pursuit of ideals. As he once told a labor meeting, "Let us not become too practical. Having realized our dreams of yesterday, let us dedicate ourselves to new dreams of a future" with no unemployment, with economic security, and with political freedom.[23] To achieve that dream, he used the power of his union, in combination with progressive businessmen such as Edward Filene and Joseph Schaffner, to bring stability to the clothing industry.

In his work with the Amalgamated, Hillman did achieve practical results. He championed the introduction of an impartial umpire to resolve industry issues, set up a union bank and housing cooperative, and pushed for industry-wide bargaining. He used the union to bring stability to the industry by establishing uniform wages and working conditions in many of its sectors and geographic areas, a result many managers in the industry accepted and occasionally applauded. His practical side was demonstrated with a truly pragmatic approach. As he described it, "In the union we always used the scientific method of trial and error. We try something, and if it is wrong, we stop it and try something else."[24] This approach was to be very acceptable to Barkin.

Barkin would also be impressed by Hillman's overriding principles for unions. First, Hillman firmly believed in the use of impartial umpires to settle disputes involving conflicting interpretations of a contract agreement. Second, he felt that the union movement must always expand by organizing nonunion areas and industries. Third, in that expansion, funds and other resources from the unionized segments should be brought to bear. Finally, he stressed the need for careful planning in pursuit of labor's goals and on never giving up on those goals until they were reached.[25] In attaining their goals, unions should also, Hillman thought, not be wary of using government action or the advice of experts. As Fraser summarizes, "What Hillman envisioned was a cross-class alliance that would link restive elements of the labor movement with reform-minded technocrats and bureaucrats and likeminded elements of business. Together they would experiment with using the machinery of government to expand mass purchasing power, to plan for economic growth and to systematically regulate business."[26] This was a vision Barkin shared.

Hillman's experiences on the Labor Advisory Board of the NRA certainly helped to focus his insights and principles on a need for organizing industrial workers.[27] Hillman recognized that the NRA could be used to bring industrial stability, much as he had strived for with his own union. The men's clothing code, with a 20 percent wage increase and a 36-hour week, secured with the help of lobbying by management, was one of the better results of the NRA codes.[28] Hillman also understood that a weak union movement or the lack of unions in many industries limited the effectiveness of the NRA labor code. He had long appreciated that the welfare of an industry's labor force depended on the health of that industry's firms. The Amalgamated had taken many steps to reduce the chaotic competition that undermined the health of the clothing industry, and Hillman saw that similar measures were needed in other industries.

Hillman's choice of textiles as opportune for an organizing drive was influenced by his principles as well as his perception that his own union was circumscribed by an unorganized textile industry.[29] In this he copied the approach of Lewis, who had organized the steel industry to protect his coal workers. He set up an organizing committee to supplement the existing AFL union, the United Textile Workers of America. He thought that his contacts with employers in the apparel industry would be helpful in organizing the textile industry. He also looked for assistance from a friendly government in Washington, including the NLRB, Sen. Robert La Follette's civil rights committee, and congressional leaders who were trying to pass the Fair Labor Standards Act (FLSA) to raise wages in the South.[30]

Hillman was instrumental in securing the passage in 1938 of the FLSA, which set minimum wages and limited hours of work. Passage of the act had been difficult, with several previous failures in Congress recorded in 1937. Business groups, especially from the South, opposed it, as did the AFL and Railway Brotherhoods, which feared that its minimum would become a maximum. Hillman testified formally for the measure and informally urged President Roosevelt to give it his support. Roosevelt, who had little knowledge of labor issues, did call a special session of Congress to debate the bill, and when it passed took as much credit as he could but did acknowledge Hillman's contribution. Lewis gave a more direct verdict on Hillman's role: "If it had not been for him there would probably have been no Fair Labor Standards Act."[31]

This exceptional performance added to Hillman's high personal prestige, and he was especially willing to exploit it in helping unions to make advances in new areas, especially textiles. But unlike steel and automobiles, where an impressive victory at a major producer could lead to gains in the whole industry, the textile industry was fragmented in part into many small firms scattered over a wide geographic area and was composed of many industrial subdivisions, such as cotton, wool, silk, carpets, and rayon, each of which were further subdivided into different markets with varying levels of competition. In the cotton branch, the industry was additionally complicated by the dominance of selling agents. The organization led by TWOC made some important gains after it started in 1937 but was soon frustrated in any further improvements by a recession that hit textiles especially hard and by an inability to make more than modest gains in the South. The South proved an especially hard area to organize and the task was made more difficult by the unexpected death of the leading organizer in the region, Steve Nance.[32]

When Hillman became ill in November 1937, he narrowed his efforts to his own union, never returning to work with the TWOC. As a result, from September 1937 through 1939, Barkin ran the TWOC central office as an executive officer, even though he retained his title of research director. Most of the organizing work was still conducted by regional directors, who were experienced; Barkin filled in the gap of central coordination but did not take power as a leader. He never wanted to hold office as president of the union, preferring to serve as a staff member on the premise that labor leaders should rise from the ranks of the union.

In May 1939, a consolidation was effected that merged the unions of the TWOC with the unions of the United Textile Workers (AFL) to form the Textile Workers Union of America (TWUA); Emil Rieve, formerly president of the Hosiery Workers and handpicked by Hillman, served as president. Only then was a formal structure developed for the union. Barkin wrote a report detailing the results of the two-year effort of the TWOC for the convention.[33]

In his later reflections on the TWOC years, Barkin recognized that Hillman in textiles was trying to do what Lewis had done in steel: use his leadership and reputation to carry through on an organization that had been bungled by the AFL union.[34] In a more recent analysis, he gave very high marks to the CIO leaders. He wrote, "They showed an understanding of the opportunities offered by the new situation by addressing themselves to the reconstruction of their own organizations. . . . They became models of dedication for other leaders. Their skills, experience, counsel in strikes and services in negotiations became available to other leaders. Their achievements made them public figures who could help others make breakthroughs in their organizing efforts."[35]

This is as fine a definition of union leadership as one could find. Subsequent chapters describe how rare such leadership was, in Barkin's view. Although he shared with Hillman a temperament that was both practical and intellectual, in his own case he was sure he did not have the personal qualities to provide this type of leadership. That is why he never sought political leadership in the TWUA, preferring to make his impact as a "staff man," in an administrative and supervisory function.

His role as a staff support person in the union did not preclude Barkin from having to deal with the problem of labor radicals and communists. As he began work with the TWOC, Barkin faced a situation wherein communists followed the strategy of "boring from within." When he had to act as union executive due to Hillman's illness, Barkin countered by sending known communists on difficult assignments well outside of New York City, "sending them to Siberia" as he described it. He also did not participate in communist-sponsored activities with regard to the Spanish Civil War, a path many young liberals followed to the Communist Party (CP), feeling that the party members were using the popularity of the war for their own gain. At the same time, TWOC offices were located in the same neighborhood as CP headquarters and many party leaders had been classmates of Barkin at CCNY. He often met them for lunch and kept abreast of what was happening within the CP. Although it was not until the late 1940s that communists were expelled from the TWOC, Barkin had always been intellectually suspicious of their ideas. He was not a determinist and did not believe that the class structure of the United States resembled what Marxists depicted. Besides, he had more important work to do.

In the course of his years as research director for the TWUA, Barkin worked on finding solutions to a variety of problems confronting organized labor. Because his writing on these problems forms the core of Chapters Four, Five, and Six, it is necessary to only mention them here; he conducted studies on the degree of concentration in the textile industry, became an expert on efficiency methods and personnel management techniques, developed a union position on tariffs, documented the impact of minimum wage legislation so as to present labor's side of that issue to Congress, tried to reach a better understanding of conditions in the South, created a program for area redevelopment and led the fight for its enactment into federal law, provided studies in support of minimum wage legislation, and devised approaches for helping workers adjust to technological change. He also devised methods of weekly reporting by organizers to report on problems encountered and progress made, and he created systems for helping supervisors to follow up on organizers' programs.

Barkin always aimed at raising the professional level of union research. Not only did he provide the information requested by union leaders, but also he tried to anticipate what information they should have. In many cases he first had to educate himself. He mastered the intricacies of efficiency techniques and time-and-motion study in order to provide textile unions with solid knowledge about those areas. He also studied the statistical techniques of quality control to determine how much responsibility workers should have for defects. During the war, he mastered the process of job evaluation to make labor's case for higher wages before the War Labor Board. He conducted research into wage incentive systems and job assignment changes. At the time that he began as research director for the TWUA, unions had no formal approach to bargaining with management over the use of these techniques; their business agents and other negotiators simply bluffed their way through the problems the techniques caused. Union staff members were incapable of developing alternatives to management's approaches.

In conducting his research, Barkin followed two courses. First, he would deal with the concrete problem at hand, analyzing what was at issue and advising the business agent what should be done. Second, he would develop the more general set of principles and procedures that the union staff as a whole could use when they encountered some variation of problem. He wrote many manuals of procedures for union members to help them understand the generalized approach to problem solving. His reputation as an expert in problem solving grew to the point where in some cases business agents for the TWUA locals could get a settlement from management by threatening to call him in.

In terms of economic research, Barkin produced a regular statement of economic trends in the textile industry. These were provided regularly for the TWUA Executive Council. Additional economic reports were developed for use at conferences held by the different branches of the textile industry. Barkin also undertook studies of labor productivity. As a member of labor advisory committees for the Bureau of Labor Statistics, he provided input into studies of wage policies, collective bargaining, price policies, and profit, all as related to the textile industry. He applied his knowledge of economics and the textile industry as a consultant to the government in addressing plans regarding how the revival of the British textile industry would fit in with the recovery of Europe after the war.

All in all, it was a full and busy life in the world of activism. But Barkin's activities on behalf of the TWUA carried over into the academic world as well. His many articles published in academic circles were based on his work with labor. They spell out in the most general terms the principles and procedures he learned from dealing as a professional expert with the problems faced by a trade union.

According to Harold Wilensky, experts hired by unions fall into three broad functional types: the "facts and figures man," who provides the hard empirical data needed by unions; the "contact man," who provides broader ideas and serves as liaison between the union and the outside world; and the "internal communications specialist," who provides ideas for inside use to foster effective relations between the leadership and the union hierarchy.[36] Given the breadth of his accomplishments and responsibilities, Barkin combined all three functions.

Moreover, Barkin was able to avoid conflicts with his union leadership, a problem many experts faced. His relations with Rieve remained workable. Rieve, he felt, viewed him with suspicion as harboring ambitions for leadership; Barkin, however, found Rieve to be one of the brightest and most effective leaders in the union movement, calling him a "wonderful guy to work with."[37] Barkin believed that the TWUA had the best research staff in organized labor, in no small part due to Rieve's respect for his staff members' professional competency.[38] Barkin often boasted that his own research was the equal of that of the technical staffs maintained in the textile industry.

As a supervisor, Barkin also respected his staff members' abilities. They in return respected him. One former employee noted that Barkin was always trying to find new approaches to research problems. Another referred to him as "The best Research Director any union ever had."[39] Throughout his tenure as research director of TWUA, Barkin constantly hired highly qualified economists and engineers to conduct research into the economic and technical conditions surrounding the textile industry. He also maintained an ongoing relationship with many former members of his research staff, such as Sumner Shapiro, Franklin Bishop, Lawrence Cohen, Dorothy Garfein, George Perkel, John Weiser, and Daniel Finkle, and he helped place members of his research staff into other positions, where they have proved to be outstanding leaders in industry, government, and academic life.

At the same time, Barkin could be difficult to work for. He was very demanding intellectually and took his mission in the union movement so seriously that few were able to put up with him very long. The few who did, especially those previously mentioned, were the survivors, an exceptional group of professionals dedicated to unions. Franklin Bishop is an example of the type of person Barkin attracted to the TWUA. Bishop came to the TWUA immediately after World War II, as a college-educated (Columbia University) industrial engineer recently employed by General Motors in the production of fighter planes. While in college he had done cooperative work with the International Ladies' Garment Workers Union. On his recollection, Barkin's example set the model of behavior for the research department's activities: long hours, meticulous attention to detail, and a staunch commitment to the aspirations of workers. Bishop found Barkin's ubiquitous hand to cause him little difficulty, because of his own confidence in his abilities to meet the exacting standards Barkin demanded.[40]

People's memories may be selective, but it is of note that other members of Barkin's staff also recall those days as very exciting and rewarding.[41] However demanding and difficult Barkin might have been to work for—and he does have an intellectual's impatience with obtuse and incompetent persons—the staff who endured were able to overlook those difficulties. In addition, they were neither obtuse nor incompetent. If they were really good, Barkin encouraged them to leave the TWUA after five years to find a wider horizon for their skills. Bishop, for example, went on to a notable career as an industrialist.

Of particular note among his projects was Barkin's active involvement on the national political scene by serving as labor's advocate for an Area Redevelopment Act under the Kennedy Administration. In addition to being a vocal supporter of the legislation, when the bill was passed, Barkin was selected to serve on the national advisory committee to the Area Redevelopment Administration. Sen. Paul Douglas, sponsor of the legislation, arranged for Barkin to be present when the bill was signed by President Kennedy, who also gave Barkin a keepsake pen from the signing.

Barkin's experiences in the labor movement culminated with his classic study *The Decline of the Labor Movement and What Can Be Done About It*,[42] published in 1961. At a time when unions seemed to be enjoying a great deal of success, Barkin, with his insider's information, recognized that they were at their apogee and accurately forecast many of the problems they would face over the next three decades, to be described more fully in Chapter Seven. The study aroused great national interest, with notice of its contents appearing in over a hundred newspapers nationally, including the *Wall Street Journal*, in an editorial. Barkin saw the advent of union decline coming from a variety of causes, and he included criticism of union leaders for not taking steps that might have forestalled the demise of the union movement. It has been claimed that Barkin's critical stance alienated him from the union leadership and made him part of an exodus of intellectuals from the union movement that took place during the early 1960s.[43] More important, Barkin saw little chance that unions, especially the TWUA, would make the critical changes they needed to continue to grow. He also was attracted by opportunities to participate on the international scene. Whatever the reason, in 1962, Barkin retired from the TWUA.

On his retirement from the union movement, he began a five-year tour in Paris as deputy to the director and head of the Social Affairs Division, Manpower and Social Affairs Directorate, of the Organization for Economic Cooperation and Development. In this capacity he wrote and directed a variety of studies dealing with manpower policy, area redevelopment, and social and technical change. The studies are described in greater detail in the Conclusion. At the end of that tour, he became professor of economics and research associate of the Labor Center at the University of Massachusetts at Amherst, where he remains as professor emeritus. On his retirement from the University, he served a year as visiting professor at Erasmus University in Rotterdam, Holland, and was Fulbright professor at Wellington University in New Zealand. During his academic years he continued to reflect upon the pressures facing unions during their recent decline and remained a staunch defender of progressive unionism in scholarly publications and before professional academic associations.

In addition to his academic interests, Barkin has been active in a variety of other areas. He has served as a member of the board of trustees of the National

Planning Association since 1950, was vice chairman of the Joint Council on Economic Education from 1952 to 1963, and was a member of the board of trustees of the National Council on Aging from 1955 to 1963. In 1964, he was elected president of the Industrial Relations Research Association. In 1952, he was elected a member of Phi Beta Kappa Associates, a more restricted grouping of members of Phi Beta Kappa. Government work included serving as a consultant for the War Labor Board in 1944 and for the Committee on Income of the White House Conference on Aging in 1971 as well as being U.S. delegate to the Negotiations of the International Cotton Textiles Agreement in Geneva in 1962. He also served as a member of the National Public Advisory Committee on Area Redevelopment during 1961–62.

In 1961, he was given the very important assignment of serving as a member of the labor delegation to the International Labor Conference in Geneva. At that conference he was elected vice chairman of the Committee on Employment, in which capacity he negotiated the committee's resolution on full employment. He was also the union spokesman designated to answer the arguments of the delegates from the Soviet bloc countries, who maintained that their economies did not suffer the widespread unemployment that the Western nations did. Barkin countered by reminding them of how much of their unemployment was hidden by their labor camps.

The point was not hard for Barkin to make intellectually, for he had always been skeptical of the claims of Marxian socialists and communists. As a reformer, he sought to find a middle way between capitalism and socialism along the lines of industrial democracy, placing himself squarely in the camp of the industrial pluralists. As a researcher on the problems of older workers, he recognized the negative features of a private enterprise economy. As an analyst and administrator for the NRA, he saw how the power of government could be used to eliminate such negative features, especially as they impinged on workers. When the opportunity to apply his knowledge and skills directly to the problems faced by workers was presented to him by work with the TWUA, he was eager and well prepared. Although the union did not give him his ideas, his work with it introduced him to a part of the world where those ideas could be applied.

All serious thinkers are influenced by the events that took place during their life. This is especially true for Barkin, however, because most of his writing was highly responsive to the events of his life. It was his role, as in-house intellectual for the CIO, to analyze events as they took place, explain them to union leaders and the labor camp, and set forth labor's views before its opponents and the general public. The events that took place in the world of labor form an important backdrop for subsequent chapters. But a proper understanding of Barkin's ideas necessitates that they be placed in the context of one of the worlds in which he worked—the intellectual world of economics.

Institutional Economics

Throughout its history, economics as an intellectual discipline has been divided into an orthodox mainstream, which proclaims the virtues of the free market, and heterodox schools of dissenters, who have questioned how well markets work. During the early years of this century, in the United States there developed an institutional school of economics, which took a dim view of the market economics of the mainstream. One of the founders of the school, Thorstein Veblen, specifically repudiated the twin pillars of the mainstream—equilibrium and rational calculation. For Veblen, the nature of the economy and economic development was that of a process that was ongoing and unteleological, with never a resting balance. Moreover, in the place of rational calculation, Veblen maintained that most economic decisions were due to habits of thought that carried over from past periods into the present.

The prime mover of economics, for Veblen, was technology, which had the power to change habits of thought, at least among those working with it. On Veblen's analysis, the market never had a fair chance to work, for businesspeople were always subverting it by withholding efficiency in order to raise prices by restraining trade or by subverting the development of new technology. To get a more effective economic system, Veblen felt that businesspeople needed to be replaced by a more progressive force that would not suppress technology.

At one point, Veblen pinned on labor his hopes for a better society. Because workers were intimately connected with methods of modern production, which required rational thinking to operate, their own habits of thought became more rational. He expected that this process would lead workers to approve of and fight for a system of industrial democracy such as the Webbs proposed. But to the extent that workers joined unions and pursued the strategy of gaining their own betterment through restrictive practices, he found them to be no better than businesspeople and disapproved of them.[44]

Other members of the institutional school took a more optimistic view of unions. Veblen's protégé Robert F. Hoxie studied unions more closely than did Veblen and concluded that they fit into four main categories: business unionism, uplift unionism, revolutionary unionism, and predatory unionism. Had he been able to continue his analysis (he killed himself in despair partly due to a feeling of failure of his analysis and partly due to his feelings that neither business nor labor was willing to work together), Hoxie might have been led to see the reduction of these types to a conflict between business unionism, wherein craft unions tried to benefit solely their members, and uplift unionism, which often aimed to act for the good of society.[45] Had he witnessed the debate between the AFL and CIO in the 1930s, this point would have been stressed even more, because Hoxie was willing to take a normative bias in favor of uplift unionism, such as the CIO was then proposing.

John R. Commons, the other leading figure (with Veblen) of the institutional school, had no qualms about reforming the capitalist system to improve labor's position. As had the Webbs, Commons observed that in modern society collective action had begun to dominate economic affairs. This collective action, when involved with economic transactions, took on more of a legal form than that of a market activity. Collective organization on one side of the market required a similar type of organization on the other side. Commons was not concerned over the source of collective organization for workers. In his view, an industrial democracy was as likely to "start with the employer as with the employees," and he urged the employer to activate a "newly awakened spirit of collective action" in "his own shop." He felt that employers would compete with each other in offering better working conditions and industrial democracy in order to gain the goodwill of workers. He also urged unions and management to eschew any type of national organization.[46]

As Ben Seligman pointed out, Commons was a conservative reformer who wanted to keep the main outlines of capitalism. But he also wanted to achieve better relations between capital and labor. Here he had a problem. As Seligman wrote, "That this [better industrial relations] might require a labor union to match a corporation in size and resources seemed to him quite reasonable. Whatever disputes would arise would be settled by a government commission anyway. It never occurred to Commons, however, that the latter might be not quite as impartial as his studies suggested they ought to be."[47]

Commons and his followers formed a Wisconsin school, which conducted research in economic conditions and then proposed reforms to correct the conditions they found unwholesome. In terms of industrial relations, Commons felt that the wage and working conditions could be based on decisions made by a government agency, much as public utility prices were beginning to be set, in part due to his efforts. He looked for a system of regulated markets to produce a "reasonable" capitalism, but he questioned whether business or unions could be reasonable on their own.

Rather, unions would develop what Commons's student Selig Perlman dubbed "job consciousness," wherein craft workers would try to use unions to gain a property in a particular job.[48] Craft workers needed guidance and even control to keep them from forming unions that went beyond the "job conscious" attitude and challenged management or the institutions of society. As Commons wrote, revealing his image of the proper place of unions, "The trade union movement looks upon itself, not as the irreconcilable opponent of capitalism, but as a member of the family. Being a member of the family it is entitled to have a row with *the head of the family* and to live apart for a time. . . . Trade unionists do not presume . . . that the members of the family can do without *the head of the family*."[49] The Wisconsin school would see labor as a subordinate partner in industrial democracy, to be taken care of by paternalistic employers or a beneficent state.

Perlman agreed. Writing in the 1920s, however, he based his view on the craft unions of the AFL. As Richard Lester has pointed out, Perlman's theory of unions was static and did not allow for an evolution of trade union practices.[50] When the CIO emerged as a force in the 1930s, he did not care for its broad-based activism. Another member of the Commons group, Sumner Slichter, was more accepting of the CIO. Following Commons's feeling for collective action, Slichter interpreted the victories of the CIO as bringing about a system of "industrial jurisprudence." For him collective bargaining was a way to set wages, but it was also a way to protect workers from being abused by management.[51] After the period of the 1940s, however, when CIO idealism and militancy were at a high point, he began to believe that unions were abusing the system and became less inclined to accept their activities. Still, his analysis, by following the institutional approach, did see wage-setting as taking place under conditions far removed from the free market.

There are two themes running through this survey of institutional economics that are essential to an understanding of Barkin's views on economics. The first concerns to what extent markets and the economic models based on them are helpful in analyzing union activities. The institutional school placed little emphasis on markets. Second is the question of how far unions should go in achieving their goals. The institutional school looked with favor on unions, but only if they behaved themselves by acting reasonably, with reasonableness determined by the institutionalists as behaving as underlings in the industrial democracy and system of goodwill that their bosses were creating for them with the help of the state.

In his own approach, Barkin would join with the institutionalists in shunning the market approach to labor economics, but he parted company with them by giving much greater approval to the activities of unions. In terms of the mainstream approach, Barkin's position went to the heart of the school's method. Following the thought of Veblen, Barkin outlined a problem with the basic assumption of the mainstream: "The assumption is that the society and economy tend to seek an equilibrium, thereby denying or minimizing a continuing state of disequilibrium of varying magnitudes which national policy makers often try to rectify. The tendency is to concentrate on movements and to subordinate the concern for divergent trends, instability and unrest."[52] As a result of this approach, mainstream economists often make faulty predictions during periods of great change or unrest. Barkin concluded that a more realistic theory was needed, one that when it failed in its prediction would give some indication of why.

The difficulty with the market approach is that it leaves out too much, especially with regard to unions. As Barkin once noted, "An exegesis on supply and demand curves hardly serves as an introduction to the beliefs of the craft-union operation."[53] The problem for Barkin is that single factors, such as market forces, are not sufficient to explain complex historical events. Commons and the Wisconsin school understood this, so their approach to labor history and labor relations was more appropriate than the mainstream in Barkin's eyes. Barkin also

would view with favor their stress on habits of thought being at least as important in economic decisions as rational, marginal calculations.

Barkin had some hope for the institutional school and the labor movement to
be of mutual assistance to each other. Commons and his associates had helped
the AFL to develop its strategies and structure, and they facilitated the push for a
system of industrial relations pluralism. Unionists shared the institutionalist's
opposition to mainstream economics, viewing "economists as apologists for the
current economy rather than objective students." Both groups also held a commitment to pluralism.[54]

But he also believed that the institutionalists did not go far enough in their
appreciation of the role of unions in the economy. For him, the institutionalists
were outsiders where unions were concerned. As a result, their economic approaches were not applicable to unions. Barkin's development of a system of
union economics is taken up in Chapter Two, as are his direct criticisms of labor
economics. But the problem of economists' being outsiders with regard to unions
returns us to the issue that began this chapter: how do intellectuals establish a
satisfactory working relationship within the union framework?

Intellectuals and the Unions

One of Barkin's aims as research director for the TWUA and as in-house intellectual for the CIO was to get other intellectuals involved with the union movement. In his own union he hired engineers and economists to conduct research on
problems facing union leaders and workers; when possible, he also used the
expert help of psychologists, sociologists, and pollsters. In recent years, unions
have hired financial consultants for advice on investments and corporate take-
overs. But despite those efforts, Barkin contended that when the union movement ran into difficulties, "There were no intellectual resources that were readily
available to it."[55] For unions to attain those resources, several problems on the
part of unions and intellectuals were left to be overcome.

Intellectuals who seek any type of employment are caught in a contradictory
position in which there arise conflicts between the demands of their employer
and the integrity of their intellectual discipline. Whether employed by business,
government, union, or university, an intellectual is placed in an awkward situation when the goals of their organization infringe on the free pursuit of ideas. All
these organizations value their own goals as paramount and the needs of their
intellectual employees as secondary; pressure is brought to bear on intellectuals
in terms of the projects they are permitted to undertake or the time they are given
to complete a project. Even in academia, the pressure to publish quickly and in
volume can skew the balanced approach an intellectual might prefer.[56]

This problem can be especially magnified with labor unions. As the supposed
protectors and spokespeople of downtrodden workers, unions have an appeal to
intellectuals. But when unions fail to live up to that role, intellectuals may

become disillusioned with them. Such disillusionment can become even greater over time. For example, as unions gained in power during the 1940s, intellectuals became more critical of them. Intellectuals followed the institutional school by being sympathetic to unions only so long as the unions behaved themselves. As Barkin noted of intellectuals, "They believed that corrections in our society could be effected by improving the balance of bargaining power. Now they are told by the press that such a balance of power has been attained and that we are faced with a struggle of monopoly powers, and they are not so certain they want to favor the unions."[57]

The abuse of power by unions and their leaders did present a problem for intellectuals in the post–World War II era. As Derek Bok and John Dunlop have described, "Almost all [intellectual critics] seem to agree that the root problem of American labor lies in the inadequacy of its leadership. They have not always held this position. In the thirties, many CIO leaders were thought to be well endowed with initiative, ability and daring. According to liberal critics, however, much of this imagination and energy has given way to bureaucratic routine."[58] As is noted in Chapter Seven, Barkin would agree with that assessment. His solution to the lack of ideals in the union movement would be fresh ideas from intellectuals.

First, intellectuals would have to win over union leaders, who would not take kindly to their critics. The problem for labor leaders with regard to intellectuals is, as Selig Perlman once observed, that they are "desirous to make their own ideology also the ideology of labor."[59] Barkin would agree, having written, "The so-called 'intellectuals' in the first decades of the American Federation of Labor tried desperately to saddle the trade-union movement with specific political doctrines. . . ." These doctrines were successfully resisted, just as the CIO resisted the influence of communists in the 1930s and 1940s. But there remained a residue of mistrust of intellectuals by union leaders.[60] As a result, mid-level union staff members found themselves hampered by having union leaders place limits on their activities.[61]

Unions have another reason to mistrust intellectuals. Many educated persons have taken positions with unions, only to leave and become a part of management.[62] As a high-ranking unionist once noted, "You can never tell when [the intellectuals with college background] will pack up their bag and fold their tent and leave the union for some other adventure. We had a lot of bitter experience with that. . . ."[63] To be sure, there were also cases of union officers and workers who took jobs with management, but there was a special question of loyalty in terms of securing academic aid for unions. Business had already gained the loyalty of the universities, where intellectuals were housed. Within a university, therefore, work for management carried more prestige and financial reward than did work for unions.

To give a more recent example of intellectual neglect of unions, which Barkin has found especially distressful, we must look at the Industrial Relations Research Association (IRRA). The IRRA was formed in 1947, in Barkin's words, "out of a desire to introduce the study of unionism and collective bargaining into the roster of academic subject matter. Academics, particularly in economics, had previously avoided and even rejected these studies as unworthy of being classed as an academic discipline." By the late 1980s, Barkin found, the IRRA was reorienting itself by taking on as part of its field the study of human resource management, which, as discussed in Chapter Seven, Barkin deemed to be a management tool used to defeat unions.[64] Union leaders would surely look askance at anyone with this background who sought to advise them.

Nevertheless, as Barkin had previously said, "The trade union movement needs more help from the organized centers of intellect and knowledge than [from] the business world."[65] It was his view that more balance of intellectual work was needed, with academic disciplines' "studying, describing and serving the union and its leaders in the same manner in which it has been assisting management in the understanding of its structure, personnel and operations."[66] How were intellectuals supposed to gain the confidence of labor leaders?

This is a question many intellectuals in the union movement must have asked themselves. Union leaders have a reputation for anti-intellectualism, based on the stress they impose to attain quick results and on their having been educated in the "school of hard knocks." To some extent, these leaders might keep intellectuals around merely for show; Harold Wilensky even determined that union staff experts might be more effective if they retained as much anonymity as possible. It was also important for them to convey a sense of loyalty by being vocally pro-labor.[67]

The way Barkin would answer a question about the role of the intellectual in unions is through his own experience. Basically, intellectuals could gain the confidence of union leaders by working for them and by supporting the fundamental tenets of unionism for a long period of time. They could also serve as contact for the union with the academic world and represent the union in public affairs. For all of that to happen, there needs to be a twofold commitment of time and ideas. In Barkin's words describing the commitment an intellectual must make to a union, "To be useful he must be a full-time person in the employ of the trade union. He must be closely identified with it to be trusted and to gain the insights necessary for his understanding of the stresses and influences combining to affect policy, and to develop an appreciation for research techniques. He must accept the purposes, the legitimacy of the activities and philosophy of the trade-union."[68]

Now such a commitment would be difficult for many intellectuals to make, as Barkin appreciated. He found benefits that would result if it were. First, society would gain from a better understanding of an important institution in its structure. Second, intellectuals would gain, for their own discipline would be improved by the development of new techniques for research and new knowledge about human behavior.[69]

Of even greater importance to Barkin, of course, were the gains that would accrue to unions. With the help of intellectuals, unions would be better able to communicate their goals and needs before management, government, and the public. They would also be able to develop better policies. Indeed, unions might even gain a respect for knowledge and intellectual pursuits and learn the value of intellectuals. Of utmost importance, intellectuals could keep alive and infuse into the union movement the idealism that marked the CIO in the 1930s. As Barkin put it:

> The task of defining a new progressive course for the trade union movement becomes the major responsibility of the realistic yet bold American progressives, both within and outside the movement. . . . However, while the "outside" liberal has access to the trade union movement, he is generally without knowledge of the trade union as an institution. He does not know how it operates, nor is he acquainted with the ways in which it articulates aspirations. He needs to gain an intimate knowledge of it if he is to serve the assignment to reconcile the aspirations and institutional concepts underlying trade unionism with the aspirations of a redefined philosophy of progressivism.[70]

Few intellectuals ever tried to serve unions, society, and their discipline in this way, and Barkin would have little patience with intellectuals, especially on the left, who were critical of unions from the "outside." To his mind they were too theoretical and too impractical for unions to be served by them. He also worried that their loyalties, to either a party or an abstract notion of a social revolution, would compromise their commitment to the union.

Intellectuals live in a world of thought, but thoughts can change at any time; they blink their eyes and it's a whole new world. Without long years of dedication on behalf of the union movement, intellectuals, Barkin felt, would remain more true to their ideas than to unions, making them unreliable compatriots. This would hold especially true of leftists who would go down the line with Marx, following ideas that were outside the realm of union beliefs. In his own case, Barkin was an insider for more than twenty-five years, serving by both following and developing the union doctrine. How that service attempted to enhance the idealism of the union movement and Barkin's own study of economics will be the subject of the rest of this book.

Conclusion

In his classic study of trade union intellectuals, Harold Wilensky constructed a group of role orientations indicative of what experts sought from their work. Of the four major categories he devised—missionaries, professional service experts, careerists, and politicos—the first two are readily applicable to Sol Barkin; the second two apply tangentially. First, Barkin was a missionary who "sees the union as a vehicle for social changes in accord with his private goals" and whose "job satisfactions come from combat on behalf of the cause."[71] His long-term service in government and the union movement is evidence of his missionary bent; he would never have contemplated a career in business. Second, Barkin shared the attributes of the second category: "The Professional Service Expert is oriented in his job role toward an outside colleague group; his primary job identification is with his profession."[72] Barkin's extensive publication record, high-level positions, and contact with academic circles attest to his professional standing.

Despite having his own mission and outside link with academic groups, Barkin parted company with most intellectuals by following the path of a careerist or politico by being "highly identified with the union hierarchy."[73] He did not follow these paths to greater income or power, as did careerists and politicos, however. It is quite clear that Barkin's mission—to help working persons to attain a better life through greater economic security and more control over their working lives—could be achieved through unions. His professional contacts were designed to convince other intellectuals of the worth of this mission and the part of unions in attaining it, and his work within the leadership hierarchy of the TWUA and the CIO aimed at reinforcing the same idea among union leaders.

Certain difficulties were involved in the attainment of Barkin's mission, as the events chronicled in this book indicate: business was not willing to cooperate, unions were losing their progressive zeal, and the government became indifferent and then hostile to labor. Something needed to be done to revive all three partners, who had seemingly worked together well during the New Deal and World War II. That something was to be found among intellectuals, who could bring a spirit of idealism to all three institutions. Intellectuals might balk at serving any group at all, especially one so readily categorized as a "special interest group" such as organized labor. In Barkin's view, every interest group had a right to be heard in a pluralistic society, and who better to make the case for the trade union movement than intellectuals?

If intellectuals balked at the role, the proper thing for them was to expand their horizons. They should adopt an interdisciplinary historical approach, similar to the institutional school, and they should get more involved with the union movement. If they fear the development of a laboristic economy, they should make efforts to make unions a viable part of a pluralistic society. For without the presence of unions there may be no countervailing power to keep the economy from being dominated by business.

The problem in maintaining a pluralistic society, according to Barkin, is that the spontaneous generation of countervailing power cannot be relied on. With his institutional approach, Barkin sees the economy as always being in a state of change; there are no states of equilibrium. Conflict of interest, as James Madison long ago recognized, is a constant in society. The way to effect social betterment is to find the interest groups that can offset the negative effects brought about by the activities of dominant groups. It then becomes the role of the activist intellectual to prod the interest group in the right direction. This Barkin tried to do with the union movement.

The prodding of the interest group must be done from within, by a member in good standing of the group. Intellectuals in their academic chairs cannot understand the perspective of a group, especially a union, unless they share the experiences of the group. Nothing in their thinking allows them to see the personal and social costs involved with human participation in the society and the economy. Antonio Gramsci introduced the term "organic intellectual" to characterize the thinkers "which every new class creates along side itself and elaborates in the course of its development."[74] Barkin hoped that the union movement would also create its own group of intellectuals to take on the role of explaining the goals and ideals of unions and of advancing them further.

As a result of holding that extremely broad view of the role of the intellectual, Barkin remains skeptical about any dogmatic approach, whether it be the free market conservatism of the mainstream or the class struggle orientation of Marxists. Ideas developed without a social context can too easily become dogma. Barkin would prefer that the intellectuals add more realism to their theories by paying more attention to and participating in what is happening in the economy, especially what is happening to unions. Then they would appreciate the benefits of developing a field called trade union economics, a subject to which we now turn.

Notes

1. Unless noted, biographical information is based on personal conversations and written communications between the author and Barkin.
2. "The Reminiscences of Solomon Barkin," Oral History Research Office, Columbia University, 1961, pp. 2–3.
3. Donald R. Stabile, "Herbert Hoover, the FAES and the AFofL," *Technology and Culture* 27 (October 1986):819–27.
4. Christopher L. Tomlins, *The State and the Unions: Labor Relations, Law and the Organized Labor Movement in America, 1880–1960* (Cambridge, England: Cambridge University Press, 1985), p. xi.
5. Ibid., p. 5.
6. Stanley Vittoz, *New Deal Labor Policy and the American Industrial Economy* (Chapel Hill, NC: University of North Carolina Press, 1987), pp. 137–38.
7. Broadus Mitchell, *Depression Decade* (New York: Harper Torchbooks, 1947), p. 239.
8. Robert H. Zeiger, *American Workers, American Unions, 1920–1985* (Baltimore: Johns Hopkins University Press, 1986), p. 34.
9. Solomon Barkin, "Labor and the Codified Construction Industry Under the N.R.A.," *Proceedings,* Twenty-eighth Annual Convention, Building Trades Department, American Federation of Labor, 1936, p. 4.
10. Columbia Oral History Research Office, "Reminiscences," p. 15.

11. Solomon Barkin, *The Labor Program Under the NIRA*, Report prepared for the President's Committee on Industrial Analysis (Washington, DC: U.S. Government Printing Office, 1937), p. 7.

12. Solomon Barkin, "Collective Bargaining and Section 7(b) of NIRA," *The Annals of the American Academy of Social and Political Science* (March 1936), pp. 174–75.

13. Barkin, "Labor and the Codified Construction Industry," p. 22.

14. Solomon Barkin, "Negotiating the Construction Code: History of Participation by Building Trades Organizations in Code Making Under NRA," *Proceedings*, Twenty-seventh Annual Convention, Building Trades Department, American Federation of Labor, 1935, p. 25.

15. Columbia Oral History Research Office, "Reminiscences," p. 68.

16. Irving Bernstein, *The Turbulent Years* (Boston: Houghton Mifflin Co., 1970), pp. 37–53, 217–317.

17. Steve Fraser, "The 'Labor Question,' " in Steve Fraser and Gary Gerstle, eds., *The Rise and Fall of the New Deal Order, 1930–1980* (Princeton, NJ: Princeton University Press, 1989), p. 71.

18. Tomlins, *The State and the Unions*, pp. 102, 147.

19. Walter Galenson, *The CIO Challenge to the AFL* (Cambridge: Harvard University Press, 1960), p. 642.

20. Steve Fraser, "Sidney Hillman: Labor's Machiavelli," in Melvyn Dubofsky and Warren Van Tine, eds., *Labor Leaders in America* (Urbana and Chicago, IL: University of Illinois Press, 1987), p. 208.

21. Cited in Matthew Josephson, *Sidney Hillman: Statesman of American Labor* (Garden City, NY: Doubleday & Co., 1952), p. 431.

22. Fraser, "Sidney Hillman," pp. 208–13.

23. Cited in George Soule, *Sidney Hillman* (New York: Macmillan Co., 1939), p. 5.

24. Ibid., p. 207.

25. Ibid., pp. 215–17.

26. Fraser, "Sidney Hillman," p. 218.

27. Bernstein, *Turbulent Years*, pp. 67–77.

28. Josephson, *Sidney Hillman*, p. 367.

29. Galenson, *CIO Challenge to the AFL*, p. 329. Barkin disputes that this was a strong motive for Hillman. See Oral History, p. 70. But he also feels that Hillman's motives were several, making any interpretation of them difficult.

30. Fraser, "The 'Labor Question,' " p. 75.

31. Josephson, *Sidney Hillman*, p. 431.

32. Galenson, *CIO Challenge to the AFL*, pp. 329–43.

33. "Building a Union of Textile Workers," a report of two years' progress to the Convention of the Textile Workers Organizing Committee, May 15–19, 1939.

34. Columbia Oral History Research Office, "Reminiscences," p. 70.

35. Solomon Barkin, "Selected Aspects of the CIO Experience," *Proceedings of the 38th Annual Meeting, Industrial Relations Research Association* (1986), p. 189.

36. Harold L. Wilensky, *Intellectuals in Labor Unions* (Glencoe, IL: Free Press, Publishers, 1956), pp. 38–97.

37. Oral history interview with Solomon Barkin, November 7 and 9, 1977, by James A. Cavanaugh, Wisconsin State Historical Society, Tape 2, Side 2.

38. Columbia Oral History Research Office, "Reminiscences," pp. 94–96.

39. Oral history interviews with George Perkel and Lawrence Rogin, May 4, 1978, by James A. Cavanaugh, Wisconsin State Historical Society, Tape 3, Side 1.

40. Franklin Bishop, "Notes Recounting 1945–41," December 30, 1990, personal communication with the author.

41. The author has viewed several videotapes of retirement parties and meetings of former TWUA officials in forming this opinion.

42. See note 1.

43. "Eggheads Are Leaving Unions," *Nation's Business* (September 1963), p. 325.

44. For an extended discussion of these aspects of Veblen's thinking, see Donald R. Stabile, *Prophets of Order: The Rise of the New Class, Technocracy and Socialism in America* (Boston: South End Press, 1984), Chapters 7 and 8.

45. Robert F. Hoxie, *Trade Unionism in the United States* (New York: Appleton, Century, Crofts, Inc., 1921), pp. 33–51.

46. John R. Commons, *Industrial Goodwill* (New York: McGraw-Hill Book Co., 1919), pp. 112–16.

47. Ben B. Seligman, *Main Currents in Modern Economics* (New York: Free Press of Glencoe, 1962), p. 177.

48. Selig Perlman, *A Theory of the Labor Movement* (New York: A. M. Kelley, 1970), as excerpted in Simon Larson and Bruce Nissen, eds., *Theories of the Labor Movement* (Detroit: Wayne State University Press, 1987), pp. 161–73.

49. Commons, *Industrial Goodwill*, pp. 194–95.

50. Richard A. Lester, *As Unions Mature* (Princeton, NJ: Princeton University Press, 1958), p. 5.

51. Sumner Slichter, *Union Policies and Industrial Management* (New York: Greenwood Press, 1968), p. 1.

52. Solomon Barkin, "A U.S. Commentary," *Rélations Industrielles* 44 (1989), p. 908.

53. Solomon Barkin, "Studies in Trade Union History: Discussion," *Proceedings, Fifth Annual Meeting, Industrial Relations Research Association* (December 1952), p. 1.

54. Solomon Barkin, "Institutional Economics and the American Trade Union Movement," *Rélations Industrielles* 43 (1988), pp. 491–508.

55. Minutes of Third Meeting, Columbia University Seminar on Labor, 1957–58, copy in Barkin Archives, Library, University of Massachusetts at Amherst, p. 4.

56. For a comprehensive overview of the difficulties of intellectuals, see Donald Stabile, "The New Class and Capitalism: A Three-and-Three-Thirds-Class Model," *Review of Radical Political Economics* 15 (Winter 1983), pp. 45–70.

57. Letter from Barkin to Professor Paul Hayes, Columbia Law School, February 17, 1958, copy in Barkin Archives, p. 2.

58. Derek C. Bok and John T. Dunlop, *Labor and the American Community* (New York: Simon & Schuster, 1970), pp. 30–31.

59. Perlman, *Theory of the Labor Movement*, p. 172.

60. Solomon Barkin, "Applied Social Science in the American Trade-Union Movement," *Philosophy of Science* 15 (July 1949): 193.

61. Lorin Lee Cary, "Middle-Echelon Labor Leaders and the Union-Building Process," in Merl E. Reed, Leslie S. Hough, and Gary M. Fink, eds., *Southern Workers and Their Unions* (Westport, CT: Greenwood Press, 1981), p. 213.

62. Ibid.

63. Cited in Wilensky, *Intellectuals in Labor Unions*, p. 272.

64. Solomon Barkin, "Critique of Committee Report," presented at Annual Meeting, Industrial Relations Research Association, December 1988, copy in author's possession.

65. Minutes, Third Meeting, Columbia University Seminar on Labor, 1957–58, p. 10.

66. Solomon Barkin, "Psychology as Seen by a Trade Unionist," *Personnel Psychology* 14 (Autumn 1961), p. 270.

67. Wilensky, *Intellectuals in Labor Unions*, pp. 270–74.

68. Barkin, "Applied Social Science," p. 196.

69. Minutes, Seventh Meeting, Columbia University Seminar on Labor, 1957–58, p. 2.

70. Solomon Barkin, "The Social Crisis of Our Time," *Labor and Nation* (January-February 1949), p. 19.

71. Wilensky, *Intellectuals in Labor Unions,* p. 125.

72. Ibid., p. 129.

73. Ibid., p. 153.

74. Antonio Gramsci, *Selections from the Prison Notebooks* (New York: International Publishers, 1971), p. 6.

2

A System of Trade Union Economics

Injury has been done not only to those persons in low-wage industries, but also to the nation itself. We, as a country, and particularly our local communities, have established a special "welfare economy" for the low-wage industries. The public and government [are] subsidizing these laggard employers, whether through direct grants or through the high cost of the social and human neglect created by low wages.
—*Solomon Barkin*

During the past three decades, the discipline of economics has gained a reputation for exercising a powerful influence on society through its policy prescriptions in macroeconomics and its preaching of the virtues of free market microeconomics. In the early 1960s, the apparent success of Keynesian fiscal policy ushered in the Age of the Economist; by the late 1980s, the advocates of deregulation and rational expectations were promising policies that would foster steady economic growth to rival what had taken place in the 1960s. To many economists there could be no doubt about the social value of their discipline.

It was Barkin's view, however, that this type of economics lost its value when it was applied to labor unions. From his own perspective of almost three decades of research on issues pertaining to unions as well as from his training as an institutional economist, he felt no qualms about claiming that his own virtues as an economist owed much to the condition wherein economics had little to say about those issues. As he once told the members of a Columbia University graduate Seminar on Labor, "No matter which subject I examined, which field of knowledge I faced, there was something original which I could say. It wasn't that I was inventive, ingenious or particularly gifted. But I had a body of experience which was not available and had not been tapped by the particular professional group which I was addressing."[1] All intellectual disciplines involved in the study of industrial relations were taking a limited approach to the subject. Political science, sociology, economics, law, management, even the humanities, Barkin felt, could gain in their interpretations and in their methods if they tried to see the world from the trade union perspective. Barkin was especially interested in seeing economists develop this approach.

In making his case, Barkin was also expressing an assumption that members of the various disciplines shared his belief that unions are and should be a permanent feature of modern society. He realized the tenuousness of that hope with regard to economics, however. His concern about economics goes right to the heart of the discipline. Economists are wary of any economic agent that exercises market power, whether it be business or labor. With business, economists have always been adept at finding forces that can be interpreted as offsetting the potential abuses of market power, such as a quasi-market effect (potential competition) or greater efficiency and lower costs (scale economies). When they analyze labor unions, no such offsets on the possible abuse of market power are found. As Barkin summarized their attitude, "It is well to note that the liberal economists' assumptions respecting trade unions are unclear. Trade unions seek to balance bargaining power. But when they attain this power, they are to be feared for being apt to be collusive."[2]

If economists looked more closely at what unions do, they might take a different perspective. At least that was Barkin's hope. As he put it, "If the economists can erect a system of business enterprise, farm enterprise and family economics, if we can challenge traditional economics with institutional and welfare economics and with Keynesian economics, why not have a system of trade union economics?"[3] According to Barkin, this plea went unheeded by mainstream economists, who limited themselves to the study of individual behavior and choice without regard to how these are socially conditioned; they also overlooked nonmonetary costs of production and omitted consideration of institutional change. In terms of developing a system of trade union economics, the dismal science has been a dismal failure as far as concerns an understanding of what values unions and their members hold.

To some extent, the failures of economics are becoming more widely recognized. Many Wall Street brokerage firms, banks, and investment firms have begun reducing the number of economists on their staffs as they realize that macroeconomic forecasting is not a reliable procedure. In addition, as deregulation has proceeded, it has brought a variety of problems not anticipated by its proponents. In defiance of Milton Friedman's strictures on predictability as the test of a theory, the economy has not proved to be easy to model, for too many random variables always come into play. Predictability in labor markets is even more uncertain, because human behavior with all its vagaries is even less susceptible to a regular pattern than is financial behavior.

Barkin never developed a systematic treatise on trade union economics in his own body of work; he was too busy working and dealing with the pressures of daily problems to set down his own approach. Most of his writings constituted responses to immediate challenges or his desire to record the lessons learned by the TWUA in meeting such a challenge. In other cases, his published works were responses to invitations to speak or write for particular audiences and journals or part of his effort to publish in a certain journal. His many publications were thus not a systematic effort at making a formal thesis but represented an effort to stimulate others to look more closely at the issues he raised.

This chapter presents a general approach to the type of economics Barkin would like to see applied to unions. A brief warning is perhaps in order: Presentation of Barkin's economics has two particular biases stemming from its relationship to traditional economics. First, there is a tendency to simplify the analysis of the mainstream and other schools of thought by keying in on what they had to say about issues of concern to Barkin; in many cases this was not much, so larger contributions made by those economists have been ignored. Second, Barkin's work and the account of it presented herein stress the differences he had with other economists; he had no time to heap praise on them for good work in areas of agreement but wanted to push them toward his concerns. Much of what is said in this and the following chapters about economics should be read within that context: that the ideas presented and the words put in the mouths of other economists are there primarily for the purpose of providing a contrast to Barkin's approach.

Central to this approach is the concept of social cost as applied to labor. The concept, one that Barkin learned from J. M. Clark, forms a backdrop for much of Barkin's trade union economics, even though Barkin rarely refers to it except by implication.

Social Costs of Labor

Nowadays, when a coal mining company practices strip mining that damages the environment, the company is expected, when operations finally cease, to repair the damages it has wrought. Cases of rural blight left behind by the mining businesses are too obnoxious to be ignored. When the repair obligation is not met by business, it falls upon government to make up the difference. Federal and state laws now require mining companies to restore the arability of soil, but even government may fail in its efforts to remedy social problems. Although it is somewhat fanciful, the same argument could be extended to urban blight. Perhaps businesses that abandon factories, warehouses, or retail stores will one day be required to transform them into parks. At least this argument has been applied to chemical dump sites, although again, when the parties inflicting the damage cannot be identified or held responsible, it is government that may remedy the damages.

When the blight left behind is of human form, the obligations of business are somehow weakened. Mountain chains and urban waterways are inanimate objects that cannot protect themselves, and endangered species do not have the right to vote. Because human beings have legal rights that supposedly enable them to take care of themselves, they do not need the special protection that is accorded to trees and spotted owls. The tragedy is that when they try to use their unions to secure similar forms of protection, they are viewed as being economically unsound and unreasonable.

The concept used by an institutional economist such as Barkin to measure the impact of these various forms of blight is that of social cost. The concept dates back to at least Adam Smith, and its further refinement took place in the 1920s at the hands of J. M. Clark. It was noted in Chapter One that Barkin studied economics under Clark at Columbia and was influenced by Clark's use of social costs. Since Barkin never set down his own views on social costs in a complete way, elaboration of Clark's theory of social cost and how it applies to labor is in order.

Clark's theory of social costs holds that there are indirect costs involved in industry that are not properly taken into account in calculating the overall costs of production. As a result, they are left out of the prices that are charged for final goods. This means that consumers do not pay the full cost associated with the resources used to satisfy their wants.

Clark's statement of the problems caused by indirect costs is found in his studies on overhead costs. Clark was concerned with difficulties that are caused by the overhead costs that have developed with the rise of the mass production economy. Because mass production relies more heavily on capital as a factor of production, direct costs of labor and raw materials become of less importance in determining the costs of manufacturing a final product, even though in many industries, labor costs remain substantial. In addition, compared to overhead costs, direct costs have the advantage of being identifiable; it is fairly easy to calculate the amount of raw material and the amount of labor used and their costs in manufacturing a product.

Calculating the indirect or overhead costs of capital used in production is more difficult. In theory, whether economic or accounting, the calculation and allocation of overhead costs are seen as being straightforward. Determine the useful life of the capital, divide the value of the capital by the number of years for which it will be used for an annual depreciation figure, and then divide the annual depreciation figure by the number of items produced in order to arrive at overhead cost per item—what economists refer to as average fixed costs. When this figure is added to the unit labor and material costs, total cost per unit can be determined.

Clark saw a host of problems in so allocating overhead costs, believing that they were not being allocated well. First, such notions as the "value of capital" and "useful life" are arbitrary; accountants have not determined whether to use historical cost (what was paid for the item), replacement cost (what the item would cost if currently bought), or exit value (what the item would sell for if the firm liquidated). A second problem arises in terms of knowing what quantity is to be produced, for the average fixed cost depends on whether the amount produced is large or small. Accountants solve this problem by way of a concept called standard burden, whereby items are allocated their share of overhead costs based on an assumed level of production. To the extent that these internal overhead costs are improperly allocated, Clark argued, prices charged by business would not reflect the true contribution of the fixed resources and could result in inefficient production and misallocation of resources.

Clark applied the same argument to the indirect costs associated with the using up of social resources—what can be accurately described as social overhead. It is now recognized that the process of production causes by-products, such as pollution, that use up clean air, clear water, and pristine land. These costs are external to production and are usually imposed on persons not necessarily connected with the product, or they are not paid for at all. Our social tendency is to see that those costs are imposed on the individuals (consumers, producers, and workers) who benefit from the production of the commodity, even though the costs are difficult to identify and calculate. Ingenious ways are devised to ensure that these social costs are figured into the process of production so that they are made part of the cost/benefit calculations on which economics is based. Only when the full costs of producing a product are weighed against the benefits of consuming it, can an efficient allocation of resources be said to have taken place. When calculation and apportionment of social costs cannot be made with accuracy, the alternative is for government to pay for them by using its taxing powers to impose them on all taxpayers, under the principle that all society gains from the production of the product.

Long before the idea became popular in economics, Clark recognized that production involved the use of social overhead. At any moment, a society has a fixed stock of what might be called social capital in terms of, for example, human talent or the environment. As with any type of capital, the more this social capital is used, the faster it will depreciate. Such depreciation of social capital is what Clark meant by social costs, and he worried about the allocation of the social costs of using that social overhead. The business system was not equipped to set aside a depreciation allowance to replace the social capital it was using.

In a provocative chapter in his studies on overhead costs, Clark gave an example of the concept of social cost by applying it to labor. For him there are a variety of social costs involved with work, including unemployment, health care, and training. Clark understood that labor, like capital, had to be maintained in order to remain useful. Labor, too, has fixed overhead costs. As he wrote, "There is a minimum of maintenance of the laborer's health and working capacity which must be borne by someone, whether the laborer works or not" or else "the community suffers a loss through the deterioration of its working power."[4]

When he looked at actual economic practices, however, Clark found that the concept of social cost as applied to labor went unrecognized. For the individual business, only capital represents a fixed cost; to businesspeople, labor is a variable cost that can be avoided simply by discharging workers. Workers are responsible for their own maintenance. But when their wages are not adequate to tide them over during periods of unemployment and if the community does not make additional provisions for them, members of the labor force might themselves deteriorate.

To bring home his point about the social costs of labor, Clark, following the analysis usually applied to business, divided the costs of work into fixed and variable costs. The fixed costs he considered to be the costs of reproducing the worker in good stead (he allowed that these costs might increase with a greater work effort); in short, the worker, to be properly maintained for work, has to be provided with adequate food, shelter, rest, and health—these are social costs that cannot be avoided. The variable cost of labor is the leisure time the worker gives up in deciding to go to work.[5] It was clear to Clark that wages determined in the labor market did not always cover the worker's fixed costs.

Overhead costs are best defined as those costs that exist no matter what level of production is chosen, even when the level chosen is zero. This holds for social overhead costs as well as business overhead costs. In the case of workers, this means that they must feed, clothe, and house themselves, whether they are working or not; if they are unemployed, sick, or elderly, they must still take care of themselves with training, medical care, and a retirement fund. If, when they are employed, workers are sufficiently compensated to provide for these contingencies, they are being paid at their full social cost level. Since these costs will not go away, if workers cannot pay them, someone else must, whether it be friends and relatives, eleemosynary institutions, or government. To the extent that these other agencies help to cover the social costs of work, the businesses that pay a wage below the social cost level are being subsidized by them. This is the problem Clark raised.

Suppose that there is a minimal amount of goods and services that must be purchased to ensure subsistence; these would represent a social cost wage that cannot be forgone by workers. If wages are low, the worker has no choice but to work enough time to pay for this minimal amount. One does not have to be pro-labor or a Marxist to argue that under free market capitalism, workers find that wages below the social cost minimum are likely to prevail. It was Adam Smith's canny observation that in conflicts between the servants and the master over wages, the master is usually the master. According to Smith, employers have advantages over workers in terms of their fewer numbers, their greater ability to outwait workers in a strike, and the weight of the law on their side. He wrote, "Masters are always and everywhere in a sort of tacit, but constant and uniform combination, not to raise the wages of labor above their actual rate"[6]

Smith's general statement on labor requires some qualification. Although employers may well keep wages low in order to remain competitive, they can also enhance their position with regard to other firms by improving their efficiency or by making a better selection among workers. For Smith such gains could be made through a further division of labor and could be used by companies even without the pressure of competition. Smith's basic proposition remains viable in a slightly altered form, however. When competition gets severe, the first option that employers are likely to consider is how to reduce wages.

Given that option, the forces of competition may compel firms to seek the lowest wages possible. If a few firms or even one firm locates in an area where buying power can be exploited to pay low wages, all other firms are forced to push their wages down to the same level. Individual bargaining by workers will not be able to prevent wages from falling, nor will individual businesses gain by using better working conditions and payment of social costs to attract superior workers.[7]

As with any problem raised with social costs, this one does not lend itself well to a market solution, due to the prisoners' dilemma paradox. Suppose we have an industry with perfectly competitive markets for products and resources. It is quite possible to imagine in this industry a situation existing in which wage levels did not cover the full social costs of labor. Even if employers realized that their workers were not adequately provided for, there is nothing they could do to redress the problem. Any employer who considered paying workers a social cost premium above the going wage, unless the employer were sure of being compensated with higher productivity, would be compelled to choose not to, for to do so would incur a competitive disadvantage and reduce profits. Other ways must be found to internalize these social costs by imposing them on all employers.

Mainstream economists might hope that social costs may be avoided or eliminated by having them internalized on a firm's cost structure or by somehow creating a market for the right to abuse the social overhead. The problem of social costs is pervasive and ongoing and not suitable to adjustments derived from an analysis based on partial equilibrium. As K. William Kapp, whose work also had an influence on Barkin, stated the problem, "All economic development is structural change and structural change tends to give rise to losses which are shifted to or borne by third parties or society at large."[8] While he was concerned about all social costs, Kapp, like Clark, worried about the social costs of work, especially when it involved the obsolescence of skills or low standards of worker safety. He pointed out that in the food and drug industries, new products were carefully screened before being put on the market to ensure that they caused no harmful side effects. This procedure could also be applied to new technology. Kapp wrote, "The burden of proof that a new technology, a new product, a new process and a particular input (and output) pattern are safe would have to rest in principle upon the producer and not upon the damaged person or society."[9] Responsibility for the social costs of production should be placed upon the producers, when possible, using government power when necessary. In the case of labor, unions could share in that responsibility, but only if there were cooperation between them and management.

Although this argument based on social costs cannot be found in this form in any of Barkin's writings, it is clear that his economic approach was influenced by it. His solution to the prisoners' dilemma problem is to bring in an outside agent to compel all employers to raise their wage levels. Two such agents appear as likely candidates to impose a social cost wage[10] on all employers. Labor unions can organize an entire industry and impose a union scale on all employers, or the government can legislate minimum wage and maximum hour laws. Although he would prefer union action to ensure a full social cost wage, Barkin would accept government responsibility to accomplish that goal, as detailed in Chapter Six.

Social costs are a constant factor of economic life. Barkin's idea that unions would be able to gain the power to impose a full social cost wage on employers goes against the grain of two centuries of thinking in economics, for it means that unions would have the power to upset the entire fabric of economic life. Their ability to achieve this power and use it responsibly has long been questioned by economists, as the next section describes.

Theories of Union Economics

Economists have never found a way to give labor the central role in their theories that it plays in the economy. No one would challenge Marx's premise that a capitalist economy is impossible without workers, but standard texts in basic economic theory rarely give labor more than a chapter, which comes near the end of the text. Yet labor's share of national income is more than 60 percent, and nearly 90 percent of the work force is employed by someone else. Despite this importance of labor, attention in economics remains focused on consumer demand as served by the small firm under market conditions of perfect competition. How this shallow end has been reached requires a brief excursion into the history of economics.

The classical economists, starting with Adam Smith, were certainly concerned with market competition and ensuring that the consumer was well served. They also understood that there was something different about labor markets. In the *Wealth of Nations*, Smith made it clear that the wealth of any nation depended on how its labor was applied and that the division of labor was central to economic growth. Smith had a theory of wages that was based on the supply and demand for labor, but just as he warned that businesspeople rarely got together without scheming to raise prices, Smith recognized that they could also combine to depress wages. Smith regretted these efforts to reduce wages, for he believed that high wages benefited society by spurring workers to greater productivity. He concluded, "Where wages are high, accordingly, we shall always find the workmen more active, diligent and expeditious, than where they are low."[11]

Smith, along with Ricardo and Marx, started from the premise that workers must be paid at least a subsistence wage, a rate Marx described as sufficient for individual workers to support themselves and their family and for the labor force to continually replace itself. Smith wrote, "A man must always live by his work, and his wages must at least be sufficient to maintain him. They must even upon most occasions be somewhat more; otherwise it would be impossible for him to bring up a family, and the race of such workmen could not last beyond the first generation. . . ."[12]

Smith worried that the condition of workers would worsen as capitalism developed. The division of labor would narrow the skills and mental outlook of workers until they became "stupid and ignorant." Their chances for attaining a higher wage would be diminished. Smith harbored some optimism that the lot of workers could be made better through overall economic growth.

The rest of the classical school was not as hopeful as Smith. Thomas Malthus set forth his population doctrine to refute any reason for hope by workers. High wages would cause them to have more children, eventually increasing the labor supply and reducing wages. David Ricardo was equally dour; high wages (caused more by high food prices than supply and demand) would cause workers to be replaced by machines, and again their wages would be reduced. There emerged in classical economic thought the notion of the wages fund doctrine, which asserted there was a fixed supply of funds available for wages, with the number of workers dividing up the fund determining the wage each worker received. The impact that trade unions might have on wages was not considered, perhaps because there were very few unionized workers and the legality of unions was in question at the time. Besides, all unions could do was affect the distribution of the wages fund in favor of their members.

Even though he stands as a towering dissenter from the assumptions of the classical school, Karl Marx shared many of its conclusions. To be specific, Marx accepted neither the population theory of Malthus nor the wages fund doctrine. Even more than Smith, he desired to see the condition of workers improved. He did not see those conditions getting better under the capitalist economy.

In Marx's analysis, the conditions of the working class were determined by its struggles with the capitalist class, the rulers of capitalism. Because of their superior economic, legal, and political power, members of the capitalist class had advantages in bargaining with workers over wages and working conditions. These advantages enabled them to exploit workers by allowing them to pay workers a subsistence wage that was less than the value of the product that workers produced. For Marx, the difference between the subsistence wage and the value of the product determined the level of profits in the economy. In their efforts to increase profits, capitalists would reduce wages as much as possible, but even Marx conceded there was a floor on how low wages could go. Further profits could be made by introducing machinery either to reduce the cost of products that formed the subsistence wage, thereby allowing the wage floor to be reduced, or to increase the amount that each worker could produce, thereby reducing the need for workers. In either case, there was created an industrial reserve army of the unemployed, which ensured that wages would not increase.

Marx could conclude, in words much stronger than Adam Smith used, that the labor market in capitalist economies was rigged against workers. His solution, of course, was to replace the capitalist economy with a socialist (and eventually communist) economy that would redress the wrongs against workers. Marx did not think that labor unions would be of any permanent help to workers; they aimed at helping workers to make economic gains within the capitalist system. Only after a revolution in which the working class defeated and eliminated the capitalist class could the conditions of workers be improved. At best, in Marx's view, the role unions might play in this revolution was to spread among workers the class consciousness they would need for it.

In sum, the classicals were pessimistic as to whether the wage would ever go above the subsistence level due to the operations of the wages fund, the industrial reserve army, or population growth. As a result, they did not find it likely that unions could accomplish anything with regard to higher wages.

In the period immediately after Marx wrote, economics itself underwent a revolution wherein the ideas of the classicals were replaced by thinkers in a neoclassical school (to be referred throughout this work as the mainstream of economics, for that is what it has become). Instead of the social turbulence depicted by the classical school, the mainstream of neoclassicals saw an economy of balance imbued with small decisions.

The two basic tenets of the mainstream of neoclassicals were, and still are, equilibrium and marginalism. Under the neoclassicals' system, markets tend toward equilibrium, a balancing of the forces of supply and demand that determine the one price that clears the market by satisfying both buyers and sellers. Underlying that satisfaction is a series of small decisions based on what small changes mean for the individuals who make up the market and make rational decisions about their options. In labor markets, for example, the buyer of labor must decide whether the additional output to be gained by hiring another worker is worthwhile in terms of the wage determined by the market, and the worker must decide if the extra money the wage offers is worth giving up additional leisure time. Outside agents, such as unions, cannot alter this outcome, although they can upset it for a time.

The notion of marginal productivity, simultaneously discovered in England by Jevons, in Austria by Menger, in Switzerland by Walras, and in the United States by J. B. Clark, is an obviously brilliant parable. J. B. Clark, for example, drove it to the point that the division of income brought about by the calculations of marginal product was fair, because both capital and labor earned an income equal to their marginal contribution to production. Modern members of the mainstream would not go this far in asserting fairness to the marginal approach but would still hold that wages cannot exist for long either above or below the marginal product of the last worker hired.

A smooth-working labor market was essential for the working out of marginal productivity theory. For a labor market to work well, there must exist conditions of perfect competition, which include a large number of firms trying to hire a large number of workers, a fairly uniform level of skill required of workers, and a high degree of mobility among workers. These conditions ensured equal bargaining power on both sides of the market and meant that if workers were dissatisfied with their jobs, they could work elsewhere. Free labor markets that resulted in a balancing of the marginal decisions of many individuals continue to be a mainstay of the mainstream approach.

The early members of the mainstream were still troubled by their approach, however. Lloyd Reynolds once observed, "Economists have always been somewhat diffident about integrating labor into the market schema. Marshall, Pigou, Taussig and other leading theorists were troubled by the 'peculiarities' of the labor market."[13] In this regard they followed the concerns of Adam Smith. The synthesizer of the neoclassical school, Alfred Marshall, exemplifies those concerns.

As a product of the Victorian era, which saw a great deal of economic progress brought about by industrialization and mass production, Marshall was very optimistic about workers' receiving an improved standard of living. Improved efficiency was the key to workers' gains, for that would bring about higher wages. Higher wages would lead to improvements in the health and mental outlook of the next generation, leading to further efficiency and even higher wages. If workers were permitted their education, gains would come even more quickly.

In his attitudes toward unions, Marshall was ambivalent. He took a favorable view of unions as being outlets for self-government, sources of self-respect, and essential to democracy. As he put it, "Unionism must be judged by its influence on the character of the workers." Moreover, unions could fight to improve working conditions and eliminate exploitation as a counterforce to "the tacit agreements among employers" to keep wages low and profits above normal. Marshall worried about drawbacks from unions, primarily their efforts to restrict output and entry to a trade. As Clark Kerr summarizes, "Marshall drew a clear balance sheet on the trade unions—as combinations they were all right; as combinations in restraint of trade they were not."[14]

How was one to judge whether trade unions were guilty of a restraint of trade? In Marshall's view, it would have to be when they failed the market test. Although Marshall believed that unions could do a lot for workers, he did not believe that unions could raise wages very much above those of nonunion workers. In the long run, the market would determine the level of wages in any industry, and unions that tried to change this by restrictive action would cause social harm in the short run without accomplishing any long-term gains.

In summary, the early mainstream, typified by Marshall, stressed market forces in its view of labor relations, although Marshall staked out a moderate position by always qualifying how applicable market theory was in practice. Unions had a place in the economy as long as they did not upset the forces of supply and demand in theory, while in practice they could make small gains for their members.

Marshall's qualifications were downgraded in the 1930s by John Hicks's major mainstream statement, *The Theory of Wages*, in which Hicks declared, "The theory of the determination of wages in a free market is simply a special case of the general theory of value." Wages were set by markets, just as happened with other commodities. The only thing that made the case special was the presence of government regulation or unions in setting wages. These made little difference. Hicks continued, "The same forces which determine wages in a free market are still present under regulation; they only work rather differently." Thus the starting point in a study of labor economics was with the free market wage. Anything else was a detrimental deviation from it. Hicks could view collective bargaining and strikes as following a pattern conditioned by markets and undertaken by rational marginalists on both sides who would be brought to an equilibrium between resistance and concessions.[15]

Hicks would later call *The Theory of Wages* "a thoroughly bad book."[16] That was only after a twenty-year challenge by a group of labor economists who were willing to take a more realistic approach to the study of labor markets. That group, which Clark Kerr has named the neoclassical revisionists (hereafter they will be referred to more simply as the union support school), took Hicks's approach seriously, for they were much influenced by his writing when in graduate school. But the key members of the group—John Dunlop, Clark Kerr, Richard Lester, and Lloyd Reynolds—worked during World War II with the War Labor Board in trying to determine what wage increases were needed to get workers into the right industries. They soon became convinced that the deviations from the free market result were more powerful than the market itself in determining wages.

More specifically, when they studied labor markets in order to reach recommendations on where to set wages under wartime controls, the members of the union support school discovered that there was not a single wage set in any labor market, as market equilibrium theory would have predicted. Rather, there was a whole range of wages for the same job in the same labor market or even the same firm. This finding led them to put more stress on market imperfections in determining wages; they especially noted that there was a lack of labor mobility between markets and among firms within a market, while within firms there existed internal labor markets wherein firms set a range of wages based on a variety of factors.[17]

When they looked more closely at company practices, members of the union support school found that in nonunionized industries, business had bargaining advantages over workers. The primary imperfection in labor markets was a buyer's monopoly (or monopsony, as economists call it). As Lloyd Reynolds and

Cynthia Taft argued in their classic study, *The Evolution of Wage Structures*, "There can be no doubt of employers' monopsony power over wages under nonunion conditions."[18] This power gave business the ability to keep wages low; market imperfections that kept workers tied to a company also permitted little chance for workers to be protected from unsafe working conditions or poor management practices.

To provide workers with a more equal footing in bargaining, the union support school took a friendly attitude toward unions and collective bargaining. As Kerr has recalled, members of his group "supported collective bargaining and were interested in its operations," which led them "to a more neutral stance between labor and management."[19] This neutrality aimed at finding a middle ground between the mainstream, which opposed unions, and the Wisconsin school, which seemingly favored them.

When it considered the activities of labor unions, the union support school developed two approaches. John Dunlop stressed the economic approach, wherein unions were viewed as trying to maximize the wages of their members. In opposition, Arthur Ross set forth a political approach, which highlighted the efforts of union leaders to keep peace with management, government, and rank-and-file members.[20] Although they were sympathetic to the plight of unorganized workers, the union support school members were also wary of too much bargaining power going to unions.

The union support school did have in common with the institutional school an effort to introduce more realism into the study of economics. Many of its members adhered to an interdisciplinary approach to the study of labor, and they used this approach to produce some exceptional studies of union behavior, which will be referenced throughout this book to form both a counter to and a confirmation of many of Barkin's ideas. By the 1960s, however, both schools had experienced sudden and sharp decline. In part, they ran out of studies to undertake. Equally important, members of the union support school, perhaps due to their sense of realism, had a talent for administration and arbitration that carried them to the high echelons of education and government. Most important, however, the 1960s saw a revival of the mainstream in labor economics, especially in the United States.

At a theoretical level, the mainstream approach to economics was revived by two powerful thinkers. Paul Samuelson placed economic theory on a mathematical basis, which added to the rigor of its analysis and gave economists a whole new box of tools to develop. Milton Friedman placed the quest for realism in a subsidiary position by arguing that it was beside the point, that the true test of a theory was not its congruence with reality, but its predictive power. The result has been a reduced effort on the part of economists to use the case study approach as a way of understanding the economy. Instead, economists devote their time to the study of high theory, and their empirical work is completed when numbers collected by someone else are subjected to sophisticated econometric analysis via a computer.

The mainstream version of labor economics has been restored to primacy, thanks to the work of both H. Gregg Lewis, who used advanced statistical methods to determine that the ability of unions to raise members' wages relative to the general wage level was strong only during recessions, and Gary Becker, who applied human capital theory to explain how education and training can influence wages and result in wage differentials within markets and firms.[21] Of greater importance, the revival of the mainstream has led to a shift in emphasis back to a study of labor markets as the starting point in labor economics, with unions' being considered as a deviation from the norm. The qualifications that Marshall had made in a bygone era were further reduced in importance.

Among the mainstream, the concept of a subsistence wage has been dropped from labor economics. The pure economics of the neoclassical school relies on an analysis of labor markets in which the wage workers are paid as determined by the forces of supply and demand. The demand for labor is held to be based on what workers contribute to production in terms of value of the final product. When the supply-side of the labor market is considered, workers are viewed as comparing the wage rate, in terms of the goods and services it will buy, with the leisure time they must give up in order to work, perhaps making a hidden assumption that the labor-leisure trade-off takes place only after a subsistence wage is met. When the forces of supply and demand are brought together, the result is an equilibrium wage that satisfies both sides and clears the market. Firms will not pay more than the equilibrium wage, and workers who are not satisfied with the equilibrium wage will leave the labor market. In this argument, no consideration is given to whether the wage covers the cost of reproducing the worker in good stead, to use Clark's term. The concept of social costs is not even mentioned in standard neoclassical treatments of labor economics.[22] Even Albert Rees, a highly perceptive observer of union economics, ignores the concept.[23]

Among the institutional and union support schools of labor economists, the concept of social costs has been applied to cases of technological displacement and layoffs.[24] Where these schools mention a full social cost wage, it remains tangential to their analysis as supplemental fringe benefits, although they do admit of union success in attaining such supplements.[25]

There are two themes running through this survey of the history of labor economics that are essential to an understanding of Barkin's views on economics. The first concerns the issue of the extent to which the markets and the economic models based on them are helpful in analyzing union activities. The issue between the mainstream and its challengers from the institutional and union support schools was the extent to which wages were determined by market or nonmarket forces. The challengers stressed the presence of nonmarket forces and the need for nonmarket solutions to improve industrial relations. The second issue concerns whether unions could be part of nonmarket solutions.

From his institutional perspective, Barkin would find the attainment of a wage to cover the full social costs of work to be a fundamental goal of unions. Two problems with basing wages on social costs are that social costs are very difficult to define and that they represent only a minimum. Barkin's own efforts in defining social costs provide a good example of how it might be done. During World War II, in hearings before the War Labor Board on setting wages in the textile industry, Barkin started with a basic minimum standard of living as defined by the 1935 Emergency Subsistence Budget of the Works Progress Administration, with the help of the U.S. Department of Labor. He then repriced the budget items underlying that standard, using prices from surveys of three New England and two Southern textile communities. Textile workers were also surveyed to determine whether household incomes were sufficient to pay for the standard budget and to show how difficult it was for textile workers to earn a standard of living that would meet their social costs. Profits of textile firms were also calculated so as to demonstrate that firms could easily afford to pay a higher wage. Barkin then digested all this information in a form that could be easily presented and understood at board hearings. In this case, the argument proved effective, for the board decided to grant the higher wage.[26]

There are other factors that need to be considered when determining wages once a minimum social cost wage has been calculated. These include productivity, changes in the cost of living, the amount of profits a firm has, industry conditions, and even the accounting methods a firm uses. Barkin's view, to be discussed more fully later, was that employers had a wide range of wage options they could pay workers, depending on their other costs and the amount of competition they faced. The maximum wage that could be paid was greatly influenced by conditions in the product market. This did not mean, however, that it had to be below the amount needed to meet the social costs of labor.

By making the concept of the social costs of labor central to his economics, Barkin establishes the attainment of it as a legitimate goal for unions. Unlike more traditional economists, he sees union efforts to gain higher wages as having a social benefit and not as just an effort to maximize the income of a select group. In taking this approach, he is a follower of Clark and Kapp and would agree with Clark's notion that a more efficient allocation of resources will take place only when all social costs, including those of labor, form a part of the final price consumers pay for goods and services. If collective bargaining by unions is necessary to place social costs where they belong, Barkin would approve of it.

Workers' Attainment of a Full-Cost Social Wage

The problem of attaining a wage that covers the full social cost of work requires that it be imposed equally on all employers. Suppose we have an industry with a large amount of competition and all firms in it utilizing similar technology with the result that productivity is pretty much equal across all firms. Because of this industrial structure, firms will be limited in their abilities to raise prices. As a result, during normal times, profits may be increased by reducing costs, and during hard times, when price cutting becomes widespread, losses may be minimized through reducing costs. There are, however, two methods for reducing costs: improving efficiency and productivity and cutting wages. In the short run, wage reductions are the quickest, easiest, and surest method of reducing costs. In the long run, improved productivity is the most progressive and socially beneficial approach. Both approaches will likely be used, for competition will force them, and the problem will be even worse in a real-life situation in which different plants have different levels of efficiency. The problem involved with wage-cutting, as an analysis of social costs should make clear, is that costs are not really cut. They are simply transferred to workers or more generally to society in the form of welfare benefits or the reduced health of a large sector of the economy. Arthur Goldberg gave the most concise statement of this view when he wrote, "There is no social advantage to be gained by allowing manufacturers to compete on the basis of sweatshop wages."[27]

Barkin was keenly aware of business's penchant for lowering wages as a quick way to cut costs and was able to document it in terms of national aggregates. The pattern he detected revealed a very deleterious effect for labor: "Wage increases, if they were granted, generally lagged behind the business upturn or the rise in prices. . . . Wage reductions, on the other hand, followed quickly upon the recognition of a downward turn in business or price reduction."[28] The pattern changed, starting in 1938, a factor that Barkin attributed to increased bargaining power on the part of unions and the effective intervention of the Roosevelt Administration in the restoration of the wage cuts in the railroad industry.

In using its power in the labor market, the union movement pursued two broad objectives of wage stabilization desired by workers—stability and security. Workers would want to see a steady wage rate and to feel secure that they can rely on it for a time. To help foster that stability, unions would aim at a target of uniform wage rates for all workers in an industry as part of a program of maintaining labor cost parity among all firms in that industry. In this way, wages could be kept out of competition, with firms spared the need to constantly change wage levels in response to the actions of other firms. As Barkin put it, "The worker, as well as the employer, wants a stable wage system. Constant changes are disturbing."[29] It is for this reason that both unions and management make wage agreements for a defined time period of several years.

To avoid many changes in wages, a union would try to impose a uniform wage standard on an industry. The easiest way was to establish a uniform wage scale for each job, as AFL craft unions had done. In industrial situations, in which separate job categories were not feasible, several strategies were possible. Uniform piece rates could be devised, even though these placed more stress on labor cost parity then on equalization of wages. This procedure would work well in industries that used standardized products and methods of production in all firms. The procedure was also very elaborate, requiring rates that had to fit each circumstance and that had to be based on efficiency studies conducted jointly by union and management. Barkin pointed out one piece-rate agreement that was fifteen pages long.[30]

Another way of imposing uniform labor costs on all firms in an industry was to set a standard minimum wage in an industry in which the product and production methods were uniform. This policy required active policing by the union, however, because some manufacturers and workers would cut wages in order to bring business into their area.

When a product was not uniform and the technology was constantly changing so that production methods were not standard throughout an industry, the best unions could do was to opt for a strategy of wage equalization, thereby keeping wages out of competition and giving employers an incentive to continue to adopt new methods of production. Wage equalization could be accomplished by setting a standard of average hourly wages in a plant and then allowing for differentials based on the type of job. Piece rates could be established that guarantee each worker a minimum hourly wage, especially if adjustments were made when new methods of production were introduced.[31]

Barkin drew on several cases for an object lesson in how wage equalization and labor cost parity worked. As he noted, "The apparel industry is a classic example of what can be done. The industry used to be chaotic. Each employer would say: 'Well, I can't pay you decent wages because the other man is cutting prices and wages.' The union came in and said in effect: 'From now on everybody is going to have the same labor costs.' " As a result, Barkin found, economic conditions in the industry were becoming more stable, and management and the union were directing more of their attention to problems of increasing efficiency. Barkin also found that conditions in the textile industry were begging for this type of stability imposed by industry-wide collective bargaining.[32]

The textile industry also presented for Barkin a dramatic example of what could be done in an extremely bad situation. The example is particularly significant because it took place in the South, at a time when that section was considered to be extremely underdeveloped and free from union pressures. Low wage levels in the South were held to be a drag on the wage levels in the entire industry. As Barkin described it,

> One of the plants in New Orleans, which the city did not particularly care to boast about, was the Lane Cotton Co., whose industrial relations history has not been of the best. Back during the depression it was not unknown for that company to pay 10, 12, and 15 cents an hour. . . .
>
> That company was finally unionized. . . . That company is not keeping all its people at the minimum wage as it did years ago, and that company is now producing more cheaply than ever before, because what has happened is that now management has begun to look into the mill to see how its plant . . . (is) operating.

The result was that management found many ways to improve efficiency.[33]

At the bottom of this process, Barkin believed, was a faith among union leaders that management was or could be resourceful enough to find ways to pay a higher wage, and he referred to it as the theory of dynamic cost. Once a full cost social wage had been imposed on all employers, they were all forced to improve their productivity. From that view, labor became a potent force "as a means of making management manage well."[34]

The key, of course, was the ability of unions to impose an industry-wide wage standard. In the textile industry as a whole, this ability had never existed, although some approximation to a standard industry wage had been achieved in individual sectors of the industry for periods of time. Unionized plants had to compete with nonunion producers, especially in the union-free South. At times, the union even made concessions to help employers compete with nonunion mills having lower wages. The final result was that "the organized segment of the industry has rapidly declined."[35] This experience should be sobering to anyone looking for givebacks to revive an industry. Uniform wage standards throughout an industry could serve the same function.

To achieve such a standard, unions had to establish industry-wide collective bargaining; they had to be able to treat all employers equally. Indeed, the problem was even greater, because different industries could gain labor-cost advantages over each other; it might be expected that profits in low-wage industries would be higher than in high-wage industries, allowing them to attract greater resources into the industry. Equally possible, and perhaps closer to reality, high profits might coincide with high wages, giving management the wherewithal to substitute capital for labor. In either case, coordination on a national level was needed. As Barkin described the needed progression:

> Individual plant negotiations restrict the unions' efforts with economic problems. Industry-wide collective bargaining opens up new horizons to correct arrangements which are unstabilizing working conditions and depriving workers of opportunities for advancement. But just as plant-wide collective bargaining has limitations, so has industry-wide collective bargaining. You can't deal with most economic courses besetting the individual workers except by national collective bargaining.[36]

Here Barkin has noted a problem of concern to all economists. A firm's ability to adjust to higher wages can be improved not by greater efficiency but, in the presence of market power, by price increases.

Economists are always worried that the presence of market power can cause distortions in the allocation of resources in an economy. Thus it has been argued that a unionized sector may attain high wages by reducing employment in that sector; those unemployed in that sector will crowd into the nonunion sector, depressing wages there. Moreover, if unionized firms have market power, they can charge higher prices. In such a dual economy, the primary sector would appear to be gaining at the cost of the secondary sector. The solution that most free-market economists propose to the problem is reduced market power in the primary sector, usually starting with unions.

For Barkin the solution would be more unions, not fewer of them. Any sector of the economy that is lagging in terms of pay would have to be brought into the union fold, with the ultimate goal being a system of national collective bargaining to impose a full-cost social wage on all employers. Such a system would ultimately evolve into a form of national economic planning under the collaborative efforts of business, government, and labor. Such was necessary, as Barkin saw, because domination of the economy by the large firms of the primary sector had vitiated the "significance of [the] market determined price."[37]

The system Barkin advocated requires a greatly strengthened labor movement compared to what existed when he wrote. Nearly all industry in all sectors of the country would have to be unionized for national collective bargaining to be truly efficient, and in the late 1940s, many saw that as a possibility. Union leaders were willing to settle for moving bargaining to the industrial level. Management has resisted this type of bargaining, wanting to keep control within the firm, even when the firm may be very large and the dominant firm in an oligopolistic industry. Instead, such firms will practice wage leadership to accomplish the same industry wage standards that could have been achieved through industry-wide bargaining.

What happens when unionization falls short of a national or industrial scope? (The problem of international competition is considered separately in Chapter Six.) Unions and their friends must use government to impose a full-cost social wage on employers, centering their efforts on legislating a minimum wage. It was for this reason that the CIO pushed for the passage of the Federal Labor Standards Act in the 1930s.

Traditional economic analysis of the minimum wage is straightforward. Given a going wage rate in a free labor market, efforts to legislate a higher wage cause unemployment. Workers are willing to supply even more labor at a higher wage, but employers are not willing or able to hire all of them. Economists typically oppose minimum wage legislation. To some extent, the degree of unemployment is lessened if a labor market is viewed as producing a zone of equilibrium, for employers are willing to grant some increases and keep the workers they are satisfied with. That number could include all workers.

Barkin also found that there was a great deal of flexibility in terms of a firm's ability to increase wages for its workers without laying any of them off. From his institutional perspective, he also saw that the labor market set limits only on the wage a firm might pay. Wage rates were determined by labor costs and the amount of competition a firm faced in the product market. Firms faced with little competition could increase wages by sacrificing some of their high profits, which is what Barkin preferred, or by raising prices on their final product. Firms with market power had a wide span of wages from which to choose to pay workers, and unions could try to force them toward the upper limit of that span. A minimum wage would also move them into that range. In neither case would there be need for a decline in the number of workers hired. This insight into the relationship between market power and a firm's ability to pay higher wages was one that Barkin gained very early in his career,[38] but it has not been followed up in a systematic way by any school of economics. As a result, economists' notion that a minimum wage law will cause unemployment remains unproven for all cases.

Business groups often are against minimum wage laws, but not so much out of sympathy for unemployed workers; they fear that their own costs will rise. Some businesses have appeared to support the minimum wage in industries in which competition has been especially fierce, as a way to stabilize the industry. In the textile industry, for example, some employers in the North supported minimum wage legislation as a way to diminish the wage differential they faced in competing with Southern firms.[39] To the usual opposition by economists and business there was also at one time—when minimum wage legislation was first proposed—the reluctance of AFL unions to support minimum wage laws, on the grounds that the minimum might become the maximum for all workers.

As chairman of the CIO Committee on Fair Labor Standards, Barkin had the responsibility of responding to critics of the minimum wage during repeated testimony before congressional committees for over twenty years. The overwhelming preponderance of support these days seems in favor of eliminating the minimum wage (or letting its impact be offset by holding it steady during a period of inflation), and it will be useful to review Barkin's arguments in favor of it.

Not surprisingly, the main part of his argument centered on social costs. As late as 1955, for example, Barkin claimed that because of low-wage industries, "Injury has been done not only to those persons in low-wage industries, but also to the nation itself. We, as a country, and particularly our local communities, have established a special 'welfare economy' for the low-wage industries. The public and government [are] subsidizing these laggard employers, whether through direct grants or through the high cost of the social and human neglect created by low wages."[40] As a specific example of the problem, Barkin cited cases in Southern textile towns where there were no medical services available and where doctors would not come unless they were guaranteed payment in advance. Making up for this lack fell then and still falls on local, state, and federal governments.[41] When they do not intercede, individuals and the community suffer, as can be seen recently in the social problems (costs) included in the plight of the homeless.

The problem of fair-minded employers' not being able to provide a decent wage was also addressed. Barkin argued that the minimum wage would "moderate the operation of the competitive process sufficiently to prevent the fringe of workers' being victimized . . . [It] provides a realistic wage floor to which no employer can truly object if he wants to pay his workers a wage which represents some modicum of decency. It should be established by law to protect fair-minded employers in industries where they are now inhibited from paying decent wages by competitive forces. That sector of employers who exploit the helplessness of workers by paying them intolerable wages should not be allowed to create unfair competition by paying" low wages.[42]

To gauge the impact of low wages, Barkin relied on figures for the cost of living, as adjusted on an hourly basis, to show that the proposed minimum wage was barely sufficient for workers to attain a subsistence level of income.[43] He was also able to show that regional differences in cost of living were minimal: "The differences in the costs of living among cities in the same region are greater or as great as the differences among regions. Variations in living costs among cities of the same size are greater than between large and small cities."[44]

As for objections by AFL unions that the minimum might become a maximum, Barkin proposed a plan of "peg-point provision," whereby a wage commission would set a small group of key rates based on job rates, to set minima for those occupations. Although such rates would not be a full wage scale, they would ensure that a wage scale above the national minimum would exist in those industries that needed one.[45] This measure was never tried, but it did bring home the message that once a society begins any form of regulation of markets, for no matter what laudable purpose, for the regulation to be effective, the society must also commit itself to a further degree of planning.

The ultimate benefits of such a system, even so simple a one as a national minimum wage, were positive in Barkin's view. First, better-paid workers were more productive; they were healthier, had higher morale, and were more ambitious.[46] Second, better-paid workers were also better consumers. Barkin had noted that in textile towns in the South, few retail services existed, because there was little market for them. A higher living standard would boost the buying power of workers locally and nationally.[47]

In terms of its impact on the textile industry, Barkin found that the minimum wage system had produced good results in helping "to eliminate the cutthroat competition which previously had threatened the better wage scales in the industry." To give a specific example, he cited the crepe silk industry, in which declining conditions and irresponsible employers had led to wages of ten to fifteen cents an hour in the mid 1930s. After passage of the Fair Labor Standards Act, the law "raised wages to the 25-cent and then to the 30-cent minimum level during this chaotic period, and protected the more responsible employers."[48]

There might be costs involved, however, if the minimum wage resulted in higher prices. Barkin defended his case by repeating his argument that higher wages would spur management's efforts to improve efficiency.[49] He also estimated, based on 1947 figures, "The effect on cost of production would have been less than one-quarter of one percent. The total increase would be less than two percent of the profit margin before taxes."[50] This bias against efficiency caused by low wages still remains a problem, because recent studies of the service sector have shown that the existence of low-wage female workers in that sector have hindered the introduction of capital with the concomitant slow growth in productivity.

The impact on business of a higher minimum wage raises another issue. If increased wages raise costs of production uniformly for all industries and erode profits—no matter how small those changes might be—would not business simply raise prices to recoup its losses? How can wage increases keep from being translated into price increases?

Barkin went to great lengths to establish that wage increases need not translate into price increases, and his case is discussed fully in a later section on inflation. At this point only the gist of his argument can be presented. First, he observed that in the past, price increases had preceded wage increases (condition 1). Second, if management did its job and improved efficiency, then costs and therefore prices need not rise and could even fall (condition 2). Third, as higher-paid workers purchased more goods, industry could expand production and reach lower points on its cost curves (condition 3). Of course, the prospects for conditions 2 and 3 required some offset to condition 1. Some force had to exist to ensure that businesses passed on to consumers the benefits of lower costs. As noted previously, Barkin would assign this task to unions and to government.

In his early study on why workers join unions, E. Wright Bakke found that fair wages and economic security were goals workers wanted unions to help them achieve. Workers' notions of what that goal meant in specific terms were very vague but could be boiled down to "enough to keep me and the family in good health."[51] In those simple terms, workers were saying that they wanted to be paid enough to cover the total costs of their existence. Barkin would agree and would favor unions' evolving a system of national collective bargaining to achieve that goal. If unionism remains weak, which seems to be the case in the United States, he would augment their strength with a legislated minimum wage. Not that a minimum wage itself is sufficient for workers to live a healthy existence, but at least it is a start in that direction. Barkin also had faith that business could pay a living wage to all workers by improving their productivity.

Conclusion

The concept of social costs has formed a constant theme of this chapter, just as it forms a constant theme of Barkin's work. But the concept that workers, indeed all members of society, are entitled to a level of pay that enables them to maintain themselves and their family is probably alien to most Americans. After all, won't a guarantee of adequate pay sap individual initiative? The concept does have some social support. It is included in the Declaration of Human Rights of the United Nations, which states in part, "Everyone has a right to a standard of living adequate for the health of himself and his family. . . ." Moreover, the past sixty years have seen a quest for security that has achieved payment of some social costs to some workers. Few would want to abolish workers' compensation, unemployment and medical insurance, or Social Security.

Even more important, as has been argued in this chapter, the individual is severely limited in terms of being able to influence income through personal decisions. Most decisions relating to the terms and conditions of employment are prerogatives of management, and there is little that the individual worker can do to change management's behavior. Groups of workers, when formed into unions, can influence management, however. If they are successful, Barkin would argue, then the incentives for making workers more productive will be placed on management. This is a view quite at odds with that of most mainstream economists.

When economists recognize the existence of social costs, they seek a variety of solutions in terms of regulations, taxes, and market incentives. When an industry's existence is threatened by the imposition of any of these solutions, economists often determine that the impact of the solutions should be softened or the industry be directly subsidized. When it comes to the issue of internalizing the social costs involved with labor, economic analysis remains barren. If industry cannot pay the full social costs of labor, then free-market economists would probably argue that the costs should be left out of prices altogether.

From his trade union perspective, Barkin sees that the problem of social costs and of the efforts made to internalize them are a part of the struggle of the human condition. Workers do not want higher wages simply because they are greedy; they want them because they desire lives that are secure and dignified. Their only way to fulfill these desires is through union or government efforts on their behalf. This is the outcome Barkin would anticipate from the development of a trade union perspective in economics.

But if economists, unions, and government began to recognize the existence of social costs and make efforts to impose them on business, a major question remains: who will ultimately pay for them? As the economy is currently structured, different firms and groups of workers have differing strengths in terms of their ability to pass these costs on to other sectors of the economy. To effect a fair allocation of social costs, either the strength of these groups must be reduced or that of the other sectors must be increased. Any orderly allocation of social costs requires coordinated efforts by all parts of society to allocate them.

It would seem inescapable, then, that recognition of the need to pay the full costs of labor also carries with it the need to develop some form of indicative planning. Perhaps that is why traditional economists shy away from consideration of paying full costs and have not developed a trade union economics. Barkin is not so bashful. His belief in the middle way of organizing the economy gives intellectual support to his conviction that indicative planning can take place without a totally collective society. That search for a middle way also constituted an integral part of the New Deal and the politics of the period of the Great Depression.

The Great Depression of the 1930s was an opportune time to raise the issue of social costs, for their existence was plain. Roosevelt, for example, identified a large portion of the population that was "ill-fed, ill-housed and ill clothed," and he and his advisers were determined to do something about it. Their initial attempt consisted of a form of cooperative planning by industry, labor, and the public under the NRA. They also designed programs such as Social Security, which enabled the elderly and disabled to subsist. In support of affordable housing, they created the often-overlooked Federal Housing Administration, which, by providing government backing for home mortgages, permitted the long-term finance that made it possible for many workers to purchase a home. Not all of this social planning was a triumph, but enough of it remains a part of life in the United States that it is still valid to refer to it as a momentous transformation. Planning there was, but it could not ever be considered as compulsory, at least not honestly. Few among the New Dealers would have opted for the system of planning being promoted by communist thinkers. Of consequence for this study, the New Deal made progress in distinguishing the social costs of work and doing something about them.

Liberals were drawn to the New Deal because it offered the prospect of a form of social democracy that would provide income security and a voice in public affairs for the mass of industrial workers. Quite often, in pursuit of social democracy, these liberals made common cause with the communist movement. When the Cold War came, with its virulent anticommunist disposition, many New Deal liberals were inclined to back away from their progressive beliefs so as to keep from being viewed as fellow travelers, either in direct response to criticism or as a preemptive measure. Barkin, however, had never made common cause with the communist movement, for his early brushes with the left had convinced him of its futility. With no concern over being viewed as "soft on communism," he retained his liberal vision of social democracy.

Barkin is and remains a product of the New Deal. He was eager to join in its fight against the social deprivation that the Great Depression only made apparent. He was an ardent supporter of the social programs set forth by Roosevelt and his advisers. He, too, affirmed the need for national planning, especially if no coercion was involved. His experience with the NRA showed him that practical planning in an industry can take place when all parties cooperate. At the same time, his keen sense of the fallibility of communism—a lesson from his youth—kept him from moving too far to the left. With the help of government it was possible for unions and management to get together and negotiate a wage that defrayed many of the social costs of work. It was even conceivable that this type of cooperative planning could avoid the ruinous wage-cutting that plagued industry during hard times. Barkin stayed committed to the advancement of this kind of planning for the rest of his life. Whether the three components of that planning—business, labor, and government—are sufficiently responsible and resourceful to carry out the planning is the subject of the following chapters. First we must look more closely at what workers seek from unions.

Notes

1. Columbia University Seminar on Labor, Minutes to the Meeting of December 18, 1957, p. 2 (copy in Barkin Archives, Library, University of Massachusetts at Amherst).

2. Columbia University Seminar on Labor, Minutes to the Meeting of March 5, 1958, p. 7.

3. Ibid., p. 4.

4. John Maurice Clark, *Studies in the Economics of Overhead Costs* (Chicago: University of Chicago Press, 1923), p. 16.

5. Ibid., pp. 361–66.

6. Adam Smith, *An Inquiry into the Nature and Causes of the Wealth of Nations* (New York: Modern Library, 1937), Book 1, Chapter 8.

7. Sumner H. Slichter, "Weakness of Individual Bargaining," in E. Wright Bakke, Clark Kerr, and Charles W. Anrod, eds., *Unions, Management and the Public*, 3rd. ed. (New York: Harcourt, Brace & World, Inc., 1967), pp. 55–57.

8. K. William Kapp, *Social Costs, Economic Development and Environmental Disruption*, J. E. Ullman, ed. (Washington, DC: University Press of America, 1983), p. 10.

9. K. William Kapp, *Social Costs of Private Enterprise* (New York: Schocken Books, 1971 reprint of 1963 edition), p. xxi.

10. This concept of a social cost wage would include either monetary payment or a combination of money and benefits. Thought would have to be directed toward the effectiveness of either approach, as Barkin has done. See his "Total Wage Package: From Wage Bargain to Social Contract," *Journal of Economic Issues* 11 (June 1977), pp. 339–51.

11. Paul J. McNulty, *The Origins and Development of Labor Economics* (Cambridge: MA: Massachusetts Institute of Technology Press, 1980), pp. 37–62.

12. Smith, *Wealth of Nations.*

13. McNulty, *Labor Economics*, p. 49.

14. Clark Kerr, *Marshall, Marx and Modern Times* (Cambridge, England: Cambridge University Press, 1969), pp. 44–47.

15. McNulty, *Labor Economics*, pp. 178–80.

16. Cited by Clark Kerr, "The Neoclassical Revisionists in Labor Economics (1940–1960)—R.I.P.," in Bruce E. Kaufman, ed., *How Labor Markets Work* (Lexington, MA: Lexington Books, 1988), p. 10.

17. Bruce E. Kaufman, "The Postwar View of Labor Markets and Wage Determination," in Kaufman, ed., pp. 149–61.

18. Cited by Kaufman in Kaufman, ed., p. 164.

19. Kerr in Kaufman, ed., p. 14.

20. Martin Segal, "Post-Institutionalism in Labor Economics: The Forties and Fifties Revisited," *Industrial and Labor Relations Review* 39 (April 1986), pp. 391–92.

21. McNulty, *Labor Economics*, pp. 191–93.

22. Don Bellante and Mark Jackson, *Labor Economics* (New York: McGraw-Hill Book Co., 1979), a standard neoclassical text, makes no mention of the concept.

23. At least in his standard text, Albert Rees, *The Economics of Trade Unions*, 3rd ed. (Chicago: University of Chicago Press, 1989).

24. See Sumner H. Slichter, *Union Policies and Industrial Management* (New York: Greenwood Press, 1968), pp. 161, 224, and 280, and Gordon F. Bloom and Herbert R.

Northrup, *Economics of Labor Relations* (Homewood, IL: Richard D. Irwin, Inc., 1969), p. 497, for examples.

25. Bloom and Northrup, *Economics of Labor Relations,* p. 336.

26. Solomon Barkin, "Preparing a Case for a Government Board," Chapter 19 of J. B. S. Hardman and Maurice F. Neufeld, eds., *The House of Labor* (Westport, CT: Greenwood Press, 1970), pp. 242–49. The actual report produced is "Substandard Conditions of Living: A Study of the Cost of the Emergency Sustained Budget in Five Textile Manufacturing Communities in January-February 1944," TWUA Research Department, 1944 (copy in Barkin archives).

27. Arthur J. Goldberg, "Fallacies of the 'Labor Monopoly' Issue," in Bakke, Kerr, and Anrod, p. 661.

28. Solomon Barkin, "The Significant Change in Wage Demands," *Labor and Nation* (February-March 1946), p. 8.

29. Solomon Barkin, "Industrial Union Wage Policies," *Plan Age* VI (January 1940), p. 3.

30. Ibid., p. 4.

31. Ibid., pp. 6–9.

32. Solomon Barkin, "National Collective Bargaining," *Personnel Journal* (November 1946), p. 7.

33. Hearings before the Subcommittee on Education and Labor, U.S. Senate, Washington, DC, September-October 1945, p. 289.

34. Barkin, "National Collective Bargaining," p. 4.

35. Sumner H. Slichter, James J. Healy, and E. Robert Livernash, *The Impact of Collective Bargaining on Management* (Washington, DC: The Brookings Institution, 1960), pp. 615–16.

36. Barkin, "National Collective Bargaining," p. 8.

37. Solomon Barkin, "Labor-Government Cooperation as a Basis of Sound Price Policy," *Labor and Nation* (May-June 1947), p. 11.

38. Barkin, "Industrial Union Wage Policies," pp. 9–10, and "Wage Policies of Industrial Unions," *Harvard Business Review* (Spring 1941), pp. 344–47.

39. William Hartford, untitled manuscript, Chapter Four, p. 10.

40. Statement to the Subcommittee on Labor and Public Welfare, U.S. Senate, April 22, 1955, p. 3 (copy in Barkin files).

41. Hearings, 1945, p. 298.

42. Statement before the Subcommittee on Labor and Public Welfare, U.S. Senate, Washington, DC, April 12, 1949, p. 6 (copy in Barkin files).

43. Statement, 1955, pp. 7–8; statement, 1949, pp. 3–4.

44. Ibid., 1949, p. 6.

45. Hearings, 1945, pp. 780–81.

46. Ibid., p. 297.

47. Statement, 1955, p. 1.

48. Barkin, "Wage Policies of Industrial Unions," p. 347.

49. Statement, 1955, p. 2.

50. Ibid., 1949, p. 7.

51. E. Wright Bakke, "Why Workers Join Unions," *Personnel* 22 (July 1945) in Bakke, Kerr, and Anrod, p. 89.

3

Workers, Jobs, and Unions

There is no one who has written a good book on labor economics because they don't understand the simple rules in the Clayton Anti Trust Law, that labor is not a commodity.

—*Solomon Barkin*

What do workers want? This question has been as difficult to answer as Freud's similar query about women. In the case of workers, the difficulties of answering the question, at least in the United States, have been due to workers' wanting many things but having few means for expressing those wants. Surveys, mass media coverage, and books by labor intellectuals may claim to discover what workers want, but none of these are produced either by or for workers. The problem of getting the information is especially difficult for management and can easily cause misunderstanding. For example, a recent survey of supervisors' perceptions of what workers wanted was matched against what workers really wanted. Supervisors thought that workers would rank income and security of employment as most important. Instead, workers put "full appreciation of work done" and "feeling 'in' on things" as their main issues (supervisors rated these as low), placing income and security near the bottom of their list.[1]

Those supervisors join a long list of persons, from Frederick W. Taylor to the mainstream school of economics, who have assumed that workers were interested only in income and keeping their job. Mainstream economics places centrality in its framework on the rational economic person, who makes all decisions on calculations of costs versus benefits. Habit, custom, and aspiration do not count in this calculation, unless they can somehow be reduced to numerical costs or benefits. In addition, under this scheme, individuals act in isolation, with the feeling, traditions, costs, and benefits of other persons never entering into their decisions. While this may be an apt description of a savvy arbitrager making a stock purchase, it hardly touches the type of thinking a worker invokes when deciding whether to join or vote for a union or making a decision concerning a job. Money matters to workers, but so does a sense of participation, and the way workers enumerate priorities on a survey depends on the questions asked and the circumstances workers face when surveyed.

It is not the purpose of this chapter to criticize the mainstream view of human nature, although much will be said implicitly. Rather, the chapter concentrates on how Barkin, as an institutionalist, viewed workers in terms of what they want and why they belong to unions. Because Barkin and the TWUA experienced difficulty and resistance in their efforts to convince workers in the South to join unions, Barkin's writings on workers were weighted toward understanding the problems they faced. This chapter follows that weighting, but despite claims of Southern exceptionalism, many of the lessons Barkin drew from the South are applicable elsewhere.

Seeing the Worker Whole

The traditional white male blue-collar worker has long been an anomaly in American life. He is often viewed as a cultural hero and the backbone of solid American values, but his affectation of middle-class values and his supposed fascination for television and sports have led him to be characterized as a philistine. Advertising may extol the importance of blue-collar work and the use of beer to celebrate its ending ("For all you do, this Bud's for you"), but it also leads to pejorative references to all the "Joe Six-Packs" out there. One thing is clear about such caricatures of workers' lives: Even though they are intended for workers, they are not created by workers. Workers themselves remain unheard from. For despite all of this attention paid to workers, Barkin's contention of more than thirty-five years ago still remains true: "We have no analysis of the worker's attitudes, conduct, social relations, and behavior."[2]

To some extent, this lack of appreciation for the psyche of the worker is due to the bias of economics. For free-market economists, our mass consumption economy exists to serve consumers. The emphasis in this economics, as well as the starting point, is on the problem of individual choice facing the rational economic person. Instead of determining what values individuals do hold, economists start with a set of values that individuals are assumed to hold. Although recent work in experimental economics may depart somewhat from that scheme, in the main, and especially in its popular versions, economics is concerned with individual behavior as it relates to making calculated choices based on cost-benefit analysis. Individual consumers make decisions that maximize their personal satisfaction; individual owners of resources make decisions that maximize their incomes.

When it comes to applying this approach to labor, economists use the same general theory of price determination that they do for all items that are bought and sold. For them, despite the intent of the Clayton Act, which states, "The labor of a human being is not a commodity or article of Commerce," and the warnings of Marx, labor is merely a commodity for sale in the marketplace like any other commodity, say, cars. This approach is much too simple, however.

In a general way it can be said that labor differs from other commodities by being one that formulates its own set of values. More specifically, labor has many differences in comparison with other commodities. Under our present economic system, for example, labor is one of the few commodities not produced by private enterprise. The supply of labor depends on a variety of nonprice factors, including population growth (a reflection of fertility rates), participation rates (a result of social attitudes to female and child labor), and the quality of the work force (a condition dependent on attitudes toward education). As a result, the costs of producing this commodity must be figured differently from the costs of producing other commodities. As noted in the previous section, many of those costs are part of a social overhead that is not included in the decision to hire a worker.

In addition, labor is one of the few commodities whose qualities cannot be determined before, or sometimes after, it is purchased. There are no guarantees that it will perform in the manner its purchaser desires. If the concept of labor includes consideration of the intensity of labor application, there can be wide variations in what is being purchased by management. The amount of work represented by a particular supply of labor depends on the skill it has, how intensely it applies that skill, its morale, and its attitude toward its purchaser (i.e., management). The problem is that humans can consciously or unconsciously alter their qualities. Because the purchasers of this commodity cannot own it, they cannot directly control it unless it is willing to cooperate. To secure that cooperation, the purchaser of labor must enlist a variety of techniques.

This last point raises what represents a significant difference between labor and other commodities: labor is the only commodity that can join together and organize a union. This quality is another element to Barkin's economics. From his perspective it is only natural that workers band together to further their collective interests. When confronted by business organizations that use a variety of managerial and technological devices to secure desired behavior on the part of workers or when faced with a labor market that does not always provide a wage that covers the social costs of labor, workers have few choices open to them for protection within the institutional structure of our economic system. From among those choices, unions would appear to be a good bet.

The process by which workers form unions as a vehicle for collective action is easily misunderstood by the traditional economics of individualism. Neoclassical labor economists focus their attention on the activities of individuals—both workers and businesses (portrayed as individual persons)—to show how the forces of competition bring them together in the labor market, with neither business nor labor having a bargaining advantage. Because of labor's unique features compared to other commodities, this approach misses the point about labor markets. For example, because new workers and new work locations are risky and uncertain, both employers and workers have a tendency to stick with those they know; each party to the wage agreement may be willing to sacrifice some income to retain the current situation. The idea of one equilibrium wage's holding in a labor market then becomes misleading. It is more appropriate, as Clark Kerr has noted, to think of the wage determined by the labor market as an equilibrium zone, with both sides' exhibiting flexibility in terms of the final wage pattern.[3] Indeed, as Kerr has also pointed out, possibly the only labor market resembling the free market set forth in neoclassical theory (i.e., having complete mobility and only a cash relationship between management and labor) is that of migrant agricultural labor.[4] The conditions faced by migrant workers are not something to inspire faith in free markets.

When workers do join unions, neoclassical economists interpret that action as the formation of a monopoly. Group behavior in this sense, especially collective action to set wages and working conditions, is viewed as an imperfection in the labor market, to be eliminated whenever possible. When unions are analyzed at all, they are, like business, treated as an individual income-maximizing unit, with some allowance's being made as to whose income is being maximized. As with any monopoly, they are interpreted as raising wages by reducing the number of workers employed,[5] although Kerr's notion of an equilibrium zone implies that it is possible to gain an increase in wages without causing layoffs.

Moreover, it is not clear that workers in unions or their leaders would abuse what market power they had. A rising standard of living is part of the American dream of the good life. Many persons join many groups to act collectively in pursuit of this dream. It is also one of the goals of unions. In response to this goal of unions, workers join with them in hope of improving their lot. The labor union is constituted to improve their condition by getting ever higher wages. Barkin sees no problem with that goal, because "we have boasted that this country is a high-wage country."[6]

In opposition to the neoclassical interpretation of unions, Barkin takes a completely positive view of collective bargaining as essential to protecting the individual rights of workers. This view has been confirmed by many labor studies, with one reaching the succinct conclusion "The origins of unions in many enterprises can be traced to a belief on the part of employees that the company has been arbitrary, discriminatory or capricious in meting out discipline."[7] Barkin stated this position in more positive terms: "The American worker wants to participate in the determination of his conditions of employment. It is not enough for him to receive wages and work under satisfactory conditions. He must be able to review such conditions and share the responsibility in their establishment."[8]

Any attempts to understand the collective behavior of workers as members of unions must be based on an accurate appraisal of the values those workers hold and why those values may lead them to seek protection by banding together with other individuals. E. Wright Bakke once hypothesized, "The worker reacts favorably to union membership in proportion to the strength of his belief that this step will reduce his frustration and anxieties and will further his opportunities relevant to the achievement of his standards of successful living."[9] Elaboration of the system of values upon which this hypothesis rested went beyond the scope of Bakke's report.

Whatever values workers do have, they share with all Americans a belief that their conditions will continually improve. Not only do all workers expect a social cost wage that meets a minimum standard of living, but also they take it for granted that a rising standard of living is almost a right. The union movement has included this belief in its own goals as part of an optimistic faith in the system. As is discussed in Chapter Five, unions have been successful in gaining higher standards of living for their members; they have also helped to gain better conditions for all members of society, until their recent decline, by prodding nonunion firms to follow the wage and benefits patterns established in unionized companies, as described in Chapters Five and Seven.

In Barkin's view, it is difficult to gather information about values from workers. Workers have no direct outlet for conveying this information themselves, and it is not likely that they will give accurate responses when they are asked— for good reason. Too often the information has been sought by management, with the sole intention of using it to manipulate workers. As Barkin states the problem, in reference to the use of opinion polling among workers, "It is dangerous because it is deceptive. It rests on the assumption that workers will talk freely to management if it professes to be interested in their attitudes. Workers know their position within the economic hierarchy. They are aware of the employer's bargaining strength and they are not going to endanger their position because of new professions of interest. The answers will be controlled primarily by the individual worker's estimate of the effect of his reply on his own position rather than by his own desire to secure a fair representation of his own views."[10] Because of the problems involved in management's efforts to learn about its employees, Barkin especially wanted help in this area from disinterested academic disciplines, such as economics. One academic study undertaken on workers' values that Barkin found valuable was performed by Robert Blauner, who felt strongly about studying alienation in an impartial, scientific way.[11]

Even with impartial questioners, a definitive statement on workers will remain elusive because work and workers are constantly undergoing change, and as Blauner notes, work takes place under a diverse set of industrial conditions.[12] In the past two decades, the structure of the economy has changed so as to cause a great decline in traditional blue-collar work in the manufacturing sector and an expansion in so-called "new-collar" jobs in the service sector. It has been recognized that this transformation results in a change in the economic well-being of workers caught up in it; pay for service work averages much less than that of manufacturing labor. Equally important, many workers making such changes are going from union to nonunion atmospheres. Such changes must have an influence on workers' attitudes.

Barkin recognized the importance of understanding the changes. His statement on the issue brings out both the problem of the analysis and the problem facing workers. He wrote, "No formal description exists of the new personality profile of the organized worker, but it is vastly different from that of the early thirties. In in-plant attitudes, the present American worker is more disciplined; he looks not to intermittent eruptions but to systematic pursuit of his grievances and regular review of contract terms for correction of irritation and attainment of new gains. . . . Within the community, the higher income and availability of alternative jobs have produced a new respect for workers."[13] Greater buying power among workers may explain why advertisers treat them as an important marketing segment.

What will happen to workers who lose this environment by changing jobs into the service sector? How will their attitudes change when they are no longer protected by unions? There are no clear answers to these important questions. Some early indications might be gleaned from the attitudes workers have held in nonunion environments. Barkin's studies of Southern textile workers have some insights to offer. Of greater importance, his case studies are paradigmatic of the type of research that he thought necessary to understand workers' attitudes and values and that is lacking now.

The Case of the South

Before Barkin's view of Southern workers can be set forth, some background information is needed. The South has long been seen as a unique region in terms of its economic development and population mix. It has also been found to be culturally different, that is, more traditional than the rest of the nation. Whether such cultural isolation has truly existed is irrelevant. The notion endures that the South is marked by a tradition of conservatism based on an elite plantation society combined with racial differences and low industrialization. Whatever the sources of that tradition, it contributed to making the South a very hostile territory for unions. When manufacturing plants did arrive in the region, as textile mills did, the idea emerged that their owners, by bringing jobs, were "public benefactors."[14]

While unions made some inroads in the South as industry appeared, the record in the textile industry was dismal. The UTWA had several periods of strife and organization in the 1920s and faced a general strike in 1934; its gains were small. The TWOC, as mentioned previously, had some success in the South during its 1937 organizing drive, but nothing such as it had in the North. Even during World War II, when the War Labor Board took many measures that were of great assistance to unions, the South remained barren ground for unions and especially for the TWUA.[15]

In early 1946, the CIO again began efforts to make inroads in the South, especially in the Southern textile industry. The CIO's organizing drive had a businesslike quality. As Barbara Griffith has written, "A Southern organizing drive had to be undertaken, both to consolidate the impressive gains labor made during the war and to remove the South as a haven for 'runaway' Northern businesses."[16] It is also true that wages and working conditions in the South, especially in the textile industry, were truly deplorable, so organizing to help those workers constituted more than a business decision. Besides, no business would ever have taken on so hopeless a venture.

The drive was financed by a $1-million fund contributed by various CIO unions and used to pay for nearly 240 organizers—impressive until it is realized that the area in question covered twelve widely dispersed states, and as Ray Marshall documents, the pledged contributions from other unions were not always forthcoming.[17] Moreover, as the TWOC experiences of the 1930s had shown, management had a host of weapons, both legal and illegal, with which to thwart organizers. In many textile mill towns, the mill owned the town, and town officials, including law enforcement agents, were often on the company payroll. Moreover, although the industry was sizable, with many large mills, it was scattered in five states (Virginia, Georgia, North Carolina, South Carolina, and Alabama) and included many small mills. This has been the standard interpretation of industry circumstances.

Barkin observes, however, that Southern industry was not as widely dispersed as it has been customarily depicted. Many of the mills were arrayed into chains of larger mills. The TWUA concentrated its efforts on these chains, but labor law required a certification in each mill in a chain, rather than for the whole chain. This requirement made organizing more difficult. In comparison to the North, where mill chains cooperated in organizing all their mills, owners in the South fought such efforts. Due to these differing conditions, an industry in the South was effectively more scattered than in the North, so union organizers were unable to concentrate their efforts for a dramatic victory.

Still, they tried. At times the organizers were from the North, which could label them as "outside agitators." Southern-born organizers could be easily painted with the red brush of communism. Efforts to organize mills were not uniformly successful. One great setback was the inability to establish a foothold at the Kannapolis, North Carolina, mills of the Cannon family,[18] a leading firm in the Southern textile industry. Workers did have grievances, but the whole apparatus of the small-town social system served to keep them from using unions as a vehicle to vent those grievances. A blend of paternalism and fear promoted by mill owners kept workers in their place, so the unions' inability to achieve gains forced workers to think twice about joining the movement, and the union had a tough time winning a majority vote for certification as bargaining agent. In sum, as Griffith has put it, "The CIO was forced to accept a contest on grossly unequal grounds. It never found a way to redress the balance."[19]

In his work with the TWUA, Barkin was intimately involved with the TWOC drive in the South. He recognized the problems that such a drive would face, having frequently surveyed local organizing efforts, operating conditions at Southern locals, and negotiating difficulties they faced, for the purpose of preparing memoranda for the union president during the 1930s. He also had cause for hope. The TWUA and the CIO had developed a strategy for organizing an industry of small firms, namely, organizing a few key firms and then calling an industry-wide strike to bring recalcitrant firms into the fold. The drive might evoke an industry-wide spontaneous uprising of workers, such as had happened in 1934. Neither of these strategies proved applicable, as few employers would stand up against the regional antiunion pressure to take the lead in seeking industry-wide wage standards. The drive was not a total failure. Barkin notes that from May 15, 1946, to December 31, 1946, the TWUA won twenty-one elections that covered 4,279 workers and got it 65 percent of the vote while it lost twenty-six elections that covered 11,847 workers and got it 33 percent of the vote. The gains were made in smaller plants, as these numbers indicate.[20] In other cases, the union did win a sizable following, but still short of a majority. Not a sterling performance, but not a total defeat.

The TWOC, TWUA, and, later, Operation Dixie did introduce new techniques developed for organizing. Union missionaries and public relations experts were sent out to make the union case before community leaders, newspaper editors, public officials, and clergy, but with only small success.[21] Local directors were allowed to divert resources to organizing smaller units in their areas, with some efficacy. Barkin instituted a policy of having standard forms on which individual organizers could report weekly on their activities and on which regional supervisors could comment on those activities.

In general, Barkin would agree that Operation Dixie failed and that business resistance was the leading cause of that failure. In his view, there was only one solution to the problem of organizing the South: government assistance.[22] Many of the early organizational drives of the CIO, especially the automobile strikes, had been assisted by state and local government officials who refused to call in the police or national guard to expel the strikers. Staff members of the NRA and the early NLRB had actively taken steps to assist unions, as had the War Labor Board.

Government intervention on behalf of unions was not likely while Operation Dixie was taking place; Congress was too busy passing the Taft-Hartley Act, which changed the legal climate of union organization. After Taft-Hartley, the NLRB, which had acted as a supporter of labor's right to organize, became more of a neutral umpire.[23] Rarely after would labor be able to count on government assistance in its efforts to organize industrial workers.

Faced with all these obstacles, Barkin judged that it was imperative to analyze the attitude of workers in the South, to see what part it played in resistance to unions. At the start of his analysis, Barkin made it clear that "The outlook of the

Southern textile worker is determined largely by his cultural heritage, his relative isolation from the mainstream of American life, his relatively low living standards, and the impact of his job and his employer." To some extent this isolation has been bridged by modern communications, so the worker is aware of a better life, but "such is his situation that he is resigned to the belief that his will not be an equitable sharing of an expanding America."[24] The cause of this resignation comes from the way that workers are treated in the plant and the manner through which that treatment is reinforced in workers' relations with the community and within their family.

Within the mill, "the worker is employed in an autocratic and paternalistic atmosphere where the employer is absolute monarch and the foreman is his emissary. Worker petitions for relief of any grievance must be presented in subdued tones."[25] In a textile mill, the worker's main task is that of a machine tender, always on the lookout for malfunctioning equipment. As a harbinger of future trends, that task resembles the trend toward robotics in manufacturing. The more the machines break down, the harder the effort required by the worker. The worker is paid for production rather than effort, however. As a result, "The average textile worker believes that the harder he works the less he will earn. . . . He is also of the view that new and better machines and improved performance are an invitation to employer reevaluation of the job. Technological change has simply come to mean more machines for the worker to tend."[26] Mill work imposes a form of conservatism on the part of workers; they are fearful of any change because they are pessimistic enough to believe that things will probably not get better for them, and things are more likely to get worse.

Outside the mill, in the community, employers still remain supreme. They keep a watchful eye on local government and social institutions, when they do not lead them themselves. Within this system, workers remain in the servile position of dependence on their employer's goodwill and discretion. As Barkin describes the situation, "The textile worker is born into a sheltered environment and mode of life which makes few demands on him other than continued hard work. All institutions in his community are designed to insure his acquiescence and submission to the prevailing way of life and to his employer."[27] Although they may be unhappy with their conditions, workers are reluctant to risk an open fight to correct them.

Instead, they may turn to their family and church for solace. The force of family life, however, only adds to their conservatism. The family, by providing a form of support in times of trouble, nurtures further feelings of dependence. Moreover, the cost of such support is conformity to a strict code of behavior, under penalty of punishment. Finally, because many members of the family are directly or indirectly dependent on the mill for their livelihood, "compliance with the mill's code and the employer's wishes is enforced for the family's security."[28] The church, frequently built, maintained, and supervised by the employer, augments this pressure by emphasizing those parts of Scripture that accent salvation through poverty and strict observance of spiritual values, including a yielding to biblical authority. As Barkin sums up, "The carry-over from the acceptance of scriptures to the codes of the employers is a simple one."[29] So emplaced, Southern textile workers have few options for improving their lot.

One option chosen, which Barkin found to be of increasing importance in the 1950s, is outmigration. Those who remain are in a more difficult position. As Barkin saw their plight, "While the people have yielded to the variety of economic, social and political pressures and seemingly have been resigned to their lot, there continues to be a greater yearning among many to rid themselves of the repressive feudal system."[30] Unions can be a vehicle for achieving this goal, but their efforts in this area are fraught with difficulty.

The resistance to unionism by Southern textile employers has been described succinctly by Ray Marshall as "a pattern of company resistance with the aid of local law enforcement officials, conflict with the union if organized, strike, violence, use of the national guard, [and] slow response from the NLRB."[31] Employers will use any and all economic, political, and cultural power they have to prevent their workers from joining unions. This places the workers in a conflict-ridden situation and causes difficulties for union organizers. As Barkin describes it, "The union is the deliverer in the eyes of the textile workers who join it. It is the 'outsider' who is to liberate them from the repression of the 'bossman.' It must become the teacher, the organizer, the spokesman and the bosses' opponent. These responsibilities it must discharge without involving the worker; secrecy is called for as the regular way of behavior. The workers want to avoid overt action."[32]

Once this resistance has been overcome, Barkin found that Southern textile workers remain extremely loyal to their unions. To some extent this loyalty may represent a transfer by workers of their obedience from the employer to the union and its leaders; their whole life has been lived on the bottom rungs of a hierarchical society, so it is not surprising that they do not aspire to a leadership position in their own union. Still, as Barkin found in a survey conducted among Southern textile workers, their major purpose in supporting the organization of a union was "to prevent unilateral action, caprice and discrimination rather than to effect any real change."[33]

Whether these attitudes still apply to Southern textile workers or to workers in nonunionized sectors of the economy is doubtful. By the 1960s, Barkin had found that the increased use of newer technology was continuing to transform conditions facing textile workers. More and more they were being transformed into "machine attendants" who must be sensitive to "deficiencies which the control mechanisms in the machine itself will have failed to record."[34] At the same time, the South has undergone widespread socioeconomic change during the past two decades, including both the ending of segregation and expansive economic growth. Much of the small-town parochialism that Barkin found important in the 1950s has been changed. Poverty-stricken workers of small towns may no longer be migrating north, as urban areas in the South have become a source of new opportunities. The advent of television and the information it brings to viewers has ended the isolation of the small Southern town, although it has yet to be determined whether it has diminished the authority of local leaders. As these equivocal statements indicate, much of Barkin's analysis is outdated and has not been significantly updated since he wrote. The pressures on Southern textile workers have changed, especially as their plants run away to other areas. As a constant, they still have the option of organizing unions to protect themselves from bad management practices at work.

The importance of unions in textile workers' lives can be seen by comparing conditions in the South with those found in New England, where, even during the prosperous days of the mid-forties, workers felt uneasy about their work. Older workers who had grown up doing mill work persisted in staying in the industry, even though they could have got a higher-paid job elsewhere. Women were particularly hesitant about moving. Their loyalty was apparently to both their job and to their home area, for they had very strong ethnic and family ties to the plant and to the town. The TWUA reinforced these ties by giving the workers more security in the plant by way of seniority, stable wages, and the like. It also recognized the need for programs to make life in the mill town more palatable by sponsoring dances, concerts, ball games, and educational classes to fill that need. Many of these efforts also aimed at having workers identify with the union, but they were aided in the identification because many local union officials were products of the same environment. Younger workers were less likely to have this loyalty to industry or town, because they had been told how bad the industry had been during the depression, had seen a bit of the world during the war, and had gained a sense of mobility. They would migrate to other jobs and areas where wages might be higher.[35] Similar changes in attitude may have taken place under the influence of urbanization and better communication on a younger generation, but any out-migration of these potential mill hands probably was offset by the increased employment of blacks in mills. Barkin's latest word on these issues is to call for further study to outline what has taken place.

In a more general study of workers' values, Blauner made the concept of alienation central to his analysis. Alienation, moreover, had four dimensions: powerlessness, meaninglessness, isolation, and self-estrangement. Powerlessness in turn derived from the worker's inability to have any say in general management policies, conditions of employment, or daily work conditions.[36] In Barkin's view, this feeling of powerlessness is a central part of workers' values and a feeling workers wish to avoid through exercise of the union option.

Equally important, their deliberations over whether to exercise that option display a variety of influences, including, but not limited to, rational calculation of personal economic gain. The approach taken by neoclassical economics, with its emphasis on competitive markets and the monopolistic departure from competition, may provide a first approximation of how workers behave, but it does not establish the wherewithal to go beyond that first approximation to the day-to-day world, where real people live. As Bakke notes, "A union is partly a business institution, but it has other features which keep it from being purely a business institution."[37]

To highlight the nonbusiness aspects of unions, the institutional approach, such as Barkin utilizes, tries to establish how workers' values are formed within a cultural context and how they translate into union activity. In this section, examples show how Barkin would try to discover the values workers have and how those values may lead workers to form unions. When workers choose to form unions, they become part of a complex institution. The next section considers the insights Barkin's trade union economics has to offer into what workers seek from unions.

What Workers Seek from Unions

As elaborate organizations, labor unions are symbolic of the paradoxical nature of collective activity in American culture. Much of the tradition of our life and law emphasizes individual behavior as the most important element of society. Yet our heritage contains many cases in which individuals have joined forces successfully to accomplish a task. We need only remember Benjamin Franklin's stricture about hanging together to avoid hanging separately to see that this is so. Even the mythical rugged individualists who settled the West went there in groups of wagon trains, banded together in posses to capture outlaws, and joined with each other to build barns. Of course, these activities were usually undertaken during times of crisis, which may explain them as desperate measures, to be avoided in normal times. It should also be recalled that the U.S. Constitution, which we so revere, was formulated as the best way to balance the power of "factions"; to secure its passage, however, its proponents were compelled to add the Bill of Rights in order to protect individual rights. The point is that somewhere between the total individual freedom of anarchy and the stultifying controls of complete collectivism lies the American way, and for Barkin, unions fall well within those two extremes. Any study of unions must, as Robert F. Hoxie cautioned long ago, be undertaken in "pluralistic terms."[38]

This position is not one that was easily accorded to unions. The constitution makes no mention of unions, and for a long time they were prosecuted as conspiracies under common law. Following an era of reform in the economy from 1890 to 1920, the rule of law changed, but still unions faced legal problems from the Sherman Antitrust Act, judicial injunctions, and yellow-dog contracts. Not until the 1930s, as described in Chapter One, with the passage first of Section 7a of the NIRA and then of the NLRA, was organized labor accorded the legal standing that would permit it to organize and represent workers. Barkin would find this granting of legal rights to unions a very wholesome outcome.

At the same time, however, labor law did not undermine the prior underlying relations between labor and management. As James B. Atleson has argued, many decisions rendered by the NLRB and the courts with regard to labor cases reflect a basic assumption that managerial prerogatives are not to be voided by labor law. Atleson feels that these assumptions were present in the law before passage of the NLRA, as part of the common law. In all cases of labor law, he notes, "An important focus is on the workplace as the property of the employer."[39] Barkin is very sympathetic to this interpretation.

Atleson's and Barkin's views on labor law are not universally shared. From one extreme, it is held that unions do nothing for their members and serve only to trample the rights of businesses.[40] As noted earlier, traditional economists typically interpret unions as economic agents, trying to maximize the income of (a) union leaders, (b) union members (who then pay more dues to union leaders), or (c) senior members (who are the last to be laid off in hard times)[41]. It may be true that unions do pursue these activities, as Barkin might admit, but they do a lot more. For Barkin, this "more" that unions do is an extremely important part of every union's activity and an appropriate justification for their existence. Unions are a vehicle for achieving the aspirations of their members. They provide basic protections to safeguard the rights of individual workers so those workers can make choices compatible with their own aspirations and provide collective support when threats to individual workers arise. Moreover, Barkin would argue that unions cannot be understood unless they are placed into the context of the total picture of how they reflect those aspirations.

Much of Barkin's writings are an effort to set forth this total picture, because he often felt that labor leaders themselves made little effort to "set the record straight." He believed that the overriding goal of unions is the pursuit of two objectives. First, within the firm, he found that the union "is a tool for gaining greater personal opportunity, correcting unsavory, irritating and debilitating conditions, and combating repressive forces in the plant."[42] Second, within society as a whole, he observes, "The fight for greater social justice is the raison d'être of the trade union movement. Unions are created and are being constantly formed by employees to achieve their goals of equality and independence in the marketplace. They represent the local skirmishes in the battle for greater democracy in the full society."[43]

In sum, for Barkin, unions represent a way for workers to secure their rights, including the right to a wage that covers all their social costs. By setting up a procedure to assist workers in forming unions, the legal system of the NLRA, which originally had the intent of promoting collective bargaining in industry and fostering the interests of all workers, enhanced the prospect that they would make headway in attaining rights. As Sumner Slichter began his pathbreaking study of unions, "Collective bargaining . . . is a method of introducing civil rights into industry, that is, of requiring that management be conducted by rule rather than by arbitrary decision." Slichter referred to this process as a system of "industrial jurisprudence."[44] Barkin would agree but, along with Atleson, would conclude that the fight for rights is ongoing. Why workers must fight for their rights in the first place is a question of great concern to Barkin.

While labor is not a commodity under law, neither is it a property. The practices of common law as well as the codification in our constitution, especially after the passage and interpretation of the Fourteenth Amendment, have been aimed at the protection of the rights of private property. To some extent, this protection was aimed at preventing the abuses of an arbitrary and sometimes unscrupulous use of power on the part of government, especially monarchs. In the United States, that protection extended at a time when property ownership was widespread. Ownership of property, especially productive property, has increasingly become skewed; few Americans directly own productive property. Thus property rights have a bias reflected in Anatole France's wry comment that the law in its majesty equally forbids the millionaire and the bum from sleeping on a park bench.

In more specific terms, labor law carries with it notions of management prerogatives that predate the modern industrial system. Management rights based on property derive from an era when property was widely held and management was in the hands of a direct owner. The industrial revolution changed those de facto ownership rights by separating ownership from control through the vehicle of corporate stock widely held by the public. Preindustrial property rights still hold in labor relations. As Atleson observes, preindustrial work was marked by a status system consisting of master versus servant; modern employment is supposedly derived from freedom of contract. The legal system has evolved as a blending of both systems. Atleson writes, "The merger of master-servant law and contract law meant that the law never treated the employment contract as the result of free bargaining and mutual assent. . . . Instead, the contract was deemed to include 'implied' terms which reserved to the employer the full authority and direction of employees."[45] The master is still the master, to recall Adam Smith's verdict, with all the detriments this holds for workers.

In the era of craft unions, skilled workers tried to attain the equivalent of a property in a job by way of restricting membership in the occupation or craft through the means of pushing for a closed shop, union shop, or closed union. In the era of industrial unionism, efforts were made to gain security clauses in contracts through collective bargaining. The primary form these rights have taken has been that of seniority, with length of prior service being held as the chief factor in determining which workers to lay off first and rehire last. Although that system has problems, it has obvious virtues for unions, as Barkin has identified: "Seniority is easy to define and it minimizes discrimination."[46]

The obvious virtue of the seniority system for labor is that it limits management's discretion, which may be arbitrary, in making employment policies. Even though seniority as an easy measure may seem to be equally arbitrary, it does convey the idea that because years of service reflect loyalty to the firm, loyalty is being rewarded. It also gives management an incentive to train and retrain workers with seniority, to make them as effective as possible.

The important point is that when a seniority system is emplaced, it gains the force of law that both parties must obey. It is the workers' substitute for legislative action and provides a system that tells workers where they stand. Unions have also had recourse to the law, with the result that they have been able "to secure limitations upon the employer's exercise of his managerial powers and to prescribe conditions for the use of property."[47] These limitations have not developed into anything resembling a property right to a job, to be taken away only after due process, for either individuals or groups, and "the courts have spurned attempts to provide the worker with equity in jobs."[48] One example, as Barkin relates, is the failure of attempts by workers to constrain businesses' decisions on plant relocation.[49] In this case, however, things have changed, as Congress did pass a law requiring advance notice of plant closings, despite the organized opposition of the business community and the Bush Administration.

Although this particular example no longer holds true, the general principle of workers' having few rights to a job remains intact. As Atleson points out, most court decisions, as in the *Darlington, Mackay,* and *Fansteel* cases, have served to limit rights purportedly granted to workers by the NLRA.[50] At the same time, however, the Supreme Court has ruled that women who leave work to have children are entitled to reclaim their job. Whether it is the rights of the women as mothers or as workers that are being established on closer par with property rights remains an unsolved question. Thus far, the courts generally have been reluctant to alter the employment-at-will tradition by protecting workers from unfair dismissals.

The basis for this reluctance on the part of courts has been a subtle reading into the constitution of free market principles by the courts and politicians in the latter half of the nineteenth century. While not fundamental to freedom, the principles were felt to be necessary to fulfill it. Regulations that violated the market, such as minimum wage legislation, were interpreted by courts as an unwarranted taking of employer rights, even if done in the public interest. The New Deal legislation program was an effort to change this view of rights by seeking to address the many defects in the market system, including those involved with labor. There was no legal or social reason, it was felt, to take the underlying conditions of a free market as acceptable or adequate for fulfilling public welfare doctrines of the constitution.[51] The problem for workers was that a cultural lag prevented the courts from taking this New Deal view, so while more rights have been granted throughout society by regulations, the legal rights of workers remain missing.

Given that workers as a whole do not have legal rights to a job on par with a property right, their only recourse is to find some protection in their collective bargaining agreements. Individual workers may prefer a certain set of working conditions, but because they compete with each other through labor markets, those preferences will not be met. Those who would end all labor-imposed limitations on property rights should recognize that unions will fight for these limitations as part of their negotiations with business as a way of fulfilling worker preferences. In any event, the present legal system in the United States still requires that some issues be resolved through collective bargaining or be left to the discretion of management.

Unions also serve as a medium for helping workers to attain better working conditions and personnel practices. In protecting workers from unfair and harsh treatment by management, unions play an important role. The best way to protect workers is through a grievance procedure designed to correct bad personnel practices. Management often resisted the establishment of grievance systems and final arbitration for fear of giving status to unions.[52] Only after unions have won recognition can effective grievance procedures be put into place.

Sound grievance procedures can be a benefit to management. Dunlop and Healy have noted "that the grievance procedure can be made to serve the function of discovering problem situations. . . ."[53] Worker complaints, especially if they are recurring, can often lead to the discovery of unsound personnel policies. In addition, by making managerial decisions on promotions subject to grievance procedures, management must be very careful in terms of the attributes it seeks to reward.

Moreover, when a sound grievance procedure has already been installed as part of collective bargaining, continual negotiations over workers' rights on the job can be kept to a minimum. In some ways, Barkin argues, strong unions are easier for management to deal with. These unions feel secure that any grievance issue can be satisfactorily resolved whatever the degree of codification in the contract. "Unions which are not granted a secure status or are established in plants with an unfavorable history of labor relations are constrained to insist upon provisions safeguarding the rights of union members and workers. It is for such plants that long and complicated agreements are written."[54]

Seniority systems and grievance procedures can serve to protect workers' basic rights on a job, but they can also be used to protect workers' pay. One reason unions hold to seniority as a security measure is that they do not believe there are any truly objective measures of employee worth. From the workers' perspective, pay is determined by the requirements of the job, not by the merits of the individual who holds the job. In recent years, managements have been concerned with having workers who have all-around skills that will enable them to handle any job; workers who attain this level of skill will want to be compensated for the extra abilities that improve their potential for taking on complementary responsibilities. The perspective is derived from workers' knowledge about the skill levels needed to work in modern industry and is influenced by their desire to be treated fairly. In addition, using promotion to reward performance becomes arbitrary, because the differences in performance by individual workers are often too subtle to be measured with any accuracy. Nevertheless, Barkin notes, management will persist in trying to develop measures that sift among workers to find the most worthy. In its negotiating efforts, the union must also deal with the employer's demands for special personnel practices such as employee rating systems, job evaluations plans, wage incentive arrangements, and methods of determining work assignments. Management has developed these techniques to establish its standards for settling problems in those respective fields.

Standards of work have their background in the development by Frederick Taylor of his "principles of scientific management" and were long opposed by organized labor. Barkin agrees that that opposition was justified on the grounds that Taylor's approach was not scientific and was biased toward employers. He feels that efficiency methods cannot go unchallenged by unions. Barkin did not recommend that unions simply continue to fight such methods. Rather, unions should accept responsibility for experimenting with the techniques so as to establish them on a sound scientific basis and ensure their proper application. They should also devise their own alternative approaches to provide techniques that are more compatible with the workers' views of appropriate measures. In holding this perspective, Barkin shares the attitude developed by Taylor's followers in the 1920s, when they sought to cooperate with unions in introducing their methods and developed approaches whereby workers could maintain their own control over efficiency methods.[55] As noted previously, Barkin was very familiar with the work of these progressive Taylorites, from his experiences of the 1920s as a member of discussion groups that included leaders of the Taylor society. The cooperative approach to efficiency had also been a favorite strategy of Sidney Hillman.

That cooperative approach would be an important addition to negotiating a labor contract. In surveying existing practices, Barkin found, "Most unions are reluctant to assume any responsibility for these practices; others are willing to experiment with management in developing satisfactory techniques."[56] As is taken up in Chapter Five, Barkin saw a role for academicians to play in devising techniques of efficiency and performance measurement that were user friendly for workers and their unions. He devised a number of such techniques, especially in industrial engineering.

The notion that unions would cooperate with management both in devising methods to evaluate workers' performance and in improving productivity, even though it has long been proposed by labor leaders and management experts, still seems an exceptional practice. It also would appear to be broadly at variance with present labor-management practices. Why business and labor have failed to live up to their respective responsibilities in attaining a cooperative approach is a complex question, so separate chapters on business and labor are necessary to deal with it. A few preliminary comments are in order here.

In assessing blame, Barkin finds enough to go around. Most commentators on the labor scene criticize unions for their retention of the outlook described by

Selig Perlman as "job-conscious." Under this outlook, unions have been seen as having concentrated their efforts on protecting their jobs and getting better pay. Barkin may agree with that characterization, but he finds several reasons why labor has not gotten beyond it, not all of which stem from union activities.

Primarily, he notes, union's efforts to overcome the job-conscious outlook have been rebuffed by business. During the era just after World War II, when the union movement was at the height of its organizational success and its idealism, efforts were made by unions to behave more responsibly in their activities. But management fought them. As Barkin describes that period, "The ascendant management group in a growing number of big businesses launched out on a new track to redesign trade union behavior. The aim was to get trade unions to accommodate themselves to, and restrain them from interfering with, business purposes and performance. . . . Management yielded on significant union demands and granted historic contracts in return for its right to exercise administrative, financial and production control."[57] General Motors was willing to endure a long strike in 1946 to make sure that unions retained the emphasis on a job-conscious outlook. It is not surprising that unions took the hint. Barkin believes that unions have a role to play in cooperating with management—a role workers would value—but it is a role that managements have never permitted. Even recent efforts at cooperation plans are limited to the job level.

There is one other lesson that Barkin thinks workers have drawn from business in terms of what they seek from their unions. He observes that workers "have known that management violates the moral codes and feel that their own first job is to get along with the improvement of their own lots and the protection of their own rights rather than the creation of effete institutions modeled on the rules of 'middle-class' morality which is observed more in the breach than in the fact."[58] Thorstein Veblen long ago worried over the development of a pecuniary society, wherein the values of making money subscribed to by the dominant business class would trickle down to workers. Barkin echoes that concern by asking why workers should be held to a higher level of probity and idealism than businesspeople. He would like for them to choose such a higher level but recognizes that as long as business sets a model of monetary gain at whatever cost, it should come as no surprise that workers will follow.

This model has one other detriment to responsible behavior on the part of labor attached to it. When workers become cynical about management's behavior, that cynicism will also be applied to expectations about the union leadership. When this occurs, it will result in a "tolerance of the membership for unethical and undemocratic conduct by some of its leaders."[59] Workers may well seek out leaders who will be ruthless, for that is what dealing with management requires. This approach would be in keeping with the spirit of political conservatives who felt that Richard Nixon's deviousness became a virtue in conducting foreign affairs; such was needed in dealing with the crafty leaders of the Soviet bloc. Whether such behavior would lead to responsibility in other areas was not a major question, at least not until it were too late. Certainly one would hope that workers would aspire to a higher level of responsibility among their leadership.

Barkin believes that unions have made progress in this area and in serving workers. He finds that unions have been responsible for building "human tests and controls into our economy to make for more progressive and stabler operations." This view is in keeping with his conclusion that "Collective bargaining must be considered a process for effecting changes in the terms of employment and the benefits enjoyed by workers and for recording workers' judgments of management." Through this process the union "is always testing the effectiveness of the economy in human terms. Are the human costs excessive? How can they be moderated?"[60]

This last point represents an important role unions can play as far as Barkin is concerned. In many places among his writings he stressed the problem of the social costs of labor. So he notes that one other positive feature of union effort is to foster a "demand for a fairer distribution of the costs of social change." As he sees it, "Advances in society bring great individual costs. The incidence should not be borne by the victims but should be spread widely among all."[61] Cases dealing with industrial health, in which workers have been compensated for damage suffered from working in unhealthy conditions, for example, working with asbestos, are indicative of the type of progress on social costs Barkin sought.

If Barkin were pressed to give one objective that unions should pursue diligently, he would reply that they should do everything possible to ensure that the human and social costs of work do not fall totally on workers. Pursuit of that objective does not mean that unions must subvert the economic system or the business firms that are its mainstay. It does mean that unions have an attitude toward the economic system that differs from that held by free market economists. As Barkin sums up that attitude, "The trade union movement believes in a free market society. It doesn't want a collective society. It wants to operate through the free market. Otherwise where would the trade unions be? But we don't think that the present system of pricing functions well. We are trying to shift overhead costs like fringe benefits on to the wage structure in order to transfer these costs into the pricing structure."[62]

Barkin credited unions with being able to behave responsibly in their efforts to increase wages. As he put it, "in formulating specific immediate demands, trade unionists adjust their goals to what is realistic and immediately practical." In the TWUA, for example, bargainers took into account what the industry conditions consisted of in the several branches with which it conducted negotiations, differentiating "between industries with limited competition and high profits and those with substantial competition." Some branches of the industry could afford to pay higher wages; others, because of their structure, could not. The final result was, as Barkin summarized, "In each of these industries the union adapted its specific demands to the economic conditions of the industry." In industries in which competition was keen or profits low, the TWUA would cooperate with firms to find ways of improving efficiency as a way of ultimately gaining higher wages.[63] If all unions held to this standard of performance, they would be able to protect the rights of workers, gain them a higher wage, and do so in a way that would protect the industry as the union promoted a healthier structure for it.

In this section, Barkin's view that unions exist to establish the rights of workers through collective bargaining has been explored. The particular rights he feels workers want to gain include job security, a say in personnel practices, protection from harsh treatment, and the ability to be represented by leadership capable of effectively representing them at higher levels of management. Unions also reflect the worker's desire for a rising standard of living. Unions can give this value concrete expression by defining it more concretely in terms of fairness, security, and benefit sharing. They may also give life to such worker aspirations as stabilized employment or lifetime job security, such as is enjoyed by workers in Japan and Europe.

In particular, it has been noted that all these rights must be negotiated with management. Unions will be misunderstood if they are viewed as following an economic policy similar to that of a business with a monopoly, first because unions must negotiate and bargain with their customers and second because a union must reflect the values of its members. This view is totally at odds with that of neoclassical economics.

Conclusion

The institutional approach to economics, as personified by Barkin, takes a richer view of workers than does the mainstream method. It establishes that workers are not the rational economic persons that mainstream economics thinks them to be, nor are they simply a commodity as the market model imagines. Workers do make rational decisions, but that is only part of what makes them tick. If workers were purely rational, as mainstream economists believe, and if unions used monopoly power to gain higher wages for their members, as those economists also allege, then it would be irrational for workers not to join unions. It would also be irrational for employers not to oppose them on the same grounds.

Not all workers choose to join unions, however. To some extent, this decision reflects cultural values and employer resistance and pressure on workers as much as cost-benefit analysis, as Barkin's studies of Southern workers confirm. But whether the decision has been freely made would be open to debate. In order to argue that Southern workers did not want unions, one must explain why, if workers were antiunion, employers had to take strong measures to see that unions were defeated.

When workers do choose unions, they seek more than personal economic gain and job security. They realize an opportunity to have their rights in the workplace defined and defended. They also acquire a vehicle for expressing their wants in the offices of management, a voice in the halls of government to secure legislation to advance their well-being and protect them from unfriendly government action, and a say in how their work life will be ordered. Finally, they secure a higher sense of personal dignity and group importance than would be accorded to them as merely "hired hands." How well they are served by their unions in meeting these wants is the subject of Chapter Five.

When employers resist the formation of unions in their plants, they deny their workers the fulfillment of their rights and ability to express themselves. Such employers may claim that the granting of these rights and abilities is too costly and that as rational, profit-maximizing entrepreneurs they cannot afford the expense of dealing with unions. In holding this conviction, they have the backing of over two centuries of mainstream economic thinking. Barkin would disagree. To him that rationality is constrained by a traditional management opinion that prevents employers from perceiving that there are gains to be had from accepting unions and cooperating with them. What management must do to realize those gains is the topic of the next chapter.

Notes

1. Frank Swaboda, "A Revised Manual for Keeping Out Unions," *The Washington Post*, October 28, 1990, p. H3.

2. Solomon Barkin, "A Pattern for the Study of Industrial Human Relations," *Industrial and Labor Relations Review* 9 (October 1955), p. 97.

3. Clark Kerr, "Labor Markets: Their Character and Consequences," in Richard A. Lester, ed., *Labor: Readings on Major Issues* (New York: Random House, 1965), p. 294.

4. Clark Kerr, "The Balkanization of Labor Markets," in E. Wright Bakke, Clark Kerr, and Charles W. Anrod, eds., *Unions, Management and the Public,* 3rd ed. (New York: Harcourt, Brace & World, Inc., 1967, p. 551.

5. Don Bellante and Mark Jackson, *Labor Economics* (New York: McGraw-Hill Book Co., 1979), pp. 170–79.

6. Solomon Barkin, "Industrial Union Wage Policies," *Plan Age* VI (January 1940), p. 9.

7. Sumner H. Slichter, James J. Healy, and E. Robert Livernash, *The Impact of Collective Bargaining on Management* (Washington, DC: The Brookings Institution, 1960), p. 624.

8. Barkin, "Industrial Union Wage Policies," p. 11.

9. E. Wright Bakke, "To Join or Not to Join," in Bakke, Kerr, and Anrod, p. 85.

10. Solomon Barkin, "Evaluation of Recent Research on Employee Attitudes and Morale," *Proceedings, Industrial Relations Research Association 4th Annual Conference*, 1951, p. 1.

11. Robert Blauner, *Alienation and Freedom* (Chicago: University of Chicago Press, 1964). Blauner's work on textile workers (Chapter 4) relied heavily on Barkin's own studies (cited in the following notes). Barkin, in turn, had recourse to data from the outpatient clinic at the University of North Carolina, which had many textile workers as patients.

12. Ibid., pp. 6–11.

13. Solomon Barkin, "Human Relations in the Trade Unions," Chapter XIII of *Research in Industrial Human Relations* (New York: Harper & Bros., 1956), p. 194.

14. F. Ray Marshall, *Labor in the South* (Cambridge, MA: Harvard University Press, 1967), pp. vii-viii.

15. Ibid., pp. 83–85, 166–70, 228–29.

16. Barbara S. Griffith, *The Crisis of American Labor: Operation Dixie and the Defeat of the CIO* (Philadelphia: Temple University Press, 1988), p. xiii.

17. Marshall, *Labor in the South,* p. 257.

18. Griffith, *Crisis of American Labor,* pp. 33–36, 46–60.

19. Ibid., p. 105.

20. Solomon Barkin, review of Barbara S. Griffith, *The Crisis of American Labor: Operation Dixie and the Defeat of the CIO,* in *Labor History* 31 (1990), pp. 378–85. For a more detailed analysis of the relative gains made by the AFL and CIO during Operation Dixie, see Marshall, *Labor in the South,* pp. 265–69.

21. Ibid.

22. "The Reminiscences of Solomon Barkin," Oral History Research Office, Columbia University, 1961, pp. 87–89.

23. Robert H. Zeiger, *American Workers, American Unions, 1920–1985* (Baltimore: Johns Hopkins University Press, 1986), p. 110.

24. Solomon Barkin, "The Southern Textile Worker," *IUD Digest* 6 (Spring 1961), pp. 88–89.

25. Ibid., p. 90.

26. Ibid., p. 91.

27. Solomon Barkin, "The Personality Profile of Southern Textile Workers," *Labor Law Journal* 11 (June 1960), p. 3.

28. Ibid., p. 10.

29. Ibid.

30. Ibid., p. 11.

31. Marshall, *Labor in the South,* p. 261.

32. Solomon Barkin, "Southern Views of Unions," *Labor Today* (Fall 1962), p. 33.

33. Ibid., p. 35.

34. Ibid.

35. "Reconversion in New England," *Monthly Labor Review* 63 (July 1946), pp. 8–14; William Hartford, untitled manuscript, Chapter Four, pp. 12–21.

36. Blauner, *Alienation,* pp. 16, 166.

37. E. Wright Bakke, "Some Basic Characteristics of Unions," in Bakke, Kerr, and Anrod, p. 140.

38. Robert F. Hoxie, *Trade Unionism in the United States* (New York: D. Appleton-Century Co., Inc., 1921), pp. 64–67.

39. James B. Atleson, *Values and Assumptions in American Labor Law* (Amherst: University of Massachusetts Press, 1983), pp. 8–10.

40. Morgan Reynolds, "The Case for Ending the Legal Privileges and Immunities of Trade Unions," in Seymour Martin Lipsett, ed., *Unions in Transition* (San Francisco: ICS Press, 1986), pp. 221–38.

41. Albert Rees, *The Economics of Trade Unions,* 3rd ed. (Chicago: University of Chicago Press, 1989), pp. 46–53.

42. Barkin, "Human Relations in Trade Unions," p. 192.

43. Solomon Barkin, "Trade Unions as an Ethical Force in a Pecuniary Society," address before the 10th Annual Conference of the International Association of Personnel Women, April 30, 1960, p. 2 (copy in Barkin files).

44. Sumner Slichter, *Union Policies and Industrial Management* (New York: Greenwood Press, 1968), p. 1.

45. Atleson, *Values and Assumptions,* p. 14.

46. Solomon Barkin, "Labor Unions and Workers' Rights in Jobs," in Arthur Kornhauser, Robert Dubin, and Arthur M. Ross, eds., *Industrial Conflict* (New York: McGraw-Hill Book Co., 1954), p. 128.

47. Ibid., p. 121.

48. Ibid., p. 124.

49. Ibid., p. 126.

50. Atleson, *Values and Assumptions,* throughout.

51. Cass R. Sunstein, *After the Rights Revolution* (Cambridge, MA: Harvard University Press, 1990), pp. 12, 18–20, 39.

52. Slichter, Healy, and Livernash, *Impact of Collective Bargaining,* p. 745.

53. John T. Dunlop and James J. Healy, "The Grievance Procedure," in Bakke, Kerr, and Anrod, p. 318.

54. Solomon Barkin, "Union Strategy in Negotiations," in *Collective Bargaining Contracts* (Washington, DC: Bureau of National Affairs, 1941), p. 27.

55. Donald R. Stabile, *Prophets of Order* (Boston: South End Press, 1984), pp. 96–106.

56. Ibid., p. 31.

57. Solomon Barkin, "The Industrial Impact of the American Trade Union Movement," *Labor Law Journal* 7 (April 1956), pp. 218–19.

58. Solomon Barkin, "Trade-Unionism: An Ethical Force in a Pecuniary Society," address delivered before the 10th Annual Conference of the International Association of Personnel Women, Statler Hotel, New York, April 30, 1960, p. 3.

59. Ibid.

60. Solomon Barkin, "Labor's Code for a Private Enterprise Economy," *Labor Law Journal* 3 (December 1952), pp. 844–45.

61. Barkin, "Industrial Impact," p. 221.

62. Columbia Seminar, minutes, December 18, 1957, p. 7.

63. Solomon Barkin, "Wage Policies of Industrial Unions," *Harvard Business Review* (Spring 1941), pp. 342–48.

4

Responsibilities of Industry

I speak of the dynamic theory of wages in talking to employers. I ask a simple question: what is the greatest compliment the union has paid you? Well, it's when they ask for a wage increase, because that's the greatest show of faith in the employer's competence to run the plant.
—*Solomon Barkin*

Ever since the age of reform that took place in the years immediately preceding World War I, society has imposed an increasing number of responsibilities on business. Gone are the good old days when a firm's sole obligation was to record a decent level of profits for its owners, the days when it was believed that since any firm making a profit must be producing goods society wanted, profits were an indication of socially responsible behavior. Recognition of some of the social costs of industry has changed this belief, and during the twentieth century, regulations such as the Food and Drugs Act (1906), Workmen's Compensation Laws (passed during 1910–20), and the Environmental Protection Act (1970) have altered business's ability to escape responsibility for meeting those social costs. In labor relations, the NLRA made it obligatory for business to permit unions to request that certification elections be held, in the partial expectations that unions would help workers to meet their social costs. Even in the present era of deregulation, businesses are still expected to act responsibly in areas such as environmental protection, affirmative action, and product and human safety.

In addition to government, there are a number of forces that seek to compel business to accept greater responsibility for the social costs it creates. Dissident stockholders of all stripes often try to influence corporate behavior directly at stockholders' meetings, with attempts to force divestiture of assets in South Africa being only a recent example. Unions, too, are a powerful force for seeing that the social costs of labor are met through the payment of a full-cost social wage. All these activities raise a critical question: How far should business be pushed toward meeting its responsibilities? It would appear that the socially accepted principle for measuring a firm's efforts at meeting its social obligations is still its profitability, and the idea remains that bankruptcy is a harsh penalty to impose on a firm for acting in a responsible manner.

In some cases, as with the pension fund legislation that established the Employee Retirement Income Security Act, it has been necessary for government to underwrite the funding of social costs in order to protect society from bankrupt firms. Unfortunately, firms may use that protection by declaring bankruptcy to shift the burden of social costs back onto society, as the LTV Steel Co. attempted with its pension fund obligations. The imposition of the burden of social costs on private firms is, for good and ill, tied to the problem of bankruptcy. In early 1991, it became evident that the social cost and the competitive elements of pension guarantees were being recognized. Congress gave the Pension Benefit Guarantee Corporation more ability to stake a claim on the assets of firms in bankruptcy, preventing them from escaping their obligations. More responsible firms favored this new power, for they "hate seeing competitors gain an advantage by off-loading their pension obligations."[1]

Should a firm that cannot pay its full share of the social costs it incurs be permitted to remain in operation? Any firm that does not pay the full social costs of its operations is receiving a subsidy from society. In the absence of an outside agent to impose those costs on business, the "prisoner's dilemma" problem will force all firms to the lowest level of responsibility in meeting social costs, with the result that they will all be subsidized by society. Firms with the highest levels of social costs are receiving the largest subsidy when they are permitted to escape payment of those costs.

When social costs are imposed on all firms, those firms with the highest level of social costs have the most to lose. They complain loudly about the harsh penalties being inflicted on them. Once it is determined that social costs must be met, however, the economic test of business performance changes. If products cannot be produced and sold at a price that covers all social costs incurred by firms in a particular industry and still includes a normal profit, society apparently does not value that product as highly as it does others. In that case it should not be produced (or if there is something essential about the product, its production should be subsidized as part of a public policy). If any firms in an industry cannot cover their burden of social costs and remain viable, they are being inefficient in other areas. In either case, for sound economic decisions to be made, Barkin believes, "The social costs of business must become a substantial part of the accounting of the enterprise."[2]

But Barkin also believes that payment of a wage that covers the social costs of labor need not lead inexorably to bankruptcy. Rather, he has espoused the view that higher wages can be offset by gains in productivity. The key to attaining that increase in productivity is through programs that incorporate labor and management cooperation. Achieving such cooperation, in turn, would require management to relinquish some of its prerogatives. It would also require that a new measure of managerial performance be established, one geared more toward labor.

Labor Measure of Performance

It should be clear, from Chapter Two, that Barkin prefers a measure of managerial performance that includes business's responsibility for paying its workers a wage that at a minimum covers workers' social costs. He would argue that any firm that cannot pay its workers such a wage might be declared insolvent. In that view, payment of decent wages joins profits as a measure of a firm's performance. This is a novel view, requiring elaboration, since it smacks of irresponsible unions' cutting of their own throats by forcing their employers out of business. After all, aren't low wages better than no wages?

Barkin thinks not. To him, the imposition of social costs on business represents a challenge that managers should be capable of meeting. In his view, as described in the previous chapter, low wages are the easy way to cut costs, but business reliance on cutting wages to restore profits adds little to economic growth. It not only reduces the demand for products on the part of workers but also depletes incentives for technical and managerial innovation, which are the most progressive force in economic growth. Moreover, low wages in one firm or industry act as a competitive drag on other firms and industries, which must cut their wages to remain competitive—thus multiplying the problem. Finally, the social costs of work do not go away; having them met by workers or other agencies creates inefficiencies in terms of how labor is allocated into different industries and how income has to be redistributed.

The problem of the competitive effects of social costs can be seen in the recent debates over universal health care. According to *Business Week*, the legislation proposed in Congress to force business to either pay health care benefits to workers or pay a tax to support national health insurance has caused concern among some sectors of the business community: "Many small companies fear that they would be forced out of business." These same companies do not think they should be the primary providers of health care for workers. At the same time, large corporations, most of which provide health benefits, feel that "rising medical costs reflect the expense of treating workers uninsured by smaller employers."[3] In effect, the *Business Week* article indicates that in terms of the social costs of health, large businesses and the government are subsidizing small businesses.

Labor unions have long recognized that higher wages are best ensured through increases in productivity. But this recognition is often lost amid charges of worker resistance to technical change: stories of featherbedding, no matter how rare such practices may be, are all too common, and the reason such practices exist at all has to do with the manner through which management has improved the methods of productivity.

Karl Marx claimed there was an unending conflict between capital and labor over how long and hard workers should work. Employers in the United States seem to have accepted that view. In this country, management, especially since the development of large-scale, mass-production industries that left direct observation of the factory difficult, has recognized the difficulties involved with determining whether workers were performing as well as possible. A number of methods—technical, social, and psychological—have been devised to ensure that workers are working properly. Management has never been reluctant to absorb the costs of these methods, presumably because of the greater benefits attached to using them.

The social costs borne by labor have usually been missing from these cost-benefit calculations when new methods have been imposed by management. The new methods may be beneficial to the firm only because workers absorb the costs of retraining or relocation that new methods create for them or because management overlooks the costs involved with hiring new workers. In addition, unilateral imposition of new methods of production has been done in ways that created conflict with workers, for workers have not had any guarantee that they will gain and not lose from such changes. Change is frightening, especially among those who are unable to protect themselves. Why should workers under these conditions trust management to take care of them if they are to be displaced by new methods of production?

Barkin would rather sidestep this question of trust by strengthening the ability of unions to redistribute the social costs of worker displacement. He feels that worker resistance to change does not come from an intrinsic desire to hold on to the older forms of work. That attitude may have prevailed among skilled handicraftsmen who derived personal satisfaction from the exercise of their skills; it is less likely to be found among industrial workers, who are fearful of losing their livelihood or being asked to perform work that is especially difficult or dangerous. If they had the assurance of earning a full social wage, they would feel more secure. If they had a say in how change would take place, they would be more accepting of it.

Programs of labor and management cooperation, which aim to reassure workers that they will have a say in what happens to their working conditions, have had a long history in the United States.[4] To a large extent, such programs have represented generalized efforts to correct for worker dissatisfaction with working conditions and to gain worker input into overall productivity. In many cases they have been tied to worker pay-incentive plans, such as the Scanlon Plans, which were popular in academic circles but not widely used during the 1940s and 1950s, and the Employee Stock Ownership Plans (ESOPs) of more recent vintage. The problem with these plans is that they remain within the sphere of managerial prerogatives, with workers having little security or input into the plan. Workers have little input into the operations of a plant or firm. Witness the recent efforts of business to recover the "surplus" in company pension plans wherein management has argued that it, and not workers, owns the pension fund.

Instances such as this point out not only that unions are useful in making labor and management cooperation work, but also that they are essential to getting cooperative plans started. In summarizing the results of studies of fourteen industries, David Cornfield states the case very well. He writes, "Formal labor-management cooperation has been established in the highly concentrated and unionized, mass production industries. . . ." At the same time, he notes, "Increased unilateral control has tended to occur in less unionized, high growth industries. . . ."[5]

The only way workers can gain security and input into management decisions is through their unions. As Barkin sees the situation, "The responsibility for this technical development rests with management. Organized labor will gladly share to the extent that management allows it to participate and thereby increase management's effectiveness."[6] In essence this would mean that virtually every change considered by management would have to be negotiated with the union, as is the case in Sweden, where unions may, under force of law, challenge changes in work standards and have them stopped pending arbitration when differences exist. To many critics of unions, such full-scale negotiations would simply burden management with meddlesome interference on the part of unions. These critics remain mired in Marx's view that labor and management must always be in conflict. Instead of holding to a conflict theory of labor relations, Barkin believes that a system of labor and management cooperation is possible and that it would impose a higher level of responsibility on both parties.

Business Response to Unions

That responsibility was not one that business managers have accepted readily. One of the reasons for the passage of the NLRA was to promote collective bargaining as a way of strengthening labor so that the NLRA would be able to promote cooperation with business. Quite often, legislation such as the NLRA changes the preferences of business groups, because it forces them to deal with organizations such as unions against whom they are biased. Familiarity gained by working with the unions might have dispelled business's prejudices against them.

The NLRA secured social legitimation because the period during which it was enacted, the depression of the 1930s, was also the lowest moment of esteem for business in the nation's history. The 1920s had been heralded as a triumph of U.S. business, so it was easy to blame the business community for the disaster of the 1930s. In the arena of social legislation, businesspeople were clearly on the defensive, while in their own domain "their power over their own employees and factories was threatened."[7]

They did not roll over and die, however. In politics they managed to regain their prominence during World War II by serving on government boards and by managing their enterprises in ways that secured efficient production for the war effort. It was easier to be loyal to the Roosevelt Administration then. In their factories, they devised a number of strategies to counter unions. Some firms remained opposed to unions through direct confrontation at every stage of an organizational campaign or negotiating round; others remained opposed but did so through subtle delaying tactics under the NLRA or outright violations of it. More moderate managements were willing to accept the existence of unions and work with them, although they took care to limit the areas in which such collaboration took place. Innovators began developing new methods for dealing with workers in ways that would co-opt the power of unions as a medium for communications between unions and management.[8] All of these strategies dawned soon after passage of the NLRA but would come into play only when the war was ended.

If businesspeople regained their prestige and influence during the war, labor was still not far behind. The War Labor Board had given unions a "maintenance of membership" rule and had intervened on their behalf in a number of organizational drives. Nevertheless, wage increases sought by unions were not often granted, and labor leaders who participated on war planning boards served only as advisers; the real planning was done by businesspeople in their own plants or acting as government-appointed administrators. And while members of the board supported the NLRA for its promotion of better industrial relations, they also strongly supported management's right to run its plants without interference from workers or their unions.[9] The real test would come after the war.

In November 1945, members of the United Automobile Workers Union (UAW) went on strike in General Motors (GM) plants throughout the nation. Shortly thereafter, other CIO unions struck in their industries in support of the UAW. The main issue of the strike was whether labor could retain the gains it had made during the war in the face of the removal of wage-and-price controls after the war. As vice president and head of the UAW bargaining team, Walter Reuther asked for a 30 percent wage increase and for no accompanying price increases by GM, arguing that GM's profits were sufficient to do so. He challenged GM to open its books to establish the need for any price increases to pay for the wage increases.[10]

The efforts to win wage increases during the 1945–46 GM strike were both a part of CIO idealism and an effort to act responsibly in dealings with management. To be sure, Reuther was seeking high wages for UAW members, and he might have been using the strike to consolidate his own position as union leader.[11] Nevertheless, his pushing GM for no price increases would, if won, have been beneficial for all consumers. The union stated that its goal was to influence pricing as a way "to achieve a full production, full employment, full consumption economy."[12] Reuther had indicated labor was "not going to operate as a narrow economic interest group."[13] As A. H. Raskin described it, "Reuther's idea was that unions performed a disservice to the community if their sole concern was to win higher wages and improved conditions and then allow the cost to be passed on to the consumer."[14] Equally important, Reuther's asking GM to open its books and to use them to justify the need for price increases constituted an attempt to eliminate the link between wage increases and price increases. Both demands were unprecedented in labor negotiations on this scale both at that time and ever since.

Top management at GM rejected both demands out of hand and accepted a 113-day strike rather than give in. Their objections to the demands were that the prices GM charged were a management prerogative and they would not give in to "an opening wedge whereby the unions hope to pry their way into the whole field of management."[15] As Robert Zeiger reports, one GM official stated, "We don't even let our stockholders look at the books."[16] Another GM executive, in refusing to submit the contract dispute to arbitration, declared, "Functions of management cannot be delegated to anyone not responsible for the continuing success of the business."[17] GM boycotted a fact-finding committee set up by President Truman to study the connection between wages and prices. The outcome of the strike was a wage gain, although it was not as large as Reuther had demanded. Reuther also agreed to cease UAW efforts to organize GM supervisors. It is easy to agree with Howell Harris's conclusion: "General Motors did not choose the ground, but it won the battle."[18]

Reuther had always tried to invade management's customary range of prerogatives as a means of bringing about a more liberal social order that would see authority over industry shared by business, government, and labor; in making his case he reproached business for its inefficiency in production and irresponsibility in social affairs. This was the spirit of his dramatic "500 planes a day" proposal during World War II. The spirit had not carried during the war, however.[19] Nor did it work during the GM strike. Not only did the UAW lose its fight for greater control in the workplace, but also GM had some counterproposals that permitted it to recapture some of the authority it had lost during the war.[20]

Although this episode set the tone for industrial relations in the auto industry and much of the unionized sector of the economy, it did nothing to nurture a greater sense of responsibility and cooperation in management or labor circles. Business stoutly maintained that it had inviolable prerogatives or rights in its operations that labor could not touch and that those rights required resistance to any union encroachment. The rights centered on functions of administration and control, which could not possibly be shared. Management must be free to develop its policies and implement them. Business might submit to government violations of its rights in the form of regulations designed to promote public welfare, but it would not accept any abridgments by nongovernment organizations such as labor unions. And while there were always limits placed on business by outside nongovernment agents, such as banks, they were limits that were based on a common acceptance of business principles.

For their part, unions were always, whether consciously or not, seeking measures that would constrain management. They could not help but do so. In the case of profits or dividends, the amount paid out could equally be used for pay increases, with wage increases being thought of as a form of profit sharing. On decisions relating to the allocation, layoff, or discipline of workers, the union clearly has an interest. Any policy that has an impact on the success of the firm will provide workers with more or less pay and work. As one union official argued, "Should any policies of the company adversely affect the wages and working conditions of its membership, the union would have to challenge management's unilateral authority over the problem."[21]

The fighting ground over managerial rights was collective bargaining. Management wanted strict limits placed on the content of collective bargaining; it wanted a clearly defined line, which unions would not cross, fearing that union involvement with corporate decisions would impair efficiency. The GM agreement of 1946 specifically prescribed a set of management's rights.[22] Unions could not agree to any limits that would impinge upon their desire to protect the security of their members. Managerial rights themselves were a matter for collective bargaining. With both sides' having such differing attitudes, it is no surprise that Neil Chamberlain concluded, "The roles of management and union in the large corporation cannot be defined by a differentiation of spheres of mutual or exclusive interest in the operation of the business."[23]

In the contest for determining where to draw the line, however, business has crucial advantages. Unions are a creation of the industry they organize and have no existence without it. This makes them passive reactors to business policy and it limits their actions by requiring they fall far short of anything that threatens the survival of the industry. In the GM strike, for example, management seemed more willing to risk the industry's survival than were unions. Afterward, unions were clearly on the defensive. They learned not to fight over basic rights of control over the work floor.

Management had made the point that it knew best, and it persisted in its faith that unilateral decisions were the most effective. Barkin disagreed with management on this issue, for he believed that cooperative resolution of differences would improve economic and social efficiency by imposing a greater sense of responsibility on labor and management.

The remainder of this chapter concerns Barkin's exploration of how management's sense of responsibility would be heightened by cooperation with labor in management decision making with respect to efficiency methods, human relations, accounting, technological change, and problems of older workers. In proposing systems of labor and management cooperation in these areas, Barkin would extend them all the way down to the shop floor. Few observers on the labor scene accepted such far-reaching cooperation, for it would impinge directly on tacitly recognized managerial prerogatives. Barkin would respond that by sacrificing its prerogatives, management could attain a higher level of responsibility and come closer to meeting a labor measure of performance.

Efficiency Methods

No specter has haunted American unions more than Frederick W. Taylor and his "principles of scientific management." In principle, Taylor promised to develop standard policies that would make both labor and management perform more efficiently. In practice, however, he was sensible enough to realize who would buy his services. He aimed his efforts at showing management how to get the most from workers. He also claimed that his methods treated workers fairly and paid them what they deserved for improvements in their productivity. With Taylor and his kind to take care of their well-being, workers had no need of unions. That workers and unions did not take well to Taylor's offer is well-known.

In applying his methods to labor, Taylor was trying to reform many of the difficulties inherent in worker incentive plans. The key to incentive plans, of course, is to give workers a direct financial stake in improving their productivity. As Barkin has written, this key breaks down into a list of purposes.

> They are: (1) to reduce overhead and unit costs by increasing man-power output; (2) to raise worker income without increasing labor costs; (3) to increase substantially the basic level of worker effort with slight additional cost to management; (4) to give management a way to recapture the benefits of improved productivity derived from sources other than worker effort; (5) to reduce the pressure on supervision by increasing the worker's personal interest in production; (6) to fix unit labor costs and thereby facilitate cost estimation; and (7) to provide management with a tool for planning and controlling the production process.[24]

All of these aims have been controversial and have encountered considerable resistance on the part of both labor leaders and workers.

The objections leveled by labor leaders against incentive plans are varied. Foremost of these, Barkin finds, is that "wage incentive systems tend to strengthen the employer's bargaining power." Incentive systems must be revised constantly, as working conditions change, with the result that the effectiveness of union wage negotiations becomes determined by the union's ability to negotiate each change, a very difficult and costly task. In addition, leaders worry that incentive systems undermine worker solidarity by making workers compete with each other. Other reasons for union resistance that Barkin finds important are that incentive plans give management too much power in terms of distributing the gains of improved productivity, that the increased productivity may be used to cut costs and not expand output and employment, and that the incentive system biases management to look to it, instead of to other areas of potential improvement, for cost-cutting measures. Barkin does note that union leaders will support wage incentive plans when they truly result in higher wages, when they set industry-wide standards of pay that eliminate competitive wage-cutting, and when, as in war, there are periods of hourly wage freezes. Thus the systems are not seen as all bad.[25]

The views of leaders on this issue would appear to be in advance of the wishes of the rank and file. "If anything," Barkin reports, "it is probable that the leaders have been more receptive and inclined to proceed with the negotiations, installations and administration of these plans, than have the workers."[26] This result should not come as a surprise, since workers are more directly affected by the plans and would be more likely to oppose them, especially if the potential for gain from the plan was not clear to them.

The basic feature of strong worker opposition to incentive plans is workers' expectations of what they deserve. As Barkin puts it, "The worker expects a living wage not as a reward for additional effort but as a normal by-product of employment. . . . The worker's primary interest is in his income rather than in his output. He does not readily associate the relationship between" them.[27] Of course the intent of wage incentive plans is to bring this point home to workers, but there are other features of the systems, which render this intent difficult.

First of all, workers who are involved with incentive systems quickly come to understand that their productivity does not derive simply from their efforts. It also depends on the tools, materials, and working conditions that management provides them. Their ability to improve their productivity and pay is not totally in their control. Second, they recognize that improved productivity can threaten their chances for holding on to their job. They realize that when they compete with each other by increasing their productivity, the result may be high income and security to exceptional workers and layoffs for the rest. Finally, workers feel that incentive measures are arbitrary and that hiring and layoff decisions based on them can become capricious.[28]

The arbitrariness of incentive measures also lends itself to abuses of the system in workers' eyes. The history of these systems produced several abuses that have fostered union and worker resistance to them. Chief among them is rate-cutting; once an incentive rate has been set and workers increase their incomes by stepping up production, managements often engage in cutting the rate. As Slichter, Healy, and Livernash observed, more changes in incentives fall into the category of "management revision without union consent" than into any other category.[29]

In other cases, workers sometimes figure out flaws in wage incentive systems that permit them to increase their pay without adding to output. When management discovers such cases, it seeks to cut the rates, setting off disputes until negotiations resolve the issue. In Barkin's experience, a typical resolution to this problem was to grant workers a onetime bonus and correct the system. Furthermore, workers have found that their inability to meet the rates has often been due to situations in which managements have not always maintained the operating conditions essential to maintenance of production standards. In practice, incentive plans have not always resulted in higher earnings for workers, and workers thus remain suspicious of them. The problems of installing and monitoring them in a manner that wins workers' trust are very difficult.

Taylor understood these problems and sought to resolve them. A basic proposition of his overall system of scientific management was that the quest for efficiency required a total overhaul of work conditions. His proposals included efforts at achieving more efficient plant design, devising better machines, and improving the qualities of the materials (witness his experiments with hardened steel). Where labor was concerned, he promised to determine, scientifically, what the expected level of work would be and what level of pay for that work should result. Once the objective standards of workload and basic pay were in place, there could be no quibbling between labor and management on these issues. Thus they could get on to more important matters of improving production.

Now these are noble objectives and, to be charitable to Taylor, worth pursuing. Even so, in the managerial context in which Taylor sought to introduce his methods, he experienced a limited amount of acceptance for his theme. Managements rarely adopted Taylor's entire program. They chose to use only those parts that would give the quickest results. One component they applied most seriously was time-and-motion study to determine the most effective level of worker effort. Here was a scientific approach to finding out just how well work was being performed.

Because of the lack of objectivity in their application, however, time-and-motion studies could never be scientific in the manner Taylor thought. At first glance, this would appear to be an unwarranted claim. What could be more objective than timing any activity with a stopwatch? We do it all the time in athletic endeavors, with world records' being recorded to the millisecond. There are difficulties involved with the measurement of time, including accuracy of the actual measurements. For example, efficiency experts themselves once applied their methods to sports, claiming in a promotional film to have helped pitchers for the Chicago Cubs to increase the velocity of their pitches into the range of 150 miles per hour. Since even modern laser guns rarely record pitches in excess of 100 miles per hour, however, this claim was not well-founded.

Measuring devices can be improved, as sports experts can testify, but improved measuring devices cannot be sufficient for establishing the proper conditions surrounding the measurement. In sports it is recognized that performance by runners is affected by wind, altitude, and drugs. Record times set under extreme cases of these effects are not counted as official world records, which should be set only when the race is run under normal conditions. But the designation of normal is somewhat arbitrary, because the advantage going to particular athletes varies depending on their size, strength, and psychological makeup. Where is the line to be drawn as to what determines too much wind?

If complicated issues can be raised over measuring something as simple as a footrace between two fixed points, then efforts to measure how and how well a worker should work will be even more complicated. But it is just these sorts of issues that Barkin raised in terms of time-and-motion studies. Very early in his career he learned that "labor is aware of the usefulness of objective measures. It is, however, skeptical about the value of time and motion study techniques in their present crude form and usage."[30]

Barkin made several complaints about the application by business of time-and-motion studies. A major defect was that the practitioners of the method were poorly trained. Because the method itself seems so simple (how much skill does it take to punch a stopwatch?), its application had been too widespread and too far-flung to produce any standards of performance on the practitioners themselves. Taylor had warned of this problem, but to no avail.

Even with competent practitioners, time-and-motion studies were still marred by the lack of a general definition of the worker's expected performance. When measuring performance, efficiency experts should understand that what is "normal" or "average" in a statistical sense might not be indicative of a worker's potential. In any system of measurement, a worker's performance displays variance above or below the norm, but that does not mean that the norm is an accurate reflection of what can be achieved by a typical worker. If statistical measures were not good predictors of how much an individual worker could produce, what measures could be used? Barkin's own research showed that time-and-motion study experts relied more on their experience and judgment as to what productivity was to be expected of the normal worker than on the statistical techniques of sampling and measurement.

In addition, Barkin found that the workers to be studied by the efficiency experts were not being chosen randomly. His research made him conclude, "All too often time study men select the workers 'from whom they can expect the best results.' Generally they are the more intelligent, skillful and consistent workers." Once the workers were selected, the process still foundered over issues of what time of day or year the measurements were made, length in time of the study, and number of cases on which the results would be based. Finally, obstacles remained both in determining the elements of the job in terms of what motions were necessary and in deciding what were proper working conditions and methods.[31] Barkin illustrated the sharp differences between the loose job descriptions used in practice, particularly in manuals, and the descriptions using kinesiological methods.

After a decade of experience in working with efficiency experts, Barkin recognized that they had tried to improve time-and-motion methods. Many of the described issues had been seemingly resolved by concentrating on human application, that is, physical effort as distinguished from actual production. This meant that human motion itself, divorced from any context, was to be measured. The emphasis would be on the speed of the motion. But the problem of choosing whose speed to measure remained, so for Barkin, "the concept of speed . . . as an index of human application is at best a mental application."[32] Methods of rating work elements by setting up an ideal approach were equally variable and therefore unfounded.[33]

After a thorough review of all the developments in time-and-motion-study techniques, Barkin concluded, "Neither management nor trade unions can turn to the time-study practitioner for a clear-cut definition of what should be measured in determining the level of human application."[34] Although there were to be no objective standards of performance forthcoming from time-and-motion experts, Barkin still suggested to management, "Labor believes that the time and motion study technique provides a valuable adjunct for management and a means of providing objective data for collective bargaining relations."[35]

The way to make efficiency methods effective, which Barkin derived from his experiences in the textile industry, centered on making production standards an item for negotiation in collective bargaining. Since the results of time-and-motion studies depended on the experience of the practitioner, those results might just as well be supplemented by the experience of the worker. For example, to establish criteria for the working conditions required for accurate measurement of worker performance, workers and their union should be able to make a case for what they considered the proper machines, layout, operating speed, and so on. Work activities could be categorized as to how frequently they were performed, ranging from scheduled to random, with allowances made for when randomness exceeded allowable variances.

Once these conditions were determined, each study proposal would be put through a trial run so as to be sure both sides agreed it could be performed within agreeable bounds. If both management and labor accepted the results of the study, the new standards could be put into operation. In cases when conditions hampered workers' performance, provision could be "made for the testing of complaints by checkers who observe the job for frequencies. Joint labor and management checkers are proposed where the management does not agree with the workers' complaint." Because the plan allowed for the union to participate in the setting up of the pilot study, the result was that under this system, "unions can participate fully in the study and bargaining process as soon as they accept the position that production standards should be set in terms of the job demands and personal effort demanded by the work."[36]

As is described in Chapter Five, Barkin later characterized this program as a "bench-mark approach" and considered how to expand its application outside the textile industry. The key to the approach, he noted, was that "the first criterion for the acceptability of a program of work measurement, therefore, must be that its techniques coincide with the workers' and unions' concepts of equitable measurement."[37] For management, acceptability depended on being able to make adjustments when necessary and to relate reward to production.

The starting point in the process was recognition of the "subjectivity in setting production standards." From this starting point it follows that the concept of a fair day's work is subject to mutual consent. As Barkin sums up, "The benchmark approach relies upon the immediately interested and knowledgeable parties to set an acceptable basic assignment and/or production quota." Instead of relying on the supposedly impartial arbiter in the form of the efficiency engineer, this system provides for each side to marshal its own set of experts in terms of setting the parameters for negotiation. As he put it, "All the expert know-how of the parties must be brought to bear, first to set up the job, and second, to analyze the job, and finally to formulate a finished model task." As to how each party would formulate its proposal, Barkin argued, "There can be no limitation on the manner in which either party may devise its proposal. . . . There can be no restriction on the source and type of recommendations, since there are fundamentally no scientific methods for formulating them. Only experience and judgment can provide answers."[38]

This approach goes a long way from Taylor's objective to replace judgment and experience with scientific practice. Unfortunately, in his own approach, Taylor overlooked how important judgment was. Nor did he believe that unions could develop a scientifically based judgment about production, which, after all, is what Barkin wants to promote. As is described more fully in Chapter Five, Barkin's ideas are in keeping with more recent findings that "Workers are ingenious at finding short cuts to beat the rates set by production engineers. Factory workers, not surprisingly, know a great deal about their jobs. They have a reservoir of knowledge that is underutilized. . . ."[39]

Barkin's position on how to tap that reservoir would be to organize labor and management cooperation programs through the medium of labor unions. Taylor's followers, in the 1920s, did try to seek cooperation from unions in getting their approach accepted by management, but their efforts had a mixed result. In the public arena, many unions remained opposed to Taylorism. One exception was in the clothing industry, where Hillman was willing to learn from scientific management.

Barkin, in line with his intellectual experiences of the 1920s and his contacts with Hillman, retained a strong commitment to the efficacy of labor and management cooperation in improving efficiency, but only if that effort included input by unions. This commitment was at odds with the view of the union support school, which felt that managerial discretion in setting efficiency standards was very important. Successful incentive plans, according to Slichter, Healy, and Livernash, included "strong top management support for the industrial engineering department" and "an adequate central and plant engineering staff." Without such a staff, rates would be set through negotiations, and "the bargaining tends to produce wrangling and ill feeling."[40] This attitude would tend to support the views of Taylor.

Barkin would be happy if management had solid engineering behind its plans, but he also encouraged unions to have equally skilled experts. In his own union, as the next chapter describes, he implemented his views by creating an engineering section in his research department. His research department was thus able to prepare several manuals for the union's membership and staff. One manual provided work duty charts that listed the operations of each textile machine so workers could use it to identify the type of worker needed to perform a specific duty in a given mill. A second manual defined time study methods and informed workers of how to deal with them; separate case studies of previous experiences with efficiency methods were also made available by the TWUA Research and Engineering Department. Barkin was very forward-looking among unionists with this approach, because at the time there was opposition among unions to the use of union time study experts, with the result that "The use of union time-study representatives is thus not common."[41] The reasons for this opposition are explored in the next chapter.

In all of his thinking and working with efficiency methods, Barkin was motivated by his recognition that they needed constant adjustment, that there was not a "one best way" to handle a job as Taylor had asserted. In some cases, work standards might become tight, as management changed other features of the work environment. In other cases, they might become loose, especially when workers made additional improvements in methods on their own. In either case, revision of the standards required the knowledge and judgment of both parties in a cooperative effort, with workers' being represented by their union. This same type of cooperation would also be helpful when management wanted to engage on changing technology, the topic of the next section.

Technology and the Worker

In the previous section, consideration was given to the problem of productivity improvements by way of changes in worker applications, as determined by time-and-motion studies. Barkin's contention was that workers are not totally opposed to changes in work methods, if they are protected from the adverse effects of the changes and if they have a voice in the final form those changes take. Barkin also contended that conflicts from efforts to improve productivity through technological innovation can be resolved in the same way. The process for resolving the conflict becomes more complicated, however, for technological innovation brings with it a more direct threat of machines' taking the place of workers. As Barkin describes the impact of this threat on workers, "The opposition to all types of technological change originates with the fear of job loss, the loss of bargaining power, through the elimination of established skills or personal qualities and changes in job methods, as well as the threat of overstrain and reduced self-reliance, and the suspicion that management is really not concerned with the present or future welfare of its workers." This last point is crucial to Barkin's contention, for it indicates to him that workers and unions have little faith in business's willingness to assume any responsibility in dealing with "the grim fate faced by the displaced worker."[42]

Workers want to share in the benefits of productivity changes. When management changes the work effort, workers feel that it is stealing away the easing in the job that has taken place under previous conditions. At a minimum, they want to share in the economic benefits of productivity changes to compensate for the more difficult work effort that the new technology or job will require of them.

Most mainstream economists believe that technological changes always result in a net gain for society, with lower production costs' and the resulting lower prices' helping consumers more than the loss of income hurts workers. This belief may be valid. But it is beside the point as long as workers themselves are not somehow compensated for their losses. Equally important, technological change can impose costs on society when it ends the effective working life of a worker. As Slichter put it, "The important thing is not how much a man produces per *hour* or *day*, but how much he produces in a *lifetime*."[43]

Given these considerations, it is not surprising that unions have always entertained mixed feelings about responding to technological change. In the United States, that response has often been one of grudging acceptance At the turn of the century, one writer in the AFL journal wrote, "I deprecate the action of organized labor . . . of striking against labor-saving machinery."[44] The AFL unions instead pushed for a reduction of the hours in the working day for each worker as a way of aiding displaced workers, a policy that would be called for by all unionists. Despite such claims by unionists, Slichter summarized the union responses to technological change as fitting into the categories of obstruction (in which unions fought the new methods), competition (in which union workers took wage cuts to compete with the cheaper production of the new methods), and control (in which the new methods were accepted but the workers using them became part of the union). Slichter took a dim view of these responses, maintaining, "The history of the attempts of unions to adjust themselves to technological change suggests that they have a strong tendency to do the right thing too late."[45]

Barkin would disagree, claiming that unions' "present tolerance and acceptance of technical change strikingly contrasts with more general opposition in the past." The main form of opposition in the past had been from craft unions. Members of these unions relied on their skills for secure employment and would resist any changes that diluted those skills. The formation of mass production industries and industrial unions within them changed this attitude. This form of union "seeks to protect all workers. Its effectiveness is not dependent upon control over a particular skill . . . [but] . . . from the determined will of the mass of workers." Since control over the form and content of jobs was impossible for it, the industrial union instead ensured that new or changed jobs remained within its bargaining unit. Indeed, Barkin asserted that industrial unions had accepted the inevitability of technical change, had acknowledged in collective bargaining contracts management's rights to make changes, and in many cases had insisted that sluggish managements adopt technical change as a way of improving productivity and pay. In return, labor expected management to provide it with adequate notification and information about the impending change, to negotiate restrictions on management's rights to use technical change to increase worker effort and pace, to agree to share the benefits of the change with workers, and to give assurances that old employees would be employed on new jobs.[46]

Barkin's writings on the area of worker resistance to technical change conform to more recent findings. One such study has suggested that workers will make adjustments to new methods when they see them as being beneficial to themselves. In the case studied, management made changes, both with input from unions and with workers' having no fear of being displaced. The author concluded, "employees are as rational as employers and not merely accept but actively encourage the introduction of technological change when they believe the changes will benefit them. So much for the hobgoblin of 'innate resistance to change.'[47] Moreover, as Cornfield argues, "Organized labor has shifted the emphasis of its measures for preventing technological unemployment . . . toward training and retraining. . . ."[48]

The problem with retraining programs is that they run into the dilemma posed by social costs. Under a free competitive system with no responsibilities imposed on business, management has no incentive to provide retraining for displaced workers. Workers who are displaced and find no new job will eventually end up on welfare. Welfare imposes no direct costs on business, whereas training programs do. By doing nothing, business lowers its costs, but it increases the costs to society of technological change, and the faster the rate of change, the higher the costs.

The pace of technological change heightened in the 1960s with the advent of automation and has continued with the present application of robotics. Barkin referred to the automation era as a "third industrial revolution." The tools of this revolution were the computer, transfer machines, and servomechanisms, he noted, adding, "Automation involves far more than these tools. It means new ways of doing things and of organization within industry. It involves a new approach which is commonly referred to as 'systems engineering.' "[49] Because of this approach, automation carried implications much more pervasive than those connected with the introduction of new machines.

A systems approach requires a rethinking of the overall operation of the firm. Automation brings with it the ability to centralize management to a greater degree than ever before, so it is not surprising that many mergers and corporate reorganizations followed the development of automated systems, spawning new fields of application in management. Equally important, however, automation required a complete redesign of the operating plant; its introduction meant something more than merely changing the machines in an existing plant. New plants need not be built on the sites of older plants, however, so another effect of automation was extensive plant relocation.

As a result of this process of reorganization and relocation, workers confronted a new series of problems. In the textile industry, the number of jobs was reduced, the content of those jobs was greatly altered, and the jobs may well have been moved to another locale. Faced with such widespread changes, workers would surely be expected to oppose them.

Barkin, however, believed that management could take positive steps to minimize this opposition. Those steps would succeed only if management agreed to share the burden of the social costs imposed on workers by the process of technical change. He had earlier noted, "Widespread employment opportunities dimmed the fears of unemployment and eased the problem of adjustment."[50] Workers had less to fear from technical change if they felt secure that the costs of their existence as well as the costs of their adjustment to change would be met. It was up to management to develop programs to foster that security.

The complex process of technical change and plant relocation, however, created two groups of affected workers with differing needs. One group consisted of workers who would be unemployed after the change. There were limits to what individual companies could do for them, and their plight is discussed in a later chapter on government policy. Barkin did assert that business had some responsibility for the social costs of that unemployment, including reasonable severance pay, vesting of pensions, and time off to look for another job or for retraining.

One program for helping displaced workers, which Barkin might applaud, was that undertaken by the meat packer Armour and Co. As summarized by Irving Siegel and Edgar Weinberg, in the early 1960s, Armour and its union used a joint study committee to help 5,000 workers displaced by the closing of six plants. The program included retraining, transfers to new plants, and early retirement benefits, helped by a fund of $500,000 provided by the company. Siegel and Weinberg judge the program to have been a success.[51] It also seems to have been an exception, at least where retraining is concerned. According to *Business Week* columnist John Hoerr, firms in the United States continue to make training for workers a very low priority, and what job training does take place is aimed primarily at managerial and professional workers.[52]

In terms of helping the second group—workers who continued to be employed—Barkin recommended that firms meet their responsibilities by adopting a systems approach of planning out the proposed changes. The approach should be guided by such questions as "Is the job content being altered? Is the job pace being speeded up? Will employee status be changed? Will the organizational relationship of individuals, groups and departments be changed? Will the system of supervision and delegation of management responsibility be altered?"[53] Affirmative answers to these questions would indicate that planning was needed to ensure the cooperation of labor in effecting a smooth transition to the new methods of production. The overall objective of such a plan must be to satisfy the purposes of the organization and its people, including workers.

Problems that arise from changed work application or skills can be solved through negotiations, as they involve workload, speed, or effort. Training can be utilized for the problems that arise from changes that call for different skills or job requirements. Even more effort, in the form of financial assistance, is necessary for change in location. For all such changes, Barkin suggests a variety of techniques, including "outright transfers to other permanent jobs, temporary or other job assignments, relocation to other areas with financial and other aids to facilitate adjustment, job redesign to enable the particular people to maintain employment and personal adjustment through medical, educational and social casework aid."[54] Management can also help by giving old employees preferential treatment in hiring at new plants and assuring them that their income will not suffer adversely through the change.

It is important that all these changes be planned in advance. One question to be asked seriously at the outset was, Would it be desirable to have employee representatives participate in the planning in order to get their views of the problem? Whether or not that course is chosen, planners must be careful to analyze the total impact of the changes on the work force and devise ameliorative methods. Once these decisions have been made, the next step is to prepare a schedule for the timing of the changes, including the demands to be made on manpower. The final, and to Barkin the most important, step in the process is "the discussions and concluding negotiations with the union representatives or employees prior to the announcements." Only when these have been made final can the program be communicated to all employees.[55]

Successful completion of the process requires great effort and responsibility on the part of management, so it is not surprising that they are more prone to sudden announcements or none at all when a plant is to be closed. The dollar costs of such a plan might also be high, but for Barkin that is merely a case of business's meeting its obligations with regard to social costs. There are benefits as well. One goal of personnel policy, as described in the next section, is establishing plant or enterprise consciousness. How can workers be expected to gain a positive attitude toward a plant that can be moved without a minute's prior notice? Why would they be loyal to an enterprise that treats them, or other workers in other places, poorly? A cooperative spirit in making adjustments to change gives workers a sense of security in their job consciousness that carries over into a heightened sense of plant or enterprise consciousness. In the specific terms of applying a cooperative systems approach to technical change, Barkin concludes, it "has the great value of assuring the rational and calculated adjustment of personnel in all changes and ultimately of creating an attitude among employees which is favorable to the process of change itself."[56]

As he had argued about efficiency methods, Barkin believed that workers had no objection to technological change per se. In many instances, they welcome the change when they are convinced that it holds benefits for them. To ensure that workers benefit from technological change, however, they must be sheltered from the social costs that those changes impose on them. To foster an atmosphere in which workers feel confident that new technology does not threaten them, management must implement the technology in a systematic way. It is also important, Barkin would remind managers, to obtain a spirit of cooperation from unions in order to smooth the transition to the new methods of production.

While Barkin was first making his proposals for labor-management cooperation in introducing new technology and methods of work, management had already begun to experiment with alternative methods by which to obtain the cooperation of workers without the intervening medium of unions. These "welfare programs," as they were called, eventually evolved into the approach known as human resource management (a topic considered at length in Chapter Seven), with the aspiration of handling the difficulties of intransigent workers. Barkin remained skeptical about their effectiveness, as the next section describes.

Human Relations Policies

Workers have always faced a set of divided loyalties. At home they are expected to be loyal to their family and, when necessary, to their country. In social and political arenas, they have been construed as being class conscious. At work, when they form unions, it is because of a feeling of job consciousness. At the same time, their employer expects their sense of loyalty to take the form of plant or enterprise consciousness.

The purpose of human relations policy is to strengthen the worker's enterprise consciousness. With the growth of large corporations, the worker's loyalty became uncoupled from any sense of personal attachment to the boss. Efforts were made, through welfare programs, employee representation plans, and social activities, to regain that loyalty for the firm itself. By the late 1920s, researchers at the Hawthorne plant of Western Electric Co. discovered that they might have some success by working directly on the problem of changing workers' attitudes to work by producing a spirit of teamwork. By the 1940s and 1950s, management's thinking culminated in a human relations approach that stressed the importance of administering labor problems and that set forth people-oriented personnel practices. In all of these efforts, Barkin argues, the underlying philosophy remained the same:

> The personnel program pursues these ends [efficiency and higher profits] by seeking to induce the worker to accept or adapt himself fully to management's code of values and management's goals. . . . Ideally (under such a program) the worker is expected to accept the logic of efficiency and management's

right to apply it, unilaterally and without review or approval by the workers. Such autocracy is most efficient since it is certain and undeviating and is in the best interests of the enterprise.[57]

Since it is believed that workers will not develop this enterprise consciousness on their own, policies must be designed to foster it.

Barkin finds five distinct practices for fostering enterprise consciousness. First, personnel administrators have devised procedures for screening workers in an effort to secure the most efficient and desirable help. Physical exams and aptitude tests are especially useful in this process. Second, they use counseling services to alleviate individual problems and to root out sources of dissatisfaction. Third, efforts are made to establish lines of communication with employees in order to show workers that they have interests in common with management; in-house magazines are a good example of this. Fourth, attempts are made to establish new groups among workers, such as sports teams, so that identification with the team will carry over into the enterprise.[58] Fifth, many benefits provided for workers, especially vesting of pension rights, are based on length of service, in part as a way of ensuring loyalty to the firm.[59]

Despite the pervasiveness of these policies, they have not been an overall success in Barkin's opinion. This opinion could be challenged on the basis of more recent experiences, including efforts that mimic the methods of Japanese companies in gaining employee loyalty. Companies in the United States have made bolder attempts to initiate workers into the corporate culture through the use of better personnel methods and the application of new systems of human resource management, as described in Chapter Seven. Many new firms in the sector of advanced technology have been ingenious at finding ways to make workers feel a part of the corporate family. Whether that family feeling will survive the strains induced by a recession and layoffs is doubtful, however.

The problem with these new approaches, as Barkin saw it, is that workers have their own loyalties. Within the work environment, that loyalty is directed toward the worker's peers in the job group. Here, through informal discussion, workers find an outlet for dissatisfaction. Ultimately, when workers' dissatisfactions become deeply felt, the informal job groups may evolve into formal unions. As a result, workers' aspirations for themselves become formalized. Even though management may try to formalize these groups through quality-of-work-life programs, their success will still be limited. In either case, as Barkin put it, "A new set of objectives, quite different from management's code, must be taken into account in operating the business enterprise."[60]

Barkin finds these objectives falling into three broad categories. First, workers want to have the smallest possible human cost imposed on them by their work— they do not want to be exploited. Second, they want the maximum human advancement in terms of the economic gains of higher wages, security from the burdens of unemployment, and full industrial citizenship, including grievance procedures and arbitration. Third, workers want their unions to be strong enough to provide the first two objectives.[61] As is obvious, these objectives do not coincide with those of management.

In order to respond effectively to workers' needs, Barkin observed, "Personnel policy must recognize the existence of two independent value systems. One is management's and ownership's tests of performance and the other consists of the objectives of workers and the trade union."[62] In general terms, the clash of values can be seen as that between management's hope for achieving a high degree of control over workers and workers' aspirations for attaining an industrial democracy. Personnel administrators have two broad choices in dealing with this situation: they can try to avoid dealing with unions in the hope that they will eventually go away or they can incorporate unions into their personnel systems.

Barkin wants them to accept the second option not merely because he is sympathetic toward unions but also because he feels that management itself has much to gain by working with unions. Because unions are formed from workers' feelings of frustration and dissatisfaction, they are outlets for the release and redress of those feelings. As he wrote, "The union's primary objective is to dispel the dissatisfaction of workers. Grievance machinery offers a formal and secure method of presenting complaints which, if necessary, will be reformulated for greater effectiveness by more articulate union members." Perhaps the worst form of tension in any plant comes from festering complaints. A sound personnel policy should be designed to uncover such complaints and address them. Workers are not likely to voluntarily reveal their complaints to the representatives of their bosses; they fear the risk of their being penalized for expressing themselves and wish to avoid the possibility of suffering from individualized criticism. Instead, they gripe to peers. If peers are part of a formal union and they feel that something constructive will come from their complaints, then they might speak out, especially if someone more articulate then speaks up for them. Unions can render a service by achieving some of the objectives sought by personnel policies.[63]

Acceptance of this service includes some obligations on the part of personnel administrators. They must revise their own goals to make them compatible with workers' objectives. First of all, they must take a more positive attitude toward unions so that workers will be convinced that personnel policies will be truly constructive. Second, the intent of employee-screening devices must be changed. There are no objective criteria for the human qualities that make for desirable employees, so the effort in personnel policy should be aimed at placement and job-assessing techniques that fit the applicants for work.

Efforts should be made to channel all communications, except for specific work instructions, through the union. Workers recognize that other forms of communication are an attempt to indoctrinate them to enterprise consciousness. What they want is information about matters that affect their life, such as changes in working conditions. They do not care to have this information handed to them as a decree from on high. If it is offered to the union for transmission, then "the communication can be evaluated and acted upon with the proper degree of worker participation and review. The response is then likely to be frank and well-considered. The workers' suspicions, antagonisms and anxieties will be reflected in the answers, so that they can be dealt with before the changes are made."[64] Here again, management can gain information about employee dissatisfaction and head it off, but with the help of unions.

This sort of information can be most beneficial to management. As Barkin wrote, "Management sorely needs data and analysis which will give it a better understanding of the 'labor problem.' Adequate personnel administration can be built only on a broad understanding of the worker."[65] Management cannot get data and analysis from its personnel experts. Their approach is too wedded to management's objectives to find out what workers' real interests are.[66] Personnel policies that ignore the positive contribution that can be made by unions will continue to be unsuccessful, would be Barkin's conclusion.

There is one final area of reform in personnel policy that Barkin recommends, and while it may appear minor, it is of great importance. He urges, "Benefit programs should be oriented toward improving workers' well-being and not used as techniques for the indoctrination of enterprise-consciousness."[67] For Barkin, benefits represent the payment of a full-cost social wage and should be recognized as such. It is odd that provision of protection for workers against the social costs of work by insurance against sickness and unemployment and provision for retirement are euphemistically referred to as "fringe benefits," as if a decent standard of living and health were somewhere on the fringe of human concern. It should not be forgotten that management usually lists expenditures for "fringes" on a paycheck, to ensure that workers realize the value of the employer's total contribution to their well-being and implicitly recognize its importance.

Management is correct in recognizing the importance of benefits to workers. Surveys of workers have shown that they consistently rank benefits as having a high priority, with many workers willing to sacrifice pay raises for higher benefits. In particular, they were most interested in retirement plans, paid vacations, and medical insurance. Surprisingly, profit sharing and stock option plans were not viewed as being important by workers.[68] These results are in keeping with the point made in Chapter Two: that workers value a pay system that covers their social costs of work.

To Barkin, realization by workers that they are being paid a full-cost social wage, especially if they recognize that their own efforts through their union helped gain it, will help keep them more loyal to their company. In addition, the union can provide better employee relations by giving workers a voice to express their grievances against the company. By highlighting this feature in his writings, Barkin anticipated the later work by Albert Hirschman dealing with the choice of voice versus exit. In keeping with the theme of this chapter, Barkin would note

that labor's voice can be especially effective when it is raised to ensure cooperation with management in terms of using personnel policies that include union
input.

Barkin's opinion on the limitations of management to use human relations
methods to gain workers' loyalty may have been overstated. For one thing,
management took this issue seriously. As Richard Lester reports, by the late
1950s, a survey of 714 companies revealed that they employed one human
relations expert for every 175 workers, whereas there existed one union official
for each 300 union members. This period also saw increasing centralization of
the function of industrial relations in corporations.[69] Unions were being out-
manned and outorganized in the area of human relations, as business put increasing resources into this function.

Although the costs of this effort might be high, management might decide that
it was more effective than cooperation with unions. Barkin felt that such expenditures were misplaced and easily avoided by cooperation with unions. The
outlays could be better used to pay higher wages because management should
recognize that the payment of a full-cost social wage confers benefits on the
corporation. Achievement of this recognition might be fostered if the expenditures were balanced with an asset gain in order to remind management that they
are not a total waste of money. Placing social benefits on the corporate balance
sheets, however, would require significant modification in the tools of accounting, a problem Barkin also investigated.

Accounting Methods for Collective Bargaining

Accounting exists as a profession whose members are charged with the express
purpose of supplying accurate and timely information for making economic
decisions. The type of information furnished by accountants depends on the use
to which it will be put, which in turn depends on the needs of the users. Accountants recognize this and agree that the most important users of their information
are management, investors, creditors, financial analysts, and the public. It is the
last category—the public—which constitutes the concern of this section, for it
includes a broad spectrum of groups, from economists to environmentalists. It
also includes labor unions. Since the public is so diverse, the information provided by accountants is geared to the groups they see as primary consumers. The
groups constituting the public are not so well served unless pressures become so
great that changes in reporting become imperative.

While part of the blame for the inadequate information available to nonbusiness groups may fall on the accounting profession, it more directly falls on
management itself, which has the capacity to put the strongest pressure on the
accounting profession. The accounting information available to unions, for example, is not very useful. One might expect, Barkin has pondered, that since a
firm's financial condition is a material factor to be considered by both parties in

management's negotiations with unions on wage issues, corporate financial reports would be an important part of the bargaining process. He wrote, "It might have been presumed that management would anxiously parade the financial facts in considerable detail before union representatives to help them realistically appraise the situation. Certainly such a procedure would have coincided with the declared objective of mature bargaining; namely, discussion on the basis of agreed-upon facts."[70] Instead, management has not been forthcoming with financial details, and when it has provided this material, it has rarely been more than was contained in its public accounting statements.

Those public accounting statements have been presented in forms promulgated as part of generally accepted accounting principles, as approved by professional accounting groups with some assistance by government regulators. As such, they may help those groups that the profession sees as its primary users to make informed economic decisions, but they are not of much help to unions.

The bottom line of accounting statements consists of the firm's profit. As a method of analyzing a firm, profits can tell about a firm's ability to meet its obligations; they also tell how well a firm's management has performed in its function of improving the firm's condition. Quite often these two measures can conflict, especially because there are a variety of acceptable ways to calculate the bottom line. For example, during the 1970s, when inflation was a serious problem, accountants were concerned with how to reflect the effects of inflation in a firm's accounting statements. If a firm gained because the value of its inventory increased due to inflation, it was held that such phantom profits overstated the firm's well-being and should be excluded from evaluations of management's performance. Yet, any organization's ability to cope with inflation depends to a large degree on whether it has kept pace with it. Failure to keep up with inflation may impinge on a firm's ability to meet its obligations. A management that profited from inflation was really doing its job well.

Barkin was keenly aware of the vagaries involved in the determination of accounting income, so he proposed two changes in accounting procedures to make the concept of income more useful to unions in their efforts to decide on a firm's ability to pay for wage increases.

Barkin's first concern was with the problem of the determination of income available for distribution. In general, items associated with the cost of production are considered to be reductions in income; payments made for ownership claims are considered distributions of income. In the days of individual proprietorship, there was no problem in making this distinction. Profits as a distribution of income were the reward for the owner's efforts and the use of the owner's capital, both of which are considered a part of the entrepreneurial function.

The growth of large, publicly held corporations separated the functions of ownership and entrepreneurial control. Accounting methods did not keep pace with this change. Dividends paid to the stockholders, as nominal owners of the firm, are considered distributions of income. Payments to top executives, members of the board of directors, and other management groups are considered costs of production on the basis that these persons are merely employees, even though they now perform the entrepreneurial function. In much the same way, payments to creditors of interest for capital loaned also represent a cost of production on the grounds that they, too, are not owners, even though the supply of capital is still part of the function of the entrepreneur.

Instead of this confusing (to unions at least) definition of income, Barkin would like to see all forms of entrepreneurial income considered part of the total profits available for distribution. Since the wage demands of unions are to some extent a request for redistribution of income, he feels that unions should be given a true picture of how much income is available.[71] His procedure would be roughly similar to that used in looking at the income side of the national income accounts. In essence, what Barkin is after is a method of determining whether a "surplus" or pool of above-normal profit is available for improving the lot of workers. This method also would be useful in gauging whether a firm had the resources to absorb all of the social costs attributable to its activities.

A second problem of concern to Barkin was in the accounting methods used for determining actual costs of production. At first glance, these methods would appear to be simple, something on the order of what Veblen termed the exact science of making change. The principles of accounting require a timely matching of costs and revenues. Once costs and revenues must be matched over a number of time periods, however, a valuation problem arises, because the value of assets can change over time. A building purchased many years ago, for a variety of reasons, could show an increase in its value. Inventory held for any length of time can undergo a similar change in value.

Accountants have devised a series of valuation techniques, such as accelerated depreciation and last-in, first-out ("LIFO") and first-in, first-out ("FIFO") inventories to reflect the changed value of these assets. Their intent is to substitute some notion of market value or replacement cost for the historical cost for which the item was purchased. Many of these techniques are employed, when permitted, to reduce the firm's tax burden. They are also in keeping with the general conservatism of accounting, which finds it prudent to understate the firm's ability to pay (often in the face of management's desires to overstate its record of performance).

In any event, it is widely suspected that corporations keep at least two sets of books—one for the Internal Revenue Service (IRS) and one for stockholders— each with differing determinations of profit. A trade union negotiator may well fear being given a doctored set of books when it comes time to open wage negotiations. As Barkin described this fear, "Any procedure which permits the accountant to modify or alter an entry, to adjust it to an outside cost or income figure will be looked upon suspiciously. It opens the accounts to manipulation and possible loss of integrity." Thus, Barkin argues, unions are interested in accounts that are based on historical costs.[72] These give the union negotiator a true picture of the firm's ability to pay any wage demands.

For example, during periods of widespread inflation, gains made in inventory value will be reflected in profits, unless some adjustment is made. LIFO takes care of this problem to some extent by valuing items sold at their latest (and highest) cost. The approach tends to understate profits, which might be necessary in terms of paying income taxes. It will not be helpful in terms of determining whether a firm can pay its workers cost-of-living increases without corresponding increases in prices. Phantom profits are not so illusory that they cannot be banked as a hedge against further inflation. They could be used to obviate the need for further price hikes to pay for cost-of-living adjustments.

The point here for Barkin is that if unions are to be expected to behave responsibly in their negotiations with business, they must be provided with accurate and timely information as to the ability of the business to meet union demands. If such information is not made available to them, the best they can do is ask for as big a wage increase as they think they can get. To help unions behave more responsibly, management and its accountants need to provide unions with answers to five primary questions:

1. What were the business profits before and after taxes?
2. What financial benefits did the entrepreneurial interests and the employees gain?
3. How does the company's financial experience compare with that of other enterprises?
4. What is the likely future business course in terms of volume of sales, prices and costs?
5. What are the present and likely future break-even points for the business?[73]

Not only unions would be interested in this information. Even financial analysts have a concern for finding out business's plans for the future, no matter how tentative. For unions this information is essential, if they are to make informed, prudent claims on their proper share of the firm's resources.

To give one example from Barkin's experiences on the importance of accounting procedures, in 1938, he conducted an arbitration case against the Bigelow-Sanford Carpet Company in which he questioned the company's accounting statement on losses. The company had revalued its inventory of wool and finished carpets to adjust the carpets for lower prices. Barkin claimed that this procedure was inappropriate because it had been done at mid-year and because his research projected an increase in prices, which did indeed take place during the next year. This argument may have been partly responsible for the arbitrator's decision to change the company's proposed wage reduction from 10 percent to 5 percent.

There is one other area in which Barkin finds that accountants need to broaden their function, and that is the provision of information for the economist concerned with the social costs of enterprise. Not only economists need to be served by an accounting of social costs; even business might be served. As things stand now, payments made to absorb social costs are included as a cost of doing business. Since they do not bring in a recognized revenue, there are no offsetting gains. To business they may appear to be a dead loss. Corporations do receive a benefit for these expenditures, even if it only trickles in as their part of a greater social good.

Where workers are concerned, these expenditures may produce direct benefits in the form of lower absenteeism from illness due to better health care or in the form of improved productivity from higher employee morale. More effort is needed to find ways to put these benefits on the books, and while some advancement has been made in the past decade, the actual accomplishment has been meager. Barkin's long-ago appraisal of the situation still holds true. He observed, "A single system of business and social accounting, which would govern business administrators, is not yet in the offing. Such a system is the best hope of linking the logics of business and of trade unions."[74]

In all of his work, Barkin has sought to find ways to give business and labor a common interest. In the area of accounting, it would appear that both groups have an interest in timely information, not only about a firm's costs, prices, and profits but also about its social costs. Barkin's interest in accounting methods is unique among labor economists, who never saw how accounting practices could influence the type and quality of information available in labor markets.

During the 1970s, forward-looking accountants tried to develop a system of social cost accounting but failed to convince business of its value. That is unfortunate, for the next two decades will see a greater need for information about social costs as an aging population forces society to come to grips with the ultimate social costs, namely, those associated with older and retired workers.

Problems of Older Workers

Another area in which Barkin wanted business to take on more responsibility was in dealing with older workers. As described in Chapter One, Barkin's first professional job was to conduct research into a system of old age assistance, which was quickly followed by a study of the problems of older workers. Barkin found that at that time older workers were among the most needy persons in society, unable "to save enough from their wages to protect them against the ordinary hazards of a lifetime."[75] He further found that older persons suffered from employment handicaps wherein "industry had deliberately undertaken to make the chronologically middle aged person also economically aged and to set them on the 'scrap heap at forty.' " The basis for this handicap imposed on older workers was simple age prejudice. First there was outright age discrimination wherein it was believed that all older persons could not handle work; no efforts were made to treat individual cases. Second, older persons eventually suffer a decline in their powers, so hiring them may impose additional costs on employers.[76] For Barkin, business's failure to meet these additional costs simply shifts them elsewhere, so a proper allocation of costs requires business to take responsibility for a full-cost social wage for workers.

For example, a plan could be proposed that required businesses to set aside a retirement fund or pay laid-off older workers a pension that guaranteed a living income. In that way, the full social costs of older workers would be imposed upon companies. In that context, the additional costs involved in retaining older workers might seem small.

Instead, Barkin recognized that pension programs result in compulsory retirement ages as part of "the drive to avoid employing older, less effective persons." Barkin believed that management must have the responsibility of "employing all persons who are willing to work." From this perspective, pensions should be designed "to facilitate the retirement of those desirous of it, who have found employment burdensome." Workers might not want to retire because they enjoy the work, the personal associations they have on the job, and the feeling of satisfaction in making a contribution to community life.[77]

There are several steps business can take to meet the responsibility toward older workers. Selective placement of workers on jobs would be beneficial. Barkin notes that during periods of low unemployment, more older persons are hired. To allow for their place in industry, younger persons are shifted to jobs for which they are fitted, and jobs are reserved for older persons for which they are adapted. In addition, jobs can be redesigned so as to fit them more readily to the abilities of older persons.

As the number of older persons in society grows, the problem of matching them with productive jobs presents even greater challenges for business. As Barkin argued, the way for business to meet these challenges is "to lift the art of adjustment of jobs to older persons and these persons to the job from a state of haphazard investigation to that of systematic, well investigated and proven principles and corroborated experiences." This would appear to be a task for which business is well suited. After all, we have seen how much effort is put into measurement of worker application and effort and the pervasiveness of personnel policies in judging the capabilities of workers. Barkin finds that "industrial engineers who have devoted themselves for a half century to the study of jobs and their design cannot provide us with adequate tools for job analysis to determine the mental and physical demands."[78]

These experts are not so equipped, because all their work has been biased toward management's interest in attaining the utmost efficiency from workers. They never gave consideration to the workers' need to have parts of the job adjusted to them. As a result, Barkin looked for help for the older worker in terms of job adjustment's coming from those experts "in the field of the placement of the handicapped [who] have developed techniques of job analysis which are more suitable" for application to the problems of older persons.[79] These experts have made progress in this area because they have avoided a bias toward management. Instead, they have considered the needs of their clients first, as they must, and then expected management to adjust to their clients' needs. In these days, many of our institutions are being asked to make adjustments in building design and job requirements in order to enable physically handicapped persons to lead a normal life. In Barkin's view, a far better approach would be to require institutions, especially business, to take on the responsibility for making adjustments so that all persons can lead a normal life.

There has been progress in following this approach. Starting in the 1950s, the discipline of ergonomics was established, and its practitioners all over the world have figured ways to redesign jobs for older workers and others. In his years at the OECD, Barkin sponsored several studies on this topic. Recently, more attention has been paid to ergonomics and job redesign, especially where the use of personal computers is concerned. Regulations governing the use and placement of personal computers in a sound ergonomic fashion are coming to be popular. What remains is to extend the benefits of this trend to all workers in all industries, but especially to older workers.

As the population ages during the next thirty years, it is quite possible that a lack of younger workers will make it incumbent on business to hire older workers. To some extent this has happened, as fast-food chains adjust to demographics by substituting older workers for teenagers, whose numbers are declining. In this area, Barkin would urge business to be systematic about its policies toward older workers. Businesses have not been reluctant to redesign jobs to control the work effort of workers, and those same techniques can be utilized to redesign jobs so as to make the work effort suitable to the capabilities of older workers. The social costs related to older workers can be provided for by business in a responsible way.

The theme of this chapter should serve as a reminder that business does not act responsibly without pressure from other agents. Barkin took a dim view of plans that offered business a financial incentive to hire older workers, including one set forth by Sumner Slichter.[80] Instead, Barkin would have older workers protected by unions, as had been done through seniority rules and by fighting against compulsory retirement. He would utilize programs of labor and management cooperation to solve the problems of older workers.

Conclusion

If Barkin were to reduce his code of the responsibilities of management to their simplest terms, he would tell managers: Run your plant so efficiently that you will be able to pay your workers a full-cost social wage and use collective bargaining as a means for cooperating with your workers in achieving this end. That statement, as we have seen in this chapter, brings out a number of issues relating to management practices. Those issues have not been resolved, for the concept of the full-cost social wage has not been given widespread recognition, much less acceptance, and the notion of labor and management cooperation certainly goes against the grain of habit in the United States.

The idea that labor and management should cooperate to achieve greater worker participation in managerial decisions is an old one, dating back at least to Robert Owen. That unions exist at all indicates that this type of participation has not been accepted by management. Workers need a union to give them a voice in management circles. Moreover, they need a strong union to make that voice effective, because, as Slichter, Healy, and Livernash have pointed out, "Some managements are opposed to seeking help from the union on the ground that such action would build up the prestige of the union."[81] Strong unions will already have prestige, which should remove this managerial opposition to cooperative plans.

There are other grounds for managerial opposition to cooperation. George Shultz once stated, "The idea of worker participation on production problems is . . . one that challenges a traditional management philosophy. Thus, the *fundamental premise* of the participation idea . . . might be stated this way: The average worker is *able* to make and, given the right kind of circumstances, *wants* to make important contributions to the solution of production problems."[82] Shultz was referring to the broad participation sought by the Scanlon Plan. Scanlon Plans were not used very much in industry and never succeeded in causing management to change its philosophy toward cooperating with workers.

Today, management attempts to gain worker cooperation through quality-of-life circles, job enrichment programs, or ESOPs. But as Siegel and Weinberg point out, "Not only are collaborative arrangements slow in developing but they also have a disappointing survival rate."[83] Perhaps this is because business tries to use cooperative policies as part of an overall strategy to avoid dealing with unions wherever possible. As Cornfield summarizes the results of fourteen industry case studies, "Empirically, collective bargaining appears to be a prerequisite for formal cooperation, rather than a mutually exclusive alternative."[84]

Barkin's position as to why efforts to promote management-union cooperation programs have so consistently failed during the past two decades is set forth in Chapter Seven. In terms of a program of cooperation that excludes unions, however, his conclusion can be stated succinctly: Whatever management thinks it will gain through programs of human resource management, quality-of-work-life plans, or labor-management participation teams, a policy of cooperation with unions remains the best option for creating an environment that would lead to a constructive resolution of labor-management conflict. Only then can workers be said to have a true and independent voice in terms of how much cooperation they want to give.

Notes

1. "The Protector of Pensions Develops Its Biceps," Business Week, March 11, 1991, p. 80.

2. Solomon Barkin, "The Challenge of Annual Wages," *Personnel Journal* 24 (April 1946), p. 271.

3. "There's Nothing Universal About Plans for Universal Health Care," *Business Week*, January 22, 1990, p. 39.

4. See Irving H. Siegel and Edgar Weinberg, *Labor-Management Cooperation: The American Experience* (Kalamazoo, MI: W. E. Upjohn Institute for Employment Research, 1982), for a history and survey of recent cooperation plans. For detailed studies of early plans, see Sumner Slichter, *Union Policies and Industrial Management*, Chs. XIV-XIX, and Slichter, Healy, and Livernash, *The Impact of Collective Bargaining on Management*, Chs. 28–29.

5. David B. Cornfield, ed., *Workers, Managers and Technological Change* (New York: Plenum Press, 1987), p. xii.

6. Ibid.

7. Howell John Harris, *The Right to Manage* (Madison, WI: University of Wisconsin Press, 1982), p. 6.

8. Ibid., pp. 23–39.

9. Ibid., pp. 42–56.

10. Joseph G. Rayback, *A History of American Labor* (New York: Free Press, 1966), pp. 389–90.

11. Kim Moody, *An Injury to All* (London: Verso, 1988), p. 33, makes this claim.

12. Neil W. Chamberlain, *The Union Challenge to Management Control* (New York: Archon Books, 1967, reprint of 1948 ed.), p. 97.

13. Robert H. Zeiger, *American Workers, American Unions, 1920–1985* (Baltimore: Johns Hopkins University Press, 1986), p. 105.

14. A. H. Raskin, "Labor: A Movement in Search of a Mission," in Seymour Martin Lipsett, ed., *Unions in Transition* (San Francisco: ICS Press, 1986), p. 5.

15. David Brody, *Workers in Industrial America* (New York: Oxford University Press, 1980), p. 176.

16. Zeiger, *American Workers*, p. 105.

17. Chamberlain, *Union Challenge*, p. 17.

18. Harris, *Right to Manage*, p. 140.

19. Nelson Lichtenstein, "Walter Reuther and the Rise of Labor-Liberalism," in Dubofsky and Van Tine, eds., *Labor Leaders in America* (Urbana and Chicago, IL: University of Illinois Press, 1987), p. 287.

20. Harris, *Right to Manage*, p. 141.

21. Chamberlain, *Union Challenge*, p. 93. The discussion presented here owes much to Chamberlain.

22. Ibid., p. 267.

23. Ibid., p. 257.

24. Solomon Barkin, "Labor's Attitude Toward Wage Incentive Plans," *Industrial and Labor Relations Review* 1 (July 1948), p. 554.

25. Solomon Barkin, "The Trade Union Approach to Wage Incentive Plans," *Time and Motion Study* 2 (June 1953), pp. 25–28.

26. Ibid., p. 29.

27. Barkin, "Labor's Attitude," pp. 554–60.

28. Ibid.

29. Sumner H. Slichter, James J. Healy, and E. Robert Livernash, *The Impact of Collective Bargaining on Management* (Washington, DC: The Brookings Institution, 1960), p. 512.

30. Solomon Barkin, "Labor Views the Working Day," *Advanced Management* VII (January-March 1942), p. 34.

31. Ibid., pp. 35–36.

32. Solomon Barkin, "Concepts in the Measurement of Human Application," *Industrial and Labor Relations Review* 7 (October 1953), pp. 108–9.

33. Solomon Barkin, "Diversity of Time Study Practices," *Industrial and Labor Relations Review* 7 (July 1954), pp. 539–46.

34. Ibid., p. 547.

35. Barkin, "Labor Views the Working Day," p. 36.

36. Solomon Barkin, "A Trade Unionist's Approach to Production Standards," *Trade Union Information Bulletin* (European Productivity Agency) (January-February 1956), pp. 1–4.

37. Solomon Barkin, "The Bench-Mark Approach to Production Standards," *Industrial and Labor Relations Review* 10 (January 1957), p. 224.

38. Ibid., pp. 223–25.

39. Richard Baker, *Clockwork: Life Inside and Outside an American Factory* (Garden City, NY: Doubleday, 1976), p. 328.

40. Slichter, Healy, and Livernash, *Impact of Collective Bargaining*, pp. 520, 811.

41. Ibid., p. 547.

42. Solomon Barkin, "Technology and Labor," *Personnel Journal* 18 (January 1940), pp. 239–40.

43. Slichter, *Union Policies and Industrial Management* (New York: Greenwood Press, 1968), p. 161.

44. George Schilling, "Less Hours, Increased Production—Greater Progress," *American Federationist* (October 1900), p. 310.

45. Slichter, *Union Policies*, pp. 201–3.

46. Solomon Barkin, "Trade-Union Attitudes and Their Effect upon Productivity," in *Industrial Productivity* (Industrial Relations Research Association, 1951), pp. 110–21.

47. Robert Zaeger, "The Problem of Job Obsolescence: Working It Out at River Works," in *Labor-Management Cooperation: Recent Efforts and Results* (Washington, DC: Bureau of Labor Statistics, 1982), pp. 84–88.

48. Cornfield, *Workers, Managers and Technological Change*, p. 19.

49. Solomon Barkin, "More Implications of Automation," *IUD Digest* 4 (Fall 1959), p. 2.

50. Barkin, "Trade-Union Attitudes," p. 110.

51. Siegel and Weinberg, *Labor-Management Cooperation*, pp. 109–110.

52. John Hoerr, "Business Shares the Blame for Workers' Low Skills," *Business Week*, June 25, 1990, p. 71; John Hoerr, "With Job Training, a Little Dab Won't Do Ya," *Business Week*, September 24, 1990, p. 95.

53. Solomon Barkin, "A Systems Approach to Adjustments of Technical Change," *Labor Law Journal* 18 (January 1967), p. 31.

54. Ibid., pp. 33–35.

55. Ibid., pp. 36–37.

56. Ibid., p. 38.

57. Solomon Barkin, "A Trade Unionist Appraises Management's Personnel Philosophy," *Harvard Business Review* 28 (September 1950), p. 59.

58. Ibid., p. 60.

59. Solomon Barkin, "Management Personnel Philosophy and Activities in a Collective Bargaining Era," *Proceedings, Industrial Relations Research Association* (December 1953), p. 7.

60. Barkin, "A Trade Unionist Appraises," pp. 60–61.

61. Ibid.

62. Barkin, "Management Personnel Philosophy," p. 11.

63. Barkin, "A Trade Unionist Appraises," p. 63.

64. Barkin, "Management Personnel Philosophy," pp. 4–6.

65. Solomon Barkin, Review of Paul Pigors and Charles A. Myers, "Personnel Administration," *American Economic Review* 39 (March 1949), p. 577.

66. Solomon Barkin, "A Pattern for the Study of Industrial Human Relations," *Industrial and Labor Relations Review* 9 (October 1955), p. 99.

67. Barkin, "Management Personnel Philosophy," pp. 11–12.

68. Gordon L. Staines and Robert P. Quinn, "American Workers Evaluate the Quality of Their Jobs," in U.S. Bureau of Labor Statistics, *Labor-Management Cooperation*, pp. 6–7.

69. Richard A. Lester, *As Unions Mature* (Princeton, NJ: Princeton University Press, 1958), pp. 116–17.

70. Solomon Barkin, "Financial Statements in Collective Bargaining," *New York Certified Public Accountant* (July 1953), p. 439.

71. Solomon Barkin, "A Trade Unionist Views Net Income Distribution," *NACA Bulletin* 32 (June 1951), pp. 1196–1200.

72. Barkin, "Financial Statements," p. 442, and "A Trade Unionist Views," pp. 1202–5.

73. Barkin, "Financial Statements," p. 441.

74. Barkin, "A Trade Unionist Appraises," p. 64.

75. Solomon Barkin, "Some Disclosures of the Report of the New York State Commission on Old Age Security," *Old Age Security Herald* (November 1930), p. 4. A complete statement of Barkin's analysis of the conditions of older workers can be found in Solomon Barkin, *The Older Workers in Industry* (Albany, NY: J. B. Lyons, 1933), 467 pp.

76. Solomon Barkin, "Economic Difficulties of the Older Person," *Personnel Journal* 11 (April 1933), pp. 393–98.

77. Solomon Barkin, "Should There Be a Fixed Retirement Age? Organized Labor Says No," *Annals of the American Academy of Political and Social Sciences* (July 1952), pp. 77–80.

78. Solomon Barkin, "Some Problems of the Older Worker," *Proceedings, Industrial Relations Research Association* (June 1953), p. 3.

79. Ibid.

80. Ibid., p. 2.

81. Slichter, Healy, and Livernash, *Impact of Collective Bargaining*, p. 23.

82. George P. Shultz, "Worker Participation on Productivity Problems," in Frederick G. Leiseur, ed., *The Scanlon Plan: A Frontier in Labor-Management Cooperation* (Cambridge, MA: Massachusetts Institute of Technology Press, 1958), p. 51, emphasis in the original.

83. Siegel and Weinberg, *Labor-Management Cooperation*, p. 100.

84. Cornfield, *Workers, Managers and Technological Change*, p. 337.

5

How Unions Serve
Their Members

The trade-union movement gains its buoyancy from its total function,
which is to act as a social critic on behalf of the employee and the
economically and socially disadvantaged, as an economic leveler, as a
stimulant to management, and as a focal point for social idealism.
—Solomon Barkin

To many members of the public, the word "union" conjures up vivid images of strikes, corrupt leaders and bureaucrats, and conflict-ridden contract negotiations, because that is how unions are most often presented by the mass media. No one seems to wonder what union leaders and their staffs do during those long periods between contract negotiations and the occasional strike. Hidden from public view are the many daily activities that unions engage in on behalf of their members. Trade unions are an organized outlet through which workers may express their wants and seek ways for satisfying them, but they are also service organizations, providing many benefits for their members. This chapter concerns how unions can be used as a vehicle whereby workers may make their wants known to management, government, and society at large and may devise ways for realizing them. It also describes some of the important direct services a union can provide for its members, focusing on what a union research department, such as the one Barkin headed with the TWUA, can do to help them.

As a means for representing workers and serving their wants, unions are and have been problematic. Unions claim to speak for all workers, but in actuality they represent only a small portion of them, a portion that has been declining for the past three decades, as Chapter Seven details. Moreover, in its perception of unions, the public does not currently hold them in high esteem; union efforts to speak for workers are often viewed as being the pleading of a special interest group.

Despite public reservations about unions, it is clear that unions render beneficial services for their members, other workers, and the community, and the public recognizes the need for their continuation. They establish educational programs; maintain publications staffs; keep legal experts available for advice; have even run banks, apartment buildings, and health clinics for members; and have maintained welfare funds. These services are furnished by both the national organization of a union and the local personnel, including nonpaid volunteers from the membership. At the local level, for example, the union hall with its auditorium can supply a meeting place for a variety of member activities and even be available for general community functions. According to Barkin, one TWUA union hall in Georgia doubled as a church for a congregation of union members. The national headquarters of a union can support a legal staff that is available to deal with problems of unfair firings and breaches of contract. Research experts can render aid in dealing with the complex problems of arbitration cases that arise at the local level; Barkin felt that his research team rendered service in the areas of economics, engineering, contract analysis, and welfare fund administration. Unions sustain their members in a variety of ways much too elaborate to be detailed in this chapter.

Setting Goals

In their efforts to express ably the wants of workers, unions have had to formulate a variety of goals in order to take into account the wants of different workers and groups of workers. The fundamental goal for unions was long ago succinctly stated in one word: "more." As time has passed, that "more" has been translated into a variety of objectives, as Barkin's experiences would attest. During the early 1940s, Barkin observed, "Trade union wage goals are determined by labor's concepts of what its share of industry's income should be and the standard of living to which workers are entitled. But these do not envisage a radical redistribution of wealth. The emphasis is on better economic returns for workers." While these goals might reflect workers' ideas as to what they wanted, few workers would be able to articulate them into specific objectives. Trade unions help to define and articulate those objectives. To give this definition, Barkin wrote of labor's goals at length. To him, labor's goals initially included "An adequate standard of living for decency and comfort (and) participation in the special economic advantages enjoyed by the industries in which they are employed." As initial goals were met, it would become important to achieve "industrial democracy in all relations between an employer and his employees. Unions consider the realization of this last goal as their first objective. The worker wants the trade union to make him free. He wants the right to complain about unsatisfactory working conditions and to have them corrected. He demands joint deliberation with employers on all matters affecting his work and wages.[1] This statement of what workers want correlates more closely to what workers say they want than does management's perception.[2]

As unions progressed in strength and responsibility during the decades of the forties and fifties, Barkin expanded his vision of their goals to include a broader outlook. Writing in the early 1960s, he added to wage and industrial relations goals another objective: "To get the enterprise to follow economic, financial, production and political policies which would tend to bring about the type of society in which employees would like to live." The standards for that society would include

> Annual wage increases together with cost-of-living adjustments; unemployment, sickness, disability, old age and death benefits; maintenance of annual employment or at least income; adequate rest and leisure through vacations, sabbaticals and shorter hours; a fair employment policy, which means jobs to all groups in the community including the handicapped; rules for transfer, promotion and lay-offs which protect long service and eliminate discrimination; and, finally, a grievance system.[3]

These are very high goals, and a section at the end of this chapter surveys what unions have done in accomplishing them. In Barkin's view, however, the means through which unions endeavored to formulate and meet the aspirations of workers was as important as the final outcome. He maintained that the process of collective bargaining furnished a field for formulating and articulating workers' goals. If management did not agree with these goals, it was up to unions to change management's mind. How far unions could go in bringing management to see the union point of view depended on the state of industrial relations and the nature of the collective bargaining process.

Providing Collective Bargaining

The industrial relations system of the United States was once thought of as one of the advanced arrangements in the world, for through the vehicle of collective bargaining, it permitted management and labor to get together to negotiate over their differences. Any system of industrial relations must set forth an orderly framework telling the parties engaged in industry how they are to deal with one another. In the United States, that framework is devised through the interactions of government, management and organized labor. Each of these three will have differing strengths at different times, and each must operate within a social climate that may also shift the balance of power among them.[4] In this section, the role that unions play in the industrial relations system through collective bargaining is considered.

Collective bargaining exists in industry, as Sumner Slichter once noted, because individual workers do not have enough information about economic conditions to conduct their own bargains over wages, because not all workers want the same working conditions, because the small gain that accrues from giving an individual worker better working conditions is often not worth management's bothering about and because employers may lose money from helping an individual worker improve his or her skills if that worker then changes jobs. In short, the individual worker is in a very weak bargaining position relative to the employer, while the employer has no incentive to make improvements on behalf of one worker.[5] Collective bargaining aims at balancing the bargaining power between labor and management.

For workers to seek improvements for themselves, they must act as a group, through collective bargaining. The only way collective bargaining can take place is through an organized entity, which, under the NLRA, must be an independent union. It is Barkin's view that the purpose of the NLRA was to provide "support for union organization."[6] There was a sound reason for support of collective bargaining, namely, that it "is conducive to industrial peace and most favorable to high productivity."[7]

According to Barkin, collective bargaining could improve productivity for a variety of reasons. Collective bargaining places management and labor on a more equal footing, which means that discussions between them can be more open and frank. In addition, once an agreement has been reached, workers have an obligation to live up to it. Finally, the bargain also defines management's authority, thereby eliminating any further problems relating to workers' refusals to accept that authority.[8] By eliminating needless controversy over the rules of the game, the parties to collective bargaining can pay more attention to improvements in the methods of work. Achieving solid collective bargaining outcomes requires a great deal of responsibility on the part of union negotiators or representatives.

For collective bargaining techniques to be effective, both parties to the process—labor and management—must behave in a responsible manner. On the union side, the key element of every collective bargaining arrangement is the negotiating committee. As Barkin notes, "The effectiveness of every negotiating committee depends on the power behind it. If the union is weak and lacks cohesion and determination, the committee is not likely to secure the best results. It is most effective when it enters upon the negotiation with the full support of the membership."[9] The role played by union leadership in securing membership support is discussed below. At this point, it is clear that for Barkin a major factor in getting membership support comes from holding meetings of the rank and file in which bargaining issues are discussed and voted upon, so workers "feel that they are participating in the negotiations."[10] In this way, unions play the important role of learning what the workers' attitudes are on the issues under negotiation, and they establish their relative priorities.

In terms of preparations for meeting with management, unions bear a demanding responsibility. Here the limitations of the analysis of union behavior as being parallel to a monopoly firm are apparent. Unlike a monopoly firm that sets its price wherever it pleases, based on its estimates of its demand, unions must negotiate with management. Its wage demands must be tempered by an appreciation for the firm's ability to meet them. In order to gain that appreciation, Barkin recommends, "In all matters affecting the cost of production of concerns whose action is not likely to affect an industry's wage level, the union must consider factors such as going wages, costs, type of management, comparative advantages, profits, prices, markets and methods of absorbing costs. It is generally advisable in all negotiations to translate the union's proposal into actual annual payroll costs. The union's demands derived from workers' needs and desires must be carefully balanced by these considerations if it is to face problems realistically and constructively."[11]

Whereas firms have more market power in terms of setting industry wage levels or prices, labor has more flexibility in terms of its demands. A union's role as income maximizer for its members is not absolute. Just as public utilities must negotiate rate hikes with government regulators, so too are union leaders constrained in the use of their supposed monopoly power. As Clark Kerr once pointed out, "The union is not involved in selling labor. It is more like a price-fixing institution. The labor is then 'sold' by the individual worker."[12] The union is a negotiator for the workers' returns.

Equally important, in their contract negotiations with management, unions are constrained in their demands by the market structure within which the firm operates. This was a phenomenon that Barkin recognized very early in his own career as a contract negotiator. Fifty years ago, based on his experiences with the TWUA, he reported that in deciding on what wages to seek in the varied sectors of the textile industry it dealt with, the TWUA "differentiates between industries with limited competition and high profits and those with substantial competition." In the rayon yarn sector, which the union felt had an oligopolistic element, higher wage gains were possible. In the highly competitive cotton textile industry, however, it would not be possible to push for higher wages. Barkin provided a similar analysis for all sectors of the textile industry.[13] Based on this experience, he believed that it was possible for unions to act responsibly in meeting management's complaint that they did not consider market conditions.

It was not enough for unions to act responsibly in considering market conditions. Business, too, had an obligation to behave well, one which it did not always meet. Leading firms in oligopolistic industries have the power to set patterns on both wages and prices. It was Barkin's conviction that these firms would hold back on their price changes in a deliberate effort to time them with wage increases granted to union workers. As a result, the public through its media pundits began to associate price increases with wage increases, oftentimes blaming unions for inflation. Despite this charge, unions had no part in determining prices, as anyone familiar with Reuther's efforts to get GM to agree to connecting prices with wages in 1945–46 would have to admit.

As the GM experience demonstrates, the ability of unions to act responsibly was related to the issue of union security that arises in contract negotiation. Barkin finds it important for labor and management to have off-the-record meetings "to dispel prejudice concerning the union's demand for security." Because managements are not sure of unions' sense of responsibility, "they are not aware of the price which management pays when the union is not secure. A union which has a guaranteed status does not usually insist on detailed provisions designed to prevent discrimination." A union that can back up its members' claims does not need to have its rights specified to the minutest detail.[14]

Another problem with contract negotiations is that they can end in strikes. This outcome is one that troubles the public, for a strike seems such a waste of time and resources. Barkin would agree that there is an expectation that parties to collective bargaining "find their own answers through peaceful negotiation." Strikes do involve high costs for both parties, which is why there are relatively few of them, with the time lost through strikes annually amounting to about 0.1 percent of the total time worked. But, he would add, they do perform the constructive function of alerting management and the public that there is an urgent need to reconsider the needs of and returns to workers.[15] Strikes are the workers' way of expressing strong discontent with the way things are, and without them it would not be as easy to push for higher wages.

Overall, Barkin would find collective bargaining to be a useful way for management and labor to reach agreement on wages and other issues, even in those rare cases when the result is a strike. It places responsibility on unions to make agreements that its members will accept and live up to. In terms of wage negotiations, he would insist that unions be realistic and take into account the market conditions that the firm and the industry face. In negotiating contracts, however, there are a variety of other issues besides wages upon which both sides must agree. With these issues—relating to such problems as work rules, technical change, and wage incentives—Barkin thinks that collective bargaining provides a very good vehicle for attaining management-labor cooperation.

Promoting Cooperation

In the previous chapter, a discussion was presented dealing with how management and labor could improve their cooperative efforts, with an emphasis on Barkin's ideas of the part that management must play to ensure better cooperation. In this section, Barkin's appreciation for the positive role that unions can play in attaining such cooperation is considered. As Barkin put it, "If increases in productivity are to be major determinants of improvement, how can unions share in their promotion?" His answer was evident, "The continuing problems relating to the economic well-being of the enterprise, the plant and the union worker will have to be dealt with by new agencies of collective bargaining."[16]

Management may resist such union meddling in its affairs. As Barkin felt, "Managerial personnel philosophies and practices in America rest on the belief in managerial autocracy."[17] More to the point, management would feel that there was everything to lose and nothing to gain by bargaining with unions over plant operations. Weren't unions simply after featherbedding to protect their members? Barkin had two main answers to management's concerns.

First, the outlook of unions had changed as a result of the shift in industry and unions from the craft unions of the AFL to the industrial unions typified by the CIO. The change was very important in terms of union response to work relations. Barkin observed, "In the earlier craft-union era, the dominant policy was to control the supply of craftsmen in order to enhance the bargaining power of those in the trade and to assure adequate employment and income for them." That attitude led to the closed shop, limits on output, and speed of work, requiring unnecessary work and resistance to technical change.

With the advent of industrial unionism, in which workers undertook a variety of jobs and the union organized an entire plant or industry instead of just one craft, there was a different outlook. In the mass production industry, workers continually became accustomed to changing technology, workloads, and job structures. To be sure, workers might have to be taught to accept the changes that technology brought, for such acceptance would not automatically happen. That outlook was another service a union or its research staff could render to workers. After World War II, for example, the TWUA's policy on technological innovation was presented in a column produced by the research department, "On the Job," which appeared regularly in the union's newspaper, *Textile Labor*.[18]

With training in the advantages of accepting technological change and no skills to protect, Barkin noted, "Industrial trade-unions have accepted the principle of the inevitability of industrial change." Their members merely wanted a set of rules to protect themselves from the detrimental impact of such change and a voice in defining working conditions.[19] Management would find workers to be more accepting of changes if workers had a way to learn in advance about the changes' existence and have influence over how changes were to be implemented.

A second way management could gain through bargaining with unions over plant policies is in the area of informal work rules. Under craft unionism, workers had the power to impose their rules on management. Although that power was eroded under the mass production methods that faced industrial unions, it did not go away. As Barkin stated the situation, "Working agreements, arrangements and understandings on the work floor existed from the earliest days of the industrial system. . . . In recent years these agreements have often taken the form of verbal pacts between the shop steward and the foreman to assure mutual cooperation on the production floor. Their existence is often unknown to the front office and is revealed primarily when formal, plant-wide rules or contracts clash with these local practices and codes."[20] When such clashes take place, the cooperative spirit can be lost. It would be better for management to bargain with unions over such rules, in which case management would become more acquainted with the existence and benefits of cooperative work rules.

For cooperation to work, however, unions need to take more responsibility for expertise in meetings with management. As Neil Chamberlain discovered, management was skeptical that union officials would have the ability to share in operating a plant, quoting one steel company executive as feeling that union leaders "don't have much to contribute."[21] This presented problems under the industrial system, because as Barkin maintained, "The intimate knowledge required of specific tasks cannot be easily acquired by the union leadership."[22] To eliminate this problem, union leaders needed to be trained in managerial methods or else turn to technical experts to assist them in understanding and dealing with management on a variety of issues relating to wages and working conditions.

As noted in the previous chapter, the main source of technical expertise dealing with work arose from the scientific management experiments of Frederick W. Taylor. Organized labor initially associated Taylor's approach with anti-unionism and maintained that his approach as applied by management was not scientific, especially with regard to time-and-motion studies and the administering of piece rates. Over time, unions, especially industrial unions, began to make peace with scientific management, which by the 1940s was operating under the rubric of industrial engineering.

As the economy evolved and unions had more contact with scientific management, according to Barkin, they began to appreciate some of the merits to Taylor's approach. During the two world wars, unions frequently worked with industrial engineers to increase productivity and found that they had reason to continue with these efficiency programs if joint consultation could be employed with them. Unions also became interested in Taylor's notion that increased productivity should be the basis for higher wages. When a second generation of industrial engineers followed Taylor's fundamental point by stressing the importance of good working conditions as crucial to improving efficiency, trade unionists were greatly impressed.[23] Hillman and the Clothing Workers had been in the vanguard of union recognition that Taylorism had some benefits for workers, if only workers were permitted to take part in setting the work standards.[24]

Acceptance of scientific management meant that the issues of collective bargaining would change. Management would insist on setting rigid technical formulas for wage plans and work rules, and the greater use of industrial engineers meant that unions were faced with persons who were "untutored in collective bargaining procedure and were trained to insist upon their right to deference to their professional judgments." Unions could either resist these professionals or acquiesce to their demands.[25]

Ultimately, the way to counter the findings of technical experts is with another set of technical experts. This Barkin did with the TWUA, hiring a technical staff consisting of "a senior and junior engineer in the national office and two field engineers."[26] This was the policy he would recommend to all unions in order to deal with scientific management. If they followed this policy, moreover, his experiences offered several suggestions.

First, union engineers should be made permanent employees of the union as early and as often as possible and not be hired just as consultants. By making them regular employees, the union would have a better chance of obtaining their loyalty. Most industrial engineers received training that stressed the point of view of management. For the union to gain its point of view on technical issues, the engineers had to be given careful training and supervision by union leaders. Moreover, service with a union would give industrial engineers a better ability to understand and formulate worker complaints. Finally, longtime work with a union would help its engineers to gain the confidence of the officers of the union, enabling them to present their findings in a way that could be understood by both union leaders and rank-and-file members.

A second important strategy for employing industrial engineers would be to integrate their activities with the union's economic staff. Ultimately, the impact of scientific management would be on wages and levels of work application. Although the responsibility for such impact would rest with union officials, the economic staff had to develop the arguments justifying wage and application changes. Its members needed input from the industrial engineers as to how changes in work methods would affect the wage structure. Indeed, Barkin found it important for all of a union's administrative personnel to be aided and trained by industrial engineers so that they could apply scientific management techniques to all phases of collective bargaining.[27]

Armed with its own engineering experts, a union is better able to enter into negotiations with management in collective bargaining over wages, work rules, technical change, and productivity gains. Although the engineering department could assist and educate local business agents, ultimately the responsibility for contract negotiation and enforcement rested with local officials. The staff at the national union headquarters could never be large enough to handle all the problems that arise at the local level. Barkin always considered his research department to be a service bureau, giving advice to union members and leaders on issues important to them and identifying areas of concern that might have been overlooked.[28] It is always in the national union's interest to seek worker participation and competence in handling local issues. The educational staff and the union press would be very important supplements to the research staff in attaining worker participation and competence.

Given a high degree of worker awareness of what the engineering staff was trying to accomplish, Barkin felt that both management and labor could gain when both used technical experts to make both sides knowledgeable about how changes in work rules, wage incentive plans, and technology would affect plant operation and worker satisfaction. Accomplishing acceptance of this type of program was not easy, because management often resisted and the issues involved were not easily resolved through the arbitration process. The outcome would, however, be worth the effort in Barkin's opinion. The joint expertise that labor and management could derive from effective use of industrial engineering would be especially helpful in the tricky area of developing wage incentive plans.

Negotiating Wage Incentives

In the area of wage determination, there is a constant struggle between labor and management over how much effort workers will make on the job, how they will apply that effort, and how much they will be paid for it. One commonly offered way of getting workers to put forth greater effort is through wage incentive plans. As noted in the previous chapter, wage incentive plans are devised to relate pay directly to output in order to give workers an incentive to increase their production. Time-and-motion study is an important part of wage incentive plans, for it establishes the base for what workers can expect to accomplish in terms of output. As previously described, the application of time-and-motion studies is neither objective nor precise. This arbitrariness explains one reason why workers and unions resist wage incentive systems.

The use of union experts can overcome that resistance by giving weight to union complaints of arbitrariness. The union will be able to back up these complaints, Barkin argues, "if it is supported by evidence such as a study by an employee or trade union time study man."[29] The union time study man need not be an engineer; he had only to be trained by a union engineer in time-study methods. Indeed, Barkin saw no reason for union engineers to be involved with time study unless the management study had been very poorly done. For him, the union engineer's "primary purpose is to define the irregularities on the job overlooked by the management's time study man. . . . His responsibility is to define the alternatives which the union may consider in formulating its counter proposals as to earnings and level of work application. His greatest skill expresses itself in converting the workers' insights and demands into mathematical form for use in negotiations."[30]

Because there are limits to how much the technical expertise workers in mass production can learn and still have time to do their job, it is necessary for them to rely on industrial engineers for the knowledge of how much work they can be expected to do. The problem is made more complicated, however, because every time the technical conditions of work change, the expectations of workers' performance and the incentive pay they are to receive for that performance also must change. Furthermore, management itself is not often technically competent to deal with these problems. Workers can gain by having their own engineers to advise them on changing work conditions and how the conditions affect wage incentive systems.

Management can also gain. About the textile industry Barkin reported, "We have many mills that specify procedures for performance. We have room conditions checked, personal and fatigue tests, machine interference studies and patrol studies. In each one of these, we, the union, have had to find a technique of testing management."[31] Only when unions have their own ability to gauge the effectiveness of management's wage incentive plans will they be able to accept such plans with confidence and cooperate with them.

Wage incentive plans have a potential to benefit both management and labor, but only if they fit the conditions in which they are introduced and if they are properly managed. In many cases this has not happened, with the result that even management can become dissatisfied and abandon them, as surveys have shown. There have even been instances when the discontinuation of an incentive plan has resulted in a reduction of labor cost per unit. A key problem can be that as working conditions change, an incentive system will yield less certain benefits for both sides. For an incentive plan to work effectively, both management and labor must cooperate to see that it is applied properly, especially as conditions change.

Adjusting to Technical Change

A cooperative spirit for technical change is also possible when union collaboration is sought. As noted previously, the legal system has consistently denied any claim to workers of an ownership right to their job, with the result that workers have an interest in fighting any change that might threaten those jobs. Because under mass production technical change has become quite common and often results in unemployment, workers resist it. If those workers are represented by a union that can give them security when technical changes are made, they will be more accepting of them.

One of the ways unions can gain that security for their members is by "getting rules which automatically define the claims of specific classes of workers." Some of these rules will impinge on management's ability to make changes in technology, but those rules are not onerous. "Seldom," Barkin writes, "is a limitation placed on the employer's right to make innovations of a technical nature. . . . Many contracts require employers to follow a prescribed procedure for informing and discussing planned changes with the union prior to the introduction of changes."[32]

By way of example of this procedure, Barkin once cited how things were done in the TWUA. Under the system used in the organized plants of the textile industry:

> Any recommendation proposed by an employer must be submitted to the union in writing, in advance of the installation. Such statement usually contains an outline of the mechanical changes proposed, as well as reasons necessitating new work assignments. . . .

The employer's proposals are carefully weighed by the general union committee, together with the representatives of the employees directly affected by these changes. When the new work assignments are posited on the existence of similar work assignments in competitive mills, the employee committee secures data on current practices in the industry from the research department of the national union. . . .

All too frequently management or engineers make improper job assignments. The conditions affecting work in a textile mill are too numerous and varied for outside observers fully to comprehend their effects. The workers' intimate knowledge of these conditions proves invaluable in correcting extravagant and improper employer proposals.[33]

There are two advantages to management's cooperating with unions on setting up procedures for technical change. First, the procedure prevents strikes and work stoppages. If workers feel they are being mistreated by a change in work conditions, they are likely to take action to stop it. Second, the system allows management to take advantage of the knowledge that workers have of the production process. Cooperating with unions is a much better way to secure this knowledge than hoping for employees to place their knowledge in a suggestion box, for it gives workers confidence that their ideas will be taken seriously. More recently, management has tried to get employee cooperation through quality-of-work-life programs, but whether these will work without the security that workers get from their union is doubtful. Few workers will make proposals that might eliminate their job, unless they are certain they will be given another one.

Establishing Work Rules

The setting of procedures for technical change raises the broader issue of just how far unions and management must go in setting procedures for all aspects of the job. The system of such procedures is usually referred to as work rules and forms a key part of any industrial relations bargain. The term "work rules" brings to mind hoary examples of featherbedding such as firemen on diesel locomotives or mandatory rest breaks. But it should be recalled that every plant or company must have rules; the question is who will make them and how. No one has ever concocted a term such as "nailbedding" to indicate cases in which management has devised work rules to give workers a less than easy time. Nor have there been many complaints vocalized over such practices, except by workers and their unions.

Management, of course, wants the power to set all work rules itself and to change them as it sees fit. Unions, in opposition, would like every rule and change in rules to be open for discussion and negotiation. As for workers, according to Barkin, they "tend to see work rules as threats to their own personal bargaining relationship. In fact, many rules are themselves the product of negotiations by individuals on the job itself and their personal achievement. Changes in these conditions will affect their individual status, earnings, job security, level of work application and even bargaining achievements."[34]

At issue in work rule changes are how workers are to be made to feel secure enough to go along with them and if the changes result in productivity gains, how the changes are to be divided between labor and management, and how displaced workers are to be protected. As with technical change, the first issue can be minimized in terms of its impact if workers have a union to bargain for them. The second issue, which relates to all changes on the job, is more complicated.

Traditional economic theory has it that wages are related to productivity, with no employer's being willing to pay a wage higher than the value of the product added by hiring the last worker. In reality, the determination of wages is composed of a variety of factors. Workers understand these factors very well, Barkin recognizes, as "they become early aware that the so-called wage bargain is composed of three separate dimensions, time, effort and/or leisure and skill or knowledge."[35] To traditional economists, these last two are part of what determines a worker's addition to output, with knowledge being considered human capital for which the worker may earn a premium. The factor of the amount of time worked does not enter into the traditional economist's theory of wage determination, which is one of static equilibrium. Nor does the question of how quickly innovation can take place in productive methods.

In an industrial system marked by rapid innovation, such as has existed in the United States, short periods often bring rapid changes in technology that offset a worker's skills and alter the value of the product being produced. These changes in technology also have a large impact on the level of productivity of the individual worker and the wage rate paid to that worker. To keep wages closely tied to productivity, managers use either production standards of performance, as determined by industrial engineers, or wage incentive systems such as piece rates or profit sharing.

For Barkin, such measures or plans define what he called human application. Human application in his sense refers to the level of effort required of workers. If output can be increased with no change in time and skill, the level of application has increased. Tight rates exist when workers feel they are being pushed to apply themselves too hard. For Barkin, in an industrial system in which individual output is difficult to measure, "Productivity is not central to the employee's rewards; it is the level of application." Since the level of application depends on a variety of factors, such as quality of raw materials, job arrangements, efficiency of complementary services, and type of product, levels of application can be quickly increased or decreased. When the output of workers increases without a corresponding change in worker application, management will claim all the resulting productivity gains for itself and not feel any need to raise wages.

Workers will resent these claims and will want a share in the productivity gains. Systems set up to monitor the gains more accurately, often with management-union collaboration, usually become too expensive to monitor. Instead, unions and management have negotiated broad measures of productivity that will assure workers they are sharing in productivity gains. As an example, Barkin noted the Scanlon Plan, which had been proposed by an official of the United Steel Workers Union "to enlist member cooperation to rescue companies from financial collapse." In other cases, measures of national productivity were used, as in the 1948 agreement between GM and the UAW. The advantage of this system, for Barkin, was that "it avoided the difficulties of calculating such indexes for the individual enterprises or industries."[36] The TWUA negotiated a "Textron formula" in 1951 that had elements similar to the GM-UAW agreement, but it failed to get it accepted in more than only a few New England mills, as William Hartford describes.[37]

Despite the fact that such broad measures could not gauge productivity so accurately that each worker's addition to output could be attained, there were advantages in their use that Barkin found important. Workers would recognize that individual measures of productivity were arbitrary and would resist them. In addition, when the measures were made part of collective bargaining, workers could feel secure that they could not be changed. Of utmost importance, moreover, by tying wage gains to a national productivity figure, as did the GM agreement, unions could assure workers of a rising standard of living; then workers would be more willing to cooperate with changes in technology or job rules once they had that assurance.

A key to the success of these productivity sharing plans, however, was that they be devised through collective bargaining with unions. Any plan set up by management and administered solely by it could be subject to unilateral change, as many workers are now finding is the case with health benefits promised to retirees. Only if workers can be backed by union representation can they be assured that they will get what the plans promise, and only then will they enter into the plans with a spirit of free cooperation.

At the TWUA, Barkin instituted a variety of procedures and proposals to foster cooperation with management but still protect workers. Overall, he tried to protect workers by seeking a tie-in between productivity gains and the industry's investment decisions. For times when technical changes were made, he developed a formula for their handling that appeared in cotton textile agreements in Northern industry. Management wanted to take advantage of every change in conditions that loosened work assignments. Workers resisted these changes because they were suspicious of management's view that conditions, as measured by time-study methods, had changed and because they did not want to give up the advantages of shortcuts they had devised on their own. The workers would thus respond to tightening of work standards by complaining loudly about the nefarious "stretchout," meaning, that they were being required to take responsibility for overseeing more machines. In weaving, for example, a worker might monitor from 50 to 150 machines, whereas in spinning a worker's job load could run to as many as 2,000 spindles. Other ways the work assignment could change might involve, for example, the pattern by which the worker patrolled the machine, in one case going from a random schedule to a scheduled circular pattern, or the introduction of new forms of raw materials and packaging. The cumulative impact of many such changes was to alter completely the terms of employment and, under an incentive wage system, the rate of pay.[38]

The TWUA engineering staff tried to find ways to help workers understand what was happening when job standards tightened and to defend their point of view. This was very difficult, as it involved their gaining an understanding of the standards involved with many different jobs; union leaders at the shop floor level were not sufficiently competent to evaluate all the changes, workers were even less prepared to undertake the full task of evaluation, and management had an overwhelming preponderance of knowledge resting with its engineering staff. To counter these difficulties, the TWUA stressed the need to have the company provide the local union with a copy of all job specifications and insisted that advance notification of changes be sent to the local union. Barkin and the TWUA engineering staff also provided workers with a guidebook that would enable them to understand and evaluate the basic components of their job.[39]

In addition to giving workers more information about the details of their job, Barkin devised a benchmark method of setting production standards that would enable them to use that knowledge. The approach was intended to remedy defects in time-study methods that both management and workers found to be causing problems. Under the benchmark system, management and the union would agree on the model job that would serve as the benchmark against which similar jobs in the plant were to be evaluated in terms of their labor input, thus implicitly admitting that time-motion studies were not objective and precise enough to set labor input standards.

The initial phase of the benchmark approach involved a description of the duties in the job to be used, rather than just a series of movements as in time study. In the textile industry, most jobs involved three components: scheduled tasks, which were standardized as to frequency and time needed to perform the task; periodic tasks, of which the frequency was known but not the time needed to perform the task; and random tasks, for which neither the frequency nor the time needed could be accurately or precisely predicted. For the description of a job, scheduled tasks could be readily defined, but periodic and random tasks could be stated only in terms of probable or average frequencies per time period, which must be agreed upon by management and the union. Thus the benchmark standard could refer only to time with periodic and scheduled tasks, with random tasks' having to be estimated on the basis of probable occurrences and the probable nature of the difficulty.

Once these elements of the model job were established, other tasks with different frequencies would be transformed into a system of equivalent operations. Studies and experiments with the actual job would be used to help develop these equivalents. The equivalents would then be built up into the standard benchmark, which would define the level of application the worker would be expected to contribute. Time-study methods usually tried to develop a standard motion and standard time for that motion to take place. The benchmark system replaced that by keying on actual operations in an experimental setting, using standards proposed by both management and labor. The result of the experiments would reflect an agreement as to what compromises of the proposed standards were needed, so the final standard would be acceptable by both parties.

By using the benchmark approach, both management and labor could benefit. In the area of technical change, since each new method adopted would require a new setting of a benchmark, both management and labor would be forced to cooperate in the introduction of the change. Once a production standard was negotiated, both workers and supervisors would have an interest in enforcing the benchmark standard. As standards became more strictly enforced, variances from the standard were quickly evident to both sides; this made corrections more likely to take place. Finally, workers would become better informed about job duties. They would have more confidence in both application levels and pay plans that were derived from a benchmark standard, especially if they had participated in the formulation of the standard. The benchmark system would help to overcome the problem of existing wage incentive systems, which can lead to wage declines when working conditions deteriorate, even if output increases.

Overall, though, Barkin felt that the impact of benchmark standards would be another way unions could help their members on shop floor issues. He concluded, "Benchmarks are designed so that the worker can be knowledgeable and able to use his collective bargaining rights in setting work standards. The benchmark is readily understood. The worker can be guided by his own extensive understanding of the actual job in negotiating the standard and he can readily count his equivalent operations to assure himself that the original bargain is being respected."[40] Through this approach, unions could give workers more control and more say in shop floor conditions, which would make workers more willing to cooperate with management.

This approach may seem to rest on an optimistic conception of workers' abilities. It is easy to underestimate what workers can accomplish, however. Even in the arcane field of scientific management, workers could make a contribution. As Slichter found in his research on time-study programs, "Time and again the workers' committees, handicapped as they were by lack of technical knowledge, were able to point out omissions and mistakes in the standards."[41] Given the technical support Barkin and his associates provided them, workers could be expected to be even more knowledgeable about their work.

To sum up these last sections, it is clear that Barkin had always believed that a spirit of cooperation between labor and management was essential to increased production. During World War II, when there was a heightened need for increasing industrial output, he promoted the idea of labor-management production committees to take responsibility for a plant's overall production gains: not that the committees would run plants on a day-to-day basis, but that they would try to determine the factors that were limiting production and then suggest methods for eliminating them. Again, the idea was to take advantage of the knowledge that workers had about plant operations so as to pinpoint conditions that hindered their efficiency.

But also, again, unions had to be a part of these committees. As part of the conditions that would make such committees successful, Barkin listed union security as number one. Trust had to exist between management and unions. He also pointed out that the program of cooperation had to protect work standards— so that workers would have no fears of being laid off—and that workers should be given a share in productivity gains—to motivate them to higher application levels.[42] Unions could also provide a service for workers by offering them information about how their jobs were formulated.

It is interesting that lessons learned in wartime are often forgotten when peace returns. In Barkin's case, the lesson learned during the war about the effectiveness of labor-management committees for cooperation to increase production was quickly forgotten, even by union leaders. By the early 1960s, Barkin was forcibly reminding them that "the labor movement's agenda must include achieving a new constructive relationship with management. Ten and fifteen years ago, the harmony in our industrial relations, born in the war years, was the envy of the free world. Now the emphasis is on conflict. . . . Leaders in labor and management have been able to find no common ground for attacking problems that affect them both."[43] Were labor leaders listening? Were they capable of making changes as Barkin suggested? These issues are the subject of the next section.

Providing Leadership for Workers

Any organization that interacts with other institutions of society must represent fairly the wants, needs, and interests of its members. This is one of the many functions of leadership. In an autocratic hierarchy, such as the military or a business corporation, that function is made easier, for the interests of the leader tend to coincide with those of the membership; indeed, it is a very important function of leadership to see that this is so. Labor unions, however, are democratic organizations, which means that leaders must be more responsive to the desires of the members. They must find out what members want. And when leaders and members disagree on the goals of the organization, it becomes a function of leadership to motivate the members to want what is good for the organization and themselves.

In his many years with the TWUA and the CIO, Barkin worked with a variety of labor leaders, from the famous, such as Sidney Hillman, John L. Lewis, and Walter Reuther, to lesser knowns, such as Emil Rieve, Charles Howard, and

William Pollock. From this experience, he derived a set of standards detailing what made for a good leader.

Barkin's highest praise for a union leader would probably go to Sidney Hillman. He would give Hillman high marks especially for his ability to inspire and motivate workers with the messages that unions were a driving force for progress and that unions have as a goal the continual betterment of society and the human condition. Although many might find Barkin's stress on the need for conveying these messages to be a harking back to the good old days of the 1930s, he would respond that it is this sort of spirit that led the CIO to its greatest successes and widest popular appeal. Hillman also recognized the need for government action to help unions stabilize an industry that was highly competitive; it was Hillman's philosophy that underlay the TWUA in its push for a minimum wage to help stabilize wage rates in the textile industry. Unfortunately, Barkin could lament, the ability of union leaders to act as "labor statesmen" in conveying the message of progress as a key part in union fights for minimum wage legislation and other government programs was rapidly dwindling by the 1960s.[44]

Union leaders needed to retain this broader idealism because of its effect on the union members and on the general population. As Barkin pointed out, "The image of the union doesn't stand high in the values of the American people. The American trade union leader is not the great moral figure he has been in the past." This effective leadership was important because of the way the public associated leaders as representatives of their unions. In addition, the activities and aspirations of leaders had an influence on the part of a union's members. In earlier, idealistic days, "unionism created a spark of new status and personal participation which extended to all aspects of the workers' lives. But when you look at the American trade union scene today you see that workers have rejected the union in all areas except the shop. In other local activity the union is not the agent of the worker."[45] By following the path of prudential unionism, the leaders of the CIO yielded the opportunity for unions to play a positive role in improving society and to gain the social respect that went with such a role.

In terms of his own union and its daily operations, Barkin accorded great favor to Emil Rieve. Rieve had the ability not only to centralize administrative functions for effective control but also to give persons in charge of the functions the freedom to operate as they saw fit. He also was an effective negotiator who enjoyed bargaining and did it in a constructive manner. He had a good sense of the realities of the economic conditions facing the textile industry and was able to get along well with employers. In dealing with subordinates, Rieve was always willing to go into the field and meet with them to discuss particular problems. With his professional staff, he displayed confidence and respect for their abilities and was willing to use their research and skills to support his own perception of economic conditions. Barkin found this especially noteworthy, for he felt that most union leaders had not developed any respect for the value of independent research. With Rieve's retirement as president of the TWUA, Barkin felt that leadership at the TWUA suffered.[46]

By the early 1960s, Barkin found the leadership capabilities of unions to be dangerously diminished. To pinpoint the problem, Barkin, together with Albert Blum, conducted a survey of union leaders and staff. Both union presidents and staff members cited technological change and a hostile government as major problems facing unions, topics discussed in Chapter Seven. Their perception of union difficulties extended to the union and its leaders. Some union presidents even attacked other presidents for poor leadership, citing a "loss of a strong sense of dedication."

Staff members were even more blunt, claiming, "Success, prosperity and a desire to emulate management [have] had a corrupting effect on many top and lower-level leaders." Among the causes for this state of affairs the survey results included "Membership apathy, the nature of bureaucracy, the increased wealth of leaders," and "lack of contact between officials and members."[47] Perhaps the clearest statement of this problem was made by a union official in summarizing his own views on the appropriate relationship between leaders and the rank and file: "A union today is like a corporation. The membership is like the stockholders and the officers are like the board of directors. As long as the board of directors pays dividends the stockholders are happy."[48] It would be hard to find a clearer statement of the business-union attitude of labor leaders.

In his own analysis of union leadership, Barkin found both good and bad. By reflecting on the fact that unions are democratically run, he typified the most common leadership at the local level as being heads of coalitions rather than dominant leaders. Because they had to keep several divergent groups happy, some coalition leaders showed "indecision and dispersion of effort." Some coalition leaders were able to put together and gain support for consistent programs, gaining them Barkin's praise as "the innovators and trail blazers, who lead with courage and imagination." In order to keep their coalitions together, these leaders also had to maintain constant lines of communication with their members. Barkin's former boss at the TWUA, Emil Rieve, recognized the problem of being too distant from workers. Having spent many years telling workers how bad employers behaved, union leaders found that when management "asks for something we think is right, we cannot even convince our people that it is."[49]

Another type of union leader Barkin recognized was "the single leader in whom power and decision-making tends to be concentrated." The number of such leaders was growing, especially at the national level. They exercised a stronger bent in terms of getting their own programs accepted by the membership, and they were becoming a permanent fixture, enjoying long periods in office because their continued success in collective bargaining had enabled them to build up a network of political power. As a result of their long tenure and power, their own policies shaped the union in their own image. Their immediate subordinates become messengers rather than thinkers.[50]

These leaders were especially detrimental for the union movement, for they stayed with what worked for them. At the same time, the top ranks of the union were filled with sycophants, who were unwilling or unable to promote new ideas or strategies for the union movement. Barkin was never a strong advocate of the type of participatory democracy in unions that kept leaders tied up with coddling the rank and file, but he certainly did not care for leaders whose power and tenure permitted them to become stultified and therefore a numbing force in the union struggle.

In an evaluation of the character traits of union leaders, Barkin found that temperament and outlook depended on outside circumstances. Most leaders were males, who had risen from among the people they represented and who therefore "reflected the predominant value systems among members." Their temperaments varied with the union's stage of development, with aggressive, uncompromising organizers and orators taking charge in the nascent days of the union, while the skilled negotiator and deal-maker emerged as the union settled into regular relations with management. The best leaders combined elements of both temperaments, gaining their skills in dealing with problems as part of their work. For such leaders, unions have served "as ladders of personal success for tens of thousands of persons who would otherwise be submerged in our society. They become an outlet for creative leadership by workers within their own field of experience."

As they rise from the ranks, Barkin would remind these union leaders to retain their idealism. Keeping idealism was important, because in his words, "Trade union leaders must fire their members with motive and conviction."[51] It was the role of the leader to take the inarticulate desires of workers and formulate them into a consistent point of view and an organizational ideology. A leader's ability to achieve this synthesis of worker yearnings and put them in a form that was both inspirational and programmatic was limited, however. At the local level, leaders became scornful of workers as they were caught between groups of workers who were militant and others who were apathetic.[52] At the national level, prominent leaders usually became too mired in the duties of office work to be able to maintain a broad vision of the direction that society and unions should be heading. The best of them could admire intellectuals, but they could not be intellectuals. As Barkin assessed the cerebral qualities of prominent U.S. labor leaders,

> In the United States, with its particular distaste for doctrine and theoretical discussion and the stress on the pragmatic, the goals and ideology have been informally and progressively shaped by internal and external pressures rather than by formal policy or specific personalities. Gompers's views on partisan politics, Lewis's and Hillman's espousal of industrial unionism and political action, and Reuther's formulations of economic goals have largely been products of the time rather than personal inventions and philosophies. Their influences have been pervasive, but they expressed rather than invented a position.

Their intense convictions [and] effective and in some cases dramatic personalities helped communicate and win support for the positions they espoused.[53]

Here Barkin has put his finger on a particular problem facing unions and their supporters in the United States. Because of their unsure legal standing and low public and government support, unions in this country remain passive responders to events. They and their leaders must react to events as their experiences and personalities permit them, but they have been unable to gain sufficient control over events to then follow them up with meaningful philosophies that put the event in broader social context. Gompers saw too many government crackdowns on unions to ever feel confident of unions' having a constant, positive influence on public policy, and Reuther, as noted in Chapter Four, was totally snubbed by management at GM when he tried to use the UAW as a counter to GM's pricing policies.

Reuther was an archetype of this leadership problem. Because of his early interest in socialism, he had a vision of the UAW as preeminent leader for social change. After years of fighting, especially with GM, Reuther settled into an era of peaceful coexistence with the automakers, surrendering worker militancy, suspending where he could a penchant for wildcat strikes by workers, and reneging on attempts to change work floor practices, all in return for better pay for workers.[54] Because Reuther was well-known as a progressive labor leader, other leaders could have been expected to do even less, because the climate was against them. They chose to follow the safer course of business or prudential unionism. As Barkin put it, "In an economic society in which management insisted upon control over price and production policies, unions could not assume any over-all responsibilities for economic policy. A policy of 'economic statesmanship' could not be pursued solely by one party to the economic bargain."[55]

Union leaders were also moved toward a strictly reactive posture by their perception of member demands. The primary function of a union leader is to deliver the goods to members in terms of better pay and benefits. That is the leader's way of maintaining with the membership the popularity necessary for continual reelection to office. Interest in broader social issues may not grab the hearts of the rank and file. In addition, union leaders may become so bogged down in the daily routine of meeting the needs of the rank and file that they have little time left over for the planning that is necessary for establishment of initiatives for union and social programs.

Satisfying members and staying in power, as goals of union leaders, may have other negative effects on the union. Leaders may spend too much time on internal politics to accomplish anything else. They may use their position to entrench themselves and their followers in leadership by appointing supporters to key positions, and they may use divisive tactics to split opposition factions. And rigged elections have been used to keep leaders in power.

Once entrenched in power, leaders may abuse their office for personal gain, in extreme cases consorting with racketeers to milk the union. Barkin was well aware of these problems, for his first assignment from Sidney Hillman was to investigate a garment market in New Jersey, where he found some companies to be racket penetrated. The very nature of the organization of unions causes problems with efforts aimed at controlling these abuses. As Barkin has written, "Members are usually not sensitive to abuses until the opposition, maladministration or absence of progress in collective bargaining, or an outside group focuses attention on these activities."[56] Feeling as he did that unions needed to aspire to the same level of ethical behavior as they expected from management, Barkin applauded "the adoption of the code of ethical practices by the AFL-CIO."[57]

The problem of ethical behavior goes beyond union leaders themselves, however, for their ethics regress toward social norms. Richard Lester once observed that the behavior of business and political leaders motivates union leaders. He wrote, "If businessmen and politicians are making money in questionable ways and 'getting away with it,' union leaders may be tempted to do likewise."[58] Unions in Europe and Canada have remained remarkably free of scandal, but so have the governments and businesses of those areas. Perhaps in the United States nothing is admired so much as the exploits of scoundrels who gain by pulling fast deals. The code of ethical practices for labor leaders must always run into the American Dream.

The code of ethical practices set forth by the AFL-CIO highlights another difficulty in correcting leadership abuses in unions. The AFL-CIO is really a loose federation of constituent member unions, with a national office that has very little say in internal local union affairs. The autonomy of local unions has been a part of trade unionism in the United States, dating from the older craft unions, but even extending to the locals of the national industrial unions. As a result, local unions operate with a great deal of independence from national union or federation offices. At best, the AFL-CIO can expel a union that transgresses its ethical or organizational standards. This power to expel has been selectively applied, with the two most well-known cases involving the Teamsters and unions that were under the influence of communists.

Much of this autonomy relates to the importance placed on democracy within the union movement. Because members elect local officers, it is felt that much of the power should rest with them. For Barkin, much of this stress on democracy was misplaced. He felt that except in cases of egregious misconduct or strongly conflicting points of view, democracy was more of an academic interest.[59] As a result, he would have no qualms about a transfer of more authority to the national federation, as had been the original intent of the founders of the CIO in their organizing drives.[60]

More centralized authority would put pressure on union leaders, but that is just where it belonged. Union members have great loyalty to their unions, having identified with their economic gains, but they have little understanding about the union movement's underlying beliefs and programs. As a result, Barkin concluded, "In crucial tests of union influence on members on noneconomic issues where broad mass participation is necessary, the union is unable to count on carrying its following with it."[61]

The lack of member appreciation had severe implications for the future of unions themselves. Union leaders had become complacent about expanding their membership among unorganized workers except in immediately competitive areas, with some exceptions taking place on the initiatives from workers more distantly located. This complacency spilled over into the membership. To revitalize the movement, Barkin hoped for national leaders to take up organizing drives as had been done in the 1930s. But the part played by union members in understanding the message of unionism was crucial. As Barkin put it, "The receptivity to unionism is to some degree determined by the degree to which present members accept, appreciate, and support unionism. They must be the ultimate preachers of the faith. The image of unionism spread by these persons helps prepare the unorganized for union appeals."[62] Only dedicated union members could keep the movement growing. And under capitalism, as Marx understood well, organizations that do not grow do not survive.

Because leadership is a key element in union success, it may be well to consider two complaints leveled against union leaders: they are undemocratic and they are not competent to understand the workings of industry. Even though those accusations have been answered earlier in some detail, this is a good place to remark that they fall just as heavily on the purported final authorities in business: stockholders and boards of directors. Although comparisons of voting records between union meetings and stockholders' meetings are not easily made, it does seem that the level of participation is not high in either; union members, like stockholders, rarely participate unless it is to voice extreme satisfaction. And members of boards of directors, who run the company in name only and rarely have more contact with the company than at the annual meeting, can scarcely have more knowledge about daily operations than a union leader would. The modern corporation is even less democratic than unions, and its legal leadership can hardly claim to be competent to run it.

To summarize this section, for Barkin, leadership in unions had a variety of functions. It could articulate the yearnings of union members and turn those desires into a consistent ideology. It could promote that ideology within society to gain a better appreciation for the purposes that unions could play in society. It could also motivate members to a better understanding of that ideology in order to maintain member interest in the union and its future growth. For Barkin, union growth was important not only for its own sake but also for the impact a healthy idealistic union movement could have on all of society.

Acting as a Countervailing Power

In the debate over the ratification of the U.S. Constitution, James Madison made much of the part played in society by factions, what today would be called interest groups. Factions would be able to counteract one another in terms of their influence. Madison wrote at a time when factions were small and widely dispersed, however. He did not face the modern problem of what happens when one faction becomes very large and powerful in its economic control and political influence, as has happened with the business community. To combat that power and influence, other organizations must grow equally strong to act as a countervailing power, to use the term John Kenneth Galbraith has popularized.

Countervailing power develops in opposition to what Galbraith called original power. It comes into being when an organization, usually a business firm, gains original power in the marketplace sufficient to control prices. If that original power goes unchecked, the firm will be able to exercise all the abuses attributed to a monopoly. More typically, that power will be checked by another entity, such as a farmer cooperative, chain store buyer, or labor union. Galbraith put great stock in unions as a countervailing power to the original power of the large modern corporation. He observed, "As a general though not invariable rule one finds the strongest unions in the United States where markets are served by strong corporations."[63]

Galbraith was interested in how unions acted as a countervailing power against business in economic matters, such as wages and prices. Barkin would agree that this was a part of what unions could do for their members. He would add that countering business on a political or social level was also an important function of trade unions. As he described the circumstances, big business had gained great power with few checks on the behavior of executives. That power had to be curtailed. As he put it, "The nation has a right to insist that business carry on its tasks with due regard for the public interest and in a way that is consistent with our democratic ways of life. The union movement can help the nation realize that goal."[64] In his writings, Barkin gave several examples of how unions have and could use their countervailing power for the public good.

His earliest proposal was for unions to take a stand against the monopoly practices of business. In Barkin's view, business geared its production and pricing policies to low break-even points, raising prices when demand was high and cutting production to maintain those high prices when demand declined. This use of administered prices to retain profits had been well established by the Temporary National Economic Committee hearings in the late 1930s. Little had been done about it.

To Barkin this was an important function for unions. He wrote, "The trade-union movement would be well advised to take a serious position in our fight against monopolistic and semi-monopolistic price and production policies." Because this was written just after the UAW failed in its efforts to gain promises of price restraints from GM, Barkin made it clear that more effort was needed. Specifically, he made two proposals. The union movement needed "a centralized agency within the national labor federations which will carry on this fight against specific prices." With all unions fighting price increases, perhaps there was a chance of winning. That chance would also be improved by Barkin's second proposal for "public forums established by government at which consumer complaints can be appraised." Unions could use these forums to present their evidence as to business pricing policies. To encourage unions in rising to this new responsibility, Barkin urged, "The establishment of such consumer price and production policy and practice panels by state and federal government must become a critical plank in the political program of the labor movement."[65]

Barkin felt unions should play a positive role in controlling prices, because he hoped they would be able to help all consumers in society. Speaking about the problems of public utility regulation, Barkin pointed out that "it is as representative of the consumer interest that the entire labor movement participates in the proceedings before regulatory bodies. No group in fact assumes this role more frequently and generally."[66] Barkin would like to see hearings similar to those by regulatory commissions held whenever any business with monopoly power raised its prices. At a later time he would point out the efforts unions had made with regard to health care costs and quality and in advocating legislation and acting as watchdogs for consumer product safety.[67] A system of review such as Barkin envisioned currently operates in Austria.

Another reason for unions to take the lead in fighting price increases by business was to help combat inflation. The fear of inflation has been widespread in our economy, and Barkin's general analysis of inflation is considered in Chapter Six. By the 1950s, much of this fear was being directed at unions by business groups in their "desire to lay the blame for rising prices on the American trade-union movement."[68] By fighting inflation, unions could avoid this blame and perform a positive service for consumers.

One other segment of society that unions could help consisted of older workers. From his early experiences in researching the problems of older workers, Barkin had learned that they were often considered by business to be unemployable. Unions could fight this discrimination in a variety of ways. Within organized plants, the seniority system gave security to older workers by way of long-term employment with a firm. They also fought the arbitrary discharge and compulsory retirement of older workers and helped to establish pension programs when retirement did come. As these practices became common in organized plants, they would be adopted in nonunion sectors as well, as part of a union spillover effect, wherein employers in nonunion firms match union gains to keep their workers from developing an interest in unionizing. In addition, unions lent their support for legislation to improve the overall opportunities for employment of all older workers.[69]

From Barkin's experiences with the TWUA, he could draw on examples of union activities that spilled over into the public interest. One such example relates to the use of charitable trusts as an instrument for corporate control. In the period after World War II, in the New England textile industry there occurred a striking episode wherein textile mills were purchased, run for a few years, and then liquidated by the separate sale of the equipment and real estate. Textron Corporation, under the leadership of Royal Little, was very active in this process.

In one such case—the liquidation of the Nashua Mills of Nashua, New Hampshire—Textron used a tax-exempt charitable trust to make the purchase. The owners of the mill had accumulated large wartime profits, which had gone undistributed because of the high wartime taxes. It was suggested that Textron use its tax-exempt philanthropic fund to make the purchase, which included the retained profits. Textron could use the retained profits to pay off the cost of the mills, while the mill owners through sale of the corporation would convert their profits into a capital gain, taxed at a lower rate. This was a very convenient tax loophole for business, and the use of the fund gave a very handy source of finance.

The case attracted Barkin's attention because it focused sharply on the process of mill liquidation and how tax-exempt institutions were accelerating the process. The closing of the mill was also very unpopular in the local community. Hearings were held in Nashua by the United States Senate, with union officials, including Barkin, testifying. As a result, a bill was passed in Congress amending the law governing tax-exempt institutions and limiting their right to use their funds to purchase corporations.[70]

In another case, the TWUA fought for legislation at the state level in the South, which would require the introduction of air-conditioning in factories. Unionists, reformers, and medical experts had noted the importance of clean air in factory work, especially with reference to reducing dust, humidity, and temperature. These problems were severe in the South, where high humidity and temperature combined to raise the effective temperature, turning a textile mill into a sweatbox, where lint and dust hung heavily in the air. To solve the problem, Barkin assigned Franklin Bishop to write articles on air-conditioning for the TWUA newspaper. Bishop fully researched the topic, talking with building and air-conditioning experts. His findings were printed as a booklet for workers, which included a set of instructions on how to check the temperature and humidity in their mill and offered a model of legislation for forcing management to provide relief.[71]

Management objected to this union interference into how they constructed their mills, even though they eventually installed air-conditioning in the mills. To push them along, the TWUA proposed legislation mandating air-conditioning in mills in Georgia and South Carolina. South Carolina already had such a regulation, so the aim was to strengthen it. The bill passed the lower house, but it was defeated in the state senate. The publicity over the bill helped speed up the use of air-conditioning in South Carolina, however. In Georgia, a model bill was introduced for the same purpose, but with less success. Bishop was scheduled to testify in its favor, but the opposition depicted him as being "employed by Emil Rieve, a Polish Communist."[72] Despite this sad failure, the TWUA did hasten the day when textile mills would attain levels of comfortable temperatures.

As these cases attest, unions can act as a countervailing power for the public good, even when they are acting in their own self-interest. When they gain benefits for their members or fight for them in other ways, there is usually a spillover effect into industries, businesses, and plants that are not unionized. In addition, social legislation sought at the behest of unions will also apply to nonunion members. To the extent that they achieve credit for these actions, unions can project a better image in the eyes of the public. Not that they are always successful or public spirited. Barkin once faulted them in the early 1960s for not taking more of a lead in the civil rights movement, and he called for a Trade-Union Commission for Self-Study to analyze, with the help of outside professionals concerned with the union movement, how unions could react more positively to external conditions.[73] Barkin would prefer that unions take the lead in performing public service and do so out of a spirit of social idealism that seeks to build a better world for all members of society.

Accomplishing Goals

Whether from a spirit of social idealism or through self-interest, unions have met their own institutional objectives, as recent evidence suggests. The "central issue in this life of modern man," Sidney Hillman once observed, is the "quest for security."[74] This was perhaps the hidden meaning in the rapid rise in labor unrest in the 1930s and in the organizational gains that followed from it. During the period of 1940 to 1960, unions and their leaders achieved for their members a degree of security unheard-of before in U.S. labor relations. By the 1950s, industrial workers had been transformed to such a state of well-being that *Fortune* referred to them as typical middle-class consumers. Poverty still remained, and organized labor helped to fight it, becoming especially active during the enactment of the Great Society programs of Lyndon Johnson.[75] As Walter Galenson has aptly written, "Unions are more responsible for the enhanced economic security enjoyed by Americans than is realized."[76]

First, they won the security of recognition by management as rightful bargaining agents for workers and by the public and the legal system as legitimate agents for influencing broad economic decisions. Second, they accomplished a modicum of income security by helping to secure legislation for the minimum wage, to initiate and then liberalize the program of unemployment insurance, and to expand the coverage of Social Security. Third, they began the process of gaining better benefits for workers, especially health insurance, pensions, and paid vacations. To be sure, many of these gains came with the help of an activist federal government, which passed favorable laws for labor during the New Deal and of equal importance, helped labor to consolidate its gains when the country went to war. A portion of labor's gains during World War II were the result of favorable decisions on the part of the War Labor Board,[77] formed in 1942 to adjudicate collective bargaining issues that would have otherwise resulted in a strike. Even though the board did not always give unions what they wanted in terms of wage increases, it did promulgate a policy of membership maintenance that helped to increase membership.[78] Unions were able to build on those gains to make the postwar era one of the most prosperous ones that workers had ever seen.

That era has seemingly come to end for workers, at least during the past decade. Despite this stop, unions have done a respectable job in maintaining the income and security of their members. In a comprehensive survey of the gains unions have accomplished, Profs. Richard Freeman and James Medhoff separate those gains into two broad categories—monopoly gains, related to Barkin's wage goals, and voice gains, comparable to his call for better industrial relations. For them, unions have two aspects: the monopoly side, through which unions use superior bargaining power to gain higher wages for their members, and the voice side, with which unions provide "workers as a group a means for communicating with management."[79] To Freeman and Medhoff, unions have been very successful in using both of these aspects to further the interests of their members.

Monopoly power usually confers on its holders the ability to raise prices above what they would have been under a free market. In the case of unions, Freeman and Medhoff find they have used their monopoly power to gain a differential over the wages of nonunion workers. Although this differential varies depending on the stage of the business cycle and on race, gender, and region of the country, they conclude, "In the 1970s, the archetypical union wage effect was on the order of 20 to 30 percent."[80] In addition, in the area of benefits, they find that members of unions are more prone to securing major benefits than nonunionized workers, about 8 percent more in benefits.[81]

The AFL-CIO reports a similar finding. In 1989, average hourly total compensation for unionized workers was $18.25: $12.11 in wages, $1.77 in legally required benefits, and $4.37 in other benefits. For nonunionized workers, the comparable figures were $10.08 in wages, $1.17 in legally required benefits, and $2.13 in other benefits.[82]

From Barkin's social cost perspective, these gains indicate that unionized workers have been able to come closer to a wage that covers the full social cost of work than have nonunionized workers. Freeman and Medhoff would disagree, for they argue that the higher wages and benefits paid to unionized workers represent a cost to society, albeit a small one, which they estimate at about 0.2–0.4 percent of gross national product. They base this estimate on their belief that higher wages cause firms to use less labor than they would otherwise, leading to economic inefficiency. At the same time, workers who lose their jobs due to unions are forced into other industries, where they are not as efficient and where they earn lower wages.[83]

The Freeman-Medhoff view of union gains from monopoly power must be qualified, however. It is not clear what unions have a monopoly over, as Edward S. Mason once pointed out.[84] Certainly no one would argue that they have a monopoly over the services of their members, when members can change jobs at will. Clark Kerr's observation that unions can only administer the wage at which workers sell their services is worth recalling in this context. It would appear that unions have market power only to some degree that is not easily determined. The market power of unions is difficult to measure because the ultimate impact of negotiations on wages and employment in a particular company depends on the market conditions facing the company's product during the term of the contract; if demand for the product increases, a union may have bargained for higher wages and then seen its membership increase.[85] Wages are only one of the economic factors that influence the demand for labor.

It is also not clear whether union wages are above what would exist in a free market. The absence of union market power does not entail a free market; as Lloyd Reynolds has argued, labor markets are full of friction in terms of labor mobility because workers are reluctant to change employers.[86] This unwillingness to move gives employers some bargaining leverage over workers, even in more-than-one-company towns. As one recent study concludes, "Within bounds set by the labor market, employers can and do set wages for their employees."[87]

There has rarely been a free market wage in labor, so it cannot be determined whether union wages are above or below what would have taken place under a free market. The point is that the market power that a union has is a countervailing power, an ability to counter the bargain that business would impose on nonunion workers. As Barkin once pointed out in the early days of union bargaining, "management . . . maintained that the wages of its employees were a matter which it alone would decide."[88] The strongest statement that can be made about the union wage is that it is more than management would have paid in the absence of the union.

The impact that unions have on nonunion workers is also subject to qualification. The typical free market argument is that unions, by winning higher wages, cause workers to be displaced from unionized industries and to enter nonunionized industries, reducing wages there. Freeman and Medhoff agree that this is possible but argue that firms in nonunionized industries often offer comparable wage packages to their workers just to keep unions out. This impact they find to be even stronger in terms of the benefits offered to workers in nonunionized plants. Moreover, this impact even carries over into the amount of fringe benefits provided white-collar workers.[89]

To Barkin, this is all evidence that unions have contributed greatly to helping all members of society to achieve a full-cost social wage. He once noted this spillover effect of unions on nonunion workers, stating, "In a desire to draw their employees away from unions and to discourage unionism, they have offered higher wages to their workers."[90] He would argue that these higher wages have a benefit to society in terms of a work force that is better fed and housed and in better health. In his view these benefits are good in themselves, but he would have no doubt that they also add to economic efficiency.

Freeman and Medhoff also consider the impact of unions on income distribution. The issue to them is whether unions have a leveling effect by making the distribution of income more equal or whether union gains benefit only unionized workers, creating a small segment of a highly paid elite. Their finding is that unions tend to create more wage equality. A union scale eliminates wage differences within a plant and within an industry; as they put it, "union standard rate policies tend to produce greater similarity across establishments than does an unorganized labor market." In addition, much of the wage difference between union and nonunion workers is due to the characteristics of the workers. Finally, unions are able to close the pay gap between blue-collar and white-collar workers. The result of the union effect is around a 3 percent reduction in wage inequality.[91]

There is another aspect of income distribution, that between labor and capital, that Freeman and Medhoff overlook. Perhaps they agree with Clark Kerr that "functional shares, whether relative or absolute, may be a rather dated way of looking at distribution, at least in the United States."[92] Besides, most studies of functional shares have determined that while the portions of income going to labor and capital may vary in the short run, especially over the business cycle, in the long run they have remained fairly constant. These studies enable Kerr to conclude that the union movement "while it can raise labor's share, it cannot raise it by much."[93]

Still, Freeman and Medhoff investigate the union impact on profits, finding that in general unions reduce profits, but the amount of the reduction varies with the structure of the industry. The more competitive the industry, the lower the unions' impact on profits. The authors conclude that in competitive industries, unions have no effect on profits, and in monopolistic industries, those highly unionized have lower profits.[94] This result would appear to justify Barkin's idea, described earlier, that unions should seek better wages from firms that have a higher degree of market power, so as to gain a share of the higher profits earned by such firms. While it is possible that unions have been successful in gaining some of the monopoly profits of big firms as part of reducing their profits, Freeman and Medhoff point out that some of the reduction in profits results from the lower productivity that they feel unions cause.[95]

The impact of unions on productivity is a controversial issue, and its strength, as Freeman and Medhoff note, depends in part on the quality of industrial relations in a unionized firm. For them, this is where the other aspect of unionism— the voice side—comes into play. When workers have no voice and working conditions are unsatisfactory, then workers' only recourse is to leave. By giving workers a voice, unions provide an option to leaving. Through the introduction of grievance/arbitration systems, workers have a way of getting a fair hearing.

As a result, they quit less frequently. A lower turnover rate has always been a goal of businesses, and for good reason. As Freeman and Medhoff note, reducing turnover can be equal to a 2 percent cut in cost or a 2 percent productivity gain.[96] Freeman and Medhoff, however, do not take into account the many other ways in which collective bargaining can improve productivity, as earlier sections of this chapter have described. Not only do good industrial relations help workers, but also they are good for the economy.

In sum, it would appear that unions have been successful in meeting their own overall objectives of higher pay, good benefits, and better working conditions for their members, although there have been some areas, such as the textile industry, in which the decline in the industry and the level of unionization precluded the possibility of wage gains. In terms of meeting the broader social goals set out by Barkin, the impact of unions is less clear. Unions have fought for social legislation and programs, but they have done so along with other groups, so unions' overall effect cannot be gauged. Besides, there is no standard by which to measure this performance. If the standard used were that raised by liberal intellectuals, it would be easy to agree with the comment by Dunlop and Bok, "Measured by this yardstick, the performance of the unions seems inevitably disappointing."[97]

The standards of liberal intellectuals are not those of workers, union members, or the general population, however. Few attempts have been made to appraise whether union members support the social programs their leaders try to promote. Union leaders cannot always deliver the vote of their members on social issues. Nevertheless, to the extent that their higher wages and benefits have had a positive spillover effect on other workers—nonunionized and white collar—unions have succeeded in moving United States society toward the type of place where workers would want to live. Much of this success has a mixed impact in terms of the public's appreciation of it.

There is public recognition of the benefits that unions generate for workers, but it is tempered by a feeling that they are not as good for the economy as a whole. Surveys taken to establish public opinion of unions usually result in a perspective that might best be called begrudging ambivalence. For example, in surveys asking, "Do you approve or disapprove of trade unions?" from 1937 to 1967, at least 60 percent approved. Other polls taken during the 1940s through the 1960s consistently showed the percentage affirming the right of workers to join unions to be even higher—80–85 percent, and a majority also agreed that unions were necessary for workers to make gains in wages.[98] Those consistently high ratings of unions continued into the 1980s, with unions' retaining an approval rating above 50 percent. The reason for these high ratings, as Seymour Martin Lipsett has concluded, is that "the majority of Americans believe that unions are essential and do more good than harm, that without unions employers would maltreat workers."[99]

At the same time, the public has expressed the opinions that unions should not grow larger, that they are too powerful, and that union leaders cannot be trusted.

In particular, the public dislikes strikes, featherbedding, and other restrictive work practices; this means there is a concern about the negative impact unions can have on productivity. Polls also rated union leaders near the bottom of a list of public officials in terms of whether they were worthy of trust and respect. Even union members, whose support for unions was stronger than that of the general public, did not express an overall confidence in unions and their leaders.[100]

Barkin was well aware of these criticisms. He noted that there had been a great expectation of unions' serving as a countering agent to business as essential to attaining a "more secure, free and equitable society." But, he continued, "Respect for unionism has diminished over the years. People began to speak of 'boss-ridden unions' and picture them as monoliths manipulated by the ambitious, tyrannical and power hungry leader."[101] As noted earlier, he would want leaders to take a more responsible role in society by retaining their social idealism.

As further evidence of public ambivalence toward unions, Lipsett reports that whereas nearly three fourths of those polled in a Harris survey in 1985 agreed that unions help their members to get higher pay and better working conditions, over half did not think workers needed unions to get fair treatment.[102] That this statement took place in the middle of the decade that saw real wages of workers decline should be a source of wonder.

Not a source of wonder is management's perception of unions. The list of managerial grievances against unions could be quite extensive. Fortunately, Bok and Dunlop once reduced it to four major "complaints against unions that would be shared by a majority of high business executives." They are that (1) unions reduce efficiency by hindering new technology and seeking onerous work rules; (2) they try to limit management's flexibility in running a plant or company; (3) they do not understand the impact of market forces on the firm; and (4) they create a climate of distrust between management and labor.[103]

Although Barkin would find these complaints familiar, both those of the public and of management, he would disagree with their validity. Indeed, much of his writing and public speaking, as outlined in this chapter, was intended to dispel these complaints against unions. He would emphasize the positive results of unions, much as Freeman and Medhoff have done, especially in the areas of higher wages and benefits, which enable unionized workers to be better able to meet the social costs of work. To the extent that union spillover effects have accorded that same benefit to nonunion workers, he would consider that another positive aspect of unions. The public, too, has recognized that unions have conferred benefits on their members but has not appreciated the spillover effects they bring. To address this lack of appreciation by the public, unions need to do a better job of presenting their case. Such presentation is not a matter of improved public relations, for the public is too skeptical for that. Rather, it requires revitalization of the spirit of idealism among union leaders and members, such as brought them to a high point of public approval in the dark days of the Great Depression.

Conclusion

In their classic study of unions, *Labor and the American Community*, Derek Bok and John Dunlop list five important socioeconomic functions of collective bargaining: setting workplace rules, helping workers to choose among different forms of compensation, establishing standard rates of compensation, letting each side set its priorities, and continually revising the methods of bargaining.[104] Barkin would agree with this list but would add to it several other important things that unions can do within the confines of collective bargaining. As this chapter has described, he would use collective bargaining to promote cooperation between labor and management, to make adjustments to technical changes that will adversely affect workers, to give labor an impact on wage incentive plans, and to act as a vehicle whereby union leadership can test its ability to lead and to set goals for the rank and file. Outside the sphere of collective bargaining, he would also see unions' providing idealism as a way of reaching progressive social goals and acting as a countervailing power to keep big business in check.

The ability of the union movement to perform these important functions, however, is determined by the state of the industrial relations system of the nation. That system reflects a balancing of the forces of business, labor, and government, and it would appear currently that that balance is unequal. Socially and legally, business has the power and prestige attached to property as a fundamental right in our society. Government has the potential to offset that power, at least legally, but rarely takes the initiative in doing so. Unions remain a countervailing power, responding to the original power of other agents, albeit often weakly.

Barkin would like to see unions grow stronger, so that their power would not be merely countervailing. Rather than passively respond to the actions of other agents, stronger unions would be able to take the initiative in performing all their important functions. Business, government, and the public might protest that stronger unions would be difficult to deal with, but Barkin would disagree. From his perspective, a stronger union would be more secure in its dealing with business, and security would bring about greater responsibility. Leaders of strong unions might be able to negotiate more effectively with management, rather than resort to the posturing that often takes place. They might also be in a better position to avoid much of the interpersonal rivalry within the union that takes so much time away from concerns about the conditions of the members. They eventually might even gain back the social idealism that Barkin feels they have lost. A union that can accomplish its members' goals is in a better position to expand those goals into the arena of social betterment. Increased strength would render unions more useful to workers, to management, and to society.

Pessimists and skeptics may see this call for social idealism by unions as an impossible dream. They would agree with Selig Perlman that only business unionism could survive in the United States, and that unions would always develop into agencies for pursuing the narrow economic interests of their members. A limited scope of interest by unions will, however, place limits on unions' ability to reach into other areas and problems of society.

The scope of union vision need not be so limited, for there is nothing inherent in the union to make it so. As Bruce Laurie has argued, the cautious approach by unions, as typified by the AFL under Gompers, owed as much to forces outside the union movement, especially the hostility of business and government leaders, as it did to a policy of business unionism. He writes, "Workers not only ran up against an arrogant and callous class of industrialists fiercely antipathetic to unions. They also encountered ruthless resistance from state and federal government."[105] Times have changed since those bad old days, but not by enough to satisfy Barkin, as Chapter Seven describes.

Moreover, unions have made gains for their members. As Freeman and Medhoff summarize, "Workers covered by collective bargaining have higher wages, better fringes, better seniority protection, better grievance systems and greater voice in determining the conditions of their employment than do other workers."[106] These gains are in keeping with Barkin's belief that workers should be paid whatever is necessary to provide them with a wage covering the social costs of work and that the primary goal of the union is to make the worker free. These are among the most important conditions and services of unions, and if these advantages of union members were extended to all workers, the result would be a society that workers at all levels would find inviting.

To extend to all members of society the advantages that union workers enjoy would require an extension of unions to all areas of the economy. The only other alternative would be for these gains to come by way of government edict. Barkin would prefer the former, for it would be a more effective way of meeting the needs of specific workers in specific industries operating under a diversity of conditions. He would be willing to see government assistance in accomplishing the establishment of better conditions for all employees. Even in a society in which unions were strong, there would still be a positive role for government to play, which is the topic of the next chapter.

Notes

1. Solomon Barkin, "Wage Policies of Industrial Unions," *Harvard Business Review* (Spring 1941), p. 342.

2. See the results of a survey by the National Association of Manufacturers, as cited in Frank Swaboda, "A Revised Manual for Keeping Out Unions," *Washington Post*, October 28, 1990, p. H3.

3. Solomon Barkin, "Are 'Human Relations' Out of Date?" *Free Labor World* 121 (July 1960), pp. 6–7.

4. Paul D. Staudohar, *The Sports Industry and Collective Bargaining*, 2nd ed. (Ithaca, NY: ILR Press, 1989), p. 5.

5. Sumner Slichter, "Weakness of Individual Bargaining," in E. Wright Bakke, Clark Kerr, and Charles W. Anrod, eds., *Unions, Management and the Public*, 3rd ed. (New York: Harcourt Brace & World, Inc., 1967), pp. 55–57.

6. Solomon Barkin, "Differentiated National Labor Policies to Meet Present Problems," *Labor Law Journal* (September 1962), p. 749.

7. Solomon Barkin, "Collective Bargaining Provides the Best Framework," *Free Labor World* 76 (October 1956), p. 5.

8. Ibid.

9. Solomon Barkin, "Union Strategy in Negotiation," reprinted from *Collective Bargaining Contracts* (Washington, DC: Bureau of National Affairs, 1941), p. 25.

10. Ibid.

11. Ibid., p. 27.

12. Clark Kerr, "Economic Analysis and the Study of Industrial Relations," in Clark Kerr, *Labor Markets and Wage Determination: The Balkanization of Labor Markets and Other Essays* (Berkeley: University of California Press, 1977), p. 207.

13. Barkin, "Wage Policies of Industrial Unions," pp. 345–47.

14. Barkin, "Union Strategy," p. 30.

15. Barkin, "Differentiated National Labor Policies," p. 755.

16. Ibid., p. 754.

17. Barkin, "Are 'Human Relations' Out of Date?" p. 1.

18. William Hartford, untitled manuscript, Chapter Four, p. 27.

19. Solomon Barkin, "Trade-Union Attitudes and Their Effect upon Productivity," in *Industrial Productivity* (Industrial Relations Research Association, 1951), pp. 110–12, 115.

20. Barkin, "Are 'Human Relations' Out of Date?" pp. 2–3.

21. Neil W. Chamberlain, *The Union Challenge to Management Control* (New York: Archon Books, 1967, reprint of 1948 ed.), p. 119.

22. Barkin, "Trade-Union Attitudes," p. 114.

23. Solomon Barkin, "The Technical Engineering Service of an American Trade Union," *International Labor Review* LXI (June 1950), pp. 5–7.

24. George Soule, *Sidney Hillman* (New York: Macmillan Co., 1939), pp. 138–9.

25. Barkin, "Technical Engineering Service," pp. 10–11.

26. Ibid., p. 12.

27. Ibid., pp. 12–13.

28. Solomon Barkin, "Expanding Functions of Union Research," and "The Union Staff Functions and Aims—Continually to Offer Advice," in J. B. S. Hardman and M. Neufeld, eds., *The House of Labor* (Englewood Cliffs, NJ: Prentice-Hall, 1951), pp. 236–7 and 500–502.

29. Solomon Barkin, "Wage Incentive Problems in Arbitration," *Labor Law Journal* (January 1970), p. 25.

30. Solomon Barkin, "Is the Industrial Engineer Finished?" *Manufacturing and Industrial Engineering* (December 1954), p. 34.

31. Solomon Barkin, "Organized Labor's Stake in Industrial Engineering," *Modern Management* (July 1946), p. 54.

32. Solomon Barkin, "Labor Unions and Workers' Rights in Jobs," Chapter 8 of Arthur Kornhauser, Robert Dubin, and Arthur M. Ross, eds., *Industrial Conflict* (New York: McGraw Hill Book Co., 1954), p. 129.

33. Solomon Barkin, "Arbitration Supplants Strikes in Stopping Textile 'Stretchout,' " *Arbitration Journal* 4 (April-July 1940), p. 88.

34. Solomon Barkin, "Work Rules: A Phase of Collective Bargaining," *Labor Law Journal* (May 1961), pp. 376–77.

35. Solomon Barkin, "Productivity Measures in Collective Bargaining," *Rélations Industrielles* 36 (1981), p. 361.

36. Ibid., pp. 363–66.

37. William Hartford, untitled manuscript, Chapter Five.

38. Solomon Barkin, "Handling Work Assignment Changes," *Harvard Business Review* 25 (Summer 1947), pp. 480–81.

39. Solomon Barkin, Franklin G. Bishop, and Sumner Shapiro, "Textile Workers' Job Primer," TWUA Research Department Publication T–113, 1953.

40. Solomon Barkin, "The Benchmark Approach to Production Standards," *Industrial and Labor Relations Review* 10 (January 1957), pp. 222–36.

41. Sumner Slichter, *Union Policies and Industrial Management* (New York: Greenwood Press, 1968), p. 415.

42. Solomon Barkin, "Stimulating Production Through Labor-Management Cooperation," *Daily News Record* (January 28, 1943) (reprint in Barkin archives, no pp. given).

43. Solomon Barkin, "A New Agenda for Labor," *Fortune* LXII (November 1960) (reprint in Barkin archives, no pp. given).

44. Oral History Research Office, "The Reminiscences of Solomon Barkin," Columbia University, 1961, pp. 130–32.

45. Minutes, Columbia University Seminar on Labor, December 12, 1956, pp. 6, 12 (copy in Barkin archives).

46. Columbia Oral History Research Office,, "Reminiscences," pp. 94–96.

47. Solomon Barkin and Albert A. Blum, "Is There a Crisis in the American Trade-Union Movement? The Trade Unionists' Views," *Annals of the American Academy of Political and Social Science* 350 (December 1963), pp. 19–21.

48. Cited in Ben B. Seligman, "Portrait of a Labor Leader," in Ben B. Seligman, *Economics of Dissent* (Chicago: Quadrangle Books, 1968), p. 340.

49. Cited in Lorin Lee Cary, "Middle-Echelon Labor Leaders and the Union-Building Process," in Merl E. Reed, Leslie S. Hough, and Gary M. Fink, eds., *Southern Workers and Their Unions* (Westport, CT: Greenwood Press, 1981), p. 212.

50. Solomon Barkin, "Human Relations in Trade Unions," in Conrad M. Arensburg, Solomon Barkin, W. Ellison Chalmers, Harold L. Wilensky, James C. Worthy, and Barbara D. Dennis, *Research in Industrial Human Relations* (New York: Harper & Bros., 1957), pp. 201–2.

51. Ibid., pp. 201–5.

52. Cary, p. 217.

53. Barkin, "Human Relations in Trade Unions," pp. 201–5.

54. Nelson Lichenstein, "Walter Reuther and the Rise of Labor-Liberation," in Melvin Dubovsky and Warren Van Tine, eds., *Labor Leaders in America* (Urbana and Chicago, IL: University of Illinois Press, 1987), pp. 280–81 and 291–93.

55. Solomon Barkin, "The Trade Union Crisis and Intra-Union Research," reprinted from *Proceedings*, Tenth Annual Meeting of the Industrial Relations Research Association, p. 3.

56. Ibid., p. 211.

57. Solomon Barkin, "New Roads in Industrial Relations," *Personnel Administration* 26 (January-February 1963), pp. 17–18.

58. Richard A. Lester, *As Unions Mature* (Princeton, NJ: Princeton University Press, 1958), p. 65.

59. Columbia Oral History Research Office, "Reminiscences," pp. 128–30.

60. Barkin, "New Roads," p. 17.

61. Barkin, "Human Relations in Trade Unions," p. 212.

62. Solomon Barkin, "The Road to the Future: A Trade-Union Commission for Self-Analysis," *Annals of the American Academy of Political and Social Science* 350 (November 1963), pp. 140–41.

63. John Kenneth Galbraith, *American Capitalism: The Concept of Countervailing Power* (Boston: Houghton Mifflin Co., 1952), pp. 114–15.

64. Solomon Barkin, "Labor Facing Economic, Technological Change," *Labor and Nation*: Timely Papers 1 (Summer 1953), p. 43.

65. Solomon Barkin, "Labor-Government Cooperation as Basis of Sound Price Policy," *Labor and Nation* (May-June 1947), p. 13.

66. Solomon Barkin, "Public Utility Regulation as Viewed by a Labor Economist," address delivered at the Great Lakes Conference of Railroad and Utilities Commissioners, June 24, 1959) (copy in Barkin archives), p. 3.

67. Solomon Barkin, "Trade Unions and Consumerism," *Journal of Economic Issues* VII (June 1973), pp. 317–21.

68. Solomon Barkin, "Economic Policies for a Leader of the Free World," *Daedalus* 88 (November 1959), p. 508.

69. Solomon Barkin, "Union Policies and the Older Worker," *The Aged and Society* (Industrial Relations Research Association, 1950), pp. 75–92.

70. U.S. Senate Subcommittee of the Committee on Interstate and Foreign Commerce, Investigation of Closing of Nashua, New Hampshire, Mills and Operations of Textron, Inc., 80th Congress, Second Session (Washington, DC: U.S. Government Printing Office, 1948); "Regulation of Charitable Trusts," statement by Solomon Barkin before Rhode Island Special Committee on Charitable Trusts, September 21, 1949; "Tax Exemption of Charitable Foundations and Trusts," statement by Solomon Barkin before Congress on behalf of the CIO, February 14, 1950; "Textile Union Asks Denial of Acquired Loss Carryover Unless Business Is Continued," *Journal of Taxation* 8 (May 1955).

71. "For Better Work from Healthier Workers: Air Conditioning in Textile Mills," Textile Workers Union of America, August 1948.

72. Franklin G. Bishop, personal communication with the author.

73. Barkin, "The Road to the Future: A Trade-Union Commission for Self-Analysis," *Annals of the American Academy of Political and Social Science* 350 (November 1963), pp. 136–37.

74. Steve Fraser, "The 'Labor Question,' " in Steven Fraser and Gary Gerstle, eds., *The Rise and Fall of the New Deal Order, 1930–1980* (Princeton, NJ: Princeton University Press, 1989), p. 78.

75. Robert H. Zeiger, *American Workers, American Unions, 1920–1985* (Baltimore: Johns Hopkins University Press, 1986), pp. 138–41, 186.

76. Walter Galenson, "The Historical Role of American Trade Unionism," in Seymour Martin Lipsett, ed., *Unions in Transition* (San Francisco: ICS Press, 1986), p. 40.

77. Joseph G. Rayback, *A History of American Labor* (New York: Free Press, 1966), pp. 378–82.

78. Zeiger, *American Workers*, pp. 87–89.

79. Richard B. Freeman and James L. Medhoff, *What Do Unions Do?* (New York: Basic Books, Inc., 1984), pp. 6–8.

80. Ibid., pp. 43–54.

81. Ibid., p. 66.

82. Shaun Gehan, "Bargaining '90," *AFL-CIO Reviews the Issues*, 1990, data calculated from Bureau of Labor Statistics data depicted on p. 8.

83. Freeman and Medhoff, *What Do Unions Do?* pp. 57–58.

84. Edward S. Mason, "Labor Monopoly and All That," in Bakke, Kerr, and Anrod, eds., pp. 667–72.

85. Arthur M. Ross, "What Is Responsible Wage Policy," in Bakke, Kerr, and Anrod, eds., pp. 533–35.

86. Lloyd Reynolds, "Competitive and Union Forces in the Labor Market," in Bakke, Kerr, and Anrod, eds., 543–50.

87. Erica Groshen, "How Are Wages Determined?" *Economic Commentary*, Federal Reserve Bank of Cleveland, February 15, 1990, p. 4.

88. Solomon Barkin, "Wage Policies of Industrial Unions," *Harvard Business Review* (Spring 1941), p. 343.

89. Freeman and Medhoff, *What Do Unions Do?* pp. 151–57.

90. Barkin, "Wage Policies," p. 342.

91. Freeman and Medhoff, *What Do Unions Do?* pp. 79–93.

92. Clark Kerr, "Labor's Share," in Bakke, Kerr, and Anrod, eds., p. 595.

93. Clark Kerr, "Labor's Income Share and the Labor Movement," in Kerr, *Labor Markets and Wage Determination*, pp. 109, 126.

94. Freeman and Medhoff, *What Do Unions Do?* p. 186.

95. Ibid., pp. 162–80, 184.

96. Ibid., pp. 94–109.

97. Derek C. Bok and John T. Dunlop, *Labor and the American Community* (New York: Simon & Schuster, 1970), p. 33.

98. Ibid., pp. 12–15.

99. Seymour Martin Lipsett, "In the Public Mind," in Seymour Martin Lipsett, ed., *Unions in Transition* (San Francisco: ICS Press, 1986), pp. 299–301.

100. Bok and Dunlop, *Labor and the American Community,* pp. 15–20; Lipsett, "In the Public Mind," pp. 304–13.

101. Solomon Barkin, *The Decline of the Labor Movement and What Can Be Done about It*, a report to the Center for the Study of Democratic Institutions, 1961, p. 27.

102. Lipsett, "In the Public Mind," p. 303.

103. Bok and Dunlop, *Labor and the American Community,* p. 27.

104. Ibid., pp. 222–27.

105. Bruce Laurie, *Artisans into Workers* (New York: Noonday Press, 1989), p. 11.

106. Freeman and Medhoff, p. 136.

6

Coordinated Government Policy

*The word "active" denotes a program of active initiative by society to
anticipate changes and to assist individuals in management and
communities in adjustment. The goal is to make it easier to shift people
to new jobs where they can be more productive and minimize the
traumatic effects of technical and economic change.*

—*Solomon Barkin*

The era of the New Deal remains one of the most intense periods of social
reform and experimentation in U.S. history. During its heyday it appeared that
government would continue to be an active force in initiating programs designed
to promote the general welfare. Since World War II, however, there has been a
conscientious withdrawal away from the specific New Deal programs and approaches and from active government policy in general. In economic affairs, for
example, broad macroeconomic policies have been deemed sufficient to promote
the public welfare, especially if they have been supplemented by the workings of
a free market. This trend toward a passive government policy has been comple-
mented by a supposition that the New Deal was mainly a failure.

To a person of Barkin's vision, however, the failings of the New Deal have
been greatly exaggerated. The problem for him has been a diminution of subsequent experimentation with active government policies. The end of the Roosevelt era saw a departure from pragmatic thinking about social affairs. To some
extent, the policies of the 1930s began to strike liberals under the influence of
later debates as too similar to the statist programs of fascism and communism.
Caught up in a conservative counterattack against the New Deal as part of the
anticommunism of the Cold War period, many liberals and social democrats
recanted their earlier beliefs in an active government, but not Barkin. He felt that
when programs fail, they should be revised. His pragmatic approach entailed
looking for policies that worked, so he regularly devised new methods for initiating government assistance to workers and redesigned and refined them as experi-

ence was gained with their implementation. This chapter traces several of his suggestions for active government policies.

To be sure, Barkin was motivated by his search for justice for workers in the area of social cost allocation. He was especially concerned with the social costs that were being created by rapid technical change and automation. Many intellectuals fear we are moving toward a society wherein all work will be performed by machines, resulting in a superfluous underclass with nothing to do and no source of income. While these fears have yet to come true, there has been the trend, nearly as bad, in which workers displaced by technology and a shrinking manufacturing base in the United States have been compelled to seek jobs in the service sector at lower wages. The problem of the displaced worker is becoming recognized even by mainstream economists and conservative politicians. But what is to be done?

A society that wishes to avoid social upheaval must find ways to ensure that the gains of increased productivity through technical change are distributed fairly to all its members. Workers should be assured higher wages, business should gain improved profits, and consumers should get lower prices. Instead of a smooth adjustment to industrial development, members of the United States economy have experienced a wrenching set of problems that have been part of an ugly process described by the ugly word "deindustrialization." Because the textile industry was the locus for the first phase of deindustrialization, much of Barkin's thinking in terms of government policy was directed at countering the economic destruction caused by it. His active government policy aimed at ameliorating the problem of deindustrialization.

Problem of Deindustrialization

In the past decade, the decline of the manufacturing sector of the U.S. economy has become a topic of concern among economists and politicians. Buffeted by reduced investment—the movement of capital to other sectors—and foreign competition, the manufacturing sector has experienced a decline in terms of employment; even when investment has taken place, it has been in the form of automated production methods, which have served to reduce the need for skilled and unskilled workers in manufacturing. It has been estimated that during the 1970s there was a decline of between 32 and 38 million jobs in the United States due to reduced investment.[1]

The main analysts of deindustrialization, Barry Bluestone and Bennett Harrison, define it as "a widespread, systematic disinvestment in the nation's basic productive capacity."[2] The process of disinvestment is complex, they argue, and involves such elements as rechanneling of investment funds away from manufacturing into other areas of the economy, milking of profits from manufacturing plants into other operations, relocating or selling off of equipment from viable plants, and closing of plants altogether.[3]

Barkin was thoroughly familiar with deindustrialization. As the nation's first mass manufacturing industry, textiles was also the first to undergo deindustrialization. The industry had a marked decline in the 1920s, when it drew a great deal of attention as a sick industry. Stabilization in the 1930s and some recovery in the 1940s seemed to revive the industry for a time, until further decline set in. The process was gradual and attracted much attention, especially that of those such as Barkin who were directly involved with it. The initial impact of deindustrialization falls most directly on workers and their communities. The history of the decline of the textile industry remains to be written, but a brief survey of Barkin's writings can give a glimpse of how it happened.

The first textile mill was built in New England in 1790. By the 1820s, the Waltham system of integrated production had been developed, and mills were being built along the many rivers of New England, since water was the main source of power. The original promoters of the textile industry were Boston merchants, who often acted in concert to control the industry. The industry remained concentrated in New England until 1890, when efforts were started to locate mills in the South, so as to be closer to the raw material of cotton and to diversify and modernize the economy of that region and open up jobs primarily for white workers. Much of the capital to build new plants in the South was from local sources. Industry in New England had to pursue a conservative approach to investment, as much of its stock shares were held in trust funds requiring a steady stream of dividends. In both North and South, the mill town previously described became the common form of organizing the industry.[4]

Starting after the turn of the century, the mills in the South began growing larger due to new construction and horizontal integration. At this time, Northern capital began to move slowly to the South to purchase existing production, reaching about a 14 percent ownership or control share of the textile industry by 1922. Simultaneously, the migration southward of Northern mills accelerated, with 51 mills moving from north to south from 1921 to 1928. In addition, competition from the South led to the scrapping of about 2.5 million Northern spindles.[5] The share of cotton textile spindles located in the South went from 22 percent in 1890 to 57 percent in 1929, with New England's share falling to 39 percent.[6] Low profits in the New England branch spread a feeling of malaise throughout the industry, but individual companies still maintained their dividends. Many firms began a strategy of deciding "to run the mills as long as possible without substantial innovation, pay large dividends, and neither change or liquidate." Ultimately, liquidation became the only recourse.[7]

Throughout the depression, the textile industry suffered from its highly competitive market structure, as prices and wages declined sharply, turning it back into a sick industry. World War II brought a brief era of prosperity to the industry, but in the postwar period, managers and owners discovered that they could gain greater yields by liquidating instead of continuing to operate. In the middle and late forties, the industry showed two trends—increasing concentration through mergers and increasing ownership by Northern interests. By the late 1940s, Barkin noted, "The old pattern of individual ownership of single mills by southern interests no longer prevails. Industrial giants dominate many branches of the industry." These giants had also gained a degree of market power, giving them the ability "to hold up production to prevent a collapse of prices."[8] While they contributed to an era of stability in the industry from 1935 to 1948, none of these trends would be beneficial to labor.

The industry was also hampered by low levels of effort in research and development. Before World War II, textile machinery was produced by New England firms, but because individual mills remained small, they did not have the wherewithal to seek improvements in the machinery they were buying. Later, as industry moved south, mills began purchasing machinery in Europe.[9] In either case, textile companies remained passive recipients of whatever technology machine makers offered them.

Starting in the late 1940s, the textile industry went into decline, even in the Southern branch. From 1947 to 1954, the number of establishments nationwide dropped by about 7 percent; from 1946 to 1956, 660 mills employing 180,000 production workers were liquidated. At the same time, new investment of $4.5 billion increased labor productivity by 47.5 percent. Even with increased productivity, however, industry output remained constant during this time. A part of the failure to increase industry output was due to a loss in the export markets. Employment in the industry fell by 25 percent from 1947 to 1956, from 786,000 to 588,200.[10]

The decline continued into the 1960s. Cumulative investment for modernization from 1946 to 1963 reached $8.3 billion. This modernization was offset by continual plant liquidations, so that the total book value of assets in the industry barely increased. These technological changes eliminated some manufacturing processes, cut the number of workers at each stage of the process, abolished much manual work, automated hand-tying of repair breaks, reduced the attention required of machine monitors, centralized control, and improved the overall layout of the mill. Productivity continued to rise and employment to fall.[11] This period also saw the beginning of an upsurge of imported textile products, which further eroded the industry.

It was clear that by the early 1960s the textile industry was in an era of deindustrialization. Employment in textiles fell, especially in the cotton textile branch of the industry. As one would expect, the TWUA felt the impact very strongly; membership fell by 160,000 between 1951 and 1958. The antiunion views of management in the South continued to hold back growth in membership in the TWUA, while the decline of the Northern branch of the industry cost members in that region. Wage differentials between the two regions became increasingly important, for lower wages in the South held back gains by unionized workers in the North.

Passage of the Fair Labor Standards Act in 1938 had established procedures for setting minimum wages for individual industries. The textile industry was the first to have minimum wages set under the act. The resultant wage increases in the South closed the wage gap between North and South. The gap widened in the early 1950s, but threats of unionization promoted some increases in the South. By the mid 1950s, the Southern textile wage began setting the pattern for the entire industry. As a result, wages in the textile industry remained below those of U.S. industry as a whole and the gap between them widened. The TWUA's twenty-year history of gaining better wages and benefits for its members was at an end.[12]

In the 1980s, the textile industry continued its decline. From 1980 to 1985, 285,000 jobs were lost in apparels and textiles, a 15 percent drop for textiles alone. While average hourly earnings in textiles more than doubled between 1960 and 1980, they were 66 percent of wages in manufacturing in 1980 compared to a 71 percent lag in 1960. Real wages in the textile industry showed an increase from $5.37 in 1960 to $6.33 in 1975; they declined to $5.17 in 1980 before the boom of the 1980s brought them back up to $6.14, still below their levels in the 1970s.[13]

It is easy to place the blame for deindustrialization on unions. In the case of the textile industry, as William Hartford has argued, the conditions of industrial decline were more complicated. Hartford found that in several textile mills in Holyoke, Massachusetts, stockholders preferred to liquidate existing profitable mills to get their money for more lucrative investments rather than reinvest it in textiles. He has also observed that even without a union scale in the North, the wage differential between the North and the South was an important factor in making business decisions to liquidate or relocate. This differential was especially important, because as other areas of the Northeast economy expanded, younger workers pursued options other than textiles, and with unsettled conditions in the industry from constant plant closings, these new members of the work force were probably correct in avoiding jobs in the textile industry. The TWUA tried to counter the declines by negotiating increased worker productivity in return for greater business investment, but such a policy of cooperation with management was to no avail.[14]

Barkin has added another element to the story of the decline of the textile industry: the decline of an entrepreneurial spirit among managers and owners in the textile industry, especially the New England branch. The industry was built, he maintained, by "the enterprising spirit of the original promoters moving their capital from mercantile to industrial pursuits, investing their gains in new mills." Later generations became passive absentee owners, "withdrawing from the operations and shifting the responsibilities to mill treasurers, agents and trust fund administrators. The preeminent concern was with dividend payments and their size."[15] This absentee ownership added to a sense of futility over meeting competition that made it preferable to liquidate rather than fight for survival.

Barkin concluded that the decline of the New England textile industry had little to do with unions or migration south. There was little actual plant relocation, and the wage differentials, which reached modest levels in the postwar period, were inconsequential. Instead, he maintained that after World War II, the managers and owners in the North had simply given up any determined effort to maintain their plants. The realization that they faced a tough problem in modernizing their plants and putting more effort and capital into running them discouraged the corporate boards of textile companies. They took the easy route that had been established earlier and liquidated their plants to get the value of the land and buildings and to resell whatever equipment remained usable. When the going got tough, they sold out, stressing short-term gain over longer-term prospects. This trend has repeated itself often in the U.S. economy in the way that many firms in manufacturing downsize through a similar process of plant closing and liquidation.

As a result, the conditions of decline that existed in the textile industry were duplicated in other manufacturing industries during the 1970s and 1980s, although no one would have believed it at the time when textiles were deindustrializing. Barkin could have observed, as, in the preface of the German edition of *Das Kapital*, Marx did for Germans who did not believe his account of English working conditions, *De te fabula narratur!* (I tell your tale!). Indeed, Barkin concluded that conditions in the textile industry, although unique at the time, could foretell of events in other industries. He wrote, "Experience in the textile industry clearly demonstrates the possibilities of erosion of union influence as a result of contraction in employment and the shift in location of industry to the southern and southwestern states, which are only sparsely organized and where employers are vigorously and openly opposed on a regional basis to the efforts of the unions to establish individual bargaining units."[16]

Barkin did more than act as a prophet of the maxim "Industrial decline, union decline." As this chapter describes, he proposed policies whereby government and unions could take steps to fight that double decline. Unions are often held accountable for the process of deindustrialization, but for Barkin the focal point of the blame has been the big business sector with its power to set administered prices free from the forces of price competition. Because of this power, large firms in concentrated industries have been able to keep the fruits of technical change for themselves and their stockholders, stock speculators, and other financial interests. Free market economists have argued that quasi-market forces will keep these firms in check, while liberal economists, following Galbraith, believe that countervailing forces will challenge the policies of big business.

As noted in previous chapters, Barkin hoped that unions could be a countervailing force in terms of imposing greater social responsibility on business. In an era when unions are in decline, he rightly asked, "As for countervailing powers, they are significant, but who is to assure that they will arise?"[17] In Barkin's experience, for example, his efforts to promote changes in the textile industry often went unaided. Even when he had assistance, it was usually independent of union leadership. Union leaders were too preoccupied with direct activities to be concerned about taking on business in the political arena. Moreover, as the TWUA research department developed sophisticated techniques of analysis and planning, it became difficult to communicate them to union leaders. These problems diminished the ability of unions to provide countervailing power for business. This waning away of union support for social power was especially true in the textile industry, where other unions did little to help the TWUA fight the problems caused by deindustrialization.

In the absence of countervailing forces' emerging as organized groups in society, such as unions, it becomes necessary for government policy makers to devise other programs for a balanced economy that shares the gains of technical change among all its members. Government itself must be prodded, however. In the absence of a powerful, motivated union movement's seeking programs, it fell to behind-the-scenes activists like Barkin to push for government action using whatever political contacts were available. The elements of this chapter are Barkin's suggested policies for government, but it should be understood that in most cases he initiated, developed, and pursued their implementation with government agencies, departments, and legislatures. As always with him, the underlying theme of all the proposed programs was how they could help workers meet the social costs of work.

Planning for Social Costs

The process of technical change, a key ingredient of deindustrialization, creates social costs even if business and labor are compelled to behave as responsibly as Barkin desired. With widespread deindustrialization, however, they would no longer be limited to one industry or area. Finding ways to allocate the burden of these social costs requires actions that exceeded the capabilities of the respective parties in any one industry. Programs designed by public policy makers become necessary.

For example, by the 1960s, automation, as Barkin has described, created an era when "plant abandonment [is] assuming an importance never before experienced in the United States. In the past, problems centered primarily [on] the displacement of individual workers in existing organizations. We are now increasingly concerning ourselves with the issues arising from wholesale displacement."[18] When a few workers are displaced, they may readily find work in their community. With the displacement of large numbers of workers, the entire community becomes distressed. Then displacement becomes a social issue.

Economists would propose a market solution to the problem, arguing that workers should seek better jobs outside their present community. This proposal carries a number of risks for workers. It is not clear how much confidence workers should place in market signals; in the early 1980s, workers in the declining areas of the Northeast were being sent signals to move to the booming area of Houston, a move that by 1986 turned out to have been a tragic error for those who did. Should the workers who followed the lead of the market to Houston move again? Is society willing to impose vagabondage on workers? In that case, workers bear a heavy burden of the social costs of their displacement, with movement to new areas requiring the relinquishment of friends, family, and home. Labor mobility imposes heavy costs on workers.

If they do not care to move, workers can choose to wait for new capital to come into their area and then take advantage of the potentially lower wages or lower taxes that a distressed area must eventually offer. But as Barkin observed, "Economically distressed areas almost invariably take decades to achieve alternate sources of economic viability."[19] Here again, workers bear a heavy social cost for waiting, with few rewards. The main advantage of a market solution to labor displacement would appear to be that markets are impersonal, so there is no one for workers to blame for their plight. If policymakers came up with a program that treated workers as shabbily as the market does, the cries of protest would be heard unto the heavens.

Because Barkin was never convinced of the efficacy of market solutions to labor problems, he proposed a series of government policies to counter the harmful effects of technical change. These policies included maintenance of a high-wage, full-employment economy; a balanced program of tariffs; area redevelopment legislation; and an active manpower policy. Before each of these policies is considered separately, it should be made clear that they are all interconnected. Each supplements the other in a calculated way. Careful thought and planning must go into their formulation. The results of the policies, Barkin argued, would be to improve on the haphazard policies currently in place.

High-Wage, Full-Employment Economy

The Employment Act of 1946 placed on the federal government, especially the executive branch, the responsibility for attaining high growth, high employment, and stable prices in the economy. The act, however, never established how these goals would be accomplished. Since then economic policymakers have followed a variety of Keynesian-inspired programs by promoting monetary and fiscal policies designed to ensure that the economy continues to grow. Most of the debate about the effectiveness of these macroeconomic policies has centered on which one was best for stimulating aggregate demand. It was argued that levels of total consumption and investment demand could be adjusted by credit or tax policies, as supplemented by compensatory government expenditures. Active and timely monetary and fiscal policy would be sufficient to meet the goals of the Employment Act. The Keynesian approach formed the basis for much of the trade union movement's theoretical outlook in economics through the early 1960s, as it developed no framework of its own.

Barkin would agree with Keynesians that recessions were caused by a demand gap. He also believed that the demand gap could be closed by expenditures. For him, the best way to ensure higher consumption demand is through higher wages. From his early days with the TWOC, perhaps under Hillman's influence, he had believed in the "dynamic theory of wages," which held that high wages were a spur for business to develop more productive methods to reduce labor costs in the face of those wages. What held true for a firm was also an appropriate strategy for the entire economy.

In order to lend support to this view, in 1946, Barkin cited the historical pattern of wages and prices in the United States. He demonstrated that prior to the 1930s, wages lagged behind growth in output during the economic upswing (by as much as three years) but were cut immediately at the outset of a recession. As a result, lagging wages tended to be a drag on economic growth during a boom, for they created a wage gap that reduced total demand; wage cuts at the onset of a recession increased that gap just when it needed to be closed. Since the 1930s, Barkin added, wage cuts in recessions had been successfully fought, through the influence of union activities and government policies, with the result that the business cycle had been moderated.[20]

The Keynesian school has been leery of underconsumptionist explanations of the business cycle. To its followers, business cycles are more likely to result from the instability of investment demand as magnified by the multiplier effect. Whenever investment changes, it has a direct impact on workers involved with producing capital goods, but when those workers spend more or less there is an effect on workers in industries supplying consumer goods. Small changes in investment can have larger changes in total demand.

Changes in investment are very likely in a modern economy, especially reductions in investment, because investment opportunities in an advanced economy can peter out if there are no innovations. As Keynes pointed out, only one railroad needs to be built between London and York.[21] During hard times, investment can be postponed, causing greater declines in economic growth. Because there are no inherent limits to consumption on the part of insatiable human beings (beyond the budget constraint) and because much consumption cannot be postponed, aggregate consumption demand is thought of as being highly stable. Because consumption demand is not a volatile factor in the economy, Keynesians have not focused attention on changes in aggregate consumption demand as part of the business cycle.

The logic of the simple Keynesian system also requires a consumption multiplier. Changes in consumption are also magnified throughout the economy, and because consumption is a much larger portion of total demand than is investment, small percentage changes in consumption can be as significant in terms of changes in total gross national product (GNP) as large changes in investment can. Moreover, as incomes grow, the proportion of consumption that can be postponed also increases. In opposition, Keynesians would argue that it is changes in investment that lead to changes in consumption.

Barkin reversed the course of this analysis through application of his dynamic theory of wages. His argument served as a reminder that whereas low wages may impair workers' ability to cover the full social cost of work, even they can postpone areas of consumption. That postponement runs the risk of long-term deprivation of workers, as occurs when consumption levels are maintained through the use of savings set aside for retirement. Low levels of consumption due to low wages or the total loss of income from unemployment may be supplemented through funds provided by the government or by other members of the community through organized charity or direct personal subsidy. These supplements still represent a drag on demand, for the burden of meeting the social costs of labor has merely been shifted.

On the other hand, high wages maintain a high level of demand, which then creates incentives for business to undertake new investment to provide new products. Inventions that result in new products can be relied on to initiate investment demand, but only if consumer demand is high enough to assure business managers that they will be able to sell what they produce. As Veblen once argued, humanity's penchant for emulation alone will maintain high levels of consumption demand, especially if there is sufficient income to make it effectual. Recently, for example, *Business Week* pointed out a study that showed that the 1990 increase in the minimum wage was expected to give a big boost to consumer spending.[22]

High wages give business another incentive for investing, which Barkin deemed important. As pointed out in Chapter Two, high wages impose on business a necessity to find ways to cut costs through changes in production. In themselves, high wages stimulate increased investment, with no upper limit on the amount of possible investment. One railroad from York to London may be sufficient, but that railroad can always be improved. As Barkin put it, "Knowing that wages are rising, management is ever alert to discover or design the new, more efficient course. Our high-wage economy has been a crucial factor in making our employers enterprising."[23] As noted in an earlier chapter, investment and innovation have come slowly in the low-wage service sector.

As a proponent of a high-wage economy, Barkin was concerned about serious side effects that high wages may cause. One way for businesses to respond to high wages may be to cut costs by relocating plants. New investment projects can be combined with movement to areas of lower wages, causing worker displacement. Even more damaging to all workers, high wages can erode the international competitiveness of the U.S. economy as producers from low-wage countries undercut domestic manufacturers. These two side effects are treated in later sections.

The largest concern in terms of the side effects of a high-wage, high-employment economy is inflation. Economists worry about the relationship between unemployment and inflation. During the 1960s, they felt that there was a trade-off between the two, with lower unemployment's bringing about inflation or inflation's being necessary to reduce unemployment. This relationship is referred to as the Phillips Curve. By the 1970s, it was felt that the Phillips Curve was vertical and that attempts to reduce unemployment resulted in accelerating inflation. Devotees of the vertical long-run Phillips Curve would maintain that the high-wage economy could become the high-inflation economy. They hold this to be especially true when unions are able to get high wages or built-in cost-of-living adjustments. A declining number of economists believe in the efficacy of the Phillips Curve argument after the experiences of the 1970s; Barkin never did.

The standard argument that blames unions for inflation is the cost-push model, wherein labor's gain of higher wages is passed on to consumers in the form of higher prices; higher prices in turn bring about a further push by labor for higher wages, and on the cycle goes. Monetary authorities can increase the upward pressure on prices by boosting the money supply and causing demand-pull inflation, thereby easing the process of passing along the wage increases and confirming labor's fears of higher prices. To break this cycle, policymakers must adopt restrictive monetary and fiscal policies that cause enough unemployment to reduce the inflation rate to acceptable levels. Under this argument, full employment is defined as the level of unemployment consistent with zero or low inflation. If the view that high wages cause inflation is accepted, Barkin's proposal for a high-wage, full-employment economy will not get very far.

Do unions cause inflation? Barkin's answer is an unequivocal no. The question of whether unions are responsible for inflation must be answered by considering the extent to which unions have the strength to affect the overall economy, to exercise an influence over pricing decisions, and to impact directly on costs.

Because unions are a very small part of the overall economy in the United States, measurement of their effect on the general level of prices must be performed very carefully. As Richard Freeman argues, the unionized portion of the work force recently existed in industries composing only 25 percent of the costs of producing total GNP. Given that unions had a premium of 9 percent above nonunion wages, Freeman concludes that during 1975–81, the net effect of higher union wages would be "to add 2.3 percentage points to the observed 68-point increase in the GNP deflator."[24] This conclusion must be adjusted for spillovers of the union effect into other labor markets, but as noted in the previous chapter, the net effect of these spillovers is difficult to determine.

It can be argued, for example, that unions achieve higher wages for their members by accepting lower levels of employment in unionized industries. By forcing surplus workers into the nonunionized sector at lower wage levels, unions could be inadvertently causing reductions in some prices because nonunionized industries would have lower labor costs. On the other hand, firms in nonunionized industries may pay their workers higher wages in order to keep them from wanting to join unions. It can also be argued that the key union wage results in higher wages and prices in all industries.

These arguments are beside the point for Barkin in terms of determining whether unions cause inflation. He would agree that many pace-setting unions are concentrated in the oligopolistic sector of the dual economy and that firms in that sector have the ability to pass higher labor costs on to consumers. He does not follow that view to the conclusion that unions cause inflation.

In a moral and legal sense, unions have no proper influence on the pricing policies of industry. In Barkin's words, the union's function "is that of stimulating or conditioning but not that of controlling management's behavior. It is the latter which sets prices." As a result, unions concentrate their negotiation efforts on raising wages to levels they feel a firm can pay, "but the later determination to boost prices to offset or improve on the increase in order to maintain or broaden existing margins is a decision in which the union does not participate in any wise."[25] Moreover, as argued in Chapter Four, unions are hampered in their efforts by a lack of solid accounting data on which to assess the financial ability of the firm to pay increased wages.

In this context, it is worth recalling that in organized labor's major attempt to link its wage demands to pricing policies in 1945–46, GM withstood a lengthy strike to win the point that it alone would decide its pricing policies. The UAW, under the leadership of Walter Reuther, had hoped to give up on self-interested business unionism and pursue a policy that would add to the economic welfare of the entire community by making a corporation justify its price increases.[26] Instead, agreements ultimately reached between GM and the UAW stressed pay increases based on an annual improvement factor, linking wages to productivity gains.

Barkin would agree on the relationship between higher wages and productivity gains but might reverse the logic of cause and effect. In an application of his dynamic theory of wages, he would argue that as long as wage increases can be paid for by productivity gains, prices need not increase. Barkin believed that higher productivity results from a variety of sources, from technical change to improved work application. High wages spur business to search for new methods of production. It is possible that high wages could pull excessive amounts of capital into a particular industry, but in a high-wage economy, they would encourage firms in all industries to expand their capital. In this view, high wages are a spur to future productivity gains, not a reward for past ones.

The dynamic theory of wages was a unique advance in economics made by the trade union movement, but mainstream economists have generally not accepted it, continuing to assume that wage increases must be passed through in higher prices. Reuther was a visible proponent of the dynamic theory of wages, and through his efforts in the 1948 settlement with GM, it was built into the U.S. wage system through the introduction of the annual improvement factor.

The link between productivity and wages remained tenuous for much of industry, however. When he examined the relevant data for the period, Barkin learned that from 1947 to 1956, productivity had increased by 40 percent in manufacturing and by 28 percent in all nonfarm private industries. During the same period, real wages rose by 32 percent in manufacturing. Using this information, he figured that unit labor costs had increased by only 14 percent. When he looked at prices, he discovered that they had gone up by an amount greater than the increase in unit labor costs. For example, wholesale prices for consumer durable goods and producer-finished goods rose by 39 percent during the same period.

As a result of this evidence, Barkin concluded that "(1) prices, particularly those of the manufacturing industries, have risen well beyond the rise in unit cost of labor and (2) real wages in the primary, unionized industries have increased less than the rise in productivity."[27] Wages might no longer be lagging behind aggregate output, but they still seemed to be lagging behind productivity and prices.

Perhaps other forces were at work. Even if high wages are eventually offset by productivity gains, in the short run they can still increase a firm's costs. Barkin maintained that increases in labor costs need not have this effect, because the most important factor in total costs is not really labor costs, but volume of output. As long as firms are able to expand their output to utilize their productive capacity at its fullest, they can spread out their high overhead costs in quantity production, thereby reducing cost per unit. The high demand that results from a high-wage economy should enable them to operate at a point where average fixed costs are low. High wages would also improve feelings of security among workers, making them more amenable to cooperating with management in promoting changes in productivity. Finally, high wages promote a stable work force for the firm that pays them, reducing the costs of training and absenteeism. Because these factors seemed to be falling into place during the period immediately following World War II, Barkin anticipated significant increases in productivity during that period. A high-wage, full-employment economy without the risk of inflation would surely be at hand.[28]

Barkin's thinking on costs was a marked departure from standard economic analysis. Mainstream economists depict the cost per unit of a typical firm as first declining and then rising as production is increased. All unit costs decline at first, in this view, because overhead costs are being spread over more output and because the costs of such variable inputs as labor do not grow as fast as output due to increasing productivity from making effective use of a greater number of workers. Then the point of diminishing returns sets in, brought about by declining productivity from additional workers, so variable costs begin rising faster than output. In the case of labor, this means that unit labor costs will begin rising, and eventually they will rise by enough to offset the decline in overhead costs.

This mainstream position is assailable on many grounds, including the one that it implicitly assumes a definition of capital as a fairly malleable substance. More important, as Richard Lester once suggested, there is evidence that in many manufacturing firms, labor is marked by increasing returns, so that labor costs per unit would decline as production increases, until full capacity is reached.[29] Barkin's position was that the rise in average labor costs would not overwhelm the decline in average overhead costs except at very high levels of output near full capacity. The problem was how to define full capacity.

In Barkin's view, the definition of full capacity related to business's pricing and costing methods. In the oligopolistic sector of the economy, price competition was no longer the order of the day. Big businesses recognized that price competition led to dangerous price wars. To avoid ruinous price wars, they adopted techniques of competition that rely on changes in product design and expensive advertising campaigns to gain new sales. Prices became administered by business on the basis of a straight markup over costs.

In an age of high overhead, however, cost estimates on which to base markup prices are open to managerial discretion. Barkin pinpointed three business practices that distorted the pricing models used by management. First, managers based their price calculations on costs that reflect how much must be spent to replace capital and inventory at current prices, so the prices of final products were automatically inflated upward when these costs were increasing. Second, businesses tended to include in their markup factor an amount sufficient to provide for future expansion through retained earning; in that way, consumers were paying future outlays for capital expansion.[30]

The third pricing technique used by business is more complicated, for it involves the allocation of overhead costs. In order to calculate unit overhead costs so as to develop prices, managers of a firm must choose an expected level of output at which they can be sure of breaking even. Prices are then based on a markup of costs at that level of output. Barkin contended that businesspeople were extremely conservative in estimating break-even points, usually setting them at 50–60 percent of capacity and in a sense marking this level as full capacity. That way they can be sure of minimizing a risk of loss, and if sales increase beyond the break-even point, their profits will improve as unit overhead cost declines without corresponding price reductions. When wages increase, managers could set their break-even point at a higher level of output, offsetting the higher labor costs with lower unit overhead costs. Instead, they raise prices to maintain the break-even point at the same low level. If, as Barkin contended, the payment of high wages also fostered increased demand, firms should be able to expand output above their break-even point and improve their profitability without raising prices.[31] As his research showed, management decided to operate with low break-even points and higher prices. In making these decisions, managers were acting on the basis of sound, conservative business principles, which they and only they were capable of judging.

Barkin did not agree with these principles and condemned managers for refusing to share the responsibility of evolving a progressive balanced economy. Given this refusal by management, labor unions are not in any position to behave responsibly themselves. Any efforts to make unions more responsible in their negotiations with management must focus on how to review the prices and profits of corporations operating in industries in which the competitive forces were weak. Without any public policy that forced those corporations to open their books or to keep them from passing wage increases on to consumers with price increases that might even augment profits, unions could not do more than make wage demands based on the reported profits of employers.

Unions base their demands for higher wages on their perceptions of the ability of their employers to pay them. Price boosts encourage wage demands, for they are seen as a measure of the firm's ability to pay. These wage demands may well set off further price increases, as a reader now familiar with Barkin's argument may see, but those increases will only heighten labor's interest in seeking additional wage gains during the next round of negotiations.

The cycle of wage-and-price increases will continue unless the public takes action that eliminates the increases' inflationary impact. Barkin set forth several strategies for achieving this public input. He called for "Federal and state panels, manned by representatives of business, labor and the consumer, . . . to review complaints on the price and production policies of individual businesses."[32] Similar panels were experimented with under the NRA and during World War II, with some success in the latter case. When they were employed by the NRA, the panels became dominated by business and were ineffectual in checking its aims. Barkin's experience with the construction industry under the NRA convinced him that when unions were strong and government was truly committed to impartial results, the panels could be made effective.

Barkin also proposed the institution of annual labor-management conferences, meetings in which issues such as wages, prices, and productivity could be considered by a broad sector of industry. If they were held annually, Barkin hoped, "management might overcome its reluctance to discuss business policy with union leaders." With a national discussion of these issues transpiring, a more comprehensive overview of the entire situation could happen.[33]

In sum, then, Barkin would favor expansionary monetary and fiscal policies to foster a high-wage, full-employment economy. As long as wages and employment were high, there would be little problem of inadequate consumption demand in the economy, and business would have an incentive to boost its investment spending in efforts to replace high-cost labor with machines. Moreover, he argued, there was no reason for high wages to cause inflation. Indeed, the blame for inflation must always fall on business, which alone has discretion over what prices will be charged. Excessive price increases should be checked by public policy, at which point organized labor could be expected to play a more positive role in combating inflation. Similarly, policies have been applied with good practical results in Austria, which follows a system of price review, and in Germany and Sweden, where annual wage conferences occur.

There was one other strategy for holding down prices that Barkin suggested, and over the long run it was the one that has been used, albeit inadvertently. In 1959 Barkin wrote, "A higher volume of foreign trade has been suggested as the means of counteracting the rising price levels in this country."[34] Barkin agreed that this policy might work, but that it must be used carefully to minimize the social costs of the restructuring of the economy that might ensue. He was sensitive to the need to protect domestic industry, but instead of calling for outright protectionism, he looked for a balanced system of trade policy.

Balanced Trade Policy

The present debate over trade policy continues to be couched in the extreme language of free trade versus protectionism. To free market economists the case is clear: Free trade promotes specialization gains; protection helps only special interests. In this view, free trade enables each country to specialize in producing those products in which it has an advantage compared to other countries and compared to other items it could produce. By specializing in fewer items, industry in all countries would become more efficient, and total output in the world would be greater at lower prices. The gains from such greater output could then be shared through free trade.

The basis for this argument—the principle of comparative advantage—was first devised by David Ricardo in the early nineteenth century. The justification for trade policy is an abstract, theoretical model, with little recourse made to evidence of the advantages of trade, other than estimates of the higher prices that consumers might pay under protectionism. The losses that workers and communities might suffer from free trade rarely enter these social welfare calculations.

Historical evidence in support of free trade is hard to come by, because it has rarely been practiced by any one country and has never been practiced by all countries. Recent anecdotal evidence by President Ronald Reagan, among others, paints a picture that the United States lived in a free trade paradise before passage of the Smoot-Hawley Tariff in 1929 and that we owe our economic success as a nation to our adherence to a policy of free trade. This picture is wrong, however.

In 1890, the United States embarked on an era of large-scale mass production techniques, which have since served it well in terms of output, growth, and employment. Tariffs remained high for the next fifty years—as they had for the previous forty—starting with the McKinley Tariff of 1890 (providing an average tariff rate of 50 percent), the Dingley Tariff Act of 1897 (raising the average level to 60 percent), and the Underwood-Simmons Tariff of 1913 (a reduction in tariff rates to about 25 percent). The Smoot-Hawley Tariff, far from being an aberration from a free trade tradition, was actually the culmination of a 150-year policy of protection in the United States. (It raised tariffs to levels comparable to the McKinley-Dingley rates and increased the number of dutiable items.) As Joseph Schumpeter once characterized the attitude of Americans, they have "consistently supported a policy of protection . . . refusing to listen to what mere economists have to say about it."[35]

The persistence of tariffs as a U.S. trade policy does not mean that the policy was correct, even though the period of high tariffs was also an era of rapid industrialization. Indeed, it would be an interesting project for economic historians adept in the use of "counterfactuals" to describe how the U.S. economy would have fared without them. As an aside, for most of its history, the U.S. government relied on tariff revenues as a key element in its finances. The historical evidence is that the United States favored protection when it had obvious good results and switched to freer trade when that policy seemed to be called for. The United States has never been able to develop a balanced trade policy that imposes tariffs where they are useful and freer trade where they are not.

It was just such a rational trade policy that Barkin sought to promote. Much of his case for balanced trade was based on the textile industry, for which he served as witness in many congressional hearings on tariffs. The case he made was also applicable to other areas of manufacturing. For a variety of reasons, textiles, as the first mass production industry, in both England and the United States, was the first to suffer from the threat of imports. Its conditions contain lessons for other sectors of manufacturing.

The standard arguments in favor of tariffs has been to ensure the survival of both infant industries and industries essential for national defense. In the past decade, new arguments have emerged. Under current trade policy, the United States is committed to GATT (General Agreement on Tariffs and Trade), an international agreement to reduce tariffs through multilateral agreements. Agreements under GATT have not always been easy to attain, however, and much of the trading world retains barriers to imports. As a result, bilateral agreements and regional trading blocs are developing into a two-tier system, with free trade within the bloc and barriers for countries outside the bloc. As part of this new view of trade there has developed a strategic trade theory, which recognizes that large-scale production methods and global oligopolies have vitiated any arguments in favor of free trade. Multinational companies, in some cases aided by the government of their home country, practice price discrimination, more commonly known as dumping, by targeting specific industries in other countries for direct assault.[36] Proponents of strategic trade theory seek U.S. government help for firms injured by this kind of unfair international trade.

Barkin's attitude toward international trade was a precursor to strategic trade theory, and he was certainly willing to use this argument to support his program of balanced trade. In the early 1960s he went further than strategic theorists by laying the foundation of his brief for tariffs on the issue of social costs.

Suppose that in an effort to protect the environment, laws are passed in one country requiring all producers in an industry to install pollution control devices. As a result, all firms are forced to bear the costs of the devices in a like manner, so no firm gains a competitive advantage by ignoring the cost of its polluting the environment. However, pollution costs will not be imposed on foreign producers, whose countries are not protective of their own environment. Foreign producers will gain a cost advantage over domestic producers, and there is no way to impose the pollution costs on them directly. Therefore, domestic producers must be given redress, through protection, deregulation, or subsidy. Free trade and a reliance on market forces do not permit any of these policies to be used. The social costs argument makes it justifiable to levy a tariff on imports to ensure that their prices reflect the payment of the full social costs of production.

Barkin extended this argument to include the social costs of labor. If, as a result of collective bargaining or legislation, workers in the United States, or any other country, were being paid a full social cost wage, countries whose industries did not pay their workers the same wage would have a cost advantage. As with the pollution example, a way must be found to offset this cost advantage. As Barkin stated the case,

> The social and human costs in some countries, particularly the underdeveloped ones, are now fully borne by the workers. In others they have been substantially shifted to the community through social security and other measures. In the United States we have transferred many of them to the government or to individual enterprises (through employee benefit plans). Prices in the first group of countries do not include most of these costs.[37]

Under the labor approach to social costs, the price of goods should include the social costs of unemployment, sickness, retirement, conservation efforts, and so on. Although unions can impose these costs on producers in the domestic economy, they cannot affect foreign producers. Social costs should not be ignored in trade negotiations. At a minimum, Barkin argued, "total domestic costs and the effects of international trade must be taken account of in the determination of comparative advantage. And as the present price system does not allow for them, they must be added through direct imposition or at least as calculations for the determination of real advantage and cost in the formulation of policy."[38]

In the case of the textile industry, the international aspects of social costs were clear. As Barkin wrote, "There is no natural advantage which any country possessed" in textiles. The raw materials could be readily grown, imported, or made synthetically; the technology was easy to replicate; and few skill demands were made on workers. The only advantage an underdeveloped country had in textile production was in labor costs.[39] These advantages were substantial, as Barkin noted; in the early 1960s, Barkin found money wages in the United States to be about ten times those in Japan and twenty-three times those in Taiwan.[40] But, he maintained, these advantages were temporary. As industrialization progressed in those countries, the workers in them would surely win wage increases and hour reductions.

In the meantime, entire industries and regions in the United States would suffer curtailment or elimination. This was especially true in the textile industry, as Barkin persistently made clear.[41] The result of free trade in textiles would be the displacement of workers from that industry, with all the social costs attached to maintaining them. These costs should also be considered in determining trade policy. As Barkin put it, "The absence of guarantees of full employment and arrangements for protection of persons affected by these arrangements must of course make all persons cautious about the adjustments which are made."[42]

Here is the situation as Barkin might have described it. A domestic industry, paying the full social costs of its operations, is suddenly confronted by competition from imports produced in countries whose only advantage comes from its firms' not paying their full share of social costs. Under free trade, the domestic industry will suffer and workers will be laid off; attempts to meet the competition through improved efficiency will create additional layoffs. The gains from trade may more than compensate for the social costs of the displaced workers, but there is no mechanism for having consumers share those gains with workers.

The foreign competition will continue to improve its efficiency, so that when its workers eventually gain wage-and-benefit increases, these will be offset by lower costs from improved efficiency. The short-term labor cost advantage may translate into a long-term comparative advantage. For example, in auto production, Japan had no advantage in productivity in 1960; Japanese auto producers simply had lower wages. By 1980, the advantage was in productivity, too. To combat this loss of competitiveness in international trade, mature industries can be granted temporary protection to give them time to adjust to the labor cost disadvantage from which they are suffering.

This temporary protection carries an implied responsibility for management in those industries to take measures to improve efficiency. It is questionable whether management will live up to this responsibility. Barkin doubted that it would and opposed protectionism that guaranteed the status quo of entrenched domestic power groups. Any realistic trade union leader "must balance his demands for temporary protection with an insistence that management aim at strengthening its long-run competitive position in order to enable it to hold or expand its domestic market."[43] As applied in the United States, protectionism has been a blanket policy provided for particular industries with no assurance that remedial measures will take place.

Barkin preferred a trade policy that was more carefully thought out, with criteria established for the use of tariffs. Moreover, the policy should be negotiated with other countries to ensure that trade is fair. In the case of the cost advantages that accrued to countries that did not meet the full social costs of labor, he maintained, "Access to the American market should be founded on compliance with minimum standards described and adopted by the International Labor Office."[44] Since this compliance was not directly enforceable by unions in the United States, negotiators should make sure that it is given full consideration in any trade agreement.

The textile industry affords a ready example of how such an agreement might work. Because of the ease with which the industry can be taken up, many less

developed countries (LDCs) find it an excellent starting point for industrialization. In using this strategy, they follow the example set by U.S. manufacturers, who obtained the technology for textile production from England. The
huge U.S. domestic market provided a source for rapid expansion of the
industry, which had spillover effects on other industries such as machine
tools and apparel. The textile industry led the way to our advanced mass
production economy.

In recent times, the LDCs added a twist to this approach to development by
using the textile industry for export-led growth. The costs of this growth are
often imposed on U.S. workers. Because they can charge low prices due to
low-wage labor, firms in LDCs are able to gain a foothold in the U.S. market. By
encouraging this behavior, governments in LDCs are able to fuel their countries'
economic development. One indication of whether labor policies in LDCs are
fair would be to see if workers in those countries were able to purchase the
textiles they produce. When workers overseas are paid wages so low they cannot
attain a decent standard of living, there is every indication of unfair competition.
Because this unfair competition is disruptive of existing industries, if LDCs are
determined to pursue export-led growth, they should at least be encouraged to
start up industries with new products and not enter into competition with older
established industries.

Pursuit of these policies requires that the protected industry in the United
States be progressive in its pricing and productivity efforts. In the textile industry, Barkin argued, there was sufficient competition to encourage low prices and
the continued increase in productivity through technical change. Protection
would have no adverse effects in terms of pricing in this industry.[45]

One special policy affecting the textile industry, however, was government
price supports for raw cotton and wool producers. Barkin noted that cotton prices
in the United States were five to seven cents higher than the world price and that
the government itself was selling surplus cotton to overseas producers at the
world price. This was putting U.S. producers at a great cost disadvantage.[46]
Indeed, Barkin uncovered a very curious policy trap. He observed, "We have
been financing the export of raw cotton to Japan. Now in order to permit that
country to pay, we are being urged to permit the Japanese to displace American
textile products so as to provide them with dollar exchange to repay in part the
cost of the cotton we sent them. The result is that we are asking the cotton textile
industry to be sacrificed for the large raw cotton growers with little ultimate
benefit to them."[47]

Such an occurrence indicates a policy that has not been carefully planned.
That, of course, was Barkin's ultimate objective—a planned trade policy. The
result of a planned policy should not be outright protection, but protection that
has a positive effect. He called for absolute minima of production to be safe-
guarded against foreign competition, such as the quota levels that were negotiated in textiles. He also realized that all industries would not be affected equally

by tariffs. While recognizing that there was sufficient competition in most branches of the textile industry to prevent firms from using a tariff barrier as a shield behind which to protect high prices, he understood that some branches of the textile industry as well as other industries in manufacturing had the power to set administered prices.

A tariff on their products would only encourage firms with this power to raise those prices. To offset that power, Barkin proposed that any trade policy must include the qualification that "no domestic industry should be granted this benefit if the prices for its products have consistently risen at a relatively higher rate than the rise in the general level of prices of products in the same group."[48] One wonders how the automobile industry would have fared under these criteria in the past decade, when its market share declined, due in part to high prices, even though it had the protection of voluntary import restraints as accepted by Japanese automakers.

The textile industry did gain some protection in no small measure due to Barkin's energy. Barkin began making proposals for a trade policy that would protect both domestic and overseas workers—by striking a balance between free trade and protectionism—offering a proposal before the House Ways and Means Committee in 1957. For the next four years, he presented his plans for balanced trade before a variety of groups, but management in the textile industry disparaged his proposals, not understanding the benefits management would gain from them. In 1960, his plan was given formal support by the International Textile Workers' Conference in Copenhagen and informal approval by the secretary-general for GATT. In a January 1961 Senate hearing, Barkin was criticized for not supporting outright protection.

During the 1960 campaign, John F. Kennedy promised Southern Democrats that he would help their branch of the textile industry. As a New Englander, Kennedy had knowledge of problems in the Northern branch and a motive to help it. His staff began to work on the problem and invited Barkin to give his views. These efforts culminated in a tariff negotiating round in Geneva in 1961, with the U.S. negotiating team headed by Michael Blumenthal (later secretary of the treasury under Carter) and joined by (now senator) Daniel P. Moynihan and Barkin. After these negotiations, a temporary arrangement was made in 1961. In 1962, the U.S. government helped to set up the Long-Term Arrangement on cotton textiles, which put limits on imports by establishing quotas with a goal of limiting import growth to 5 percent a year. The Multifiber Arrangement, set up in 1974 and renewed in 1978, 1982, and 1986, permitted only a small annual growth in textile imports to be negotiated bilaterally when an importing country's industry was disrupted. Thus textile imports have been reduced from what they would have been.[49]

Many of these agreements are still in effect, and they have prevented a complete collapse of the United States textile industry. By the late 1980s, there were thirty-seven bilateral agreements in textiles and apparel, with 1,300 different quotas imposed on textile items. Tariff rates on textiles averaged 18 percent compared to about 4 percent for all imports for 1982–85.[50] In the 1990 Uruguay round of trade negotiations, however, the multifiber agreement was on the table for cancellation, and its continuation is doubtful.

Most mainstream economists would see this use of tariffs as a misfortune. Dominick Salvatore, for example, sees the issue of tariffs as "the fact that small and well organized groups in a nation stand to benefit greatly by protectionist measures at the expense of the mass of 'silent' consumers."[51] Free traders continually tried to eliminate these agreements, succeeding in 1990 with President Bush's veto of textile trade legislation. There are economists who would disagree with this "fact," however.

In an unconventional view of foreign trade, for example, John Eatwell argues that free trade can be detrimental in a world where most countries restrict trade. He also notes that industries that have been hurt by trade start on a downward spiral of lower productivity gains, due to their weakened condition, and that these spill over into other industries via the multiplier effect. England, he concludes, declined in just this way, especially because a special interest group of international bankers, who gained from a maximum amount of international trade, successfully resisted tariffs.[52] Keynes made a similar argument when he pointed out that the free trade argument applied only under conditions of full employment; with unemployment and labor immobility, trade could cause serious job disruptions.[53]

Eatwell would want to see England pursue a more effective trade policy, including protectionism. He would be in agreement with the AFL-CIO, which, on discovering the loss of nearly a million jobs to imports over the previous five years, in 1971 began to push for protection of its unionized industries.[54]

Whenever unfair trade practices exist, mainstream economists would counsel that those practices be handled through negotiations. Trade restrictions might be useful for reducing the impact of transitional adjustments on workers' lives, but even here it is felt that direct subsidies would be a better policy.[55]

In the area of determining trade policy, Barkin tried to steer trade unions toward a middle ground between protectionism and free trade. To him, trade unionists could not defend protection for the economic status quo. The problem with protectionism is that it proceeds willy-nilly, without regard to who really needs it. Moreover, it does not place any obligation on those industries that were protected. In sum, protectionism was misguided because it was not well thought out. In its place Barkin would put a planned trade policy centered on the ability of industries and workers to meet the social costs that were incurred in production. As he remarked, "The criterion of trade union policy is that people—not production—must be protected."[56]

To some extent Barkin's view on trade has become a part of U.S. policy. Under the Trade and Tariff Act of 1984, worker-rights provisions were made a part of a generalized trade agreement with over 100 developing countries. As part of the Omnibus Trade Act of 1988, countries that gain a comparative advantage through abridging workers' rights are considered to be practicing unfair trade. The recent conservative administrations of Ronald Reagan and George Bush have not been very effective in applying these laws, however.[57]

Even with policies like these in place and effectively enforced, changes in the overall structure of the economy are to be expected. By borrowing a page from mainstream economists on the usefulness of subsidies to counteract disruptions from foreign trade, Barkin formulated policies that would facilitate the adjustment that workers underwent in making these changes. Trade policies must be supplemented with programs that would facilitate the adjustment of industry, people, and communities to impending change. If workers were assured that they would not bear solely by themselves the social costs of being displaced, they might be more supportive of free trade.

This view has become more common in the United States in recent years. An editorial in *Business Week* echoes Barkin's concerns about the disruptive features of trade by observing "The United States will pay an unacceptably high social cost for the gains from freer trade if displaced workers end up on unemployment or in low-skill, low-productivity jobs." It continued by pointing out that without some program to support these workers, free trade proposals would be defeated in Congress, "and rightly so."[58] Barkin would agree. He held high hopes that supplementary policies would be adopted. Referring to one example of such a policy, he wrote, in 1962, "The adoption of the Area Redevelopment Act has reduced the urgency of special laws to aid communities adversely affected by imports."[59] He had every reason to be hopeful, for he had been one of the chief architects of the Area Redevelopment legislation and had pushed for it as part of an overall strategy of shifting social costs of displacement from the individual worker to the community at large.

Area Redevelopment Policy

In 1961, President John F. Kennedy signed into law the Area Redevelopment Act as a means of providing new employment opportunities in economically distressed areas. Because of his longtime interest in and active support and promotion of such legislation, Barkin was given one of the pens used by President Kennedy in signing the law. Passage of the act had required a hard fight on Barkin's part, for Congress had passed similar legislation in the past, only to see it vetoed by President Dwight Eisenhower.

The need for redevelopment legislation had long been obvious to Barkin. Because of the decline and relocation that had taken place in the textile industry, he was well aware of worker displacement from both technological change and foreign competition. He had seen whole communities that had been dependent on employment in the textile industry suffer the consequences of high levels of unemployment. The problems these communities faced were too serious to await market solutions; adequate policy measures to help them were needed. As Barkin saw the issue, "It is not enough to extend unemployment insurance even though it is essential to maintain people. The challenge is to redesign the area and create new locational advantages to substitute for those which had formerly attracted the basic industry."[60] To meet this challenge, he had lobbied Congress to pass the Area Redevelopment Act as one way of giving local communities the funds for planning and redevelopment as well as retraining workers.

The push for an area redevelopment program was begun by Barkin in 1954, as declines in war orders began to reveal the weaknesses of the textile industry. As Sar Levitan described the effort, along with William L. Batt Jr., Barkin "was a co-organizer of the Area Employment Expansion Commission, a lobbying group established in 1956 to encourage the passage of the legislation."[61] Sen. Paul Douglas of Illinois, who was also a respected economist, was interested in this type of program because it would apply to the distressed coal-mining communities of his state. Barkin further enlisted the assistance of John Edelman, legislative representative of the TWUA, who proved vital in organizing other union lobbyists into what became the critical force for promoting the area redevelopment program. Batt served by organizing political contacts and support. The program was unique at the time in calling for local planning bodies, public works to rebuild distressed areas, and training for workers in anticipation of later manpower programs.

A redevelopment program was especially needed because firms in a private enterprise system rarely accepted any obligations with regard to assisting displaced workers. In some collective bargaining agreements, unions had been able to provide for the transfer of redundant workers to other plants in the area and to require early vesting of pensions to help older displaced workers to survive. These work rules imposed a share of the social costs of displacement onto firms, in some cases causing management to reconsider its relocation plans. The rules had limited application when the process of automation caused a wholesale obsolescence of skills and plants in a particular region.

Attempts by individual communities to reestablish themselves through the formation of local development councils were not likely to accomplish much. Because many communities in the country had started up a development council in trying to attract industry, they actively competed with each other in terms of the generosity of the inducements they offered to lure business into their area. Distressed areas were especially handicapped in the type of inducements they could offer in the competition, because they lacked the financial resources and stability required to provide tax breaks and training programs for prospective employers. In addition, development councils were usually dominated by local businesspeople who had their own interests to protect. As Barkin told Congress, from his own experience he had concluded that in textile communities, "the dominant textile interests have very often resisted new industry from coming into their community."[62] Dominant business interests might prefer to see a high level of unemployment in their community as a way of keeping local wage levels low.

Barkin wanted to avoid similar business domination of the national area redevelopment program. He recommended to the legislators drafting the act that administration of the program should not be placed under the Department of Commerce. As he saw it, "This agency seeks to promote general business and commercial activities. . . . It has not specialized in depressed areas as such." Barkin believed that the department and its secretary (Luther Hodges) were opposed to federal assistance programs and wanted to continue to rely on local business efforts. Barkin felt that the department had been unduly "influenced by its Business Advisory Committee which is dominated by big business, and the primary spokesman for American business, N.A.M. and U.S. Chamber of Commerce. These organizations and groups have not been sympathetic to area redevelopment programs."[63]

Instead of housing the area redevelopment program in the commerce department, Barkin proposed that an independent administrator be chosen to oversee the program. Believing that the person responsible for the program had to have sufficient stature to ensure the cooperation of the many government agencies that would be involved in the program, he even suggested at one point that the person in charge of the program should be given cabinet-level status.[64]

To ensure that the Area Redevelopment Agency consider broad community interests in formulating its plans, Barkin also recommended inclusion in the act of a citizens' advisory committee to guide the redevelopment agency. The purpose of the advisory committee would be to keep the program from becoming enmeshed in the federal government bureaucracy. As Barkin stated his case, "There is one provision in this bill which must be made vital, namely the 25-man citizens' committee. When this provision was written into the bill, we wanted a public agency of citizens who would be sitting on the tail of that Administrator and making him perform and execute and do this job." It was also important that the citizens' committee be broadly based to provide a spectrum of input from all sectors of the community. Barkin added, "But this requires the coordination of people of the highest caliber in every walk of life, of planners, of practitioners, of engineers, of industrialists, of civic officials, of labor people, everybody there is in the community, and not one walk of life."[65]

The most important task of the program and its administrator consisted of designating the areas that needed redevelopment programs. Although the bill provided minimum conditions for that designation, the administrator would have to exercise a great deal of judgment in making the final selections. Next, the administrator had the responsibility of coordinating all government agencies concerned with any particular project, as well as providing guidance for the citizens' advisory committee. The administrator also had to deal with specific industries that were causing high levels of unemployment and help them to devise redevelopment activities. Finally, technical assistance had to be made available to local communities in preparing their own programs for development and in applying for assistance for financing the program.[66]

The actual membership of the citizens' advisory committee formed under the act consisted of a healthy cross section of businesspeople, labor leaders, local politicians, and academics, with Barkin included as one of the labor representatives. As a member of the committee, he was able to try to influence the activities of the program and to evaluate their effectiveness.

It has become popular recently to brand all the social programs of the 1960s as ineffective, so a full analysis of one of the first such programs, Area Redevelopment, is useful. Unfortunately, such as task is beyond the scope of this work. Levitan has provided such an analysis and given a succinct statement of the issues Barkin faced. He wrote, "Solomon Barkin, a member of the National Public Advisory Committee, was the strongest proponent of A.R.A. assistance for economic planning. A.R.A. officials sympathized with this position, but had strong reservations about assuming responsibility that should normally be handled by the communities." These officials favored having planning rise from local areas, despite Barkin's pointing out that many areas had no leadership capable of initiating planning.[67]

In a review of Levitan's evaluation of the Area Redevelopment Administration, Barkin noted three areas where the administration faltered. First, the administrative body had been set up with no clear underlying philosophy and strategy, partly because the act itself had never stated such issues clearly. It became too bureaucratized and the administrator became more responsive to outside pressures than to the advisory committee. Second, the agency never developed the expertise to evaluate or improve local programs. Third, the lack of expertise was exacerbated by the failure of academic experts in the discipline of regional development to add their own knowledge to the program. As Barkin lamented, "No individual or collective sense of responsibility to this legislation had yet been developed among those students in an area which is central to their own interests."[68]

Barkin identified several aspects of the area redevelopment program that required further study. One issue was how the program should allocate its resources: Should resources be concentrated in single areas or be spread over as many areas as possible? Obviously some areas were so poorly developed that the costs of helping them were prohibitively high. Other areas needed no help. What kind of assistance should go to the many communities in the middle?

This issue was further complicated because less developed areas would not show immediate results from their programs. Administrators and community leaders might become discouraged when quick results were not obtained and blame the program itself. Areas with inadequate infrastructure were especially disadvantaged in terms of getting favorable results quickly. Plans had to conform with each area's special needs.

The differing levels of entrepreneurial talent in each area could alter the prospects for a successful program. As Barkin noted, "the cultivation of entrepreneurship within communities is quite important in determining the ultimate success of a community in redeveloping."[69] Programs in the United States that had tried to tap local enterprise had often been unrewarding, because many times the local community hoped for outside help, not seeking ways to promote and encourage local enterprises.

In resolving the issue of determining which areas to help, Barkin counseled that a redevelopment agency itself had to become entrepreneurial. He advised, "Economic growth in all cases requires gambling with public funds in the long term interest of the country. There is no sure formula. Choice must be made and it is well that [alternative] approaches are pursued."[70]

Communities in rural areas or areas with inadequate infrastructure required special consideration in formulating redevelopment plans. Because of modern transportation and communications systems, very few areas have locational advantages. In determining where to locate a plant, businesses have a wide range of choices that are economically feasible. The final decision may depend on nothing more than the whimsical tastes of an individual entrepreneur. Although entrepreneurs might be expected to be drawn to economically distressed areas because of the low labor costs that exist there, there is also evidence that they will prefer to locate in areas with a well-established infrastructure and the presence of social and cultural amenities. As Barkin described locational choice, "In the free market operations . . . the tendency is for entrepreneurs to follow the patterns followed previously and settle in places where other competitors are found. The resistance to business daring in the field of business location is as strong, if not stronger, than in many other fields of business decision making."[71] Especially hard-hit areas find it difficult to attract new industry.

Another way of fostering area redevelopment that Barkin found important was to make an effort to revitalize existing industries by expanding their product lines and markets. Drawing his lessons from the textile industry, Barkin proposed that a Textile Development Agency be initiated, with government funds, to contribute basic research for the textile industry. The textile industry had been unable to fund such an industry research unit on its own, because individual firms that survived the industry's decline felt that they would do better within a reduced arena of competition. Instead, the industry was being hit by competition from abroad and from domestic manufacturers of synthetic fibers.[72]

Not only were textile firms complacent about this competition, but also they did not have adequate resources to conduct the research to combat it. Barkin cited estimates that while all of U.S. industry was spending 2 percent of gross sales on research, the textile industry spent 0.1 percent and that out of 4,000 textile firms in the country, about 12 had real research programs. University research centers for the textile industry existed, but they were underfunded.

Even more important, most of the research went into finding better ways to produce existing products. A problem, Barkin stated, was that "nowhere is the emphasis placed on basic research which can open new vistas, new markets or truly new products for the textile industry."[73]

The textile industry was also woefully behind the times in marketing. Mills continued to produce what they had been selling until unsold inventories piled up, when they would then look for something new to produce. No marketing research was undertaken to anticipate demand, and no motivational research into what new needs might be filled existed. It was difficult for individual firms to contribute basic research, but because of what Barkin called the "rugged individualism" of mill owners, no cooperative efforts could be fashioned to produce industry-wide research.[74]

To provide or support the basic research that the textile industry desperately needed, Barkin proposed the formation of a government-funded research agency. This type of agency was not totally unusual for the United States. For years, the Department of Agriculture has furnished a similar service for farmers, who are incapable of doing it themselves for reasons similar to those found in the textile industry. Congress supplied funds for a study of the possibilities for a textile research agency. The study was undertaken by an ad hoc committee set up by the National Research Council of the National Academy of Sciences. Barkin served on the committee, and its report supported his position when it recommended in favor of the agency. It also endorsed aid for graduate education and research in textiles, expansion of the government's information gathering and reporting on worldwide textile developments, and grants to universities and individuals for writing textbooks.

To implement these proposals, the committee advocated a National Institute for Textile Research under the direction of the National Research Council and an Office of Textile Industry Research in the Department of Commerce.[75] Its report indicated the need for greater education and information in the textile industry. One project for partially automating garment production was funded but did not see any impact until the 1980s, after the government's textile research effort had been supplanted by the Textile/Clothing Technology Corporation. This new organization was supported by government, business, and the Amalgamated Clothing and Textile Workers Union of America. A Textile Information Users Council was also established to set up a network of data on the textile industry to be available for all industry members.[76]

The proposals were never seriously supported by the government, however. At the time they were being made, 1962, the Kennedy Administration was offering its own seven-point program for aiding the textile industry, including the tariff negotiations previously described. While the proposal for a textile research agency might have been overlooked by proponents of the seven-point plan, Barkin believed there was industry resistance to the research agency. Textile managers on the ad hoc committee were from large firms that could pursue their own research and that opposed government-subsidized research for private business, especially their competitors.

Despite setbacks, it was clear to Barkin that something had to be done to redress the pockets of uneven development produced in the modern economy. In the discussion over area redevelopment programs, he stressed the need for careful planning as part of the overall process and constantly criticized those plans that were drawn up as being pro forma in character and not blueprints for an active program. He also emphasized that it was necessary to supervise the planning process and monitor the implementation of the plans, relying on citizens' advisory committees to accomplish this. Moreover, he recommended strongly that when area redevelopment plans were insufficient for new firms to be enticed into a distressed area, programs in those areas had to be supplemented by an active manpower policy.

Active Manpower Policy

In a market economy, workers are supposed to respond to incentives, in terms of wages and employment prospects, by moving to those areas and industries where prospects for employment at higher wages are better. Labor markets are marked by a great deal of friction that hinders the mobility of workers, however. This friction arises from such diverse causes as poor information, difficult search processes, and high transportation expenses. Because workers themselves bear the burden and risk of overcoming these costs, they are likely to try to avoid them for as long as possible.

An active manpower policy recognizes these frictions and tries to find ways to overcome them. Under such a policy, as Barkin described it in 1963, government, communities, and industry cooperate in "a program of active initiative by society to anticipate changes and assist individuals, management and communities in adjustment. The goal is to make it easier to shift people to new jobs where they can be more productive and minimize the traumatic effects of technical and economic change."[77]

The need for manpower policy has come from the new requirements of automated industry. When automation and technical change proceed, they impose a variety of requirements on the work force in terms of maintaining skill flexibility. As Barkin understood, the modern area of high technology was putting increasing demands on workers to be able to adapt to new circumstances. Few workers would have a single career for their lifetime. As they were compelled to change careers, they would find that their formal education was inadequate to provide the knowledge and skills required of a career change. Because individuals alone are unable to gain knowledge or skills, it is up to social policy makers to create programs to assist them. These programs would also help to prevent worker opposition to change.

The obvious need is for training programs, through the educational system and from on-the-job training. Firms themselves, as noted in an earlier chapter, should undertake internal personnel relations programs to provide for transfer of redundant employees to other areas of the firm, job redesign and training programs to fit them to the new work environment, and aids to geographical transfer to help displaced workers move to other plants operated by the firm.

Where areas are distressed and firms cannot provide this assistance, government policies may be necessary. Not only must workers be helped with moving expenses, but also they must be assisted in adjusting to a new pattern of life, as in the case in which rural workers are introduced to urbanized areas. In addition, there must be the provision for social protection needed to assure the individual that the costs of adjustment will not fall heavily upon workers or their dependents. Although the need for these adjustments to take place is apparent, the fact that the market is a poor instrument for allocating the social costs that workers incur in making these adjustments has not been so well recognized.

In addition to redistributing these social costs, an active manpower policy confers social benefits on individual firms as well, especially when the policy is pursued as part of a high-wage, full-employment economy. Even during prosperous times, areas of poverty and unemployment will exist. At the same time, areas of high labor demand will experience a shortage of workers. Friction in the labor market will hinder the movement of workers between these areas.

To assist firms facing labor shortages in high employment areas, manpower authorities can take on increasing responsibility "(1) to identify labor bottlenecks . . . and to advise on policies which will help in the reallocation of labor to expanding employment areas [and] (2) to locate the labor surpluses of the unemployed, underemployed, and underutilized, and to define the policies for their recruitment and allocation to more useful employments." To meet this responsibility, policymakers will find it necessary to develop the skills to forecast specific labor market conditions and the prospects for mobility on the part of workers.[78]

These skills were crucial in order to prevent abuses of manpower policy. Job training programs can teach skills that are not linked to any useful jobs, and they may serve to profit training schools, as has recently happened with the application of the student loan program to vocational schools. Business may also use the facilities of manpower programs as a vehicle for recruiting low-wage labor. Although he did not raise these problems specifically, Barkin had to be aware of them and hope that solid planning on the part of policymakers would alleviate them.

National manpower policy in the United States has a long if weak history, dating to vocational education programs in 1917. There were also manpower provisions initiated by the Area Redevelopment Act of 1961, as previously noted. A large step was taken with the passage of the Manpower Development and Training Act of 1962, to retrain technologically displaced workers. Later programs included the Equal Opportunity Act of 1964 and the Comprehensive Employment and Training Act of 1973. One problem with these programs has been that in local areas, communities have not cooperated in implementation. Under the Manpower and Development Training Act of 1964, for example, advisory committees at the local level, much as existed under area redevelopment, were to be established. In the case of manpower programs, the advisory committees were slow in getting started and did not often draw in members from labor and management. Professional help was not always available or used.[79]

In formulating an active manpower policy to overcome friction in the labor market, Barkin recognized the difficulties inherent in such a policy, including the lack of knowledge and research in these areas. He felt that greater effort and planning are needed, if the haphazard approach of market adjustment is to be replaced by the carefully planned policy that automation has now come to require.

Conclusion

The policies discussed in this chapter are separate parts of a whole. To bring home this point, Barkin wrote, "Local programs should supplement rather than supplant national efforts for economic growth. Similarly, national economic programs should not rule out local programming and redevelopment efforts. They complement each other."[80] In Barkin's case, the four policies discussed in this chapter were intended to complement each other. An effective trade policy can slow down the pace of displacement and adjustment, giving all participants—labor and management—time to readjust; management is given breathing space to develop new methods of production, and workers have the time to acquire new skills through retraining. Area redevelopment and active manpower policy can be utilized to help both labor and management to speed up the pace of adjustment or completely change to new areas of production. A national policy of high wages and full employment will provide an atmosphere of security that will make workers more receptive to change. Finally, whenever possible, citizens' advisory committees are to be employed so as to ensure that all members of society are represented in formulating the policies and plans. Barkin also anticipated that participation in the formulation of all the programs that constituted his overall policy would foster cooperation among the parties involved.

Government policy was vital to that cooperation, however. As a New Deal social democrat, Barkin had faith that government programs could be devised that would nurture cooperation. This faith was optimistic, because there were few political strategies available to Barkin in pursuing his proposals. As described in the next chapter, the union movement was becoming weaker, and it is hard to see how Barkin's recommendations could be legislated and implemented as he wanted without the strong support of a politically powerful union movement. It is possible that by spending as much time as he did in government circles, Barkin committed a glaring oversight. As noted throughout this work, Barkin was called on often to give expert testimony before congressional committees, which he must have found gratifying per se. His writings at the time (1950s and 1960s) rarely mention labor politics. Being the realist that he was, Barkin did not consider his efforts an effective substitute for union activism. Instead, he used whatever influence he could muster to push for programs that union leaders either could not or would not support in the climate of the Cold War years.

These programs and the spirit of cooperation they engender are a far cry from current conditions in the U.S. economy, where adversarial competition in the marketplace is still being encouraged. In the place of area redevelopment assistance, we now have "free enterprise zones," where businesses are free to take advantage of distressed persons and a low minimum wage to produce cheaply but not to add to community growth. Instead of active manpower policy, we have an immigration policy that encourages undocumented workers to flock to the United States, pitting them against present workers. In national macroeconomic policy, we have an expansionary deficit, the impact of which is lost through an uncoordinated trade policy as the stimulative effect of the deficit leaks out into the import market and tax cuts for business are invested overseas, while tight monetary policy often fights inflation by causing unemployment and declining real wages in the manufacturing sector. In trade policy, we have protection granted to some special interests that seek it, such as the automobile industry, with no quid pro quo being exacted in terms of plans to improve efficiency, hold the line on prices, or help displaced workers. The overall result has been a decade of distorted economic growth in the United States.

Given such poor results from present policy, it is tempting to have government stop pursuing policy at all. But an absence of policy is not the answer to a poorly formulated policy. Poor policies must be replaced by improved policies. The formulation of policy is a dynamic process in which policies can be continually refined. As Barkin once described the process, "We are all engaged in a new search for ideas and techniques for improving our efforts. . . . No group has a monopoly of them. We have learned that economic programming must embrace all sectors and interests in a community. The approach must be integrated and allow all interests to be represented. The goals are clear. They are economic growth, rising living standards, full employment and a more satisfying life for each individual."[81]

Notes

1. Barry Bluestone and Bennett Harrison, *The Deindustrialization of America* (New York: Basic Books, 1982), p. 9.
2. Ibid., p. 6.

3. Ibid., pp. 6–8.

4. Solomon Barkin, "Management and Ownership in the New England Cotton Textile Industry," *Journal of Economic Issues* 15 (June 1981), p. 464.

5. Solomon Barkin, "The Regional Significance of the Integration Movement in the Southern Textile Industry," *Southern Economic Journal* 15 (April 1949) pp. 397–98.

6. F. Ray Marshall, *Labor in the South* (Cambridge, MA: Harvard University Press, 1967), pp. 13, 101.

7. Barkin, "Management and Ownership," quoting Thomas R. Smith, p. 472.

8. Ibid., p. 409.

9. "The United States Textile Industry: Challenges and Opportunities," Massachusetts Institute of Technology Commission on Industrial Productivity, 1989, pp. 8–9.

10. Solomon Barkin, "Labor Relations in the United States Textile Industry," *International Labor Review* LXXV (May 1957), pp. 393–94.

11. Solomon Barkin, "The Effect of Increased Productivity of the Labour Force and Its Deployment in the United States Cotton Textile Industry," *Productivity Measurement Review* 39 (November 1964), 39–43.

12. Barkin, "Labor Relations," pp. 395–410.

13. Calculated by the author from data in the Massachusetts Institute of Technology Commission on Productivity and from U.S. Bureau of Labor Statistics sources.

14. William F. Hartford, "Unions, Labor Markets, and Deindustrialization," in Kenneth Fones-Wolf and Martin Kaufman, eds., *Labor in Massachusetts: Selected Essays* (Westfield, MA: Institute for Massachusetts Studies, 1990), passim.

15. Barkin, "Management and Ownership," p. 474.

16. Barkin, "Labor Relations," p. 411.

17. Solomon Barkin, "Big Business Must Answer to the American People," *Proceedings*, League for Industrial Democracy (April 1954), pp. 21–23.

18. Solomon Barkin, "Implications of Developments in Automation for Our Economy," in *The American Economy* (New York: Joint Council on Economic Education) (undated reprint in Barkin files, ca. 1957), pp. 104–5.

19. Ibid., p. 105.

20. Solomon Barkin, "The Significant Change in Wage Demands," *Labor and Nation* (February-March 1946), pp. 8–10.

21. John Maynard Keynes, *The General Theory of Employment, Interest, and Money* (New York: Harcourt, Brace & World, 1965), p. 131.

22. "Will Consumers Shop Away the Recession?" *Business Week*, March 19, 1990, p. 16.

23. Solomon Barkin, "Boost Wages," *Challenge Magazine* 1 (June 1953), p. 40.

24. Richard B. Freeman, "Effects of Unions on the Economy," in Seymour Martin Lipsett, ed., *Unions in Transition* (San Francisco: ICS Press, 1986), p. 183.

25. Solomon Barkin, "A Unionist's Program to Meet Inflationary Threat," Proceedings of the New York University Twelfth Annual Conference on Labor, 1959, pp. 142–49.

26. David Brody, *Workers in Industrial America*, (New York: Oxford University Press, 1980) p. 176.

27. Solomon Barkin, "Wages and Inflation," *Challenge* (December 1957), pp. 29–31.

28. Solomon Barkin, "Union Labor's Views in Wage Controversy," *Factory Management and Maintenance* (February 1946), pp. 1–2.

29. Bruce Kaufman, "The Postwar View of Labor Markets and Wage Determination," in Bruce Kaufman, ed., *How Labor Markets Work* (Lexington, MA: Lexington Books, 1988), p. 176.

30. Barkin, "Boost Wages," p. 39.

31. Solomon Barkin, "Who's to Blame for High Prices?" *The Nation* (August 16, 1947), p. 164.

32. Ibid., p. 164.

33. Barkin, "A Unionist's Program," p. 147.

34. Ibid., p. 153.

35. Cited in Stanley Lebergott, *The Americans: An Economic Record* (New York: W. W. Norton & Co., 1984), pp. 139–40.

36. Richard S. Belous and Rebecca S. Hartley, "Regional Trading Blocs and International Trade: Challenges in the 1990s," *Looking Ahead* (Vol. XI, No. 4), pp. 17–19.

37. Solomon Barkin, "Labor's Position on Tariff Reduction," *Industrial Relations* 1 (May 1962), pp. 50–51,

38. Solomon Barkin, "A Trade Union Approach to Foreign Trade," *Free Labour World* (February 1961), pp. 2–3.

39. Solomon Barkin, "Statement by the Textile Workers Union of America, CIO," Committee for Reciprocity Information on Proposed List of Textile Items Subject to Negotiations in Reciprocal Trade Agreements, December 21, 1946 (copy in Barkin files), p. 6.

40. Solomon Barkin, "International Trade in Textiles and Garments: A Challenge for New Policies," in Carl J. Friedrich and Seymour E. Harris, eds., *Public Policy*, Volume XI (Cambridge, MA: Graduate School of Public Administration, Harvard University, 1961), pp. 389–90.

41. Solomon Barkin, "Statement to the United States Tariff Commission," December 22, 1954 (copy in Barkin files), pp. 2–4; "Statement of the Textile Workers Union of America, AFL-CIO, to the Committee for Reciprocity Information, on Woolen and Worsted Tariffs," ca. 1955 (copy in Barkin files), pp. 3–4; "Hearings Before the Committee on Finance, United States Senate: Trade Agreements Extension," March 15–18, 1955 (Washington, DC: United States Government Printing Office, 1955), p. 1666.

42. Barkin, Statement of 1946, p.3.

43. Barkin, "Labor's Position on Tariff Reduction," p. 51.

44. Barkin, Statement of 1946, p. 13.

45. Ibid., p. 8.

46. Solomon Barkin, "American Cotton-Textile Industry and Foreign-Trade Policy," excerpt from the Compendium of Papers on United States Foreign Policy Collected by the Staff for the Subcommittee on Foreign Trade Policy of the Committee on Ways and Means (Washington, DC: U.S. Government Printing Office, 1957), p. 861.

47. Barkin, Statement of 1954, p. 12.

48. Barkin, "A Trade Union Approach to Foreign Trade," p. 7.

49. Dominick Salvatore, "The New Protectionism and the Threat to World Welfare: Editor's Introduction," *Journal of Policy Modeling* 7 (1985), p. 7.

50. Massachusetts Institute of Technology Commission, *U.S. Textile Industry*, pp. 16–18.

51. Ibid., p. 5.

52. John Eatwell, *Whatever Happened to Britain?* (New York: Oxford University Press, 1982), pp. 124–43.

53. Belous and Hartley, p. 17.

54. Brody, *Workers in Industrial America*, p. 240.

55. Salvatore, "The New Protectionism," p. 10.

56. Barkin, "Labor's Position on Tariff Reduction," p. 52.

57. Matt Witt, "Needed: A New Day for Labor," *Washington Post*, September 3, 1989, p. C2.

58. "Free Trade with Mexico? Set a Safety Net," *Business Week*, November 12, 1990, p. 166.

59. Barkin, "Labor's Position on Tariff Reduction," p. 62.

60. Barkin, "Implications of Developments in Automation," p. 105.

61. Sar A. Levitan, *Federal Aid to Depressed Areas: An Evaluation of the Area Redevelopment Administration* (Baltimore: Johns Hopkins University Press, 1964), p. 31.

62. Solomon Barkin, Testimony, Area Redevelopment Act, Hearings Before Subcommittee No. 2 of the Committee on Banking and Currency, House of Representatives, February-March 1961 (Washington, DC: U.S. Government Printing Office, 1961), p. 583.

63. Solomon Barkin, Testimony, Area Redevelopment, Hearings Before a Subcommittee on Banking and Currency, U.S. Senate, January-February 1961 (Washington, DC: U.S. Government Printing Office, 1961), p. 172.

64. Press Release, Textile Workers Union of America, AFL-CIO, January 25, 1961 (copy in Barkin files).

65. Barkin, Testimony at House Hearings, pp. 580–82.

66. Barkin, Testimony at Senate Hearings, p. 173.

67. Levitan, *Federal Aid*, p. 203.

68. Solomon Barkin, Review of Sar Levitan, *Federal Aid to Depressed Areas*, *Industrial and Labor Relations Review* (April 1965), pp. 446–48.

69. Solomon Barkin, "Manpower and Social Aspects of Rural Redevelopment Programs," in *Regional Rural Development Programmes* (Paris: Organisation for Economic Co-operation and Development, 1966), p. 162.

70. Ibid., p. 163.

71. Solomon Barkin, "Regional Development and Active Manpower Policy," *Bedriftsokonomen* 5 (1966), p. 191.

72. Solomon Barkin, "Statement Before the Subcommittee of the Senate Interstate and Foreign Commerce Committee Investigating the Textile Industry," July 9, 1958 (typed copy in Barkin files), pp. 4, 23.

73. Ibid., pp. 24–26.

74. Ibid., pp. 27–29.

75. National Academy of Science–National Research Council, *Current Needs in Research Relevant to the Interests of the United States Textile Industry*, by Ad Hoc Textile Research Committee, March 1962, pp. 15–21.

76. Letter from Stanley Backer to Solomon Barkin, November 8, 1990, copy in author's possession. See also R. C. Sheldon, R. A. Roach, and S. Backer, "Design of an On-Line Computer-Based Textile Information Retrieval System," *Textile Research Journal* 38 (January 1968), pp. 81–100, and Darlene L. Ball, "The Textile Information Users Council," *Special Libraries* (February 1978), pp. 66–70.

77. Solomon Barkin, "Manpower Policies of the Organisation for Economic Co-operation and Development." *Business Topics* (East Lansing, MI: Michigan State University, Autumn 1963), p. 10.

78. Solomon Barkin, "Issues and Research Needs Relative to Manpower," in Solomon Barkin, William R. Dymond, Everett M. Kassalow, Frederic Myers, and Charles A. Myers, eds., *International Labor* (New York: Harper & Row, 1968), pp. 264–65.

79. Sar A. Levitan and Joyce K. Zickler, *The Quest for a Federal Manpower Partnership* (Cambridge, MA: Harvard University Press, 1974), pp. 1, 42, 47, 110.

80. Barkin, "Manpower and Social Aspects," p. 164.

81. Ibid.

7

Decline of the Labor Movement

*Unilateral benevolence has seldom satisfied free men. It nurses a
despotism—inequitable economic returns and biased work rules—that
ultimately will precipitate large-scale social conflict.*
                                                    —*Solomon Barkin*

"The American economy is a laboristic economy," wrote Sumner Slichter in
1948, "or at least is rapidly becoming one. By this I mean that employees are the
most influential group in the community and that the economy is run in their
interest more than in the interest of any other economic group." Slichter worried
that this growth in the influence of workers had the potential to undermine the
foundations of the progressive capitalist economy that had been the central feature of U.S. economic development, because he feared that wage-and-salary
workers would not maintain or appreciate the spirit of enterprise that had made
the industrial system dynamic. Unions were the leaders in this transformation to
a laboristic economy, and despite his sympathy for them, Slichter felt that they
were becoming too powerful.[1]

In writing about the role of unions in the laboristic economy, Slichter expressed his concerns as a series of questions: Would the rise of unions lead to
cooperation or conflict in industry? Would an equality of bargaining power be
reached between unions or management or would unions get the upper hand?
Would unions rise above their special interests to work for the good of the
community?[2] Although Slichter considered these to be open questions with uncertain answers, he was doubtful that the laboristic economy would be progressive. That doubt resulted from his belief in a very important trend: "The
trade-union movement will remain powerful and aggressive, and will undoubt-
edly become more so."[3]

Rise of Unions

Slichter's forecast of growing union strength was in keeping with the social concerns of the period of the late 1940s and 1950s. Many in the business community felt that union gains were growing and would continue "to penetrate more and more into managerial spheres until we have reached some form of a complete labor-management system or socialism."[4] Union confidence in being able to have a greater say in business affairs was never higher. It also led to an attitude that made managerial fears of encroachments on its affairs appear warranted. As Neil Chamberlain says, union leaders could be found who admitted, "If unions are *planning* a drive to secure a greater voice in management, I haven't seen it. Of course, it may work out that our program will lead into socialism, as they fear, but it won't be because we planned it that way."[5]

During the late 1930s, industrial unions had grown rapidly under the CIO. Throughout the war, unions continued to make gains, especially under the aegis of the War Labor Board's policy of "membership maintenance." In addition, the board "socialized much of the trade union movement's prewar agenda, thus making seniority and grievance systems, vacation pay and night-shift supplements, sick leave and paid mealtimes, standard 'entitlements' mandated for an increasingly large section of the working class."[6] Through their wartime activities, labor leaders gained personal prestige, which they used to support union activities.

When the war ended, labor was in a strong position. Membership had grown from almost 9 million workers in 1940 to nearly 15 million in 1946, with about 35 percent of the work force organized—including over 80 percent in basic manufacturing and mining.[7] Moreover, since the turning tide of the war had been determined by industrial production, aided by a no-strike pledge by organized labor, unions could call upon a high degree of social esteem. It is only in retrospect that this period can be seen as organized labor's high point.

Despite their high level of social esteem, unions had exposed a few flaws to the eyes of the public during the war. Even though he was presumably part of the no-strike agreement, John L. Lewis had called the coal miners out on strike four times in 1943, inciting a great deal of public disapprobation. The issue was over the need for cost-of-living adjustments and the manner through which they could be attained during wartime price controls. In the early years of the war, prices had risen more rapidly than wages, and it was only after labor protests that price controls were strictly enforced.[8] After the war, labor would want to regain what it had lost.

To regain the lost real income of its members, organized labor went through a large number of strikes immediately after the war, including the GM strike described earlier. CIO unions were not interested in gains for their own members only. As Philip Murray, president of the CIO argued not long after the strike period, "Organized labor in the United States has one basic objective—an ever

improving standard of living for all workers everywhere." Murray cited government statistics to show that immediately after the war, from 1945 to 1948,
inflation rose by 31.4 percent while wages went up by only 11 percent; profits
meanwhile had jumped by 90 percent.[9] The idea that all workers were hurt by
inflation and that all should be the beneficiaries of any gains in production was a
key part of stated CIO policy at this time. Murray established with great detail
that workers were not doing well in the immediate postwar years.[10]

Although the CIO unions lost out in their efforts to challenge management's
authority at GM in 1946, they did secure higher wages. Subsequent contracts at
GM, starting in 1948, added escalator clauses to protect workers from inflation
and included an annual "improvement factor" wherein wage increases for GM
workers would be tied to gains in national productivity. GM, of course, retained
its ability to set prices and change them as it felt necessary.

Despite these gains, the GM settlements had some losses for the CIO. In the
aftermath of the GM strike, unions in the CIO began a system of pattern bargaining in which one of its big unions would try to set a pattern in its negotiations,
which the others would follow. Unions and companies that followed the pattern
saved themselves much strife. Unions with special needs for higher wages were
free to promote them. To the extent that nonunionized plants followed the pattern, the union gains would be made more secure as an industry cost structure
would be stabilized. Workers in those industries might recognize that their employers had given them increases comparable to union plants, while union leaders and organizers could point out to them that only with unionization could they
be assured of retaining and possibly adding to those gains.

There was a cost to pattern bargaining in terms of the public perception of
unions, however. When a pattern of wage increases in the basic unionized industries was followed by a series of price increases, the public began to feel that part
of the blame was due to unions. Whether the price increases were needed or even
limited to covering the wage increases was beside the point. As Barkin later
concluded, "As became evident in the latter part of the fifties, the public did not
erase its suspicions and drop charges of collusion between unions and management on matters of price determination. . . . This perception haunted unions and
estranged the liberal middle class from its former sympathies for the trade union
movement."[11] It became much easier to brand the CIO with that hated epithet—
"business unionism."

The trend toward business unionism in the CIO was heightened by a maneu-
ver that was supposed to strengthen the union movement. In 1955, the breach
that had severed the AFL and CIO was finally closed. Although the final steps
that approved the merger took place quickly, the movement for the merger had
been building for some time. Efforts to attain unity among organized labor had
started in 1946, when the changing political climate brought about by congressional victories of the Republican Party, which resulted in passage of the Taft-
Hartley Act, made the need for a stronger union voice apparent. Personality

differences between Philip Murray, president of the CIO, and William Green, president of the AFL, which dated to the first schism of the two organizations, seemingly prevented an amicable union. Both men died in 1952, however, and steps were soon taken to reunite the two groups. The original split over craft versus industrial unions was now beside the point, as the AFL had been increasingly involved with organizing industrial workers.[12]

The merger was much heralded at the time. A. H. Raskin recalled, "The merger convention rang with predictions that unity would bring a doubling of union membership within a decade plus a great burst of renewed dynamism in all aspects of union affairs."[13] The merger, however, did not produce any significant results for the labor movement as a whole. The AFL may have gotten the better part of the deal; its leader, George Meany, was elected president of the AFL-CIO, and the AFL supplied seventeen vice presidents compared to ten for the CIO. An industrial union department headed by Reuther was also created.[14] Personal relations between these two different types of union leaders were never cordial, and Reuther would eventually take steps that would lead to the removal of the UAW from the AFL-CIO in 1968, as part of his quarrel with Meany.

Whatever Reuther's objections to Meany's policies, the merger continued to push the CIO further in the direction of business unionism. As Kim Moody states the view at the time, "The belief that the 1955 merger of the AFL and CIO reflected an adaptation by the CIO leadership to business unionist norms was widespread."[15] Business unionism meant a narrowing of the goals of the CIO, as it was pushed to a strategy of prudential unionism, to use Bruce Laurie's apt term.[16] Instead of being a champion for all workers, the CIO was relegated to a position of special advocacy of its members; from being a social movement in politics, the CIO began to be perceived as another special interest group.

To be sure, the CIO had been moving in that direction. The War Labor Board had encouraged unions to engage in responsible collective bargaining in return for assistance in organizing and setting wages. There were members of the board who thought of collective bargaining in the constricted business sense; their influence probably served to push the CIO closer to prudential unionism. As a result, CIO unions became more interested in a confined approach to collective bargaining that was more reflective of AFL attitudes. This also made the merger between the two groups easier to complete. The CIO still differed from the AFL in its development of a policy of seeking government assistance through national legislation, and this policy was retained after the merger.

Barkin recalled that among the TWUA leadership there was indifference to the merger; even though he would be a vice president of the AFL-CIO, TWUA president Emil Rieve was skeptical about its prospects. Once the merger was in place, however, Barkin saw no need to break it apart. After all, it was only a loose confederation and had minimal effect on the daily operations of its member unions.[17] He did agree with Moody's assessment of the drift of the merged organization. He wrote, "After the merger of the two federations, the organization reflected the outlook of the original AFL orientation rather than that of the CIO."[18]

This outlook came through especially in the AFL-CIO leadership's ignoring of labor unrest among unionized industrial workers in the late 1950s and early 1960s and an indifference bordering on being cavalier about continuing to organize the unorganized mass of workers. This outlook can now be seen as quite destructive of the union movement, but it was not apparent at the time. Slichter's concerns noted earlier were certainly overwrought, especially since they continued beyond the period of postwar labor unrest. The revision in 1960 of his classic study *Union Policies and Industrial Management* contains a clear statement of his bias. Slichter and his coauthors claimed that the book was "intended to help *both* managements and trade unions." There was a limit to how evenly they would give this help, since the two sides were often in conflict. As a result, they conceded, the leaning of their book was: "In cases of conflict, therefore, its orientation is provided by the goals of management." Slichter and his coauthors did not mean for the book "to show management how to crush unions." Nevertheless, they did applaud GM for taking a strong stand against the UAW when it saw that "the rise of unions threatened the freedom of management to run the plant."[19] As Barkin summarized this view, Slichter "warned management to set up defenses to protect its rights."[20]

Slichter's concerns were as misplaced as his forecasts were wrong. The United States has not evolved into anything close to a laboristic economy, despite the continued growth in the percentage of the population who are wage earners. Nor have unions continued to grow in strength and numbers. Even more important, however, managers had no need of Slichter's warnings, for they were quite capable of devising their own methods to counteract unions, and those actions were not purely defensive. The antiunion stance of management and the methods used to accomplish it were very familiar to Barkin, as a consequence of his experiences in the textile industry.

It is the purpose of this chapter to examine Barkin's views on the decline of the union movement, what caused it, what implications it has had for workers and society, and what might be done to reverse it. At a time when Slichter was concerned about the growing union strength, Barkin had already seen the beginnings of decline. In coming to this appreciation so early, Barkin was unique among labor economists. Even the union support school of Dunlop, Kerr, Lester, and Reynolds, as Richard Freeman reports, did not foresee the problems unions would face.[21] Barkin had the advantage of being an insider in the union movement and of functioning within a union that faced first the decline that other unions would feel later. With his background, he was able to pinpoint many elements leading to union decline, including economic restructuring, management resistance, problems intrinsic to unions, union reform, development of advanced management techniques (especially human resource management), and a changing economic environment. Each is considered in turn followed by

Barkin's views on the ultimate goal of management resistance—what he calls "unilateralism"—and his assessment of what unilateralism implies for workers, intellectuals, and society. First, we must look at some indications of how unions have declined.

Decline of Unions

By every measure, unions in the United States have experienced a long period of decline. To be sure, that decline followed a period of rapid growth. As a percentage of the labor force, union membership increased from 6.8 percent in 1933 to a high of 25.9 percent in 1953 before declining to 16.1 percent in 1984 and rising slightly to 16.4 percent in 1989. Part of the decrease in the percent of workers belonging to unions resulted from a large increase in the labor force, because the number of union members actually grew for several years after the percent of unionized workers declined. In terms of number of members, the figures are 3.5 million in 1933 to a high of 22.2 million in 1975, with a decline to 18.3 million by 1984. Among blue-collar workers—the heart of union membership—the percentage unionized fell from 79.5 percent in 1959 to 49.6 percent in 1984. This has not been offset by the modest gains made among white-collar and service-sector workers. Although this impact has varied by industry and by national union, the trend for all has been downward.[22] The area of union certification elections also shows the increasing weakness of unions, with fewer workers being involved in elections and a lower rate of victory.[23]

These trends are apparent now, but they were not so obvious to social commentators in the immediate postwar period, as previously indicated. In his prescient statement on the problem, *The Decline of the Labor Movement*, Barkin noted the particular irony in the concerns of thinkers like Slichter, pointing out most of the main features of union decline in an opening statement:

> The anomaly of the day is that the opponents of trade unions are seeking to restrain the economic and political activities of unions at a time when their growth has been halted. Many individual unions are shrinking in size, and the membership of the total movement has declined. The proportion of union members in the total workforce has also gone down. Not only are employees not joining unions in the vast numbers they once did but employers are increasingly resisting the spread of union organization and are challenging the mightiest industrial unions in outright economic battle, in several instances forcing unions to withdraw economic demands and in other instances weakening and even destroying the organization.[24]

Published in 1961, these words capture the essence of what was to come, especially as Barkin would accord management's resistance to unions as the most important factor in causing the union decline. There were other factors as well, including policies of the NLRB, impact of right-to-work laws passed under the aegis of the Taft-Hartley Act, the Landum-Griffin Act, and the impact of low levels of unemployment. Barkin even found that unions were also the source of some of their problems. A key variable was the changing structure of the economy.

Economic Restructuring

The first cause of decline that Barkin outlined was what has come to be called the structural argument. In this argument, decline in union activity is held to be the result of a reduction of employment in unionized industries. In those industries, changing technology, competition of new products from other industries, an increase in imports, altered consumer demand, and increased productivity all reduced the need for workers. Industries Barkin noted as following this pattern included mining, railroads, textiles, tobacco manufacturing, lumber, petroleum, primary metal, and rubber. As part of this restructuring of industry, he also noted the geographic shift of plants from the highly unionized Northeast and Midwest to the nonunionized areas of the South, as well as the entrance of more females and blacks into the industrial labor market.[25] As Richard Edwards sums up his own study of unions, "Industrial restructuring has generally meant union losses."[26]

The structural argument has received much closer scrutiny in recent years as an explanation for the decline of unions. Henry Farber has done econometric work suggesting that about 40 percent of the union decline from the mid-1950s to the mid-1970s can be attributed to structural changes.[27] Freeman and Medhoff also present evidence that the structural argument can be useful in explaining union decline. It creates problems, too. For example, the rise of blacks and females in the labor market does coincide with the decline of unions, but these groups, as surveys have shown, are at least as likely to vote for union organizations as are the white males who formed the bulwark of early membership in industrial unions. It would appear that structural changes are a cause for union decline, but not a major source. The structural argument, however, can highlight why union organization has become harder.[28]

Management Resistance

Another problem with the structural argument is that it masks what may be the most powerful cause for union decline—management intransigence. Many of the structural changes that have taken place in the economy may be due to the strategies used by individual businesses to fight unions. As noted earlier, plant relocations to nonunion areas may be undertaken simply to avoid unions. Kochan, Katz, and McKersie have noted how companies have "directed any expansions in capacity to new plants but, more importantly, shifted capacity from old union plants to new plants"; they also present data showing that business spending per employee on plant and equipment in union plants has consistently lagged behind nonunion plants, especially new nonunion plants.[29] Here we have the impetus behind much of the deindustrialization that has taken place in the Northeast and Midwest.

Obviously, Barkin was well aware of such management strategies. As he observed, "One of the most serious obstacles to the growth of unionism in America is the unwillingness of employers to accept unions and collective bargaining as an integral part of the industrial system."[30] In Barkin's view, the management fight against unionism took shape within the firm with the use of personnel and industrial relations systems that were designed to make workers more loyal to their company than to their union. As noted in Chapter Four, by the 1950s, the human relations approach had been cited by Barkin as a tool being developed in management circles to fight unions. These new methods would eventually evolve into the field of human resource management, to be described later, and Barkin recognized their use in an antiunion strategy at the start. This last point is worth mentioning, for it contradicts the statement by Kochan, Katz, and McKersie that "no one in the 1950s or 1960s foresaw the changes in managerial behavior that would slow and then stop the expansion of collective bargaining and union membership in the private sector of the economy."[31] Sol Barkin did see these changes, because he was fighting them. Moreover, he would have characterized them as a change in tactics, not strategy; to him management had always followed a strategy of opposing unions, overtly when they could, but covertly when necessary.

Another way management fought unions was through the political and legal systems. Management never really accepted the NLRA, and when the act's constitutional standing was ensured, management sought other ways to offset it. The purpose of the NLRA was to strengthen the ability of workers to unionize and engage management in collective bargaining, but the outcome of that bargaining and the process through which it took place were not features of the labor law. In the early years of the NLRA, the NLRB decided many cases in favor of unions, giving a liberal interpretation to the NLRA.

By the 1950s, however, this somewhat friendly legal climate for labor had changed. Again, Barkin recognized this very readily. He wrote, "The Taft-Hartley Act of 1947 and the decisions by the National Labor Relations Board since 1952 have given a new freedom to anti-union activities."[32] To his mind, the NLRA had been designed to protect the rights of workers to organize while taking into account the rights of management, and the early NLRB had upheld these rights. In the area of employer communications with workers, for example, it had been held that in-plant speeches and speeches that were part of coercive practices would be deemed unfair practices.

In the new legal climate, however, the employer's right of free speech was expanded to include predictions of plant closings if the union won an election, unwarranted characterizations of unions and union leaders, and the use of pressure from third parties such as local chambers of commerce. In addition, the NLRB began placing curbs on its own procedures. The Taft-Hartley Act also reduced unions' ability to organize, by permitting right-to-work laws and eliminating supervisors from coverage by the NLRA.[33]

As Freeman and Medhoff point out, the legal climate does have an influence on union organizing efforts, and management's use of the legal system can turn that influence negative. As the system now operates, management can mount very tough legal campaigns to dissuade workers from voting for a union and can take measures to delay the election as long as possible, thereby increasing their chances to win. In addition, management can take illegal actions such as firing pro-union workers or refusing to bargain once a union wins an election. In either case, the legal remedies—reinstatement with back pay or a possible fine—are small enough to make their risk worth taking. Not surprisingly, the incidence of these and other unfair labor practices has risen sharply since the early 1960s. The result, as many studies have shown, is that management resistance and counterattack as well as its illegal actions in fighting unions are an extremely powerful force in explaining the negative outcome of NLRB election results.[34]

The failure of unions to win elections can also be explained by good economic conditions. Barkin's contention, shared by many, was that union expansion usually followed or coincided with severe economic downturns. The organizational gains of the CIO in the 1930s were an example of this cycle. By the 1960s, a healthy economy had produced a period of economic expansion that had brought general prosperity. It is likely that continued prosperity would reduce the need for unions.[35] While this argument may have some validity—witness the belief expressed in Chapter Five that the public does not feel unions are needed for incomes to rise—it does not seem to have worn well. The 1970s and 1980s have seen some periods of severe recession, but these have not halted the decline of unionism. Why unions have not been able to take advantage of these adverse economic conditions may be due to the unions themselves.

Union Problems

Barkin was alert to problems within the union movement that were making it more difficult to gain new members. First among those problems he considered was the poor image unions were projecting by the early 1960s, when he observed, "Politicians have found it possible to build careers on exposures of union corruption." This condition was in sharp contrast to the 1930s, when political liberals and much of society had given unions broad public support as "essential to attaining the New Deal objectives of a more secure, free and equitable society." Moreover, as a disparaging opinion of unions became prevalent, union leaders did nothing to reverse it, "assuming that all they needed to do was to settle specific grievances and negotiate better contracts." The leadership had become conscious of this problem and was trying to use public

relations to give unions a better image. Barkin felt, however, that the movement was hampered in this because of its decentralized national organizational
structure and lack of unity.[36]

Unions had also experienced great difficulties in organizing the unorganized
workers, as Barkin's own experiences in Southern textile campaigns had proved.
To a large extent that failure was due to extremely hostile management resistance, combined with a social setting that served to bolster management. Part of
the problem for unions was that they had not done enough to counter that social
setting. They had not offered their campaigns as part of a program that would
lead to economic growth and development, leaving themselves open to the
charge that they would cause a loss of jobs. Nor had they ardently preached a
gospel of human rights and group solidarity for workers to counter the appeal to
individual rights that management and its friends used on workers.

Unions had also faced problems in the South with respect to race relations.
Barkin pointed out that blacks represented a growing segment of the union camp
and that unions, in response, were ending their previous policies of race discrimination. National leadership had pushed for equal treatment of all workers by
local unions. Unions had missed a chance for greater support among blacks
because despite union contributions to better race relations, "the manner and
content of the battle has done little to enhance the prestige of unionism among"
them. At the same time, blacks pushing for greater civil rights understood the
help unions gave them, but they had a problem in "how to achieve their goal
without dampening the ardor for union membership itself among their followers." The problem was that black workers had a divided allegiance between the
civil rights movement and the union movement, and the division was more likely
to be resolved against unions.[37] Unions had lost a claim to the idealism that was
now attributed to the civil rights movement.

In addition to lacking an idealism to give themselves a broad social appeal,
Barkin found that "the apathy of unions themselves to new organization constitutes a barrier to expansion in some economic sectors." This apathy was especially common among craft unions, which were not interested in organizing
lower-wage workers within their jurisdictions. The problem was acute in small
towns, where unions had made few inroads; in some cases the local union body,
such as the central labor union, had become the force for new organizing, a
procedure Barkin approved and urged the national AFL-CIO office to use. Industrial unions had always organized in large industrial centers and had not devised
a strategy for dealing with small concerns in rural areas. Barkin suggested multi-
union organizing drives as a solution to this problem. He stressed the need for
developing a strategy for organizing in small towns, because of his prediction
that they would play "an increasingly important part in our industrial system as
plants and services are decentralized."[38]

Unions also faced a big problem in recruiting new members because "there
are whole areas in the American economy where the apathy of workers to union-

ism is the primary obstacle." In particular, Barkin enumerated five representative groups: workers belonging to independent unions, women in manufacturing, nonmanual workers, blacks, and service workers. Those in the first category were hard to organize because they had a high loyalty to their employers. The problem with women and blacks started as prejudice among unionists, but even when that was removed, the vestiges of it remained a problem in the minds of the blacks and women; even though national union leaders had been in the vanguard in the fight for equal rights, there had been resistance at the local level in some regions. The other categories, which included white-collar and professional workers and low-wage service workers, had been very difficult to organize; white-collar workers, especially office workers, and wage-earning professionals had to some degree been recipients of the union spillover effect and so had no need for unions, and service workers were too scattered to be organized effectively using current practices.[39]

There has been some progress in organizing these unorganized groups since Barkin made his analysis, but it is nothing for unions to be proud of. Among all workers, 27 percent of males are in unions compared to 17 percent of females, and 20 percent of white workers are unionized as against 27 percent of non-whites (the figure for nonwhites represents a disproportionate number of them in unionized blue-collar jobs). These might represent small gains, but there is evidence that unions could do better. Among all workers, 41 percent of females and 69 percent of nonwhites favored having a union compared to 27 percent of males and 29 percent of whites. The percentage of white-collar workers organized remains at less than 10 percent, even though 28 percent favor having a union. Levels of union gain among professional workers remain equally low, as is the case among service workers.

Progress has been made in gaining union members among female and black workers.[40] In some areas, such as recent organizing efforts at Harvard and Yale, unions have made progress in overcoming these barriers, but the overall results remain meager. Freeman and Medhoff attribute these low levels of union density to low effort by unions, concluding that "the decline in union organizing effort contributed substantially to the drop over the past quarter century in the percentage of nonagricultural workers newly organized."[41]

Barkin would agree with this assessment. In his analysis, there were severe limitations within the union movement that were contributing to this lower effort. A primary limit, previously mentioned, was the structure of the union movement itself. The center of the movement was the national headquarters of the AFL-CIO, which played a weak role in organizational drives. Barkin contrasted this weakness with the early days of the CIO, when the national headquarters spearheaded organizational drives, using manpower and funds from established unions. Even after its original successes, the CIO continued to mount wide-scale organizing drives such as Operation Dixie. After the merger of the CIO with the AFL, the AFL view—"that the responsibility for new organization rests with the individual internationals"—prevailed. The national staff of the AFL-CIO served merely in an advisory capacity.[42]

The advice that the national office might give was not encouraging either. Under the leadership of George Meany, the AFL-CIO took a cavalier attitude toward the need to organize. As Meany stated his position, "Why should we worry about organizing groups of people who do not want to be organized? If they prefer to have others speak for them and make decisions which affect their lives without effective participation on their part, that is their right." Meany went on to describe how he had been concerned about the number of members in the union, but he stopped because he felt that the workers who were organized were the ones who were important in getting things done.[43]

This attitude at national headquarters did not serve well in terms of union expansion, because individual international unions, with some exceptions, were absorbed with administrative tasks. The TWUA was one exception. Older, established unions concentrated on securing gains for existing members and became complacent or even resistant to acquiring new members. In other industries that were relatively unorganized, the unions did not have the resources to mount major campaigns. Another problem with the structure was that members and officers of established unions had lost their organizing zeal. During the CIO drives of the 1930s, many union members themselves served as organizers, convincing other workers about the need for unions; some unions in those early days organized themselves.

As unions matured, they hired a full-time organizing staff, but these individuals, Barkin believed, lacked the "missionary spirit" that was so pervasive among early CIO organizers. In addition, when unions succeeded, they became more concerned with the administration of existing contracts than with the winning of new ones. The importance of the organizing staff declined as a result, and the best staff members were rarely given duties in organizing. In addition, organizing techniques themselves changed. With the settling down of organization into a set of NLRB procedures, organizers began measuring success by the number of signed cards they got and the election victories they achieved. Less emphasis was placed "on developing understanding of and devotion to unionism. The prevailing assumption, derived from earlier experience, is that people already understand and are basically in sympathy with unionism and will ultimately support unions as the solution for their complaints. This conclusion has not been reevaluated for its pertinence today."[44]

The main problem for unions, then, was that they had lost their idealism; union members and leaders were no longer willing to make sacrifices to organize other workers and seemed to have lost faith in unions as an agent for social progress. This condition was in sharp contrast with the 1930s, when sacrifice and faith were extensive. Since Barkin wrote his analysis of union decline, others have written on the same topic. And although they might agree with Barkin on the importance of the loss of idealism, they would disagree with his reasons for it.

Michael Goldfield, for example, finds that much of the high standards and militancy of the CIO were the result of its "mass rank-and-file initiatives." The rank and file lost out due to the ascendancy to power of CIO leaders like Hillman and Lewis, who were really AFL politicos accustomed to acting within a labor bureaucracy. Part of that ascendancy may have been the result of Hillman's and Lewis's having government assistance from the New Deal politicians, but it was also due to communist support for them under a united-front strategy. Unlike Barkin, Goldfield sees the bureaucracy that dominated the AFL-CIO by the early 1960s as being a part of the CIO from its early days.[45]

The development of bureaucracy in the CIO also plays a part in Kim Moody's explanation for the decline of unions. Moody also regards Hillman and Lewis as bureaucratically oriented, citing the organizational structure that existed in their unions under the AFL, and characterizes Reuther's strategy in the 1945–46 GM strike as an effort to bring himself into power and centralize that power at the national level. A result of this centralization of power with such labor bureaucrats was to minimize the influence of dissidents who might have retained some of the idealism that Barkin saw as crucial to the union movement.[46]

Barkin would not agree. In terms of the influence of radicals, Barkin would deny that they had accomplished much, except in a few urban centers, such as New York, San Francisco, and Detroit, where they played a minor but noisy role. There were few key organizers among them. In the TWOC, the smattering of communists who carried over from the united-front days were not very effective, and when, in 1938, they began pushing for separate caucuses, he reassigned them to more difficult areas where their efforts were no more productive than those of other organizers. Barkin's strong opposition to communism may have blinded him to the contributions these radicals could have made in the union movement, especially in keeping alive the social idealism often found lacking in unions.

Barkin was mistrustful of left wing idealism. As noted in Chapter One, Barkin appreciated that the CIO leaders' affiliation with the New Deal was based on their recognition that government help was needed to revitalize the labor movement, especially among industrial workers. He, too, sought a middle way and felt that the New Deal offered it. As long as the spirit of New Deal social idealism permeated union leadership, as it did with Hillman and Rieve, than the movement itself would remain idealistic. That spirit was less necessary among organizers, and it could be detrimental when it used slogans and doctrines inspired by Marx, Lenin, and Stalin. Without inspirational organizers, however, how was the spirit of idealism to be communicated to workers, especially as the union organization grew in size and complexity?

From his vantage point in the upper echelons of the CIO, Barkin had an understanding of how the CIO's bureaucracy had formed. To his mind, the internal problems of the union movement came from a lack of strong, innovative leadership. The reverses of the late 1940s discouraged union leaders from continuing to fight over managerial prerogatives in the 1950s. They began to focus almost exclusively on economic gains for their members and did not respond with any sympathy to the unrest on the shop floor that was created by management's new measures to increase control over workers. They concentrated on narrow issues and increased the power of their staffs, becoming so absorbed in sheer economics that they did not recognize the need for a policy to offset the growing power of management.

In this view, the key element to union leadership was finding innovative ways to counter the resistance of management, and Barkin would not give unions a high grade in this regard. In his memorial to the CIO experience, Barkin recalled that in the 1930s, the CIO did overcome the direct and brutal attacks made on workers by management, but that management responded with newer techniques that were less direct. Against these the unions were not very effective, because they did not "display the determination, insights, skills, and expertise needed to contend with management's innovations or to design alternative approaches." Barkin attributed this ineffectiveness to the leaders' lack of interest in technical problems and failure to employ technical experts to help them.[47]

The issue of technical expertise goes deeper than this, moreover, because management was using such technical measures as job standards, work measurements, and quality control as a way to retain control over the shop floor. Without any savvy where these technical measures were concerned, leaders of industrial unions lost control of the shop floor struggle with management, giving the initiative to them. "Unlike the major role which unions played in the more traditional industries," Barkin has written, "they were assigned an outsider's position in the large industrial structure."[48] By the 1980s the clamor for "competitiveness" would completely undermine whatever resistance unions and their members had toward managerial control. It is doubtful that a group of purged radicals could have made a difference.

It was not a purge of radicals that made unions conservative; in Barkin's view, it was the failure of union leaders to develop technical expertise comparable to that of management that put them on the defensive on shop floor issues. The leadership never defined a set of goals to accomplish on the shop floor for their unions. The question of union bureaucracy raised by left wing critics of the CIO, such as Goldfield and Moody, is really a red herring. Any union must have a staff, as Barkin's own work with the TWUA exemplifies, if its leaders are to meet business managers on an equal level of expert knowledge. The important question is how that staff is to be used. The lack of technical experts in economics, engineering, or personnel management will greatly inhibit union leaders from innovating policies to expand their role in the economic and industrial systems. It was an abuse or misuse of staff, not the existence of such a staff, that caused the problem referred to as bureaucracy.

As this section has argued, Barkin would agree that unions have become conservative in their approaches to labor relations. As unions became more stabilized, they lost the high standards that had made them the primary agent for change at all levels, from the shop floor to the nation. The problem was further magnified by a lack of central authority in the labor movement; each independent union became a separate enclave and a force on its own. Were unions still powerful, that kind of organizational structure might have been successful. When unions began to decline, in the face of management opposition, the decentralized leaderships could not mount a suitable response. Meanwhile, management continued to innovate in the techniques of its opposition. In response, according to Barkin, "National unions have hardly begun to wrestle with the significance of these innovations for the design of their policies and structures. They have often dealt with them on an ad hoc basis, leaving local unions stranded and often helpless in the face of management's aggressive pursuit of its objectives."[49] Unions are responding now, however, and that is the topic of the next section.

Union Reform

To regain a high level of activism and to allow for union growth, the movement must put itself, Barkin concluded, "through a drastic overhaul of spirit and structure." While this transformation might prove difficult, Barkin reminded unionists that many older unions had undergone much change in their attitudes during the 1930s. To foster such a spirit of change, he set forth a series of guides as friendly advice to union leaders.

One of these guides involved more centralization of power with the national AFL-CIO office. As Barkin recalled, the CIO had been "led by men of strong personality who assumed they were indeed at the helm." Hillman, Lewis, and Murray, for example, were in charge of the organizing drives that took place outside their own industries. They helped to build many of the unions that made up the CIO and used the total resources of the CIO in new organizing drives. This gave the union movement a feeling of interdependence wherein the interests of the movement were greater than those of the separate unions. To regain that feeling, he suggested, would "involve giving to the national labor center certain prerogatives that up to now have been exclusively exercised by the constituent unions." Those unions need not lose their identities or independence, but the union movement would be able to stress gaining new members and not having to worry over jurisdictional disputes.[50]

A powerful national union effort would then be able to pursue another of Barkin's recommendations: putting innovative programs into effect. In Barkin's view, unions needed to develop programs such as the minimum wage and government benefits for all citizens comparable to union benefits packages in order to fight poverty and exploitation, to devise policies for economic growth and foreign trade, to establish ways to make markets work in the public interest in such areas as monopoly pricing, social costs, and environmental pollution, to prevent financial manipulation and exploitation of our corporate structure, and to consider new approaches so both labor and management did a better job at running industry. It would also help if unions educated the public on the import-ance of taking collective action to solve social problems; as part of this educa-tional process unions should make it clear that the means of unionism, collective bargaining, and economic gains led to the better end of social advance. The union must push for progress in all areas so as to cultivate among workers a faith in a continuously improved life; without that faith, which is the basic foundation on which unions build, workers may become resigned or seek drastic changes in society. Finally, Barkin maintained that unions needed to be strictly democratic in decisions on issues directly involving workers. Through communication and education and competent local leadership, support can be ensured for these ends. All of the programs Barkin was suggesting have been described in earlier chap-ters, so there is no need for further elaboration of them here.[51]

Promotion of these policies would be helped by a restructuring of the AFL-CIO to give the national office more responsibility. Centralization would also be useful in the area of organization. A national center could serve as the source for expertise on organizing for local unions. It should also, Barkin argued, be given the authority to initiate organizing drives in areas and industries where local unions were not putting out sufficient effort. The recent establishment of an agency at national AFL-CIO headquarters to advise locals on organizing tech-niques is a modest step in this direction. Equally important, a national center could revive the talent of organizers by recruiting them from among college-educated persons and providing them with adequate training, something they did not generally receive under the current conditions.[52]

A national center would be useful in politics. Barkin felt that union support was crucial to many politicians, except in the South. Union leaders who took on positions of civic responsibility in local affairs gained some political clout, but as long as unions were viewed by the public as another big organization seeking to fulfill the narrow interests of its members, that political presence would be limited.[53] As things stood, unions and Barkin with them faced a contradiction. Without a strong political presence to push for their programs, they had to rely on lobbying efforts, such as Barkin had made with area redevelopment and textile import quotas. Reliance on lobbying, however, further gave them the negative image of a narrow public interest group. It is not clear whether Barkin discerned this contradiction as it faced him. It is clear that he wanted a union presence in all aspects of political life, from lobbying to active campaigning. The way to keep the union image from slipping in politics was to make sure it was tinged with social ideals.

Overall, Barkin wanted unions to regain the spirit of idealism that had been engendered in the 1930s. For that spirit to be regained, however, union leaders could not simply look backward to the 1930s. New programs were needed. Included in Barkin's suggestions for new programs was an implicit requirement that intellectuals be brought into the union movement in order to help it formu-late those programs. The call for more professionalism in union organizing teams along with the inclusion of college graduates on those teams would give intellectuals more opportunities to serve the union movement. With their commitment to democratic values, intellectuals could help to keep a centralized union movement from becoming authoritarian.

The response to Barkin's analysis was widespread and varied. The press services reported heavily on his book about union decline, and references to it appeared in newspapers throughout the nation; there was even reference to it in *Tass. The Wall Street Journal* ran an editorial on it under the headline "Call to Class Warfare," arguing that it was not clear how "unions fit into the emerging social order."[54] In another review, Irving Bernstein characterized Barkin's analysis as "commonplace" and questioned whether workers or leaders in the CIO ever accepted the philosophy of CIO intellectuals; he observed that the union movement was still growing in numerical strength if not in proportion to the labor force and that unions had gone through cycles of growth and decline in the past, so "Barkin need not lose all hope on the side of size."[55] The *New York Times* made note of Barkin's "perceptive study." Its article applauded his suggested reforms and recommended to labor leaders that they view the book seriously in order to make the AFL-CIO "into a much more effective instrument for serving labor and the nation."[56] Much later, the Barkin study formed the core of an article on stemming the decline of unions in the Labor Research Association's *Economic Notes.*[57]

It is not clear that labor leaders were ready to listen to Barkin, however. Several years later, reporting on the response by labor leaders to a variety of diagnoses about the decline of unions, Ben Seligman recounted how "George Meany roared at an AFL-CIO convention that such predictions fall wide of the truth, that labor has lost none of its militancy, that its success could be measured in the dollars and cents of high wages."[58] Comments like this and that of Bernstein cited earlier were more indicative of the complacency among unionists and their intellectual sympathizers that Barkin complained about.

It is possible that these unionists had good cause for complacency, because they could believe they were on an equal footing with business. In their analysis of the current crisis of unions, Richard Edwards and Michael Podgursky, among others, contend that the good years of unionism, which emerged after an intense period of conflict from 1934 to 1950, were part of a "labor accord" wherein the industrial relations system resulted in an era of cooperation between labor and management; management agreed to accept unions and collective bargaining and offer high wages in return for peace and the right to run its plants unhindered by union pressure. Firms with market power were especially able to make such an accord, for they could pass its costs on to consumers. Labor leaders agreed, for they acquired power and prestige for achieving gains for their members. In this view, the decline of unions came about because, for a variety of reasons, the accord fell apart when management became less willing to keep its end of the bargain.[59] This view begs the question of why unions were not strong enough to force management to live up to its bargain, unless they were already in a period of decline and weakened strength.

Barkin maintains that such an accord never existed. Rather, union leaders were obliged, by a number of factors described in the previous section, to acquiesce to management's forceful stand on shop floor issues. Based on his experiences in the textile industry, Barkin could find no truce that existed between management and labor in the 1950s.[60] As he later wrote, "There were no specific understandings between unions and management. Actually they were not needed. The leaders in the fight for broadening the role of trade unions had become frustrated by the setback. The could not match management's powers, even with prolonged strikes."[61]

By way of example as to how strong this antiunion attitude was among management, it can be pointed out that efforts aimed at attaining labor-management cooperation came from academic and government circles outside the industrial relations framework and were not a direct part of the industrial relations system. Management was antiunion, and even if it implicitly accepted an accord, that acceptance would only serve to mask management's unremitting opposition to unionism. If there were an accord in the form of a social contract between management and labor, it was certainly one-sided. Labor had to fight for any gains it made under this accord. Business might acquiesce to labor in specified areas, but it rarely gave up without a fight.

The previous sections have outlined many possible reasons for the decline of unions. The most important one was management resistance. Revolutions often beget counterrevolutions, and in the case of labor relations in the United States, this has been especially true. Sometimes the counterrevolutionaries need breathing space. Businesses in the United States adopted an uneasy truce with unions as a way to contain union growth until both the conditions and the techniques were right to launch an offensive against unions. Under that truce, union members were permitted to seek better wages and working conditions in return for union acknowledgment of management's right to control the firm. Struggles still existed between management and labor, for the truce dictated only where the battles took place.

In Barkin's case, the terms of the truce were much harsher, if indeed a truce were ever made. Barkin was associated with an industry, especially in the Southeast, where management relentlessly fought unionism during a period when other firms were compelled to wait for the right conditions to counterattack unions where they had gained a foothold. The conditions have been described earlier under the changing structure of the economy and deindustrialization. While it awaited these conditions, management was busy devising a new technique for dealing with union members and other workers, under the aptly named title of human resource management, which is the subject of the next section.

Human Resource Management

Ever since the growth of mass production facilities in industry and the large corporations that go with them, management has been seeking ways to integrate workers into the factory system. As manufacturing plants increased their scale, workers became uncoupled from monitoring, close supervision, and other interpersonal relations with their ultimate bosses in top management. As workers lost their individual ability to deal directly with the members of management who mattered, they became more interested in forming industrial unions to serve as a mediator for them. Management, as described in Chapter Four, devised a number of techniques to retain the loyalty of workers and to maintain control over worker behavior. By the 1950s, these efforts culminated in the human relations approach, often to counter the in-plant activities of unions.[62]

The human relations approach drew its inspiration from the Hawthorne experiments of the 1920s and from the psychological ideas propounded by Abraham Maslow. The Hawthorne experiments had determined that work groups improved a worker's sense of fulfillment. Maslow indicated that humans had a hierarchy of needs; after the basic needs of food and shelter were met, such higher needs as personal gratification and a sense of accomplishment could lead to worker frustration if unmet. Unions were a way to help workers satisfy these needs. Human relations experts maintained that if business took measures to appeal to workers' higher needs, then workers would transfer their loyalty from unions to the company. The proper strategy was for a firm to cultivate individual relationships with workers.

During the 1940s and 1950s a number of human relations strategies were developed with this aim in mind. Communications experts devised newsletters, education brochures, techniques of personal correspondence, and movies to make workers feel more a part of the "corporate family" and to explain workers' place in the family. Lessons in the virtues of the free enterprise system and the part profits play in it were provided. Surveys of worker attitudes were taken, and these were often used to downplay the union message. Supervisors were given better training in getting along with workers. The idea, as pointed out in Chapter Four, was to inculcate workers with an "enterprise consciousness."[63]

At the same time as firms in unionized industries were trying to minimize the influence of unions on workers, management in nonunion areas determined to avoid unions. This it did by offering wages and benefits comparable to what union workers were getting, causing the spillover effect noted in Chapter Five. As also noted in Chapter Five, unions provide workers with more than better wages and better benefits. Unions also provide a way for workers to be free to express their dissatisfaction with the way the plant is being run. The human relations approach stopped well short of giving workers this freedom.

As described in Chapter Two, John R. Commons once suggested that business had an interest in attaining "industrial goodwill" through better employee relations. By maintaining that competition would force all businesses to adopt programs of industrial goodwill, Commons accurately foretold of the human relations movement. In this foretelling, moreover, he inadvertently pinpointed the drawback of human relations when he drew the analogy that called the labor movement a member of the family, but a subordinate member. Human relations intended to give workers a feeling of participation, but not real participation in the shaping of their work life.

Workers could identify the extent to which their involvement in company affairs was effective. When it was ineffective, they were bound to become skeptical about the value of human relations programs. They would even be cynical about filling out survey questionnaires about their degree of satisfaction. As long as human relations programs fell short of giving workers full membership in the corporate family, their efficacy was questionable. To avoid unions, management would have to devise better methods to give workers more direct involvement. This it did. The general approach management developed is now called human resource management (HRM), or what was once known as organizational behavior.

HRM is an approach that aims to increase employee involvement in production problems and methods at the plant level in order to improve working life and ultimately to enhance productivity. It is based on the premise that the work force is one of a firm's most important assets, and if properly motivated, workers can contribute their abilities and creativity to solving production problems. The philosophical basis for HRM rests on Douglas McGregor's path-breaking approach to management wherein he promoted a change from a Theory X assumption that workers disliked work and had to be constantly directed to a Theory Y assumption that workers were self-directed and willing to take on greater responsibility.[64]

As often happens with management theories, McGregor's new approach mirrored events that had been taking place in industry. IBM Corporation, for example, had already been using an approach that was a precursor to HRM. Its personnel policies aimed at treating workers with respect and included features such as opinion surveys, interview programs in which workers could meet with higher management, and a policy whereby workers could submit grievances and suggestions anonymously to all levels of management.[65] Until recently, IBM was noted for not laying off its workers and for building a spirit of enterprise loyalty. The result of experiments in HRM, such as at IBM, was to develop nonunion systems of industrial relations.

By the 1970s, however, the results of HRM were being used to foster a new era of industrial relations in a union setting. The term under which this new approach was being applied—quality of work life (QWL)—quickly became a buzzword in management circles. QWL is an HRM approach that accepted unions when they were deeply entrenched and endeavored to develop a cooperative approach with them; it has as its aim the involvement of all workers at each level of the firm in making decisions about work and work conditions. The purpose of such involvement is to eliminate management-labor conflict and enhance employee motivation. It is also designed to reduce the number of work rules and make for a more flexible work force. The use of these new methods coincided with the decline of unions and the attendant weakened position of workers.

The central feature of HRM and QWL programs is the total restructuring of the work environment. In theory, the idea is to replace hierarchical decision making with worker participation by giving workers more say in how they will perform on the job floor. Experiments in QWL started in Europe in the early 1960s, and in the United States in the 1970s. Management sought to improve productivity, while some union leaders saw QWL as a way to gain more participation in managerial decisions.[66]

Although he was now on the sidelines of industrial relations, Barkin kept abreast of the development of HRM and QWL and provided his own analysis of its applications. To him, HRM was part of management's long-standing "determination to weaken unions within the work place or, if possible, eliminate them." While the methods may be new, the aim was the same. He continued, describing HRM: "The techniques have become more sophisticated but the goals have remained the same. They sought a shop of contented workers who would acknowledge management's prerogatives to manage and assent to its direction."[67] The main advantage of HRM in this aim was that "the use of the phrase 'human resources' allows the votaries of the new packaging to use a neutral label without having to endow it with new contents."[68]

Barkin raised a good point. All of the management methods have had finesounding names to cover up some negative features, at least negative to workers. Who, for example, could be opposed to programs that sought to improve the quality of work life? Union members could, as Barkin duly noted. He observed, "While these plans were implemented at management's pace in non-union plants, they encountered suspicion, doubts, and resistance in organized shops. . . . Some QWL programs were little more than projects previously rejected by unions." Where they were introduced in union plants, their success was shortlived. Barkin continued, "QWL programs became a source of new irritations between unions and management, which were rarely able to overcome a dichotomy of interests: management stressed cost reductions and unions sought humanizing goals and employment and union security."[69]

One study of QWL programs in the auto industry would lend some support for Barkin's views on HRM. Linda Kaboolian has found that QWL programs have a variable effect on workers, depending on the type of job and the amount of skill and freedom workers enjoy. Low-skilled assembly workers find QWL to be an advantage: higher-skilled manufacturing and trades workers were less positive about it. More important, workers in these latter groups saw QWL programs as short-term methods that management used only during periods of low profits when worker cooperation was needed.[70] Other studies have shown that although productivity may increase under QWL programs, the results are usually short-lived and the programs ultimately fail, often due to lack of company commitment.[71] The programs of HRM and QWL are not enough to help management achieve its long-term goal of a docile, highly productive work force.

This long-term management goal is the hidden message of QWL programs. In a critique of QWL from a unionist perspective, Mike Parker finds that management has five goals it wants to achieve through QWL programs: It wants to take advantage of the knowledge that workers have about their job in order to use that knowledge to improve productivity. It would like to foster a cooperative spirit with workers that would enable it to introduce new technology more readily. It wants workers to be more flexible in terms of moving workers to new jobs, changing worker rules, or eliminating jobs. It wants workers to develop a better understanding of management's need for concessions. Finally, it expects that if the first four goals are met, the QWL program will help to undermine the strength of unions.[72]

A second study of QWL programs, one undertaken by Donald M. Wells, strengthens this last point. Wells establishes that the intention of QWL programs is to shift power to management and away from workers and unions. Management retains the ability to make overall decisions, even the decision to curtail the QWL program. The purpose of a QWL program is to make workers more amenable to management control by making them feel more responsible for industrial conflict. Advocates of QWL and HRM interpret industrial conflict as being the result of the personal faults of individual workers and managers, not as intrinsic to the system of industrial relations: if managers and workers cooperated to address their personal faults, harmonious relations would ensue without the intervention of outside agents such as unions. By encouraging direct relations between workers and supervisors, QWL bypasses this traditional union function. In addition, QWL programs do not give workers any say in whether their job will be kept. They do not improve job conditions or offer more security or workplace participation.[73]

All these failings were familiar to Barkin, for they were nothing new to him. The overall ambition of management in applying QWL—the undermining of unions—involves HRM advocates in a peculiar conundrum. In their analysis of HRM, Kochan, Katz, and McKersie stress the importance of winning the trust of workers in order to implement effectively the HRM program and gain worker participation. Their own understanding of the workings of the industrial relations system led Kochan et al. to the conclusion that "for workplace participation to be successful in the long run, a strong union presence and active support for the process are also essential. Nonunion firms or firms with weak unions are unlikely to develop or sustain this full form of worker participation."[74] If QWL programs are intended by management to undermine unions but unions are necessary for QWL programs to foster workplace participation, it is not likely that workplace participation will get very far under QWL. This is especially true because QWL programs are generally applied directly on the shop floor, the one place where even strong unions find workers resisting their counsel. A study by Maryellen Kelly, for example, has shown that plants with worker participation plans actually had lowered productivity, compared to unionized plants, which experienced a positive efficiency gain.[75]

Barkin agrees that HRM would require strong union support to work well. As he argued about previous efforts to gain worker participation in management programs, the programs work only when unions are strong enough to negotiate with management over how the programs will be used and how the gains from such programs will be divided. Because management has a strong desire to keep the provisions of HRM outside of the considerations of collective bargaining, it is hard to see how unions could be convinced to cooperate with management in programs of HRM.

Instead of wanting cooperation and union support for HRM, Barkin believes that some of its advocates merely "reaffirm their dedication to the primacy of management." He notes that in one major study of HRM, "the authors observe that in plants pursuing these policies 'management normally retains unilateral control' and they are 'likely to reflect management's notion of appropriate employment rules.' "[76] Ultimately, HRM advocates have a problem in that their techniques will not be successful without union support, but as long as they aim at exclusively achieving management goals, they will not get that support. For this reason, Barkin would be justified in claiming that most HRM advocates, especially in the area of industrial relations, are really aiming their appeals to management.

In making their appeals, HRM experts are following in the hallowed tradition of Frederick Taylor, who claimed that his system would help to pacify labor, but in reality elicited union opposition. Only when unions came to recognize that they could share in the gains of scientific management were they willing to cooperate. As described in Chapter Five, that cooperation had to be embedded within the collective bargaining system. Barkin would make the same case for HRM and QWL programs. He wrote, "It is true that bona fide employee participation in decision making requires a formal structure insuring independence and equality of power. These qualities must be realized in reality. Otherwise, the formal structure will be a cloak for unilateralism."[77]

Human resource management was devised as a way to gain worker input into the decisions at the job level that influences industry, but it was not intended to be concerned with influencing the formal system of industrial relations. Instead, it was designed to work outside collective bargaining. In industries in which no collective bargaining existed, HRM could prove effective as a substitute for collective bargaining, but only to a limited degree. As long as workers had no independent means of altering the HRM program, they had to accept what management considered to be the best part of the HRM system. In industries in which collective bargaining did exist, the effectiveness of HRM would vary greatly depending on the degree of management's acceptance of collective bargaining, the urgency of changes, and the employment and earnings consequences of the experiments for workers.

At its best, HRM aimed at substituting its approaches to cooperation with workers for the union's approach; its bottom line, however, would be to replace the union with a reassertion of managerial prerogatives. The spread of HRM was tied to the decline of unions. Its application in nonunion areas served as a check against union expansion into those areas. As unions declined, there would be more areas where HRM could be introduced, and weaker unions would be compelled to make concessions to management in the implementation of HRM programs. Despite the conclusion of HRM proponents such as Kochan, Katz, and McKersie, that strong unions were needed for HRM to succeed, the pace of introduction would seem to be more directly correlated with the weakening of unionism. These proponents had simply ignored the bottom line in management's goals to which HRM was the means. Ultimately, HRM would be used as a "cloak for unilateralism."

Unilateralism

In the United States, the long-term goal of management as it concerns labor relations has been to avoid union interference in management decisions whenever and however possible. As the National Association of Manufacturers put it in 1956, "Employers hold no brief for the retention of 'sacred prerogatives' as such. They only contend for the freedom which is required in order to do a good job. . . ."[78] Doing a good job can encompass many things, and any attempt to interfere with management's right to run its plant can lead to reduced managerial performance, as measured by profits. Unions keep management from doing everything it wants. For management to be doing a good job on its terms, it must eliminate unions. By the 1980s, for example, the National Association of Manufacturers was actively pushing for the end of unionism by way of its Committee for a Union-Free Environment.

It is questionable that the National Association of Manufacturers speaks for all of management in the United States. John Dunlop once pointed out that such statements were slogans that did not "have to confront the reality of the industrial workplace," where peace with unions was more important.[79] Although it is true that associations have no official authority to speak for all of management, their statements may well be representative. The truth of managements' attitudes to unions may have been contained in *Business Week*'s sanguine observation, "American business has by and large never really accepted unionism."[80]

Barkin characterized this attitude as unilateralism, a policy wherein management seeks unhindered "rights to control the work place and to dispose of its work force in ways which would most satisfactory contribute to its production and cost goals."[81] This unilateral control was the primary short- and long-term goal of management and its conservative supporters. Democratic principles were to be avoided in managing the firm, as they would only increase costs. It was especially necessary to keep costs low during the present era, when international competition was causing so much economic distress.

Unilateralists mounted a propaganda drive that laid the blame for current economic problems on unions. Many of the programs unions had fought for, both in the firm and in society, were infringing on management's rights and adding to higher costs. Management recognized that a naked assault on union gains as part of an assertion of unilateralism might lead to worker militancy. That was one reason for following a program of HRM and getting cooperation from workers and their unions when possible.

In addition, management called for greater flexibility on the part of workers. In order to keep costs as low as possible, management wanted the freedom to hire and fire workers as it saw fit, thereby eliminating some restraints that have been put on it by law and by collective bargaining contracts. Managers also wanted greater freedom with regard to making job assignments, monitoring work effort, and control of working time (including vacations, holidays, overtime, second shifts, and part-time work). Finally, management wanted to be able to make a distinction between core and peripheral workers, which would result in a two-tier system consisting of highly paid workers with security and a lower-paid group without seniority rights.[82] As the information in Chapter Four implies, a program of flexibility would completely eliminate just about everything unions have accomplished for their members.

The push for unilateralism in the United States also entered the political sphere during the Reagan Administration. Reagan took a tough stance against unions, eliminated any contacts between his administration and unions, maintained that he was interested in the needs of labor as a whole and not just unions, and curtailed the staff and many activities of the Department of Labor. In addition, NLRB became dominated by Republican appointees, giving it an even more conservative outlook, with its chairman's asserting, "collective bargaining means labor monopoly, the destruction of individual freedom and the destruction of the market place for determining the value of labor."[83]

Union Response

In the face of such a strong counterattack by management groups, the AFL-CIO began taking action, but it was a long time coming. As Barkin noted, there had been earlier warnings, including his own, yet they had been "dismissed by the President of the AFL/CIO. Mumbled concerns were heard in the ranks of the leadership and the rank and file of the membership but no deliberate steps were taken to reexamine the strengths and weaknesses of the trade union movement until 1985."[84] Barkin considered this situation astounding, especially since he had called more than twenty years previously for a union commission to be formed to appraise its state.[85]

A report by the AFL-CIO, titled "The Changing Situation of Workers and Their Unions," did provide some analysis of the problems being faced by unions and their members. It gave unions some credit for resiliency—as unions had indeed retained a steady membership in the face of very adverse conditions—pointing out that unions still held 28 percent of workers eligible for union membership but noting that that figure was down from a high of 45 percent in 1954. (The figures differ from those given at the beginning of the chapter because they are percentages of eligible workers who belong to unions, not the percentage of the labor force; not all members of the work force are eligible for union membership, including the author in his present employment.) The committee cited as reasons for this decline the elements of the structural argument presented above and the failure of the NLRA to be applied effectively.[86] These were elements of decline that Barkin had previously identified, but the study did not include a direct reference to any of the internal problems of unions and their organizational structure such as he had noted.

There was an implicit reference to Barkin's criticisms of union effort and organization in some of the recommendations the study committee set forth to counter the decline of unionism. First, several methods were proposed for making new approaches to workers, including new forms of representation, new types of membership, new services to be provided for members outside of collective bargaining, and a pilot program of experimental organizing committees.[87] All of these methods were aimed at organizing the unorganized and making unions a broader part of the life of workers outside the plant, both of which were reforms Barkin had previously suggested.

A second set of recommendations aimed at giving workers more chances to participate in their union. Not only would members learn more about their union through better communications, but also programs that included interaction with leaders would give them a greater commitment to the union movement—as would another proposal for giving special orientation programs for new members. Moreover, leaders and potential leaders would be given special training programs to make them more effective. The committee also suggested several measures for communicating the union message to the general public.[88] Barkin had always stressed the need for better communications with members and the general public.

In the area of changing the way organizing drives took place, the committee made recommendations along the lines of reforms Barkin had previously suggested. It was proposed that a more exacting screening process be used in the selection and training of organizers. Equally important, union leaders and members should be more actively brought into organizing drives; members were especially important, for their participation would bring them into closer contact with union activities and make them better advocates for unionism. Finally, it was time for more effort to be made to organize small plants, especially "since 35 percent of the national work force is employed in companies with less than 25 employees." In all of these organizing efforts, use should be made of modern polling techniques, advanced communication technology, and experimental organizing techniques.[89] These recommendations, too, were in line with the reforms Barkin had offered twenty years before.

In its proposals for changing the structure of the national effort of the AFL-CIO, however, the study committee was not willing to go so far as Barkin in pushing for a centralized effort. It did propose that the AFL-CIO Executive Council take a stronger role in setting guidelines and offering assistance for affiliates to merge with each other. The decline of the movement had created a number of smaller unions, which could be made stronger through merger.[90] No effort was to be made to strengthen the national headquarters in, for example, organizing, as Barkin had wanted.

Barkin also came up with some new proposals to help foster the development of unions. One proposal called for a new representation system for workers, wherein "representational units should be created by employee petitions speaking for 25 percent or more of the employees of an establishment, exclusive of executive personnel, with certification by a national government agency." In this way, workers who wanted representation before management, even if they were a minority, could have it. If two or more of such units were formed, they should coordinate their efforts; any organization seeking to be the sole agent for workers would have to get signatures of more than half of the employees.

A reason for relying on signature petitions instead of elections after signatures are collected, as is current NLRB practice, is to speed up the election process. Delays in elections are always of benefit to management. Barkin also proposed that the employer be required to bargain with these units on a variety of issues such as plant closing and relocation and subcontracting, in addition to wages and benefits. Because employers often drag their feet in bargaining with newly formed unions as a way of weakening union appeal, Barkin wanted the NLRB "to be able to impose upon an employer who has violated his bargaining obligations appropriate rates of change in compensation and other terms and conditions of employment."[91] Although these proposals would help workers to get more opportunities for representation and might be of benefit to the union movement, it is doubtful that the AFL-CIO has enough political clout to get them enacted into law.

Efforts were made by the AFL-CIO in the political arena, but these proved unsuccessful. Much lobbying was undertaken to bring about labor law reform at the national level, but Congress, in the 1976 proposal, for example, had proved unwilling. The AFL-CIO's work in helping Walter Mondale to secure the Democratic Party nomination for president in 1984, although successful, backfired as Mondale went down to defeat, partly because of being branded as a captive of the labor movement. In 1988, the AFL-CIO backed off from that strategy and supported a variety of candidates in the Democratic Party presidential primaries. This approach, too, failed.

All of these responses by the union movement were well within the range of what Barkin had proposed, as previously described. Barkin had felt that many changes were needed within the movement, which is why he had written so urgently in the 1950s and early 1960s. He wanted to awaken union leaders and sympathizers from their complacency. It is possible, simply to speculate, that if union leaders had been more vocal supporters of civil rights legislation and Great Society programs as passed by the administration of Lyndon Johnson, they might have been in a position to push for labor law legislation that was later thwarted. In the early 1960s, they had not even perceived that changes in labor law were crucial. Had they paid more attention to Barkin's analysis, they might have made their proposals for reform in the law and in their own affairs much earlier. Instead, they waited until the decline of the labor movement had become a crisis, one that would have a very detrimental impact on the state of workers, unions, and their friends.

Impact of Decline

The two decades from 1970 to 1990 represented a period of great decline for labor unions. They were also a period of economic change and crisis in the United States, with two energy shocks, four recessions, and an increase in international competition in manufacturing. These are all a part of the restructuring of the economy that has added to the decline of unions. Additional pressure on unions has come from a program of deregulation of industries, which has weakened the ability of unions to gain wage increases and members in such formerly regulated industries as air travel and trucking. Many of these changes were made under Republican administrations, which believed that they would lead to greater growth for the whole economy.

Economic growth has taken place, but it has not benefited the whole economy. Instead, it has changed a long-term trend that was the heart of the American way of life. As Barkin describes it, "For more than a century American employees enjoyed the highest earnings and benefits and independence. No other country could claim to be in reach of these standards. During the last two decades the position has been changed. Recent improvements in earnings in the United States have hardly been sufficient to keep abreast of spiraling living costs." In Europe, by comparison, "their earnings are the highest, their jobs more secure, the social benefits are more numerous and extensive."[92]

Barkin's 1980 appraisal of earnings of workers in the United States are actually optimistic, for real wages have since declined. At the start of 1973, the index of real hourly earnings of nonfarm production workers was at 102.3 (using 1977 as a base year). As a result of ensuing inflation and recession, they fell and never reached that level again, hitting a lower level of 100.9 in early 1978. In July 1981, during the next recession, they fell to a level of 92.0. The recovery brought them back to a peak of 95.3 in November 1986, from which they began falling to 92.7 in December 1988, after which the series was redefined. The trend was clear, from a peak in 1973—real hourly wages of workers had declined by more than 10 percent by 1988, and that was not a recession year.[93] To put this trend in dollar amounts, in 1978 average weekly real earnings (1988 dollars) were $363; they fell to $323 during 1981, rose to $332 in 1983, but then fell to $317 by June 1989.[94]

The impact of these trends on union workers has also been negative. The 1980s were a time of union "givebacks" and concessions. Freeman and Medhoff report that the automobile industry saw labor cost estimated at a 7–12 percent reduction and the airline industry showing wage reductions of 10–15 percent. Given the rate of inflation at the time, these were substantial pay cuts for union workers, but Freeman and Medhoff remark that they really brought the wage differential that union workers were receiving back to earlier levels compared to nonunion workers.[95]

The fact that union workers had increased their advantage over nonunion workers in terms of pay meant that unions were better able to protect their members from the inflation that had preceded the 1980s. The 1980s were a different story, as all workers, probably including union members, experienced continued decline in their real wages. As unions became weaker in the 1970s, their spillover effect on other industries probably declined as well. By the 1980s, they were barely able to help their own members.

While workers saw their real wages fall during the 1980s, top executives showed substantial pay gains, estimated at 13 percent average annual increases for 1980–89 compared to 4 percent for factory workers.[96] By 1990, the average head of a large corporation in the United States was making thirty-five times the pay of the average worker in manufacturing, compared to a 20:1 ratio in Europe and a 15:1 ratio in Japan, and up considerably from a decade earlier. This disparity of pay was also impinging heavily on mid-level managers in those corporations.[97] As noted in Chapter Five, the overall impact of unions on income distribution was to tend toward equality. In the 1980s, as unions weakened, this impact was more than offset by other factors, including higher executives' getting more pay. Thus a union proponent such as Barkin would not be surprised by Congressman Lee Hamilton's comment about income distribution changes during the 1980s: "This disparity in income shares is the largest since these statistics were first compiled in 1947."[98]

In the area of benefits, as Barkin had observed, the United States has been lagging. In early 1990, the U.S. Bureau of the Census reported that 63 million persons in the United States (28 percent of the population) did not have health insurance coverage for large amounts of time.[99] Pension coverage was also declining. In 1979, half of the work force had employer-financed pension plans, an amount that declined to 46 percent in 1988. This decline was especially notice-able among males under the age of 35, whose pension coverage fell from 46 percent to 37 percent. By comparison, 89 percent of union workers are covered by pensions.[100]

The reduced coverage for younger males in pension programs is probably indicative of their finding jobs in a nonunion environment. As part of the restruc-turing of the economy, deindustrializing industries have cut back on their hiring of new workers. Instead, new workers have been more likely to find work with small companies, often in the service sector. These companies have been less willing to shoulder the burden of social costs that is imposed on their workers, and without unions to compel them to do so, they will shift them to the commu-nity as much as possible.

In political matters, the decline of unions has also led to a weakened relation-ship between unions and their political allies. In the United States, the CIO in the 1930s became part of the alliance that elected Franklin Roosevelt to the presi-dency and supported a variety of liberal programs. In 1955, the AFL-CIO, just after the merger, formed the Committee for Political Education to help foster the alliance between unions and the Democratic Party. As unions have weakened, they have diminished in their ability to deliver labor's vote to the Democratic Party. As Barkin reports in a survey of conditions facing unions in the early 1990s, union member support for Michael Dukakis in the 1988 election was only moderate. In return, "even though the Democratic party has commanded majori-ties in both houses of Congress during most recent years, labor's powerful and skillful lobbies have not gained significant union legislation."[101]

Here again can be seen the contradiction facing unions as they pursue politi-cal goals. In the United States, political parties have traditionally eschewed being the voice of a particular group, such as organized labor. Without this direct political connection, unions cannot openly influence elected government offi-cials during an election campaign, nor can they make their agenda a campaign issue. They must then resort to lobbying, the established channel in the United States for special interests to influence policy. Lobbying strength by unions, however, often diminishes their overall vitality when they are painted as being another special interest group. Barkin understood that unions had to push for specific programs, but he always believed that those programs should be placed within the context of the basic purposes of the union movement, to offset "the abuses of authority" and "to minimize the human costs of industrial progress."[102] Other than appealing to social idealism, Barkin never formulated a political strategy for unions that was specific to their problems yet could elicit a broad social appeal. Nor did anyone else.

Unions have thus become weaker at gaining legislative support for their own programs. By forming alliances with other groups, however, they can be success-ful in gaining victories in areas of broader social and economic reform. Social legislation and other benefits have been obtained through the pressure of such broader coalitions: witness the improvement of benefits for older workers when unions have been a help. Thomas Edsall, after reviewing comparative international measures of union strength, has concluded, "Those countries with strong labor union movements have in place policies of taxation, employment, and social spending advantageous to the working class."[103]

Lack of success by unions in winning political gains for themselves or for society has tended to lend a more conservative bent to government. It has also made for a greater spirit of conservatism among intellectuals. As the union movement became more narrowly focused, it began losing the support among intellectuals that it had once enjoyed. By the 1960s, many social thinkers had shifted their allegiance away from unions and to the civil rights movement, for the struggle to gain political equality for minorities had an idealistic quality to it. As that movement gained its political successes, its aims were felt by many to be accomplished. It, too, began promoting economic headway for its constituents. Idealists are less concerned about such basic issues as rate of pay above the minimum.

In general, intellectuals live difficult, alienated existences, albeit through their own choosing. Their ideal is the free-floating thinker, beholden to no one, free to pursue the truth. They often will see themselves as above the struggle for existence. Their loyalty is to ideas, which alienates them from consideration of practical affairs. It also makes them shifty characters, for ideas are open to metamorphosis. Free-floating entities, alienated from complete loyalty to social institutions, are easily buffeted by social transformations. Although ideas are not power, they can be used in the service of power. It is not surprising that intellectuals seek shelter in the pursuit of ideas that appeal to the powerful. Academics interested in labor issues have been especially prone to such intellectual drift.

As the spirit of unilateralism began to prevail in industrial relations, Barkin wrote, "Academics were sure to follow, outlining rationales for submerging bilateral decision-making and the independence of the unions."[104] Particularly disheartening to Barkin were the inroads being made among membership of the Industrial Relations Research Association (IRRA) by advocates of the HRM approach, especially because Barkin had been its president in 1964.

In the era immediately following World War II, schools of industrial relations were formed at many U.S. universities. These schools usually remained separate from the programs in business administration and management, in which the philosophy of management is strongest. Faculty at the industrial relations schools could usually be counted as advocates for collective bargaining as a key element in the attainment of good relations between labor and management. As unions declined, however, student interest in industrial relations waned. As a result, as Barkin saw it, "The spokesmen for these industrial relations (labor) departments or schools in universities in their haste to recoup their position in the student market are ready to succumb to the managerial pressures for teaching the unilateral approach to employment relations." As these schools become more like business programs, they might become superfluous and their existence would be threatened by those in charge of university budgets. Nor would unions have any reason to lend political support to them.[105]

As the primary professional association for industrial research, the IRRA might be expected to be unwilling to compromise its long-standing support for collective bargaining and unions. Barkin found many instances wherein its leaders were willing to make deals with management-oriented groups and arranged an annual meeting that "offered an array of one-sided papers, deliberately excluding labor's voice. The Distinguished Speaker crassly slurred unionists and unions."[106] Not that the entire membership of the IRRA was willing to abandon the association's commitment to collective bargaining. Rather, Barkin attributed the deficiencies in the IRRA's programs to the advocacy of a strong group of HRM supporters. By yielding to their influence, the IRRA did unions a disservice. As Barkin summarized his position, "In urging the substitution of Human Resource Management programs for bilateralism and collective bargaining, the proponents are counterposing a unilateral system of industrial governance. Such action is incompatible with the purposes and spirit of an organization born of the desire to introduce the study of unionism and collective bargaining into the roster of academic subject matter."[107]

That was the rub for Barkin. Among academics, he had always strived to promote interest in and support for unions. He had especially hoped that academics would develop ideas to help unions solve their problems; he would also want to see them infuse intellectual idealism into the union movement. As unions declined, their need for ideas and idealism was even greater, and academics were more and more standing on the sidelines on labor-management issues, when they were not actively supporting management.

In a letter to Clark Kerr outlining his thoughts on the struggle in the IRRA against the HRM advocates, Barkin noted, "It reminds me of the battle cry of the thirties when we declared that 'it is later than you think.' "[108] Barkin worried that in the struggle between unions and management, it is getting late. As with the IRRA, he felt that with unions the struggle could be won. With unions, however, he would want a victory not just to preserve them as a feature of industrial relations that merely served their members. As this section has argued, the decline of unions has had a number of side effects on society as a whole. Their weakening has not only lowered the pay of their own members but also reduced the impact of the union spillover effect on nonunion workers and other salaried employees, in terms of both pay and benefits. A powerful voice for liberal reform has been quieted. Finally, intellectuals have lost an area that should have been of great interest to them, and academics have taken on a stronger bias toward management. These are all unhealthy results that Barkin would greatly deplore.

Conclusion

If Barkin had done nothing more in his life but produce his study on the decline of the labor movement, he would still have been worthy of recognition. As one of the first intellectuals to recognize the weakening status of unions, he was able to alert others to the threats facing this valuable social institution. The value of the study was more than prophetic, however. In that study, Barkin also suggested some possible remedies. If unions had followed his advice when it was first offered, their position today might have been stronger. They would have been better able to protect themselves with legal reforms whose enactment might have been possible in the more favorable climate that then existed.

Even a favorable climate, however, would not have saved unions from the many adverse conditions they faced. Elements such as automated technology, plant relocations, and international competition have undermined the bargaining strength of unions and their members. These could have been offset by a variety of policies that Barkin suggested, especially a dedication to new organization. Particular polices for management, as described in Chapter Four, and government, as described in Chapter Six, if followed, certainly would have made unions stronger than they are today. They would also have led to a more equitable society.

Such policies were not followed by management and government. Instead, as Barkin has pointed out, the decline of unionism in the United States has been the result of "a collaborative attack by government and management."[109] No revisions of the labor laws were passed, and the NLRB became increasingly conservative in its interpretation of the existing laws. Management became more willing to break existing labor laws as a way to defeat unions, determining that the fines and penalties that followed were worth paying if unions could be avoided. Between 1970 and 1980, the number of workers ordered reinstated by the NLRB as a result of unfair labor practices by business rose by 216 percent, the number of workers awarded back pay in such cases increased by 128 percent, and the number of unfair practices filed against business went up by 130 percent, all during a time when the number of representation elections remained virtually constant.[110] The climate became openly hostile to unions.

As a result of this hostile climate, management groups could boldly reveal their long-held but latent desire to seek a union-free environment. Although a union-free environment might have advantages for management (Barkin would disagree that those advantages outweigh the costs of poor industrial relations), they are of very dubious value as a public policy. Consider the case of North Carolina.

North Carolina is still the home of much of the nation's textile industry. As a right-to-work state, it is also a stronghold of management resistance to unions (only 6.5 percent of its labor force belong to unions), with the result that the average wage in manufacturing in the state—$7.45 an hour in 1990—

is the lowest in the nation. This low wage may be a benefit to employers battling international competition, but it has not been a blessing for the residents of North Carolina. The state has the highest level of infant mortality of any state, and its youth have the poorest record of educational achievement in the country. In both these areas, this dismal effort reflects low levels of state support for public health centers and schools, a result of the low tax base from an underpaid work force.[111] Low wages also make it very difficult for workers to pay for these social services on their own, so that few private health facilities are available, and families are often forced to remove children from schools prematurely to send them to work.

This gloomy picture would not come as a surprise to Barkin. His own experiences among Southern textile workers would have alerted him to the difficulties they had encountered in attaining a full-cost social wage. Thus he would be well aware that a union-free environment would do the same for the entire nation. In effect, he maintained, the antiunion strategy of management and its government partners aimed at reducing the responsibilities of meeting the social cost of workers. He wrote, "Now we are being asked to scrap a wide variety of regulations developed through collective bargaining, law or administrative orders. Management wishes to shed itself of costs and transfer them back to individuals or society. This course will not eliminate the effects or their costs. It will merely relieve the entrepreneur of their immediate incidence and thereby remove the incentives for improved practices."[112]

Mainstream economists are fond of reminding us that there is no such thing as a free lunch, that all economic activities use resources. They rarely apply their concept to the problem of social costs, especially the social costs of work. By this omission, they are tacitly supporting the point of view of management, which would abandon payment of social costs in the name of international competitiveness. The decline of unions has helped to reduce the business contribution to payment of the social costs of work, and a union-free environment would help even more. That environment would not lead to the type of society that most U.S. citizens would care to see. For these reasons, Barkin hoped for a revival of the union movement. Although some union leaders have identified the causes of slow growth, they still have a bigger problem in identifying themselves with the broader social issues that face all of society. If they fail, all of society will be the loser.

Notes

1. Sumner Slichter, *The American Economy: Its Problems and Prospects* (New York: Alfred A. Knopf, Inc., 1948), pp. 4–7, 212.

2. Ibid., pp. 35, 39, 60.

3. Ibid., p. 170.

4. Neil W. Chamberlain, *The Challenge to Management Control* (New York: Archon Books, 1967, reprint of 1948 book), p. 140; see also p. 210.

5. Ibid., p. 90.

6. Nelson Lichtenstein, "From Corporatism to Collective Bargaining: Organized Labor and the Eclipse of Social Democracy in the Postwar Era," in Steven Fraser and Gary Gerstle, eds., *The Rise and Fall of the New Deal Order, 1930–1980* (Princeton, NJ: Princeton University Press, 1989), p. 125.

7. Kim Moody, *An Injury to All: The Decline of American Unionism* (London and New York: Verso, 1988), p. 17.

8. Joseph G. Rayback, *A History of American Labor* (New York: Free Press, 1966), pp. 380–83.

9. Philip Murray, "The Gap Between Wages and Prices," *Atlantic Monthly* (July 1948), reprinted in Arleigh P. Hess Jr., Robert H. Gallman, John P. Rice, and Carl Stern, *Outside Readings in Economics* (New York: Thomas Y. Crowell Co., 1951), pp. 267–68.

10. Ibid., pp. 278–79.

11. Solomon Barkin, "Selected Aspects of the CIO Experience," Proceedings of the Thirty-eighth Annual Meeting of the Industrial Relations Research Association, 1986, p. 192.

12. Rayback, *History of American Labor,* pp. 422–428.

13. A. H. Raskin, "Labor: A Movement in Search of a Mission," in Seymour Martin Lipsett, ed., *Unions in Transition: Entering the Second Century* (San Francisco: ICS Press, 1986), p. 12.

14. Rayback, *History of American Labor,* p. 427.

15. Moody, *An Injury to All,* p. 60.

16. Bruce Laurie, *Artisans into Workers* (New York: Noonday Press, 1989).

17. "The Reminiscences of Solomon Barkin," Oral History Research Office, Columbia University, 1961, pp. 103–5.

18. Barkin, "Selected Aspects of the CIO Experience," p. 190.

19. Sumner H. Slichter, James J. Healy, and Robert E. Livernash, *The Impact of Collective Bargaining on Management* (Washington, DC: The Brookings Institution, 1960), pp. 6, 12.

20. Solomon Barkin, "A New Environment Confronts Trade Unions in Advanced Industrial Countries," in Bruce Nissen, *U.S. Labor Relations, 1945–1989, Accommodation and Conflict* (New York: Garland Publishing Co., 1990, p. 250.

21. Richard B. Freeman, "Does the New Generation of Labor Economists Know More Than the Old Generation?" in Bruce E. Kaufman, ed., *How Labor Markets Work* (Lexington, MA: Lexington Books, 1988), p. 214.

22. Leo Troy, "The Rise and Fall of American Trade Unions: The Labor Movement from FDR to RR," in Seymour Martin Lipsett, ed., *Unions in Transition* (San Francisco: ICS Press, 1986), pp. 81, 86, 87, 92. Figure for union density in 1989 from Gary N. Chaison and Joseph B. Rose, "New Directions and Divergent Paths: The North American Labor Movements in Troubled Times," Industrial Relations Research Association, *Proceedings of the 1990 Spring Meeting*, May 2–4, 1990, p. 591.

23. Thomas A. Kochan, Harry C. Katz, and Robert B. McKersie, *The Transformation of American Industrial Relations* (New York: Basic Books, Inc., 1986), p. 77.

24. Solomon Barkin, *The Decline of the Labor Movement and What Can Be Done about It*, a report to the Center for the Study of Democratic Institutions, 1961, p. 5.

25. Ibid., pp. 10–11.

26. Richard Edwards, "Introduction," in Richard Edwards, Paolo Garonna, and Franz Todtling, *Unions in Crisis and Beyond: Perspectives from Six Countries* (Dover, MA: Auburn House Publishing Co., 1986), p. 8.

27. Cited in Kochan, Katz, and McKersie, *Transformation of American Industrial Relations*, p. 54.

28. Richard B. Freeman and James L. Medhoff, *What Do Unions Do?* (New York: Basic Books, Inc., 1984), pp. 224–28.

29. Kochan, Katz, and McKersie, *Transformation of American Industrial Relations*, pp. 72–73.

30. Barkin, *Decline of the Labor Movement*, p. 16.

31. Kochan, Katz, and McKersie, *Transformation of American Industrial Relations*, p. 8.

32. Barkin, *Decline of the Labor Movement*, p. 20.

33. Ibid., pp. 20–22.

34. Freeman and Medhoff, *What Do Unions Do?* pp. 230–36.

35. Barkin, *Decline of the Labor Movement*, pp. 25–26.

36. Ibid., pp. 27–28.

37. Ibid., pp. 50–51.

38. Ibid., pp. 36–37.

39. Ibid., pp. 38–52.

40. Michael Goldfield, *The Decline of Organized Labor in the United States* (Chicago: University of Chicago Press, 1987), pp. 130–36.

41. Freeman and Medhoff, *What Do Unions Do?*, pp. 28–30, 229.

42. Barkin, *Decline of the Labor Movement*, pp. 53–54.

43. Cited in Thomas Byrne Edsall, *The New Politics of Inequality* (New York: W. W. Norton & Co., 1984), p. 151.

44. Barkin, *Decline of the Labor Movement*, pp. 55–59.

45. Goldfield, *Decline of Organized Labor*, pp. 236–38.

46. Moody, *An Injury to All*, pp. 28–33, 45–51.

47. Barkin, "Selected Aspects of the CIO Experience," p. 191.

48. Solomon Barkin, "Pure and Simple Unionism: An Adequate Base for Union Growth?" (manuscript in author's possession), p. 5, later published in George Strauss, Daniel G. Gallagher, and Jack Fiorito, eds., *The State of the Unions* (Madison, WI: Industrial Relations Research Association, 1992), pp. 353–60.

49. Barkin, "Selected Aspects of the CIO Experience," p. 194.

50. Barkin, *Decline of the Labor Movement*, pp. 68–69.

51. Ibid., pp. 70–72.

52. Ibid., pp. 73–74.

53. Ibid., pp. 62–63.

54. "Review and Outlook," *Wall Street Journal*, December 4, 1961.

55. Irving Bernstein, review of "The Decline of the Labor Movement and What Can be Done about It" *Industrial and Labor Relations Review* 15 (January 1963).

56. "Union Self-Criticism," *New York Times*, December 6, 1961.

57. "Time for a Change," *LRA's Economic Notes* 58 (November-December 1990), pp. 1–4.

58. Ben Seligman, "New Views on Labor," in Seligman, *Economics of Dissent* (Chicago: Quadrangle Books, 1968), p. 399.

59. Richard Edwards and Michael Podgursky, "The Unraveling Accord: American Unions in Crisis," in Edwards, Garonna, and Todtling, *Unions in Crisis and Beyond*, pp. 19–27.

60. Solomon Barkin, "Pure and Simple Unionism," p. 6.

61. Ibid.

62. Solomon Barkin, "A Trade Unionist Appraises Management's Personnel Philosophy," *Harvard Business Review* 28 (September 1950).

63. This discussion of human relations programs owes much to Elizabeth Fones-Wolf, "Beneath Consensus: Capital, Labor and the Post-War Order" (Ph.D. dissertation, University of Massachusetts at Amherst), ch. 4.

64. Douglas McGregor, *The Human Side of Enterprise* (New York: McGraw-Hill, 1960), pp. 33–57.

65. Kochan, Katz, and McKersie, *Transformation of American Industrial Relations*, p. 95.

66. Irving H. Siegel and Edgar Weinberg, *Labor-Management Cooperation: The American Experience* (Kalamazoo, MI: W. E. Upjohn Institute for Employment Research, 1982), pp. 140–44.

67. Solomon Barkin, "The Current Unilateralist Attack on Unionism and Collective Bargaining," *Rélations Industrielles* 41 (1986), p. 15.

68. Solomon Barkin, "Critique of the report of the IRRA Comprehensive Review Committee," 1988 (copy in author's possession).

69. Solomon Barkin, "The Dark Side of Quality Circles," *Workplace Democracy* 52 (Spring 1986), reprinted in *A Quartet of Economic Book Reviews* (University of Massachusetts at Amherst: Labor Relations and Research Center, Reprint Series Number 89, 1982), p. 18.

70. Linda Kaboolian, "Auto Workers Assess 'Employee Involvement,' " *Proceedings of the Forty-Second Meeting, Industrial Relations Research Association* (December 1989), pp. 344–52.

71. Siegel and Weinberg, *Labor-Management Cooperation*, p. 150.

72. Mike Parker, *Inside the Circle: A Union Guide to QWL* (Boston: South End Press, 1985), pp. 23–26.

73. Donald M. Wells, *Empty Promises: Quality of Working Life Programs and the Labor Movement* (New York: Monthly Review Press, 1987), pp. 2–5, 91.

74. Kochan, Katz, and McKersie, *Transformation of American Industrial Relations*, pp. 176–77.

75. Cited in Gene Koretz, "Economic Trends" column, *Business Week*, April 1, 1991, p. 18.

76. Solomon Barkin, "Human Resource Management Examines Itself and Its Limitations," *Rélations Industrielles* 44 (1989), pp. 691–93.

77. Solomon Barkin, review of Harry C. Katz, *Shifting Gears: Changing Labor Relations in the United States Automobile Industry, Journal of Economic Issues* 20 (September 1986), p. 879.

78. Cited in Bakke, Kerr, and Anrod, p. 230.

79. John Dunlop, "Consensus and National Labor Policy," in Richard A. Lester, ed., *Labor: Readings on Major Issues* (New York: Random House, 1965), pp. 492–93.

80. *Business Week*, December 4, 1978, p. 56, as cited in David Brody, *Workers in Industrial America* (New York: Oxford University Press, 1980), p. 248.

81. Barkin, "Current Unilateralist Attack on Unionism," p. 15.

82. Solomon Barkin, "The Flexibility Debate in Western Europe," *Rélations Industrielles* 42 (1987), pp. 30–31.

83. Barkin, "Current Unilateralist Attack on Unionism," pp. 8–9.

84. Ibid., p. 12.

85. Solomon Barkin, "The Road to the Future: A Trade-Union Commission for Self-Analysis," *Annals of the American Academy of Political and Social Science* 350 (November 1963), pp. 138–45.

86. *The Changing Situation of Workers and Their Unions*, a report by the AFL-CIO Committee on the Evolution of Work (February 1985), pp. 5–11.

87. Ibid., pp. 18–22.

88. Ibid., pp. 23–26.

89. Ibid., pp. 27–28.

90. Ibid., pp. 30–31.

91. Solomon Barkin, "An Agenda for the Revision of the American Industrial Relations System," *Labor Law Journal* (November 1985), p. 859.

92. Solomon Barkin, "European Industrial Relations: A Resource for the Reconstruction of the American System," *Rélations Industrielles* 35 (1980), p. 443.

93. Data are derived from Datadisk Computer Information Service, Cambridge Planning and Analytics, Inc., August 1990.

94. AFL-CIO, *The Pocketbook Issues* (Washington, DC: AFL-CIO, 1989), p. 9.

95. Freeman and Medhoff, *What Do Unions Do?* pp. 56–57.

96. AFL-CIO, "Excessive Executive Pay," *AFL-CIO Reviews the Issues*, Report No. 42 (June 1990), p. 1.

97. Joani Nelson-Horchler, "What's Your Boss Worth?" *Washington Post*, August 5, 1990, p. D3. Conservative author Kevin Phillips, in his recent *Politics of Rich and Poor*, shows a pay ratio between workers and board chairmen of 29:1 in 1979 and 98:1 in 1988, as cited by Richard Morin, "The Curious Politics of Greed and Envy," *Washington Post*, October 21, 1990. p. C2.

98. Lee Hamilton, "Tax Fairness," *Washington Post*, August 5, 1990, p. D7.

99. Spencer Rich, "28% in United States Seen Lacking Steady Health Insurance," *Washington Post*, April 12, 1990, p. A19.

100. Aaron Bernstein, "In Search of the Vanishing Nest Egg," *Business Week*, July 30, 1990, p. 46.

101. Solomon Barkin, "New Environment Confronts Trade Unions," p. 238.

102. Barkin, *Decline of the Labor Movement*, p. 69.

103. Thomas Byrne Edsall, *The New Politics of Inequality* (New York: Oxford University Press, 1982), p. 147.

104. Barkin, "New Environment Confronts Trade Unions," p. 248.

105. Solomon Barkin, "Comments on the Proceedings of the Fortieth Annual IRRA Meeting" (1988) (copy in author's possession), pp. 8–10, forthcoming in a volume sponsored by the IRRA.

106. Ibid., p. 1.

107. Solomon Barkin, "Critique of the Committee Report" (1988) (copy in author's possession), p. 6.

108. Solomon Barkin to Clark Kerr, August 25, 1988, author's copy.

109. Barkin, "New Environment Confronts Trade Unions," p. 248.

110. Edsall, *New Politics of Inequality*, p. 152.

111. Nan Chase, "North Carolina's Beauty Masks a Bleak Social Reality," *Washington Post*, March 20, 1990, p. A4.

112. Barkin, "Flexibility Debate in Western Europe," p. 37.

Conclusion: Full Productive and Freely Chosen Employment

Throughout this study, a constant theme has been that Barkin's life and work were motivated by a desire to see all workers earn a wage that covered the costs of life—a social cost wage. This is a desire he shared with members of the New Deal and with liberals of any era. Because liberalism and the New Deal were declared obsolete during the conservative period of the 1980s and early 1990s, it would be easy to conclude that Barkin's ideas are also outmoded and of interest only to intellectual historians. Conservative thinking cannot eliminate the problems of social costs, however. It can only ignore them. For this reason, many of the ideas illustrated in this book as ways to compensate workers for the social costs they undergo as part of productive effort remain applicable. Not only are they applicable, but they are the only ideas available. Effort has been expended to create methods to deal with the social cost of the environment, but the search for solutions to the difficulties inherent in the social costs of work lag behind. As this is being written in the spring of 1992, for example, the news is still filled with stories of victims of the current, slow-to-end recession—workers whose unemployment benefits have run out or been eliminated from coverage by the unemployment compensation system and who must skimp on food and shelter to survive. Corporate downsizing has produced much of the unemployment and touched the lives of even professional and managerial employees.

It doesn't have to be that way. The New Deal, whatever its shortcomings, was an effort to establish attainment of workers' social costs as a right. In 1944, President Roosevelt set forth a "second Bill of Rights," which included rights "to a useful and remunerative job," "to earn enough to provide adequate food, clothing and shelter," and "to adequate medical care and the opportunity to achieve and enjoy good health."[1] As an ardent supporter of the New Deal and a liberal, Barkin found this economic Bill of Rights acceptable and worthy of support.

An element of this "rights revolution" was the securing for unions the right to organize and bargain collectively. Barkin has been unstinting in his support of this change in attitude toward rights and unions. He has spent his life steadfastly on the union side. Those not so thoroughly imbued with union values will at least tacitly accept that management has rights with regard to running its plants and that these rights cannot be abridged. Barkin never accepted the idea that there was a set of sacrosanct managerial rights, instead arguing that management had many explicit and implicit responsibilities that it neglected. This perspective made him highly argumentative with labor economists and industrial relations experts when those groups fell short of full-fledged support for the union position. He believed that a worker's right to a wage covering all the costs of work had to have the highest priority and that unions were a way to usher in that sense of priority. He was in the union and sanctioned the union process of securing higher wages, both nominal and real.

When he left the union movement, Barkin retained its ideals. He also gained the freedom to pursue research projects that were important to him and in his judgment necessary to devise ways to help workers obtain the wages and benefits he felt they deserved. His work in his postunion days consisted of a culmination of many ideas that had been germinating previously. Projects that Barkin worked on during his period abroad are analyzed, followed by an assessment of his overall approach and contributions to labor economics and labor relations.

International Experiences

In 1961, Barkin was appointed by the secretary of labor to be a delegate to the International Labor Conference in Geneva, sponsored by the International Labor Office (ILO). At the conference, he was elected chairman of the workers' group and vice chairman of the Special Committee on Employment; he represented the workers' group in negotiating the ILO resolution on full employment. The Special Committee was composed of representatives from business, labor, and government, including representatives from the Soviet bloc. The final resolution, which Barkin presented at the plenary session, was titled "Full Productive and Freely Chosen Employment."

The content of the resolution created a new norm by "joining the objective of full employment with continuing economic growth, rising standards of living and respect for humanity and individual freedom." The inclusion of respect for humanity and individual freedom was intended as a counter to the Soviet delegates, who claimed to have always attained full employment. Barkin would give no quarter to a government that eliminated unemployment by way of slave labor camps. His intellectual honesty kept him above mere Soviet-bashing, however, and the resolution recognized that all was not perfect in the Western democracies. As he described both aspects of the resolution, "People had . . . to be offered job opportunities which most adequately utilized their capacities and attainments, for they then could make their maximum contribution. People also have a right to choose their employment and their locations without the compulsions of a police state or coercion by employers."[2]

This reference to coercion by employers is linked to the notion of social costs. It is easy to criticize the type of intimidation posed by a gun in the hands of an agent of the state, so it becomes less obvious that the threats of job loss, wage reductions, and hunger carry equal force. For workers in an unfettered market economy to freely choose their job, they must have adequate options and information about those options; for those jobs to be fully productive, they must match the skills workers have or can attain. To the extent that workers must maintain themselves on their own when unemployed, they have little time to discover all their options or to get the retraining they need. Earlier chapters have indicated the type of policies Barkin advocated for helping workers to be free to choose. His international experiences enabled him to refine those policies.

In 1963, at the recommendation of the U.S. Department of Labor, Barkin was appointed deputy to the director of Manpower and Social Affairs Directorate and head of the Social Affairs Divisions of the OECD in Paris. He was responsible for preparing proposals for studies by the division, for conducting annual reviews of the manpower policies of member countries of the OECD, and for defining the subjects for special studies and selecting the personnel to conduct those studies. He also had charge of the conduct of seminars for unionists, managers, government officials, and academics from the OECD countries. Given this job and the flexibility to carry it out, Barkin could seek answers to questions about how workers could be helped to freely choose productive employment at a social cost wage. Under his direction, the OECD published thirty-three separate reports on employment and manpower, held twenty-two international seminars on the same issues (also published), and undertook thirty-two international missions evaluating the employment and manpower policies of the OECD member countries. Of the published reports and seminars, Barkin was a firsthand contributor to forty-one of them by writing a preface, foreword, introduction, or chapter. These published reports of the OECD, produced during his tenure of 1963–67, are a reflection of his ideas.

The theme of the reports advocates the need for an active manpower policy, a concept described in Chapter Six. The concept of social costs as applied to labor may easily be construed as giving all workers equal pay, which would offset the effectiveness of markets and higher wages as methods of allocating labor to where it was needed most. Barkin never intended for a social cost wage to be more than a minimum guarantee, with workers' getting higher pay based on skills and the demand for those skills. Even that guarantee, it might be argued, would offset the market allocation process, for workers granted a living wage might not be willing to move to areas with higher-paid jobs.

That view, however, ignores that there are costs to moving. There are the human costs of being uprooted from a familiar location and the economic costs involved in gaining information about where to go, how to live there, and what skills are needed. These costs are also an impediment to the market allocation process. The challenge for workers is to take the risks inherent in moving. The problem for policymaking bodies, as Barkin saw it, is to "be responsive to current changes and informed about medium and long-term developments in the labour market so that it may provide adequate counsel to individuals, groups and the government."[3]

In his final report to the country members of the Manpower and Social Affairs Committee, Barkin gave a lengthy list of major conclusions to be drawn from his five years of work. Despite his plea that those conclusions could not be considered "exhaustive or present a detailed integration of the work or reports of the Social Affairs Division," still the list contains too many items (thirty) to be considered in full here. Several of them, however, can give insight into Barkin's thinking.

Based on his institutional approach to economic analysis, it is not surprising that Barkin would conclude, "An active social programme is an essential part of an active manpower policy. It concentrates on those members in or those potential recruits for the labour force whose productivity or participation is constrained by personal underdevelopment and maladjustments or against whom social practices have discriminated or who have been rejected." As a result, he continued, "an active manpower policy is a broader concept than an active labour market policy." Among other things, it must include consideration of "the internal personnel and industrial relations systems as they affect manpower."[4]

This last consideration was especially important, for success of a manpower program required "careful understanding of enterprise personnel and industrial relations policies" on the part of policymakers. Any workable policy would depend on "the competence, goals and activities of the enterprise personnel and [their] working relationship with the public bodies." A good working relationship with management was crucial, because the policy was "not restricted to compensating for the inefficiencies of the performance of the enterprise as employers," but included "guides to them on methods of operating more consistently and effectively in harmony with national manpower objectives." Unions were also important, Barkin concluded, because "the collective bargaining systems in most European countries have still to be oriented toward facilitating employee accommodations at the job level."[5]

Here we have the Barkin plan in a nutshell. An active manpower policy, under government auspices, must touch on all aspects of work at all levels. Within the macroeconomy, growth is not sufficient as a tool for full employment if bottlenecks in labor markets develop, causing labor shortages in some areas and unemployment in others; overall coordination by government agencies is needed. At the microeconomic level of the firm, policies must be in place to help workers adjust to changing work conditions; these policies need the cooperation of management and labor, also under the organizing influence of government.

These policies could serve to supplement the market allocation process, and they might also replace it. This possibility makes for a convenient starting place for an evaluation of Barkin's ideas.

Comprehensive Evaluation

In recent years, the idea that any type of national planning, which Barkin's proposal for active manpower policy requires, can be used to replace the market has been severely challenged by events in the Soviet Union. National planning is doomed to fail, mainstream economists argue, because planners cannot get the information that market transactions provide in terms of individual wants and desires. Moreover, faced with this lack of information, planners often take their own wants and desires and apply them to society as a whole. Planned economies are more reflective of the values of planners than they are of the values of society. In evaluating Barkin's approach, free market economists would identify this as a big problem.

Barkin would see it as a challenge rather than a problem, however. Nor was he foolish enough to overlook the issue. As he put it, "The effective promotion of an active manpower policy gives rise to its own special manpower, e.g., the recruitment and training of competent staff in sufficient numbers." His solution was to establish "professorships in the universities in manpower economics, sociology and statistics to raise a potential body of professionals. . . ." Detractors might add that this would create a dictatorship by the professorate, but Barkin quickly countered by observing, "Tests of administrative effectiveness in attaining goals are an essential part of the process of realizing the goals of an active manpower policy and need still to be developed for most activities."[6]

Barkin's whole approach is the experimental (pragmatic) method of trial and error. The professionals of a government manpower agency would learn by doing—hadn't Barkin done the same in his work with the NRA and TWUA? At the same time, other groups in society, including elected officials, would learn to produce procedures to assess the performance of professional experts in planning. Opponents of planning who base their opposition on the experiences of the Soviet Union should be reminded that its system was installed from above and without a democratic system of checks and balances. In the United States, a system of planning could evolve pragmatically under democratic traditions that would include programs of assessments and checks on the power of professionals. Barkin had tried to inveigle intellectuals prepared to undertake research about social costs into the labor movement to provide it with tools for assessing its programs as well as the government's.

The failure of such a system to evolve in the United States can be traced to a problem of market failure. Expertise in social and economic planning has not developed because there has been no market for it, and the same can be said for methods of assessing planning. A manpower policy such as Barkin proposed might have given an impetus to development of a system of social cost accounting capable of providing policymakers with the information they need. A strong union movement might have provided sustenance for intellectuals interested in researching the problem of social costs.

Another problem associated with planning in the United States involves the propensity to separate government from other sectors of society. In particular, Barkin stressed the lack of any consultation between government agencies and interest groups on policy. Even though there are legislative hearings, lobbying efforts, and occasional advisory groups, little is done to encourage direct working arrangements among all parties to a policy, such as took place under the NRA codes. In Europe, consultation with interest groups on policies is much more common and is often used to resolve disputes among them. Barkin was impressed with this European approach to interest-group cooperation, as would be expected from someone with his experiences, and he tried to promote its use in the United States. Instead, the United States seems determined to rely on markets to solve its social cost problems, no matter what the cost, as was evident in the Bush Administration's energy policy.

Barkin does not have such faith in markets. Rather, he falls into the camp of New Deal liberals in seeking a middle way between markets and statism by having a government-negotiated system of cooperative action by management and labor. This was an idea, of course, that predated the New Deal and was not limited to liberals. It is exemplified by Herbert Hoover's remarks to engineers in 1920: "If we could secure cooperation throughout all our economic groups we should have provided a new economic system, based on neither the capitalism of Adam Smith nor the socialism of Karl Marx."[7] Hoover, however, hoped for voluntary cooperation between American business and labor under government sanction. Barkin understood that business would never cooperate with labor unless government action pushed it in that direction.

As happens to those choosing the middle ground, Barkin can be criticized from both sides. The crude followers of Adam Smith would find most of Barkin's proposals to be subversive of the market allocation process; lacking Smith's compassion for workers, these free market conservatives would fault any policy that gave advantage to unions. To them, the primary function of markets is to provide an outlet for the competitive drives of humans. Humans, according to traditional economists, are motivated by self-interest, and competition in the marketplace serves to hold self-interest within reasonable bounds. In this view, markets are held separate from the rest of social action, and the concern for students of the market consists of the prices determined in each market by the forces of competition.

Modern industrial production requires cooperation as much as competition, however. Competitive transactions on an open market are oriented toward the short term: buy today, gone tomorrow. To address long-term goals, economic actors must get together and determine what those goals are as a preamble to doing something about them. The area of energy, for example, requires a joint decision among users and producers concerning how to maintain supplies and at what level. In the labor market, cooperation is essential if workers are to be maintained in good stead. Unfortunately, cooperation is not something that can be bought in a market transaction—it must be nurtured. The spirit that nurtures cooperation, nevertheless, cannot be made compatible with competition. Nor can it take place in markets where labor is in a subordinate position. Only when they are protected by unions can workers feel free to choose to cooperate, and only with government sanctioning of unions can unions become strong enough to protect workers.

The followers of Marx would be critical of Barkin and his idea of government-promoted union-management cooperation. There is a long history among Marxists of concern that unions, by making peace with management within the ground rules of capitalism, will help to inculcate a false consciousness among workers. This interpretation is the basis for the Marxian notion that unions had reached an accord with business in the postwar era. While the idea pervades Marxist and new left thinking, one example will make the point: "In what amounted to an effective quid pro quo, organized workers were deprived of their power to use industrial action (general strikes, sit-downs, secondary boycotts, etc.) in pursuit of class-wide gains; union resources and militance were directed instead to contestation over state policy and electoral politics. Thus, class conflict over minimum wage legislation, safety and health issues, provision of medical care, antidiscrimination policy, and so forth was deflected from the industrial to the state policy sector."[8]

From this view Barkin could be construed as a well-meaning tool of the capitalist class, who collaborated with the government to buy off the aristocrats of American labor and channel their militancy into safe streams. All his ideas, perhaps unwittingly, contributed to the demise of worker militancy. Trade union members, according to Marxists, are destined to lose their ideals.

Barkin would reject this characterization out of hand as typical of the rhetoric he faced from communists in the 1930s and 1940s. Moreover, it would be hard to characterize the dismal experiences of the TWUA as the result of an accord. In spite of this experience, Marxists might be tempted to assert that if Barkin had given Marxist thinking more careful consideration, he might have gained an earlier appreciation for the difficulties intrinsic to relying on government aid: What comes from the government depends on who controls it. This assertion ignores the question of what Barkin or any unionist might have done to change the outcome of conservative government policies. Trade unionists in the 1930s were aware that Roosevelt could withdraw his support of them at any time, and he did occasionally change his relations with them and resisted many of their demands. They could try to pressure Roosevelt, either directly or through friendly advisers, to see their view. The suspicion and caution behind Lewis's final break with Roosevelt in 1940 differed only in intensity from those felt by other labor leaders, at least in Barkin's view. The New Deal gave those leaders the only card they could play, and they played for all they could.

Sidney Hillman was once asked if he were steering unions into collusion with business and reducing the possibility for a social revolution. He answered, "Labor unions cannot function in the atmosphere of abstract theory alone. Men, women and children cannot wait for the millennium. They want to eat, mate, and have a breath of ease now. Certainly I believe in collaborating with employers! That is what a union is for. I even believe in helping an employer function more productively, for then we have a claim to higher wages, shorter hours, and greater participation in the benefits of a smooth industrial machine."[9] Hillman's credo for unions applies as well to Barkin. It is somewhat ironic that the accomplishment of attaining a wage- and benefit-package that enables workers to cover some of their social costs is viewed as a sellout to the bosses.

Barkin often professed that he was open-minded and willing to use any good ideas, no matter their source. In the case of Marxian analysis, however, he had a blind spot and remained opposed to any results that might be derived from it. Because Marxists reach analytical results that disparage the gains made by unions, Barkin's anti-Marxism is understandable. Marxists place great stock in the concept of working-class consciousness wherein workers see themselves as a class with class interests. How they will attain that consciousness is left vague, except for the Leninist idea that a professional revolutionary elite is necessary to teach it to them. Trade union officials, in the Marxian view, can impart to workers only a false consciousness that stresses the gains of the group or separate individuals. Workers have more of a chance of understanding their interests on their own than would under the guidance of union leaders and bureaucrats, so Marxists allege.

Richard Lester reports on a case that is pertinent to this issue. In the 1950s, a study of union and management officials found that both sides agreed that workers preferred wage increases over improved benefits. The author of the study attributed the final granting of benefits to sound union direction. As he described it, "Although shortsightedness prevailed among the rank and file, the officials, by exercise of proper leadership, never submitted such an absolute alternative [i.e., wages versus benefits] and hence never had to fear the shortsightedness nor face the possibility of disapproval."[10] By helping workers make decisions that were beneficial to them, even in light of their lack of information and analysis, as this case typifies, unions provide a service that Barkin finds valuable. Lester agreed, pointing out that union efforts to gain better benefits on behalf of workers was "one of the principal factors in replacing the commodity concept of employment with a social welfare conception of the employer-employee relationship."[11]

To Marxists, however, labor is and always will be a commodity under capitalism, and no granting of benefits can change that. With this attitude, Marxists interpret gains accruing to workers through union efforts, such as the case just cited, as a compromise of working-class principles through deals with management by union officials as opposed to evidence of their effective leadership as Barkin would construe it. Their position would make them and anyone who followed their arguments skeptical about Lester's conclusion that the commodity concept of employment was subsiding. Barkin already had that skepticism, however, for he perceived that management would always treat labor as a commodity unless forced to do otherwise, and no amount of accord with managaement would change its attitude. His analysis determined that it was up to unions with the help of government to compel management to stop treating workers like a commodity and that the way to do it was to push for the payment of wages that made businesses pay for the social costs involved with their production and bring about a rising standard of living and a fairer distribution of income.

Mention of social costs brings us to another criticism of Barkin's work. In the union movement, the payment of wages was based on a "quest for security." Too often this quest has been construed as selfish seeking by labor, for its own benefits, and completion of it has been identified with reducing the motivational aspects of the wage system. From society's perspective, the quest for security should have been considered a legitimate search for the proper allocation of all costs involved with production. Barkin comprehended the importance of this way of looking at the labor issue and severely criticized mainstream economics for neglecting it. As he wrote, in a review of Albert Rees's *Economics of Trade Unions*, "Many economists have recognized the importance of social overhead and personal costs in assessing the 'true' price of goods. But the market does not allow for those costs until the appropriate fringe benefits or taxes are imposed. Nowhere is this calculus of price and cost, so essential to economic judgements, alluded to in Rees's analysis. Isn't this form of total social business and personal accounting the appropriate setting for evaluating the 'economics of trade unions'?"[12]

Barkin's critique goes right to the heart of the issue of social costs. Nevertheless, it must immediately be asked, if mainstream economists were neglecting the concept of social costs in their interpretations of unions, why didn't Barkin do something about it? Why didn't he write his own "economics of trade unions"? The question is far from trivial, because unions were losing out by having society regard a reasonable request for a social cost wage as a selfish quest to protect their own members. The point may have been made from time to time in speeches by union leaders and in Barkin's many writings. It was never made definitively.

In terms of business's being able to pay better wages, Barkin had three arguments that set him apart from other labor economists. First was his dynamic theory of wages, wherein he held that high wages were an incentive for business to find ways to make workers more productive. Traditional economists might argue that this led to an overuse of capital in industries that were unionized, but in a unionized, high-wage economy, it would lead to greater use of capital in all industries. This is the path to economic growth that Barkin advocated. Few economists, aside from a smattering of Marxists, have followed up on this idea.

Second, in a less than fully unionized economy, the ability to pay higher wages depended on the market structure of the industry in which the firm was located. Barkin elaborated this notion in 1940–41[13] based on his experiences in the textile industry. He found that firms with market power were better targets for wage increases than firms facing competition. This is a very important idea that was not followed up in a consistent way until recent concern with wage-and-price relationships and dual labor markets and their impact on the macroeconomic problems of inflation and unemployment. Microeconomists in the areas of industrial organization and labor economics have not yet produced systematic treatises on this topic.

A third source of better wages for workers was in the redistribution of the shares of industrial production. As noted in Chapter Four, Barkin once proposed a system of accounting that used a method similar to the one used in national income accounting to show how national income is distributed. Under the proposed system, the share of corporate income going to different claimants—workers, managers, banks, and stockholders—would be reported. The aim of this proposal was to determine how much income was available in total to be divided up, including pay going to management, in order to ascertain the feasibility of giving workers more by taking away from other recipients of corporate proceeds. Most economists believe that the distribution of income results from each producer's marginal contribution to the output and revenue of the firm and that those individual contributions are independent. To Barkin, production is a joint undertaking, with one person's contribution depending on another's, so any distribution of income is subjective. Once the total available was known, unions would be better able to lay claim to a larger share for their members. This topic has become of great concern in recent years, especially as a recession has caused companies' profits, stockholders' dividends, and workers' wages to be cut, even as the salaries of top executives have continued to climb. An accounting system such as Barkin proposed would have clarified this result, but accountants never formulated one. To be fair, however, neither did Barkin.

Barkin might respond by maintaining that he was too busy with the press of other obligations, and as has been shown in this book, he was certainly busy. His activities and writings range over wide subjects, such that few individuals, or certainly this author, would be able to replicate his breadth of knowledge. Nor was that knowledge shallow in those areas. As Russell T. Fisher of the National Association of Cotton Manufacturers once begrudgingly complimented his union foe, "Mr. Barkin consistently puts on an unusually good performance as a witness, as he not only knows his story but is able to tell it."[14]

Barkin's knowledge and abilities did owe much to his personal talents, his Institutional approach was also an asset. As has been narrated throughout this book, institutional economics eschews any form of determinism. As a consequence, its method does not lead to any predetermined result. There is no tendency toward equilibrium as exists in the neoclassical paradigm, nor is there a disposition for classes to struggle as Marxists would have it. The only things certain are change and that adjustment to change must be made. An economist such as Barkin must be prepared to revise his ideas under the pressure of events and take those events one case at a time. General theories may be helpful to an institutionalist, but revisions are always in order. For this reason, Barkin had to continuously monitor the labor scene and to constantly add to his knowledge of it. This approach required him to attain expertise in many areas, as has been detailed, and it is to his credit that he did so. The well-worn paths of economic theory lead to good company, but not to better information about the problems workers face. Barkin used institutional economics and blazed his own trail, a tortuous one that led to an understanding of labor from a variety of perspectives.

In terms of telling the overall story of labor, Barkin displayed both the strengths and weaknesses of a polymath. He could argue in depth on an array of subjects, but he could not appreciate that others did not have his great diversity of knowledge and could not have all the insights into unions that he did. At the same time, his mental concentration was such that he could not focus on one topic long enough to produce a monograph. Thoughts fluttered too quickly through his highly active mind for him ever to be able sit patiently and at great length developing one idea, such as social costs as applied to labor, to its fullest extent. Yet it is safe to say that no one else associated with the union movement could have done the job. At least no one did.

In early 1953, after Walter Reuther had written asking him to consider a nomination as assistant secretary of labor, Barkin replied that he could not accept because of problems that existed at the TWUA. Then he added, in a telling phrase, "I am ever anxious to serve in whatever capacity."[15] The notion of service in the union cause was what motivated Barkin, but the union itself was merely a vehicle for a greater cause. As Barkin had written in 1949, "My early training and upbringing had emphasized the desirability of servicing the common man in his effort to realize his rightful place in a just society."[16] Unions were essential to establish this just society and to help workers find their rightful place in it.

Barkin remains above all else a social unionist, a term that distinguishes him from the business unionist on one hand and the revolutionary unionist on the other. His efforts were aimed at improving the income and social and political status of workers, and he was prepared to use trade unions, political lobbying, and social promotion to achieve the reforms that would accomplish such improvement. Unlike other proponents of industrial democracy, he has not given up on unions as a means for achieving a better society. The trade union movement was his ideal locale for operating. He understood its potential to accomplish social good and sought to influence the internal workings of the TWUA to make it an instrument for industrial change and improvement on behalf of workers. He wanted it to be more than a single-issue lobbying group and negotiator for higher wages. He felt it could be a secular force for bringing a spirit of idealism into the economics and politics of the United States This feeling has not been fully realized, because it is not one that has been held dear by management, union officials, intellectuals, or the general public of this country.

Throughout the eerie time of the Cold War and the harsh years of union-busting, Barkin had a tough-minded independence that kept his faith in unions and in the liberal spirit of the New Deal. With an intellectual outlook that stressed the constancy of change, he understood the importance of experimenting with programs and policies and revising them when they did not work. When union leaders and liberals were losing their vision in response to social change, he asked them to broaden their outlooks. He criticized union leaders as a way of warning them that unions without ideals are doomed to fail. Because he believed that by attaining a social cost wage unions had made capitalism tolerable by guaranteeing workers full and freely chosen employment, Barkin concluded that capitalism without unions is also bound to be a failure. Whether this conclusion will ever be grasped by society remains to be seen.

Notes

1. Cass R. Sunstein, *After the Rights Revolution* (Cambridge, MA: Harvard University Press, 1990), p. xi.

2. Solomon Barkin, ' "Full Productive and Freely Chosen Employment'—the ILO Program," *Labor Law Journal* (December 1961), pp. 1177–8.

3. Solomon Barkin, "Introduction," *International Joint Seminar on Geographical and Occupational Mobility of Manpower*, International Seminar, Final Report (Paris: OECD, 1963), p. 12.

4. Solomon Barkin, "Report by the Head of the Social Affairs Division on Its Activities for 1963–1967," January 9, 1967 (copy in author's possession), p. 6.

5. Ibid., pp. 8–9.

6. Ibid., p. 7.

7. Cited in Donald R. Stabile, "Herbert Hoover, the FAES and the AF of L," *Technology and Culture* 27 (October 1986), p. 822.

8. David M. Gordon, Richard Edwards, and Michael Reich, *Segmented Work, Divided Workers* (Cambridge, England: Cambridge University Press, 1982), p. 170.

9. Matthew Josephson, *Sidney Hillman: Stateman of American Labor* (Garden City, NY: Doubleday & Co., 1952), p. 439.

10. Allan I. Mendelsohn, "Fringe Benefits and Our Industrial Society," *Labor Law Journal* 7 (June 1956), p. 383, cited in Richard A. Lester, *As Unions Mature* (Princeton, NJ: Princeton University Press, 1958), p. 137.

11. Ibid., p. 138.

12. Solomon Barkin, review of *The Economics of Trade Unions,* by Albert Rees, *Industrial and Labor Relations Review* 16 (January 1963), p. 320.

13. Solomon Barkin, "Industrial Unions Wage Policies," *Plan Age VI* (January 1940), and "Wage Policies of Industrial Unions," *Harvard Business Review* (Spring 1941).

14. Cited in Hartford untitled manuscript, p. 7.

15. Solomon Barkin to Walter Reuther, January 19, 1953, copy in Barkin archives.

16. Solomon Barkin, "Why I Am in the Labor Movement," National Planning Association, Special Report No. 20, June 1947, p. 9.

Bibliography

The Works of Solomon Barkin

All references to Barkin's works made in the text are included in this listing, as are many other works not used. An almost complete collection of these works, along with other material related to Barkin's career, is located in the Special Collections of the library of the University of Massachusetts at Amherst.

1929

"The Normally Unemployed: A Neglected Phase of Unemployment," *American Federationist* 36 (November 1929), pp. 1328–34.

1930

New York State Commission on Old Age Security, Report, Old Age Security, Legislative Document (1930), no. 67, Albany, NY: J. B. Lyon Printers, p. 692 (author of chs. IV, VI-X, XIX—economic sections, and parts of XIII, XIV).

1932

"The Employment of the Older Worker," *Journal of the American Statistical Association* (March 1932), pp. 102–8.

1933

"Economic Difficulties of the Older Person," *Personnel Journal* 11 (April 1933), pp. 393–400.
"The Middle-Aged Worker—His Chances in Industry," Proceedings of the 6th Annual Conference on Old Age Security, American Association of Old Age Security, 1933, pp. 20–28.
"The Older Worker Adrift," *Social Security* (July 1933).
The Older Worker in Industry, a study of New York State Manufacturing Industries—a report to the Joint Legislative Committee on Unemployment, prepared under the aus-

pices of the Continuation Committee of the New York State Commission on Old Age Security, Legislative Document no. 66 (Albany, NY: J. B. Lyon Co., 1933), pp. 467.

1935

"Negotiating the Construction Code: History of Participation of Building Trades Organizations in Code-Making Under the NRA," *Proceedings, Twenty-seventh Annual Convention, Building Trades Department, American Federation of Labor,* Washington, D.C., 1935, pp. 49–53.

1936

"Child Labor Control Under the NRA," publications of the National Recovery Administration, Division of Review, Labor Studies, 1936.

"Collective Bargaining and Section 7(b) of the NIRA," *Annals of the American Academy of Social and Political Science* 187 (March 1936), pp. 169–75.

"Labor and the Codified Construction Industry Under NRA," *Proceedings, Twenty-eighth Annual Convention, Building Trades Department, American Federation of Labor,* Washington, D.C., 1936, pp. 3–24.

NRA Policies, Standards and Code Provisions on the Basic Weekly Hours of Work, National Recovery Administration, Division of Review, Labor Studies, 1936.

"Safety and Health Work Under the NRA," publications of the National Recovery Administration, Division of Review, Labor Studies, 1936.

"Wages and Hours in American Industry—NRA Source," publications of the National Recovery Administration, Division of Review, Labor Studies (3 vols.), 1936.

1937

"Regulation of Hours," *Plan Age* 7 (September 1937), pp. 170–79.

"Revival of NRA Labor Program," *Journal of Electrical Workers and Operators* 34 (March 1937), pp. 103–36.

"The Experience with the Labor Program Under the NIRA," *American Federationist* 44 (June 1937), pp. 596–601.

The Labor Program Under the NIRA, report prepared for the President's Committee on Industrial Analysis (Washington, DC: U.S. Government Printing Office, 1937).

1939

Brief presented in behalf of the TWOC in connection with the establishing of a minimum wage in the woolen and worsted industry, TWOC, New York, 1939, p. 29.

"Building a Union of Textile Workers," report of two years' progress to the Convention of United Textile Workers Organizing Committee (CIO), Philadelphia, Pennsylvania, May 1939, p. 79.

1940

"A Labor View of Management," *Daily News Record,* January 26, 1940, Textile Profits Issue, Sec. 2, pp. 12–13.

"Arbitration Supplants Strikes in Stopping Textile Stretchout," *Arbitration Journal* 4 (July 1940), pp. 85–90.

"Industrial Union Wage Policies," *Plan Age* 6 (January 1940), pp. 1–14.

"Technological Displacement and Problems in the Textile Industry," 66th Congress, 3rd Session, Temporary National Economic Committee, Concentration of Economic Power, Part 300, pp. 16, 667, 831–78, 17, 248, 433, "Testimony," vol. 11, April 22, 1940, pp. 16, 831, 17, 342, Washington, D.C., 1940.

"Technology and Labor" *Personnel Journal* 18 (January 1940), pp. 237–44.

1941

"Labor Union Research Department" *Personnel Journal* 19 (February 1941), pp. 290–99.

"Methods of Wage Adjustment—a Panel Discussion, the Point of View of Organized Labor," National Industrial Conference Board, *Studies in Personnel* 33 (1941), pp. 10–12.

"The Economics of Union Agreements," a review and commentary on *Union Policies and Industrial Management*, by Sumner H. Slichter, *Personnel Journal* 20 (October 1941) pp. 147–52.

"Union Strategy in Negotiations," *Collective Bargaining of Contracts* (Washington, DC: Bureau of National Affairs, 1941), pp. 23–34.

"Wage Policies of Industrial Unions," *Harvard Business Review* 19 (Spring 1941), pp. 342–51.

1942

"Arbitration of Job Assignment Disputes," *Arbitration Journal* 16 (Spring-Summer 1942), pp. 102–7.

Book review of *The Dynamics of Industrial Democracy*, by Clinton S. Golden and Harold J. Ruttenberg, *American Economic Review* 32 (September 1942), pp. 633–36.

"Labor Views the Working Day," *Advanced Management* VII (January-March 1942), pp. 32–37.

Statement on behalf of the Textile Workers Union of America on proposed wage increases for the Southern cotton textile industry, hearing before War Labor Board, May 25, 1942.

"Union Policies in Wartime," *Personnel Journal* 21 (June 1942), pp. 54–64.

1943

"Stimulating Production Through Labor-Management Cooperation," *Daily News Record*, January 28, 1943.

"Unions and Grievances," *Personnel Journal* 12 (June 1943), pp. 38–48.

1944

Book review of *Union Rights and Union Duties*, by Joel Seidman, *Management Review* XXXIII (December 1944), pp. 467–69.

"Cotton," 78th Congress, 2nd Session, House of Representatives Committee on Agriculture, Subcommittee on Cotton, Hearings, December 4, 1944, pp. 299–304.

"Labor Seeks Maintenance of Nation's War Gains," *Industrial Engineer* 4 (March 1944), pp. 7–8, 20–21.

Substandard Conditions of Living: A Study of the Cost of the Emergency Sustenance Budget in Five Textile Manufacturing Communities in January-February 1944," A TWUA Research Department Report, 1944, 91 pp.

"Substandard Wages," 78th Congress, 2nd Session, Senate Committee on Education and Labor, S Con Res 48, Part I, November 1, 1944, pp. 12–50.

1945

"Bargaining Table or Battle Field," *Labor and Nation* (December 1945), p. 69.

"Fair Labor Standards Act," 79th Congress, 1st Session, House Committee on Labor, Proposed Amendments to the Fair Labor Standards Act, October 1945, pp. 129–84.

"Reorganization of the U.S. Department of Labor," *Labor and Nation* (October 1945), pp. 15–17.

1946

"A Critical Evaluation of Some Phases of Incentive Wage and Time Study Techniques," *Modern Management* VI (July 1946), pp. 50–59.

"It Is Impractical to Limit Scope of Collective Bargaining," *Labor and Nation* (April-May 1946), p. 17.

"Labor Policy on Productivity Gains," *Commercial and Financial Chronicle*, December 12, 1946.

"Labor's Dilemma on Wage Price Policy," *Labor and Nation* (November-December 1946), pp. 20–22.

"Labor's Wage Policy in our Transitional Controlled Price Economy," *Advanced Management* XI (March 1946), pp. 17–20.

"National Collective Bargaining," *Personnel Journal* 25 (November 1946), pp. 150–60.

"Organized Labor's Stake in Industrial Engineering," *Modern Management* (July 1946), pp. 50–60.

"Regulation W and the Free Choice of Consumer Goods," Northern New Jersey Chapter, American Marketing Association Distribution-Credit Conference, December 10, 1946, pp. 69–72.

"Should It Be Wages Up or Down; Boost Wages," *Challenge* 9 (1946), pp. 34–40.

"Significant Changes in Wage Demands," *Labor and Nation* (February-March 1946), pp. 8–10.

"Testimony," Committee for Reciprocity Information on Proposed List of Textile Items Subject to Negotiations in Reciprocal Trade Agreement, Hearings, December 21, 1946.

"The Challenge of Annual Wages," *Personnel Journal* 24 (April 1946) pp. 269–73.

"Union Labor's Views in Wage Controversy," *Factory and Management* (February 1946).

"Wage Determination: Trick or Technique," *Labor and Nation* (November-December 1946), pp. 24–26, 53–54.

1947

"Adequate Industrial Statistics," *Proceedings of the American Statistical Association*, December 1947.

"America's Resources Sufficient to Meet All Needs," *Labor and Nation* (September-October 1947), pp. 46–48.

"Economic Outlook for 1947," *Commercial and Financial Chronicle*, January 29, 1947.

"Handling Work Assignment Changes," *Harvard Business Review* XXV (Summer 1947), pp. 473–82.

"Have Clothing Costs Risen Too High?" *American Forum of the Air*, September 30, 1947, pp. 3–9.

"Industrial Price and Production Policies Need Revision," *Commercial and Financial Chronicle*, April 3, 1947.

"Industry-Wide Bargaining Reduces Labor Strife," *Labor and Nation* (May-June 1947), pp. 41–42.

"Industry-Wide Collective Bargaining," *Labor and Nation* (March-April 1947), pp. 12–13.

"Joining the Issues on the Wage Controversy," *Labor and Nation* (January-February 1947), pp. 19–21.

"Labor-Government Cooperation as a Basis of Sound Price Policy," *Labor and Nation* (May-June 1947), pp. 11–13, 47.

"Labor's View of Safety Problems," *Journal of the American Insurance Institute* (April 1947), pp. 31–32.

"New Wage Levels and Fringe Benefits," *Proceedings of the American Statistical Association*, January 24, 1947.

"Report on Political Weather in Washington and the Labor Pressure Agent," *Labor and Nation* (September-October 1947), p. 8.

"Some Aspects of Industrial Relations," Proceedings of the Second National Textile Seminar, sponsored by the Philadelphia Textile Institute, May 12, 1947, pp. 191–99.

Testimony, 80th Congress, 1st Session, House Committee on Education and Labor, Subcommittee no. 4, Minimum Wage Standards, June-October 1947, vol. 1, pp. 132–77; vol. 2, pp. 1342–72; vol. 4, pp. 1780–1852.

"TWUA & Mills Smoke Peace Pipe," *Daily News Record*, January 28, 1947.

"Who's to Blame for High Prices," *The Nation*, August 16, 1947, pp. 164–65.

1948

Air Conditioning in Textile Mills, New York, TWUA, 1948, p. 60 (Coauthor, Franklin G. Bishop).

"As the Practitioners of Arbitration See Their Problems," Labor and Nation (July-August 1948), pp. 19–24.

Comments on article by Professor Robert Lynd, "Labor's Watching Its Step," *Labor and Nation* (January-February 1948), pp. 4, 41.

"Crisis in Western Civilization: The Survival of the Middle Course," New York, TWUA, 1948.

"Evaluation of the Arbitration of TWUA Cases" (187 cases from July 1947 to July 1948), TWUA Research Department publication.

"Labor's Attitude Toward Wage Incentive Plans," *Industrial and Labor Relations Review* 1 (July 1948), pp. 553–72.

"Labor's Field Notes," *Labor and Nation* (January-February 1948), p. 45; (July-August 1948), pp. 3, 48.

"Labour Utilization and Machinery," *Textile Mercury and Argus*, December 3, 1948, pp. 803–4.

"Monopolies, Laws and Collusion Bar Price Reductions and Full Employment," unpublished paper, TWUA, February 27, 1948.

"Price Reductions Not in Sight," *Labor and Nation* (March-April 1948), pp. 11–13.

"Relation of Wages to Productivity: A Union View," *American Management Association, Personnel Series no. 122* (September 1948), pp. 38–42.

"Social Crisis of Our Time," *Labor and Nation* (January-February 1948), pp. 17–19, 30.

"Symposium on Arbitration Issues in Labor-Management Disputes," *Labor and Nation* (July-August 1948), pp. 19–24.

The Nation's Most Prosperous Industry, an accounting of the postwar financial experience of American textile manufacturers, a TWUA Research Department Economic Report, January 1948.

Toward Fairer Labor Standards (Washington, DC: CIO Committee on the Revision of the Fair Labor Standards Act, 1948), 100 pp.

"Wages and Salaries," *Problems of our American Economy*, a digest of presentations, New York University, Workshop on Economic Education, 1948, pp. 21–22.

1949

"Accelerated Depreciation Would Mean Higher Prices, Higher Government Deficits and Less New Investment," a TWUA Research Department Report, November 1949.

"Applied Social Science in the American Trade-Union Movement," *Philosophy of Science* 16 (July 1949), pp. 193–97.

Book review of *Personnel Administration—A Point of View and a Method*, by Paul Pigors and Charles A. Myers, *American Economic Review* XXXIX (March 1949), pp. 575–77.

"Collective Bargaining—Law and Practice," *Labor and Nation* (September 1949), pp. 47–48, 94.

Conference on Productivity, Round Table Session, Washington D.C., February 11, 1949 (evaluation of the British textile industry).

"Regulation of Charitable Trusts," statement before Rhode Island Special Committee on Charitable Trusts, September 21, 1949.

"South Carolina Textiles: Southern Workers, Northern Bosses," a TWUA Economic Report, 1949.

Statement before the Massachusetts Special Commission on Textile Industry, October 31, 1949.

"Statistical Procedures in Union Administration." *Industrial and Labor Relations Review* 2 (April 1949), pp. 406–10.

Testimony, 81st Congress, 1st Session, House of Representatives, Committee on Ways and Means, Old Age Benefits, April 12, 1949.

Testimony, 81st Congress, 1st Session Senate, Senate Labor and Public Welfare Committee, Revision of Fair Labor Standards Act, April 12, 1949.

"Textile Barons Keep Southern Mill Hands in 'Their Place,' " TWUA Research Department Publication, June 29, 1949, p. 6.

"The Evaluation of the Arbitration of TWUA Cases," TWUA Research Department, October 19, 1949.

"The Imbalances in Our Private Economy: Present Danger Signals for the Future," paper, Eastern Annual Conference, American Association of Advertising Agencies, October 1949, pp. 2–6.

"The Importance of Cost Finding Information to Labor," *Journal of Accountancy* 87 (May 1949), pp. 373–77.

"The Problems Besetting Constructive Labor Relations," Proceedings of the Symposium on Industrial Relations, Toward More Constructive Labor Relations, University of Buffalo School of Business Administration, April 22–23, 1949, pp. 12–16.

"The Regional Significance of the Integration Movement in the Southern Textile Industry," *Southern Economic Journal* 15 (April 1949), pp. 395–411.

"Unemployment Among Marginal Labor Groups and Areas Must Be Highlighted in Era of High Employment," paper delivered before American Statistical Association, December 1949.

"Union's Viewpoint on Human Engineering and Relations," lecture, Society for the Advancement of Management, Providence, Rhode Island, Chapter, 1949–50.

"Wage Incentive Systems and Industrial Productivity," Proceedings of New York University, *Second Annual Conference on Labor*, 1949, pp. 189–213.

"Welfare Issues in Collective Bargaining," *American Management Association, Personnel Series, no. 131*, September 26–28, 1949, pp. 29–36.

"What Shall We Have—Retirement Benefit or Superannuation Plans?" *Proceedings of the 2nd Annual Conference, Industrial Relations Research Association*, 1949, pp. 138–47.

"What's Wrong with the Tax Law?—From the Viewpoint of Labor," *New York Certified Public Accountant* XIX (January 1949), pp. 9–12.

"Why I Am in the Labor Movement," *National Planning Association, Special Report, no. 20* (January 1949), pp. 6–10.

"Why Wage Increases in 1949," *Labor and Nation* (May-June 1949), pp. 15–16, 34.

1950

"A New Spirit of Economic and Political Expansion," *Labor and Nation* (Fall 1950), pp. 4–5.

"A Trade Unionist Appraises Management's Personnel Philosophy," *Harvard Business Review* XXVIII (September 1950), pp. 52–64 (also appearing in *Human Relations for Management*, ch. 17, pp. 361–72, New York: Harpers, 1956).

Book review of *Cotton Textile Wages in the United States and Great Britain*, by Donald Gibson, *Industrial and Labor Relations Review* 3 (April 1950), pp. 457–58.

Book review of *The Problem of Employment Stabilization*, by Bertil Ohlin, *Labor and Nation* (Summer 1950), p. 60.

"Bosses Better Learn Workers are Human Beings," *CIO News*, October 1, 1950, p. 5.

"How to Raise Real Wages," *Labor and Nation* (Summer 1950), pp. 7, 51.

"How to Raise Real Wages," *Labor Law Journal* 1 (October 1950), pp. 994–95, 1090.

"Human and Social Impact of Technical Changes," *Proceedings, 3rd Annual Meeting, Industrial Relations Research Association*, 1950, pp. 112–27.

"Public Policies in a Democracy to Realize Industrial Peace," Fifteenth Annual Economic Conference, Rollins College, Winter Park, Florida, February 1950, pp. 125–41.

"Some Problems of the Older Worker," *Proceedings of 3rd Annual Meeting, Industrial Relations Research Association*, 1950, pp. 1–3.

Statement before the Committee for Reciprocity Information, "Concerning Possible Tariff Concessions on Textile Items in the Negotiation of Reciprocal Trade Agreements," June 1, 1950, p. 19.

Statement on behalf of the CIO re: Tax Exemption of Charitable Foundations and Trusts, February 14, 1950, p. 27.

Statement, 81st Congress, 2nd Session, Senate Committee on Labor and Public Welfare, Subcommittee on Labor-Management Relations, S. Resolution 140, December 7, 1950, pp. 39–71.

"Tax Exemption of Charitable Foundations and Trusts," statement before Congress on behalf of CIO, February 14, 1950.

"The Metropolitan Collegiate School of Business and Organized Labor," in S. M. Middlebrook, ed. *Centennial Addresses* (New York: City College of New York, 1950) pp. 150–54.

"The Technical Engineering Service of an American Trade Union," *International Labor Review* XI (June 1950), pp. 609–36.

"Union Policies and the Older Worker," *The Aged and Society*, Industrial Relations Research Association, 1950, pp. 75–92.

1951

"American Trade-Unions in the Present Emergency," *Monthly Labor Review* 73 (October 1951), pp. 409–13.

"An Analytical Look at Labor—a Reply to Kermit Eby," *Labor and Nation* (Fall 1951), pp. 42–44.

"A Trade Unionist Views Net Income Determination," *NACA Bulletin* XXXII (June 1951), pp. 1193–1206.

"Basic Shortcomings of Defense Mobilization Program," *Labor and Nation* (Winter 1951), pp. 18–20.

Book review of *Effective Labor Arbitration*, by Thomas Kennedy, *Industrial and Labor Relations Review* 4 (July 1951), pp. 610–11.

"Evaluation of Recent Research on Employee Attitudes and Morale," *Proceedings, Industrial Relations Research Association 4th Annual Conference*, 1951.

"Expanding Functions of Union Research," "Preparing a Case for a Government Board," and "The Union Staff Functions, and Aims—Continually to Offer Advice," in J. B. S. Hardman and M. Neufeld, eds., *The House of Labor* (Englewood Cliffs, NJ: Prentice-Hall, 1951), pp. 23–67, 242–55, 500–503.

"Experiences in Collective Bargaining: Cooperation Substituted for Wage Incentives," *Labor and Nation* (Spring 1951), pp. 45–47.

"Financial Roots of the Current Textile Situation: A Survey of 1950 Financial Returns of Textile Companies," December 1951.

"Human and Social Impact of Technical Changes," *American Labor Review*, March 1, 1951, pp. 1–14.

"Labor-Management Relations in the Southern Textile Industry," hearings before Subcommittee on Labor-Management Relations of Senate Committee on Labor and Public Welfare, 81st Congress, 2nd Session, Senate Resolution No. 140, Part 2, pp. 39–71, December 1951.

"Management Insists on Wage Incentive Systems to Assure Its Own Efficiency," *Labor and Nation* (Summer 1951) pp. 53–55.

"Management's Attitude Toward Wage Incentive Systems," *Industrial and Labor Relations Review* V (October 1951), pp. 91–107.

"Redesigning Jobs in Industry for a Maturing Population," statement before the New York State Joint Legislative Committee on Problems of Aging, December 1951.

Statement, 82nd Congress, 1st Session, House of Representatives, Committee on Education and Labor, Consumer Price Index, hearings, May 1951, pp. 201–61.

"The Economic Revival of New England," *New Republic*, August 20, 1951.

"The New York Disability Benefits System," *Industrial and Labor Relations Review* 4 (April 1951), pp. 428–31.

"Trade Union Attitudes and Their Effect upon Productivity," *Industrial Productivity*, published by Industrial Relations Research Association, Champaign, Illinois, 1951, pp. 110–29.

Work Duty Charts for Textile Operations, TWUA Research Department, 1951, p. 216 (coauthor Franklin G. Bishop).

"Working Under WSB Regulations," TWUA Research Department publication, November 1951.

1952

Book review of *Financial Reports of Labor Unions*, by George Kozmetsky, *Industrial and Labor Relations Review* 5 (April 1952), pp. 62–63.

Book review of *The Economics of New England*, by Seymour Harris, *New Republic*, July 14, 1952.

Dissent from "Changing Concepts of Business Income," *Report of Study Group on Business Income* (New York: MacMillan Co., 1952), pp. 112–17.

"Factors Affecting Occupational Trends in Job Patterns," address before Columbia University Labor Seminar, February 1952, pp. 1–7.

"Factors Affecting Occupational Trends in Job Patterns," National Manpower Council, Labor Seminar, Report No. 6, May 29, 1952.

"Jobs for Older Workers," *Journal of Gerontology* 7 (July 1952), pp. 426–29.

"Labor's Code for a Private Enterprise Economy," *Labor Law Journal* 3 (December 1952), pp. 840–45.

"Labor's Code for a Private Enterprise Economy," *Manufacturing and Industrial Engineering* (May 1952), pp. 15–22.

"Labor's View on Actuarial Requirements for Pension Plans," Proceedings of Panel Meeting on "What Is Actuarial Soundness in a Pension Plan," December 29, 1952, pp. 26–39.

"Labour's Code for Private Enterprise," *Canadian Unionist* 26 (May 1952), pp. 134–36, 140.

"Opinion Surveys in Labor Management Relations," 7th Annual Conference of Public Opinion Research, Vassar College, Poughkeepsie, New York, June 14, 1952, p. 13.

"Redesigning Jobs in Industry for a Maturing Population," New York State Joint Legislative Committee on Problems of the Aging, Legislative Document No. 35, 1952, pp. 92–96.

"Should There Be a Fixed Retirement Age? Organized Labor Says No," *Annals of the American Academy of Political and Social Science* (January 1952), pp. 77–80.

Statement before the President's Commission on the Health Needs of the Nation, Philadelphia, Pennsylvania, August 11, 1952.

Statement before the Senate Committee on Banking and Currency on bills to amend and extend the Defense Production Act of 1950, Washington, D.C., 1952 pp. 2683–90.

Statement before the Surplus Manpower Committee, March 24, 1952, on the Textile Industry, *Congressional Record*, A2091-A2093.

"Studies in Trade Union History and Development," *Proceedings of the 5th Annual Meeting, Industrial Relations Research Association*, December 1952, pp. 1–7.

"The Casual Wage," an interview by Clive Howard in the *New York Herald Tribune*, November 9, 1952, pp. 13–14.

"The Future of Collective Bargaining," *Labor and Nation* (January-March 1952), pp. 45–46.

"The Sickness of a Region," book review of *The Economics of New England*, by Seymour Harris, *New Leader*, July 14, 1952, pp. 24–25.

"Unions' Dynamic Force in Industrial Relations," *Daily News Record*, January 2, 1952.

"What the ULPC Accomplished," *Institute of Social Studies Bulletin* 1 (January 1952), p. 38.

1953

"Concepts in the Measurement of Human Application," *Industrial and Labor Relations Review* 7 (October 1953), pp. 103–18.

Dissenting opinion in Bates Manufacturing Company decision (arbitration), TWUA Research Department, June 17, 1953.

"Financial Statements in Collective Bargaining," *New York Certified Public Accountant* XXIII (July 1953), pp. 446–49.

"Labor Facing Economic, Technological Change," *Labor and Nation* (Timely Papers) (Summer 1953), pp. 34–42.

"Labor's View on Actuarial Requirements for Pension Plans," 17th Annual Meeting, American Association of University Teachers of Insurance, *Journal of Association* 20 (March 1953), pp. 204–38.

"Management Personnel Philosophy and Activities in a Collective Bargaining Era," *Proceedings, 6th Annual Meeting, Industrial Relations Research Association*, Washington, D.C., December 1953, pp. 121–31.

"Should It Be Wages Up or Prices Down," *Challenge Magazine* 1 (June 1953), pp. 34–39.

"Techniques for Developing Job-Employee Coordination," address at the Conference on Age Barriers to Employment, Temple University, Philadelphia, Pennsylvania, Bureau of Economic and Business Research, June 1953, pp. 277–82.

Textile Workers Job Primer, Vol. I, TWUA Research Department Technical Report, 1953, p. 217 (coauthors, Franklin G. Bishop and Sumner Shapiro).

"The Trade Union Approach to Wage Incentive Plans," *Time and Motion Study*, London, England, June 1953, pp. 24–29.

"Trade-Unionism in the Republican Era," TWUA Research Department Report, February 1953, p. 26.

"Trade Unions in America and Australia," *Industrial Victoria* (November 1953), pp. 467–71 (from a broadcast).

"Trade Union Utilization of Quality Control Techniques," Proceedings of the 7th New England Quality Control Conference, November 1953, pp. 1–22.

"Workload Problems," address before Wharton School Conference, Labor's Approach to Production Standards, 1953.

1954

"A Labor Program for Full Employment," *Commercial and Financial Chronicle*, July 8, 1954.

"An American Trade Unionist Meets His Counterparts Abroad," *Congressional Record*, July 7, 1954, pp. A45363-A45364.

"An Evaluation of Personnel Philosophy," *Monthly Labor Review* (February 1954), pp. 153–55.

"An Evaluation of Predetermined Time Standard Systems," *Time and Motion Study* 3 (August 1954), pp. 24–32.

"Big Business Must Answer to the American People," *Proceedings of the 49th Annual Conference, League for Industrial Democracy*, New York, April 1954, pp. 18–26.

"Discussion," *American Economic Review, Proceedings, 67th Annual Meeting*, December 1954, pp. 351–53.

"Diversity of Time-Study Practice," *Industrial and Labor Relations Review* 7 (July 1954), pp. 534–49.

"Freedom in an Age of Bigness: A Critique of Big Business," address at Conference on Values in the American Tradition, Wellesley College, reprinted in *Commercial and Financial Chronicle*, December 30, 1954.

"Governmental Action Necessary for Full Employment," address, 12th Annual Summer Conference, Labor Education Association, Haverford College, Haverford, Pennsylvania, June 1954, reprinted in *Commercial and Financial Chronicle*, July 8, 1954.

"Job Protection After 40," *Journal of Living* (January 1954), pp. 11–14.

"Job Redesign: A Technique for an Era of Full Employment," in *Manpower in the United States: Problems and Policies*, William Habor, Frederick H. Harbison, Lawrence R. Klein, and Gladys L. Palmer eds., for the Industrial Relations Research Association (New York: Harper and Bros., 1954), pp. 39–50.

"Labor Unions and Workers' Rights in Jobs," ch. 8 of *Industrial Conflict*, Arthur Kornhauser, Robert Dubin, and Arthur M. Ross eds., (New York: McGraw-Hill Co., Inc., 1954), pp. 121–31.

"Modern Science and Management Creating a New Industrial Revolution," *Proceedings, 7th Annual Conference, Industrial Relations Research Association*, Detroit, Michigan, December 1954, pp. 1–9.

"Older Workers in Textile Industry Desperately Need Improved Social Security Legislation," testimony before the Senate Committee on Finance, *Congressional Record*, July 24, 1954, pp. A4886-A4888.

"Scientific Methods Tackle Work Assignment Problems," *Daily News Record*, January 21, 1954.

"Statement Concerning Possible Tariff Concessions on Textile Items in the Negotiation of Reciprocal Trade Agreements with Japan," testimony before the United States Tariff Commission, December 22, 1954.

Testimony before Task Force on Water Resources and Power of the Commission on Organization of the Executive Branch, hearings in U.S. Courthouse, New York, New York, June 1954.

Textile Workers' Job Primer, Supplement II—"Forms for Calculating the Frequency of Periodic Work Duties," TWUA Research Department Technical Report, 1954, p. 56.

"The Application of Quality Control Techniques in Determining Work Assignments and Standards," *Proceedings of the 8th Annual Conference, American Society for Quality Control*, June 1954, pp. 471–81, reprinted in *Industrial Quality Control* XII (December 1954).

"The New Labor Approaches to Industrial Engineering," *Manufacturing and Industrial Engineering* (November 1954), pp. 15–18, and Part II (December 1954), pp. 32–35.

"When Wage Incentive Plans?" *Personnel Practice Bulletin* X (September 1954), publication of Department of Labour and National Service, Australia.

1955

"American Imports," supplementary statement to the report on American imports, a study jointly sponsored by the Twentieth Century Fund and the National Planning Association (New York: Twentieth Century Fund, 1955).

"A Pattern for the Study of Industrial Human Relations," *Industrial and Labor Relations Review* 9 (October 1955), pp. 95–99.

"A Trade Union Viewpoint of Statistical Procedures in Industrial Engineering," address before the 6th Annual Conference of American Institute of Industrial Engineers, May 12, 1955, St. Louis, Missouri, reprinted in *Time and Motion Study* 4 (December 1955), p. 10.

Book review of *The Structure and Government of Labor Unions*, by Philip Taft, *Monthly Labor Review* (June 1955), pp. 694–95.

"Comments on Views of Adlai Stevenson on Relations of Business and Government," *Fortune* (November 1955).

"Depression in the Textile Industry and the Way Out," *Commercial and Financial Chronicle*, March 31, 1955.

"Fair Labor Standards Fact Sheets," CIO Fair Labor Standards Committee, 1955.

"Government's Role in Promoting Fair Labor Standards," *Commerce Journal* (University of Toronto Commerce Club, 1955).

"Human Relations in Industry in an Age of Automation," *Proceedings, 50th Anniversary Conference, League for Industrial Democracy*, New York, April 1955.

"International Trade Union Activity—Vehicle for Greater World Security," Aspen Institute for Humanistic Studies, Aspen, Colorado, August 1955, *Labor Law Journal* 6 (December 1955).

"In Textiles the Question Is Survival!" *Connecticut State CIO 1955 Yearbook*, pp. 17–18, 97.

"Labor Approaches to Industrial Engineering," *Labor Law Journal* 6 (February 1955).

"News and Notes," *Industrial and Labor Relations Review* 8 (January 1955), pp. 316–17.

"Productivity Changes in the Textile Industry," *Congressional Record*, May 2, 1955, p. A2888.

"Programs for Lifting the Status of Low-Income Groups," testimony before the Joint Committee on the Economic Report, Washington, D.C., November 23, 1955, pp. 696–709.

"Quality Control and Wage Incentives," *Proceedings, Annual Conference, Philadelphia Chapter, Society for Advancement of Management*, February 1955, p. 100–108.

"Quality Control Techniques—an Approach to Textile Work Assignments," Proceedings of Chattanooga Section, American Society of Quality Control, Conference, November 4, 1955, reprinted in *Time and Motion Study* 5 (April 1956), pp. 34–37, 46–47.

Statement before 84th Congress, House Committee on Education and Labor, on Amendment to Increase the Minimum Wage, June 1–30, 1955, pp. 419–37.

Statement before 84th Congress, Senate Committee on Labor and Public Welfare, Subcommittee to Investigate Unemployment or Causes of Unemployment in the Coal and Other Domestic Industries, March 7–April 20, 1955, pp. 359–422.

Statement before the Joint Committee on the Economic Report, January 27, 1955, pp. 200–206, 266, 292.

Statement before the Senate Committee on Finance, 84th Congress, on Trade Agreements Extension, March 15–18, 1955, pp. 1663–88.

Statement before the Senate Subcommittee on Antitrust and Monopoly, Senate Judiciary Committee, on Study of the Antitrust Laws, June 14–July 1, 1955, pp. 763–815.

Statement in rebuttal of Dr. Schmidt's testimony on Fair Labor Standards Act, before Subcommittee of the Senate Committee on Labor and Public Welfare, April 26–May 5, 1955, pp. 751–54.

"Textile Workers Need a $1.25 Minimum Wage," testimony before the Subcommittee of the Senate Committee on Labor and Public Welfare, April 22, 1955, Part I, pp. 305–448, and Part II, pp. 1541–48.

"Textile Workers Union of America Research Department," in "News and Notes," *Industrial and Labor Relations Review* 8 (January 1955), pp. 316–17.

"The Challenge to Automation," *The Nation* 181, December 10, 1955, pp. 510–12.

"The Merger Movement in the Textile Industry," testimony before the Subcommittee on Antitrust and Monopoly of the Senate Committee of the Judiciary of the 81st Congress, June 29, 1955, reprinted in the *Congressional Record*, August 1955.

"Unemployment in the Textile Industry," testimony (with supporting statements by TWUA representatives) before the Senate Committee on Labor and Public Welfare, Subcommittee to Investigate Unemployment, hearings, March 23, 1955, pp. 359–431.

"What Automation Means to America," *Factory Management and Maintenance* 113 (September 1955).

1956

"A Trade Unionist's Approach to Production Standards," *Trade Union Information Bulletin* 6 (European Productivity Association, January-February 1956), pp. 16–19.

Book review of *Money and Motivation: An Analysis of Incentives in Industry*, by William Foote Whyte, *Industrial and Labor Relations Review* 9 (July 1956), pp. 657–60.

"Discussion," *American Economic Review*, Papers and Proceedings, 69th Annual Meeting, American Economic Association, 1956, pp. 381–85.

"Human Relations in Industry—Collective Bargaining Provides the Best Framework," *Free Labor World* 7 (October 1956).

"Human Relations in the Trade Unions," ch. XIII, and "Commentary" to ch. VII, "Authority," by Herbert A. Simon, in Conrad Arensberg et al., *Research in Industrial Human Relations* (New York: Harper & Bros., 1956).

"Labor's Code for the Operation of Private Enterprise in Our Economy," Proceedings, Faculty-Alumni Seminar of School of Industrial and Labor Relations, Cornell University, New York, December 1956.

"New Industrial Giants in the Textile Industry," *Analysts Journal* (February 1956).

"Opinion Surveys in Labor Management Relations," Second Annual Conference on Public Opinion, Vassar College, Poughkeepsie, New York, June 13–16, 1956, p. 13.

"Organization of the Unorganized," *Proceedings of the Ninth Annual Meeting, Industrial Relations Research Association*, Cleveland, Ohio, December 1956, pp. 232–37.

"Quality Control and Wage Incentives," *Time and Motion Study* 5, London, England (January 1956), pp. 1–8.

Statement before the Committee for Reciprocity Information on the Proposed List of Textile Items Subject to Negotiations in Reciprocal Trade Agreements, hearings, December 21, 1956, p. 14.

Statement before the House Committee on Banking and Currency, 84th Congress, on Area Assistance Act of 1956, April 12–26, 1956, pp. 177–203.

Statement before the House Committee on Ways and Means, 84th Congress, on Administration and Operation of Customs and Tariff Laws and Trade Agreements Program, September 24–28, 1956, pp. 737–53.

Statement before the Senate Committee on Agriculture and Forestry, 84th Congress, on Foreign Trade in Cotton Textiles, July 16, 1956, pp. 24–28.

Statement before the Subcommittee on Labor of the Senate Committee on Labor and Public Welfare, 84th Congress, on Area Redevelopment, February 24–April 26, 1956, pp. 787–831.

Statement to the Committee for Reciprocity Information on Woolen and Worsted Tariffs, March 1956.

Statement to the Royal Commission of Canada's Economic Prospects, January 1956.

Testimony before the Subcommittee of the House Committee on Banking and Currency on Assistance to Depressed Areas, April 23, 1956, pp. 177–203.

"The Industrial Impact of the American Trade Union Movement," *Labor Law Journal* 7 (April 1956), pp. 216–24.

"The Merger Movement in the Textile Industry," statement before House Committee to Amend the Clayton Act Relating to Mergers, 84th Congress, pp. 102–18, printed in *Congressional Record*, March 14, 1956, pp. A2318-A2320.

1957

"American Cotton-Textile Industry and Foreign-Trade Policy," excerpt from the Compendium of Papers on U.S. Foreign Policy collected by the Staff for the

Subcommittee on Foreign Trade Policy of the Committee on Ways and Means, December 1957, pp. 837–72.

"Bankruptcy of Human Relations Personnel Programs," *IUD Digest* 3 (Winter 1957), pp. 77–84.

"Bankruptcy of Personnel Policy," *IUD Digest* 2 (Fall 1957), pp. 74–84.

Book review of *Human Relations in the Industrial Southeast: A Study of the Textile Industry*, by Glenn Gilman, *Industrial and Labor Relations Review* 10 (April 1957).

Book review of *Why Wages Rise*, by F. A. Harper, *Southern Economic Journal* XXIV (October 1957), pp. 202–5.

"Current Trade Union Crisis and Intra-Union Research," *Proceedings of the 10th Annual Meeting, Industrial Relations Research Association*, New York, New York, September 1957, pp. 242–48.

"Expansion of Governmental Responsibilities," hearings before Joint Economic Committee of Congress on Governmental Expenditures, November 18, 1957, pp. 39–74.

"Hearings on Proposals to Extend Coverage of Minimum Wage Protection," 85th Congress, before Subcommittee on Labor of the Senate Committee on Labor and Public Welfare, February 25–March 25, 1957, pp. 797–824.

"Industrialists, U.S. Blamed for Inflation," *Christian Science Monitor,* October 10, 1957.

"Labor Productivity and Prices," *Challenge Magazine* VI (December 1957), pp. 27–31.

"Labor Relations in the United States Textile Industry," *International Labor Review* LXXV (May 1957), pp. 391–411.

"Labor's Views on Medical Care," statement to panel on "Welfare Funds and Medical Care Plans," meeting of Kings County Medical Society, Brooklyn, New York, February 1957.

"Labor Views of Secondary Education's Goals," *Proceedings of the 2nd Annual Conference on Frontiers of Secondary Education*, Syracuse University, Syracuse, New York, July 17, 1957, pp. 40–50.

"Meaning of Three Studies to Labor on Older People and the Industrial Community." a report of the 1957 spring meeting, National Committee on the Aging of the National Social Welfare Assembly, 1957, New York, New York, pp. 5–7.

"Older People and the Industrial Community," National Committee on the Aging, report of 1957 spring meeting, "Meaning of Studies to Labor," pp. 5–7.

Statement before the 85th Congress, 2nd Session, House Ways and Means Committee, Renewal of Trade Agreements Act, "Historic Levels of Domestic Production," February 1957, Part I, pp. 758–86.

Statement before the 85th Congress, 2nd Session, Senate Committee on Finance, Trade Agreements Act Extension H.R. 12591, "Historic Levels of Domestic Production," June 30, 1957, Part II, pp. 1079–90.

Statement before the Subcommittee on Foreign Trade Policy, 85th Congress, 2nd Session, House Ways and Means Committee on Foreign Trade Policy, December 2–13, 1957, pp. 546–53, 644–47.

Statement before the Subcommittee on Production and Stabilization, Senate Banking and Currency Committee on Area Assistance Legislation, May 8, 1957, hearings, Part I, pp. 710–37.

Statement on Amendments to the Antidumping Act of 1921, before House Committee on Ways and Means, 85th Congress, July 29–31, 1957, pp. 164–68.

Statement on Area Redevelopment before Subcommittee of the Senate Banking and Currency Committee, 85th Congress, March 6–May 15, 1957.

Statement on Proposals to Extend Coverage of Minimum Wage before the Subcommittee on Labor of the Senate Committee on Labor and Public Welfare, 85th Congress, 1st Session, March 8, 1957, pp. 797–823.

"The American Textile Industry: Labor Conditions and Standards," a TWUA Research Department Report, April 15, 1957.

"The American Textiles Industry: Labour Conditions and Standards," Problems of the Textiles Industry in Europe, Final Report of the Milan Conference, EPA-OEEC, May 1957, pp. 53–55.

"The Bench-Mark Approach to Production Standards," *Industrial and Labor Relations Review* 10 (January 1957) pp. 222–36.

"The Shorter Work Week," papers delivered at the Conference on Shorter Hours of Work, sponsored by AFL and CIO, Public Affairs Press, Washington, D.C., 1957, pp. 21–24.

"The Trade Union Crisis and Intra-Union Research," *Trade Union Information*, EPA-OEEC, 1957, no. 16, pp. 16–19.

"Two Views on Why Wages Rise," *Southern Economic Journal* XXIV (October 1957), pp. 202–5.

"Wages and Inflation," *Challenge* VI (December 1957), pp. 27–31.

1958

Book review of *Introduction to Work Study* (Geneva: ILO, 1957), *Monthly Labor Review* 81 (January 1958).

Book review of *Work, Workers and Work Measurement*, by Adam Abruzzi, *Industrial and Labor Relations Review* 11 (April 1958).

"Expanded Government Capital Key to U.S. Economic Recovery," *AFL-CIO Free Trade Union News* 13 (June 1958).

"Implications of Developments in Automation for Our Economy," *American Economy*, Conference at Sarah Lawrence College, Joint Council on Economic Education, Bronxville, New York, August 1958, pp. 97–113.

"Is the Dupont Thrift Plan a Proper Way to Share Profits?" Solomon Barkin Archives, May 16, 1958.

"Maximum Employment and a Selective Economic Control Policy," statement before Joint Economic Committee in 85th Congress, 2nd Session, October 31, 1958, pp. 1–42.

"Meeting the Problems of the Shifting Location of American Industries," AFL-CIO Conference on the Changing Character of American Industry, Washington, D.C., January 1958, p. 13.

"Problems in Industrial Migration," *IUD Digest* 3 (Summer 1958), pp. 115–22.

"Problems Raised by Industrial Mobility," *Christian Science Monitor*, May 2, 3, 5, 6, 1958.

"Requirements for a Constructive Employer Industrial Relations Program," *Western Business Review* 2 (August 1958).

Statement before the House Banking and Currency Committee, May 1958, Area Re-employment Legislation, pp. 799–929.

Statement before the House Committee on Banking and Currency, 85th Congress, 2nd Session, April 14–May 22, 1958, Legislation to Relieve Unemployment, pp. 800–929.

Statement before the House Committee on Ways and Means, 85th Congress, 2nd Session, January 31–February 7, 1958, General Revenue Revision, pp. 3101–18, Need for Revision of the Internal Revenue Code of 1954 Relating to Carryovers of Net Operating Losses.

Statement before the House Ways and Means Committee, 85th Congress, 2nd Session, February 17–March 7, 1958, Renewal of Trade Agreements Act, pp. 758–86.

Statement before the Joint Economic Committee, "The Relationship of Prices to Economic Stability and Growth," October 31, 1958, 85th Congress, pp. 1–42, discussion, December 15, 1958, pp. 4420–29.

Statement before the Senate Committee on Finance, 85th Congress, June 27–July 3, 1958, Trade Agreements Act Extension, pp. 1079–90.

Statement before the Senate Subcommittee on Interstate and Foreign Commerce, Investigating the Problems of the Textile Industry, July 9, 1958.

Statement before the Subcommittee of the Committee on Interstate and Foreign Commerce, U.S. Senate, 85th Congress, December 2, 1958, "A Study of the Textile Industry of the United States," pp. 1893–1948.

Statement before the U.S. Tariff Commission on the petition of the Carpet Institute for escape clause relief for the Velvet and Wilton Carpet Industry, June 1958.

Statement in support of petition for determination of $1.165 minimum wage in the cotton, silk, and synthetic textile industry, Walsh-Healey Hearings, October 1958.

"Streamlined Operation Seen Altering Textile Labor Setup," *Daily News Record*, January 16, 1958.

"Textile Union Asks Denial of Acquired Loss Carryover Unless Business Is Continued," *Journal of Taxation* 8 (May 1958).

"The Depression: Causes and Prospects," *Jewish Frontier* XXV (April 1958).

"The Politics of Rising Prices," *New Leader*, December 1, 1958.

"The Significance of Minimum Wages for the Textile Industry," 20th Anniversary Conference of the Fair Labor Standards Act, December 4, 1958.

"Third Revolution Laid to Automation," *Christian Science Monitor*, October 11, 1958.

1959

"A Unionist's Program to Meet Inflationary Threat," *12th Annual NYU Conference on Labor, Proceedings*, May 1959, pp. 139–54.

Book review of *As Unions Mature: An Analysis of American Unionism*, by Richard Lester, *Social Research* 26 (Winter 1959), pp. 458–91.

Book review of *Labor and the New Deal*, by Milton Derber and Edwin Young, *Industrial and Labor Relations Review* 12 (April 1959), pp. 468–69.

Book review of *The Affluent Society*, by John Kenneth Galbraith, *Teachers College Record* 61 (October 1959).

"Dangers and Opportunities of Economic Growth," *Free Labour World* 105 (March 1959), pp. 110–13.

"Economic Policies for a Leader of the Free World," *Daedalus* 88 (Summer 1959), pp. 505–17.

"Exclusion from Taxable Income of Interest on Municipal Bonds to Subsidize Industry Should Be Discontinued," statement before the House Ways and Means Committee hearings, November 16, 1959, Tax Revision Compendium, 1, pp. 729–35.

"Implications of Developments in Automation for Our Economy," in Proceedings, "Impact of Contemporary Scientific and Technological Developments upon the American Economy," of the Science-Economics Workshop, sponsored by Joint Council on Economic Education in cooperation with National Council for the Social Studies, National Science Teachers Association, Sarah Lawrence College, Bronxville, New York, August 3–22, 1958, pub. 1959, pp. 97–113.

"More Implications of Automation," *IUD Digest* 4 (Fall 1959), pp. 115–23.

"Principles for Area Redevelopment Legislation," *Labor Law Journal* 10 (August 1959), pp. 525–33.

"Public Utility Regulation as Viewed by a Labor Economist," address at the Great Lakes Conference of Railroad and Utilities Commissioners, Greenbrier Hotel, White Sulphur Springs, West Virginia, June 24, 1959, printed in *National Utility Fortnightly* 64, pp. 297–300.

Statement before House Ways and Means Committee on Tax Exemption of Interest on State and Local Bonds, November 24, 1959, pp. 343–94.

"Structural Improvement Required in Our Economy," U.S. 86th Congress, 1st Session, Joint Economic Committee, January 1959, Economic Report of the President; hearings, February 3, 1959, pp. 299–310, 337–65, Washington, D.C., 1959.

Testimony before the House Subcommittee of the Committee on Government Operations to Amend the Employment Act of 1946, 86th Congress, 1st Session, Washington, D.C., April 1959, pp. 197–200.

Testimony before the Senate Subcommittee of the Committee on Banking and Currency, Area Redevelopment Act, U.S. 86th Congress, 1st Session, Part I, February 25, 26, 27, 1959, pp. 464–71, 655–806; Part II, pp. 979–83.

"The American Textile Industry: Labour Conditions and Standards," and discussion comments in Problems of the Textile Industry in Europe, Final Report of the Milan Conference, by Jacques Michollin, Paris, France, 1959, pp. 53–55, OEEC-EPA Trade Union Information and Research Service.

"The Function of Management," address at 6th Annual Personnel Institute, Labor and Industrial Relations Center, Michigan State University, East Lansing, Michigan, printed in *Business Topics* 8 (Winter 1960), pp. 28–44.

"The Personality Profile of American Southern Textile Workers," a study of industrial and cultural influences on personality, for the Fourth World Congress of Sociology, Stressa and Milan, Italy, September 8–15, 1959, printed in *Labor Law Journal* 11 (June 1960), pp. 457–72.

"The Principles and Guides for Adequate Area Development Legislation," U.S. 86th Congress, 1st Session, Area Redevelopment Act, hearings before Subcommittee No. 3 of House Committee on Banking and Currency, March 9, 1959, Washington, D.C., pp. 19–166, reprinted in *Congressional Record*, March 12, 1959, pp. A2136-A2138.

"The Textile Union Work Study Conference," *Monthly Labor Review* 82 (July 1959), pp. 761–63; also in *Trade Union Information Bulletin* 23 (European Productivity Agency, March-April 1959), pp. 6–9.

"Unemployment Problems," 86th Congress, Senate Special Committee on Unemployment Problems, S. Resolution 196, October 6, 1959, pp. 1440–72.

"Union Economic Researcher Calls U.S. Deficit Inflation Threat," *Christian Science Monitor*, January 5, 1959.

"Union Programs for Economic Development of North Carolina," address delivered at 2nd Annual Convention of North Carolina State AFL-CIO, March 27, 1959.

"U.S. Private Foreign Investment," 86th Congress, 1st Session, Senate Committee on Banking and Commerce, July 13–15, 1959, pp. 112–25.

1960

"A New Agenda for Labor," *Fortune* LXII (November 1960), pp. 249–55.

"Area Redevelopment—History and Comparison of Pending Bills," *Congressional Record*, March 29, 1960, pp. 1–8.

"Are Human Relations out of Date?" *Free Labor World* 121 (July 1960), pp. 281–87.

"As a Trade-Unionist Sees a Changing Work Force," address delivered before the National Industrial Conference Board, Waldorf-Astoria Hotel, New York, New York, May 20, 1960.

"Automation and Its Social and Economic Challenges," address delivered before the Society for the Advancement of Management, March 1960.

"Automation and the Community," address delivered at Governor's Conference on Automation, June 1, 2, 3, 1960, Cooperstown, New York, pp. 93–137.

"Education for Personal and Economic Growth in a Dynamic Technological Society," Proceedings of the 45th Professional Conference on Vocational and Practical Arts Education, State University of New York, Glens Falls, October 9, 1960.

"Employment Act Amendment, 86th Congress, 2nd Session, Senate Committee on Banking and Currency, Sen. 640 and 2382, February 24–26, 1960.

"Is the U.S. the Model for World Labor and Industrial Relations?" *Labor Law Journal* 11 (December 1960), pp. 1120–30.

"Outline of Considerations for the Formulation of a Trade Union Foreign Trade Policy," memorandum for speeches, April 18, 1960, p. 24.

"Price Control," testimony before Subcommittee on Production and Stabilization, Senate Committee on Banking and Currency, 86th Congress, 2nd Session, Employment Act Amendments, S. 64, February 25, 1960, pp. 268–322.

"Time Study and Statistical Quality Control," *Trade Union Information Bulletin* 28 (European Productivity Agency, June 1960), pp. 22–25.

"Trade Unionism: An Ethical Force in a Pecuniary Society," address delivered before the 10th Annual Conference of the International Association of Personnel Women, Statler Hotel, New York, New York, April 30, 1960.

"Trends and Problems in Textile and Garment World Trade," ITGWF, London, England, October 16, 1960.

"Unions Meet Automation, a Program for Action," Conference on Automation, sponsored by New York City Central Labor Council, November 29, 1960.

"Where Are the Teachers?" *Empire State Teacher* (March-April 1960).

1961

"Area Redevelopment," testimony before 87th Congress, 1st Session, House Subcommittee on Banking and Currency, Subcommittee No. 2, Area Redevelopment Act, HR 4569, March 1961, pp. 532–84.

"A Trade Union Approach to Foreign Trade," *Free Labor World* 128 (February 1961), pp. 51–57, 62.

Book review of *The Servants of Power: A History of the Use of Social Science in American Industry,* by Loren Baritz, *Monthly Labor Review* (March 1961), p. 293.

Book review of *The Steel Industry Wage Structure: A Study of the Union Management Job Evaluation Programs in the Basic Steel Industry*, by Jack Stieber, *American Economic Review* 51 (December 1961), pp. 1118–20.

"Economic Problems of Expanding and Declining Communities," *Social Action* XXVII (February 1961), pp. 5–13.

"Educating Students for Personal and Economic Growth," *American Vocational Journal* 36 (November 1961), pp. 17–21.

"Full Capacity Employment Essential to Maximum Economic Growth," statement before the International Labor Conference, June 14, 1961, printed in *Congressional Record*, June 26, 1961.

"Full Productive and Freely Chosen Employment," *IUD Digest* 6 (Winter 1961), pp. 97–108.

"International Trade in Textiles and Garments: A Challenge to New Policies," in Carl J. Friedrich and Seymour E. Harris, eds., *Public Policy, a Yearbook of the Graduate School of Public Administration* (Cambridge, MA: Harvard University, 1961), pp. 366–400.

"Psychology as Seen by a Trade Unionist," *Personnel Psychology* 14 (Autumn 1961), pp. 259–70.

"Rationalized Economic Relations with the Pacific Nations," Fourth Saint Mary's College (California) Symposium for Business and Industrial Executives, February 2, 1961, pp. 35–36.

"The Changing Work Force: Labor's Problems," *American Enterprise: The Next Ten Years*, Martin R. Gainsbrugh, ed., (New York: Macmillan Co., 1961), pp. 366–75.

The Decline of the Labor Movement and What Can Be Done About It, a report to the Center for the Study of Democratic Institutions, 1961.

"The Southern Textile Worker," *IUD Digest* 6 (Spring 1961), pp. 88–97.

"The Textile Industry in 1961: Its Problems and Needs," 87th Congress, 1st Session, Senate Interstate and Foreign Commerce Committee, Problems of the Domestic Textile Industry, hearings, February 6–7, 1961, pp. 286–340.

"Towards a 'Full Productive and Freely Chosen' Employment Economy," *OECD Trade Union Information*, no. 35 (1961), pp. 3–9.

"Towards an International Instrument on Full Employment," *Free Labor World* 135 (September 1961), pp. 379–82.

"Work Rules: A Phase of Collective Bargaining," *Labor Law Journal* 12 (May 1961), pp. 375–79.

1962

"Automation Gets a Union Boost," interview in *Christian Science Monitor*, April 27, 1962.

Book review of *Real Wages in Manufacturing, 1890–1914*, by Albert Rees, *Technology and Culture* III (Summer 1962).

Book review of *Trade Union Democracy in Western Europe*, by Walter Galenson, *Annals of the American Academy of Social and Political Science* 339 (January 1962), p. 192.

Comment from *The Worker in the New Industrial Environment*, a report of a seminar sponsored by the Institute of Labor and Industrial Relations, University of Michigan and the Foundation for Research on Human Behavior, 1962, pp. 12–13.

Comments on Clarence D. Long's paper "An Overview of Postwar Labor Market Developments," from *Proceedings of the 4th Annual Social Security Conference*, University of Michigan, published by W. E. Upjohn Institute for Employment Research, Kalamazoo, Michigan, July 1962, pp. 25–132.

Comments on Leo Teplow's paper on "Friends in Collective Bargaining," in *Symposium on Labor Relations Law*, Ralph Slovenko ed., Tulane University School of Law, New Orleans, Louisiana, 1962, pp. 20–22.

Comments, School of Labor and Industrial Relations, Section on Labor Relations Law, University of Michigan, 8th Annual Industrial Relations Conference, April 18–19, 1962, pp. 51–63.

"Differentiated National Labor Policies to Meet Present Problems," *Labor Law Journal* (September 1962) pp. 747–57.

"Full Employment on a World-Wide Scale," *Challenge* 10 (June 1962), pp. 37–41.

"Greater Shrinkage in Production Workers in the Textile Industry," *Commercial Bulletin*, September 22, 1962.

"Investment in Foreign Enterprises," *A Positive World Trade Policy for Labor*, International Association of Machinists, Washington, D.C., 1962, pp. 19–22.

"Labor's Position on Tariff Reduction," *Industrial Relations* 1 (May 1962), pp. 49–63.

"Making Democracy Work—Can the Labor Movement Be Revitalized?" *Current* 21 (January 1962) pp. 42–43.

"Southern Views of Unions," *Labor Today*, 2nd introductory issue (Fall 1962), pp. 31–36.

"Textile Research Plan Drafted," *Christian Science Monitor*, April 12, 1962.

"The Crisis of the American Trade Union Movement," *Report Card* X (May 1962), New York State School of Industrial and Labor Relations, Cornell University, Ithaca, New York.

"The Worker's Needs and Values," in *The Worker in the New Industrial Environment*, a report of a seminar, Foundation for Research in Human Behavior, 1962, pp. 12–15.

"Training for a Lifetime," *Free Labor World* 149 (November 1962), pp. 436–38.

1963

"An Active Manpower Policy," *Free Labor World* 161 (November 1963), pp. 11–15.

Book review of *The Economics of Trade Unions*, by Albert Rees, *Industrial and Labor Relations Review* 16 (January 1963), pp. 319–21.

Book review of *Trade Unions in an Age of Affluence*, by William Mierynk, *Annals of the American Academy of Social and Political Science* 349 (September 1963).

Coeditor, "The Crisis in the American Trade-Union Movement," *Annals of the American Academy of Political and Social Science* 350 (November 1963), p. 147 and the following chapters: "Foreword," pp. ix-xii (coauthor); "Is There a Crisis in the American Trade-Union Movement? The Trade Unionists' Views," pp. 16–24 (coauthor); "The Road to the Future: A Trade-Union Commission for Self-Analysis," pp. 138–47.

"Full Employment on a World Wide Scale," *American Journal of the U.S. Information Service in the Philippines* III (June 1963), pp. 65–72.

"Manpower Policies of the Organization for Economic Cooperation and Development," *Business Topics* 11 (Michigan State University, East Lansing, Michigan, Autumn 1963), pp. 7–16.

"New Labor Relations Policies and Remedies Suggested by Different Industrial Relations Settings," *Labor Law Journal* 14 (February 1963), pp. 166–77, and in Industrial Relations Research Association, *Proceedings of the Fifteenth Annual Meeting*, December 1962, Pittsburgh, Pennsylvania, pp. 220–36.

"New Roads in Industrial Relations," *Personnel Administration* 26 (January-February 1963), pp. 15–23.

Radio address: "Unions—Who Needs Them?" *Christian Science Monitor*, February 16, 1963.

"Sicherung des Soziales Besitzstandes bei Technischen Fortschrift in den U.S.A.," in Gunter Friedrichs, "Automation in der Technischer Fortschrut in Deutschland und den U.S.A," 1963, pp. 216–38.

"The Worker in the New Industrial Environment," *Industrial Medicine and Surgery* 32 (June 1963), pp. 214–15.

"Training for a Lifetime," *Eastern Worker* 3 (March 1963), pp. 91–94.

1964

"A Current Focus for Industrial Relations Research," presidential address, *Proceedings of the 17th Meeting of the Industrial Relations Research Association*, Chicago, Illinois, December 28–29, 1964, pp. 1–17.

Book review of *A Positive Labor Market Policy*, by E. Wright Bakke, *Industrial and Labor Relations Review* (October 1964).

Book review of *The Political Role of Labor in Developing Countries*, by Bruce H. Millen, *Annals of the American Academy of Political and Social Science* (January 1964), p. 216.

Book review of *The State of the Unions*, by Paul Jacobs, *Monthly Labor Review* (January 1964), p. 79.

Book review of *Trade Union Growth, Structure and Policy: Comparative Study of Cotton Unions in England*, by H. A. Turner, *Industrial and Labor Relations Review* (April 1964), pp. 495–98.

"Introduction" to OECD International Joint Seminar on Geographical and Occupational Mobility of Manpower, Castlefusano, November 19–22, 1963, final report, Paris, France, 1964, pp. 7–14.

"Job Redesign for Older Workers," address before the United Kingdom Ergonomics Research Society, April 6, 1964, abstracts of papers, pp. 2–3.

"Manpower and Social Aspects of Rural Redevelopment Programs," *Regional Rural Development Programmes with Special Emphasis on Depressed Agricultural Areas, Including Mountain Regions*, OECD, 1964, Agricultural Directorate Publication No. 66, pp. 157–64.

"Preface," OECD International Trade Union Seminar on Economic and Social Programming, final report, Paris, France, October 1964, pp. 5–6.

"Programming of Technical Changes and Manpower Adjustments," address before International Institute for Labor Studies Conference on Employment Problems of Automation and Advanced Technology, July 20–24, 1964.

"The Effects of Increased Productivity on the Labor Force and Its Deployment in the United States Textile Industry," address before the ILC meeting of Experts on Automation, March 16–25, 1964, printed in *Productivity Measurement Review*, OECD, No. 39, November 1964, pp. 39–57.

"The Evolution of the Concept of an Active Manpower Policy in O.E.C.D.," International Trade Union Seminar on Active Manpower Policy, Vienna, Austria, September 17–20, 1963, final report, Paris, France, 1964, pp. 5–6.

"Unions and Economics and Social Programming," in OECD International Trade Union Seminar on Economic and Social Programming, supplement to the final report, Paris, France, 1964, pp. 3–6.

"What's to Be Done for Labor? The Trade Unionists' Answer" (with A. Blum), *Labor Law Journal* 15 (March 1964), pp. 177–87.

1965

Book review of *Federal Aid to Depressed Areas: An Evaluation of the Area Redevelopment Administration*, by Sar A. Levitan, *Industrial and Labor Relations Review* 18 (April 1965), pp. 446–48.

Book review of *Fringe Benefits: Wages or Social Obligation*, by Donna Allen, *Industrial and Labor Relations Review* (October 1965).

Book review of *Transition to Automation: A Study of People, Production and Change*, by Otis Lipstreu and Kenneth A. Reed, *Annals of the American Academy of Political and Social Science* (March 1965), pp. 219–20.

Book review of *Unions in Emerging Societies: Frustration and Politics*, by Sidney C. Sufrin, *Annals of the American Academy of Political and Social Science* 359 (May 1965).

Book review of *Workers Council: A Study of Workplace Organization on Both Sides of the Iron Curtain*, by Adolf Sturmthal, *Annals of the American Academy of Political and Social Science* 362 (November 1965).

"Foreword" to Allain Touraine et al., *Workers' Attitudes to Technical Change* (Paris, France: OECD, 1965), pp. 7–10.

"Foreword" to OECD Secretariat, Social Affairs Division, *Acceptance and Resistance* (Paris, France: OECD, 1965), pp. 6–9.

"Industrial Relations Policy and Action-Oriented Research," *Monthly Labor Review* 88 (February 1965), pp. 142–43.

"Introduction," International Joint Seminar on *Adaptation of Rural and Foreign Workers to Industry*, Wiesbaden, West Germany, December 10–13, 1963, final report, OECD, Paris, France, 1965, pp. 5–9.

"Introduction," International Management Seminar on *Active Manpower Policy*, Brussels, Belgium, April 14–17, 1964, final report, OECD, Paris, France, 1965, pp. 7–11.

"Introduction," International Management Seminar on *Job Redesign and Occupational Training for Older Workers*, London, England, September 30–October 2, 1964, Final Report, OECD, Paris, France, 1965, pp. 5–8.

"Manpower and Management in an Automated Age," *OECD Observer* 14 (February 1965), pp. 21–24.

"Manpower Problems and Management in an Automated Age," North American Joint Conference on *The Requirements of Automated Jobs*, Washington, D.C., December 8–10, 1964, final report, OECD, Paris, France, 1965, pp. 53–63.

"Problem Rond Arbeids-Krachten en Leiding Geven in een Eeus Van Automatising," *Social Maanblad Arbeid* 20 (March 1965), pp. 17–20.

"Report on Activities of Social Affairs Division, OECD," *Industrial and Labor Relations Review* (October 1965).

"The Manpower Policies in O.E.C.D.," *Employment Service Review* 2 (March 1965), pp. 61–66.

1966

"A Systems Approach to Adjustments to Technical Change," International Conference on *Methods of Adjustment of Workers to Technical Change at the Plant Level*, November 1966, reprinted in *Labor Law Journal* 8 (January 1966), pp. 29–36.

Book review of *Europe and the Dollar*, by Charles P. Kindleberger, *Monthly Labor Review* (October 1966).

Book review of *Manpower Policies for a Democratic Society*, by National Manpower Council, *Social Work* (July 1966), pp. 114–16.

"Foreign Worker in Europe," *Britannica Book of the Year 1966*, pp. 281–83.

"Foreword" and "Conclusion," OECD International Seminar, *Manpower Aspects of Automation and Technical Change*, final report, OECD, Paris, France, 1966, pp. 7–9, 93–104.

"Foreword" and "The American Debate on the Poor," *Low Income Groups and Methods of Dealing with their Problems*, supplement to the final report, OECD, Paris, France, 1966, pp. 121–29.

"Foreword" to A. O. Smith, *Redundancy Practices in Four Industries*, OECD Social Affairs Division Publication, Paris, France, 1966, pp. 7–9.

"Foreword" to Bent Anderson, *Work or Support*, OECD Social Affairs Division Publication, Paris, France, 1966, pp. 9–12.

"Foreword" to OECD International Management Seminar, *The Public Employment Service and Management*, final report, and *The Evolving New Public Employment Agencies*, supplement, OECD, Paris, France, 1966, pp. 11–15.

"Industrial Change and Growth Area—from the Workers' Point of View," *Proceedings of the XIVth International Management Conference*, Rotterdam, Netherlands, 1966.

"Introduction" and "Concluding Address," OECD Regional Seminar on *The Employment of Older Workers*, final report, OECD, Paris, France, 1966, pp. 1–2, 33–36.

"Introduction" and "Foreword," OECD International Trade Union Seminar on *Non-Wage Incomes and Prices Policy*, final report and supplement, OECD, Paris, France, 1966, pp. 3–4.

"Regional Development and Active Manpower Policy," *Bedrigfsokonomen* 5 (1966), pp. 191–93.

"Significant Themes at the Madrid OECD Seminar," *Employment Service Review* 3 (March 1966), pp. 23–24.

"Trade Union Policies and Programmes for National Internal Rural Migrants and Foreign Workers," *International Migration* 4 (1966), pp. 3–19.

1967

Book review of *Automation and Economic Progress*, by Howard R. Bowen and Garth L. Mangum, and *Technology, Economic Growth and Public Policy*, by Richard B. Nelson et al., *Monthly Labor Review* (October 1967), pp. 86–87.

Book review of *Compulsory Arbitration and Government International Intervention in Labor Disputes*, by Herbert V. Northrup, *Annals of the American Academy of Political and Social Science* (May 1967), pp. 205–6.

Book review of *The Labor Revolution: Trade Unions in a New America*, by Gus Tyler, *Challenge* 5 (May-June 1967), pp. 44–45.

"Concluding Remarks," discussion of "International Experiences: U.S. Contributions and Contributions to the U.S. in Industrial Relations," *Proceedings of the Twentieth Meeting of the Industrial Relations Research Association*, Washington, D.C., December 28–29, 1967, pp. 239–41.

"Een Actier Arbeidsvoortzieningsbeleid voor Nederland," *Social Maanblad* 22 (July-August 1967), pp. 461–66.

"Foreword" and "Dimensions of an Active Manpower Policy," *Scandinavian Regional Seminar on Active Manpower Policy*, Oslo, Norway, November 23–24, 1965, final report, OECD, Paris, France, 1967, pp. 1–8.

"Foreword" and "Issues and New Policy Directives Suggested by the Seminar," OECD International Seminar, *Emigrant Workers Returning to Their Home Country*, Athens, Greece, October 18–21, 1966, final report, pp. 7–8, 81–87, and "Foreword" and "A Scheme for Analysis of Country Studies," supplemental Report, pp. 3, 71–72, OECD, Paris, France, 1967.

"Foreword" and "Major Issues and Conclusions," Regional Trade Union Seminar, *Geographical and Occupational Mobility of Workers in the Aircraft and Electronics Industry*, Paris, France, September 21–22, 1966, final report, pp. 507, 43–48, and "Introductory Statement and Questions" in supplement to final report, pp. 3–9, OECD, Paris, France, 1967.

"Foreword" and "Manpower Problems of an Expanding Sector," *Manpower Problems in the Service Sector*, background report of a trade union seminar, International Seminars, 1966, final report, OECD, Paris, France, 1967.

"Foreword" and "Personnel and Industrial Relations and Programmes: Part of an Integrated National Active Manpower Policy," OECD International Conference, *Adjustment of Workers to Technical Changes at the Plant Level*, Amsterdam, Netherlands, November 15–18, 1966, final report, OECD, Paris, France, 1967, pp. 95–111.

"Foreword" and "Preface," E. Jay Howenstine, *Compensatory Employment Programmes*, OECD, Paris, France, 1968, pp. 15–20.

"Foreword" and "Summaries of Sessions," OECD International Conference, *Adjustments of Workers to Technical Change at the Plant Level*, Amsterdam, Netherlands, November 15–18, 1966, supplement to final report, OECD, Paris, France, 1967, pp. 7, 41–42, 76–77, 114–15, 181–82, 225–26, 203–4, 352, 412–14, 470–71, 547–47.

"Foreword," Gertrude Williams, *Counseling for Special Groups*, OECD, Paris, France, 1967.

"Foreword," L. H. Klaassen, *Methods of Selecting Industries for Depressed Areas*, OECD, Paris, France, 1967, pp. 11–12.

"Human Values and Technology," statement before the International Conference, *Automation, Full Employment, and a Balanced Economy*, Rome, Italy, June 1967 (New York: Foundation on Automation and Employment Ltd., 1967).

International Labor (New York: Harper and Row, 1967), ed. and contributor, pp. 1–11, 249–69.

"Introduction," OECD Social Affairs Division Publication, *Promoting the Placement of Older Workers*, OECD, Paris, France, 1967.

"Introduction," Pierrette Sartin, *The Employment of Women in Spain*, OECD, Paris, France, 1967, p. 1.

"L'Homme en col blanc," *Janus* 14 (February 1967), pp. 85–91.

"Mankracht Een Verwaarloosde Factor?" *Mededelingenblad van de Vereningen van Afgestudeerden der Nederlandse Economische Hogeschool* 15 (1967), pp. 2–9.

"Manpower—a Neglected Factor," *Mededelingenblad van de Vereningen van Afgestudeerden der Nederlandse Economische Hogeschool* 15 (July-August 1967), pp. 1–9.

"Meeting the Demands of an Active Manpower Policy with the Assistance of the Academic Disciplines," *De Economist* 115 (1967), pp. 1–21.

"Preface," Maurice Lengelle, *The Growing Importance of the Service Sector in Member Countries*, OECD, Paris, France, 1967, pp. 1–2.

"Report by the Examiners," *Manpower and Social Policy in the Netherlands*, OECD, Paris, France, 1967, pp. 133–275 (coauthor, Bertil Olsen).

"Statement of Activities of Social Affairs Division of Manpower and Social Affairs Directorate," *Industrial and Labor Relations Review* (April 1967), pp. 537–38.

Negotiated Savings Plan for Capital Formation, final report, Regional Trade-Union Seminar, Florence, Italy, May 23–24, 1967, OECD, Paris, France, 1967 (with Derek Robinson).

Technical Change and Manpower Planning: Coordination at Enterprise Level, ed., OECD, Paris, France, 1967, p. 287.

"The Economic Costs and Benefits and Human Gains and Disadvantages of International Migration," *Journal of Human Resources* (Fall 1967), pp. 495–516.

"The Meaning for Social Policy of Structural Changes in the Labour Market," *International Rehabilitation Review* XVIII (October 1967), pp. 12–14.

The Role of Trade Unionism in Independent Developing Countries, ed., OECD, Paris, France, 1967, p. 162.

"The Social Setting for Modern Personnel Management," delivered at third International Conference, Stockholm, Sweden, June 19–22, 1967, European Association for Personnel Management.

"Vollbeschaftingung Freiheit und Wohlstand," *Arbeit und Wirtschaft* (1967).

"Workers' Attitudes to Industrial Change and Growth," *Management and Growth*, 14th International Management Congress of CIOS (Conseil International pour l'Organisation Scientifique), Rotterdam, Netherlands, September 19–23, 1967 (Rotterdam, Netherlands: Rotterdam University Press, 1967), pp. 358–61.

1968

Book review of *Manpower and the Public Employment Service*, by Alfred L. Green, *Industrial and Labor Relations Review* 21 (April 1968), pp. 463–64.

Book review of *The Common Market's Labor Program*, by Mark J. Fitzgerald, *Annals of The American Academy of Political and Social Sciences* (March 1968), pp. 195–96.

Book review of *The New Sweden: The Challenge of a Disciplined Democracy*, by Frederick Fleisher, and *The Social Program of Sweden: A Search for Security in a Free Society*, by Albert H. Rosenthal, *Journal of Economic Issues* 2 (June 1968), pp. 246–49.

"Foreword," OECD Regional Trade Union Seminar, *Negotiated Workers' Savings Plans for Capital Formation*, Florence, Italy, May 23–24, 1967, final report, OECD, Paris, France, 1968, pp. 3–4.

"Issues and Research Needs Relative to Manpower," Solomon Barkin et al., eds., *International Labor* (New York: Harper and Row, 1968), pp. 249–69.

"Main Issues in Trade Union Housing Policy," OECD Regional Trade Union Seminar *The Role of Trade Unions in Housing*, Hamburg, West Germany, January 17–19, 1967, final report, OECD, Paris, France, 1968, pp. 7–13.

"Manpower Policy in a Labor-Scarce Economy" and "Summaries of the Sessions of the Conference" OECD International Conference, *Employment Stabilization in a Growth Economy*, March 24–27 and October 1967, final report, OECD, Paris, France, 1968, pp. 9–21, 23–60.

"Retraining and Job Design—Positive Approaches to the Continued Employment of Older Workers," U.S. 90th Congress, 2nd Session, Senate Special Committee on Aging, Adequacy of Services for Older Workers (Washington, DC: U.S. Government Printing Office, 1968), pp. 206–11, 294–312.

"Worker Attitudes to Industry Change and Growth," *Free Labor World* 212 (February 1968), pp. 13–15.

1969

Book review of *Europe's Postwar Growth*, by Charles P. Kindleberger, *Journal of Human Resources* 4 (Fall 1969), pp. 523–24.

Book review of *Labor Relations in the Netherlands*, by John Windmuller, *Industrial and Labor Relations Review* 23 (October 1969), pp. 147–49.

Book review of *Manpower Tomorrow: Prospects and Priorities*, Irving H. Siegel, ed., *Industrial and Labor Relations Review* 22 (January 1969), pp. 288–89.

Book review of *The Political Imperative: The Corporate Character of Unions*, by Gus Tyler, *Annals of the American Academy of Political and Social Science* (May 1969), pp. 201–10.

"General Education for the Preparation for Work Life," OECD Regional Trade Union Seminar, *Education and Training for the Metal Workers of 1980*, Paris, France, October 8–11, 1968, final report, OECD, Paris, France, 1969, pp. 201–10.

"Industrial Automation," *Encyclopedia Americana*, 1969, p. 115.

"Mésures, prixes pour influencer ou modifier les courants migratoires, assister les migrants vers les zones urbaines," in United Nations Groupe d'experts sur les aspects sociaux des migrations de la compagnie vers les villes en Europe et problèmes connexes (New York: United Nations, 1969).

"Meeting the Inflation Problem," U.S. Bureau of Labor Statistics, *Proceedings of North American Conference on Labor Statistics*, June 19–20, 1969, Kiamesha Lake, New York (Washington, DC: U.S. Government Printing Office, 1971), pp. 295–304.

"The Resolution of Conflict," *Collective Bargaining Today*, Proceedings of May 1969 Collective Bargaining Forum (Washington DC: Bureau of National Affairs, 1970), pp. 82–97.

"Trade Unions Face a Western Capitalistic Society," *Journal of Economic Issues* 3 (March 1969), pp. 49–65.

"Workers and Union Participating in Decision-Making," in G. Sommers, ed., Industrial Relations Research Association, *Proceedings for Twenty-Second Annual Meeting*, December 29–30, 1969 (Madison, WI: Industrial Relations Research Association, 1970), pp. 62–63.

1970

"Manpower Policies: Scandinavian Experience," *Labor Law Journal* 8 (August 1970), pp. 534–43.

Manuscript of an address: "Labor Education and Manpower Policy."
Memorial addresses: Ben B. Seligman and Walter Reuther.
"Pension Systems and Continued Employment for the Aging," *Flexibility of Retirement Age*, OECD, Paris, France, 1970, pp. 7–20.
"Retraining and Job Design: Positive Approaches to the Continued Employment of Older Persons," in H. L. Sheppard, ed., *Toward an Industrial Gerontology* (Cambridge, MA: Schenkman, 1970), pp. 17–30.
Statement in U.S. 91st Congress, 1st Session, Special Committee on Aging, Subcommittee on Employment and Retirement Incomes, *Economics of Aging: Toward a Full Share in Abundance*, Hearings 9, Employment Aspects (Washington, DC: U.S. Government Printing Office, 1970), pp. 1417–20.
"The Social Setting for Modern Personnel Management," M. Ivens, ed., *Industries and Values* (London: George G. Harrap, 1970), pp. 210–22.
Translation into Greek of "Trade Unions Face a New Western Capitalist Society," *Epitheoresis Koinonikon Ereynon: Revue de Recherches Sociales*, 1970, pp. 222–34.
"Wage Incentive Problems in Arbitration," *Labor Law Journal* 21 (January 1970), pp. 20–27.

1971

Book review of *Education and Jobs: The Great Training Robbery*, by I. Berg, *Journal of Economic Literature* 9 (June 1971), pp. 523–24.
Book review of *Labor and the American Community*, by Derek C. Bok and John T. Dunlop, *Labor History* 12 (Fall 1971), pp. 629–30.
Book review of *Labor Relations and the Law in West Germany and the United States* and *Labor Relations and the Law in Belgium and the United States*, by Seyfarth, Shaw, Fairweather, and Geraldson, *Annals of the American Academy of Political and Social Science* 393 (January 1971), p. 192.
Book review of *Migrants in Europe: Problems of Acceptance and Adjustment*, by A. M. Rose, *Industrial Labor Relations Review* 26 (July 1971), pp. 637–39.
Book review of *Trends in Industrial Relations Systems of Continental Europe*, by Paul Malles, *Industrial Relations* 2 (April 1971), pp. 508–10.
Book review of *Western European Labor and the American Corporation*, Alfred Kamin, ed., *Monthly Labor Review* 94 (April 1971), pp. 83–84.
"Trade Unionism in an Age of Pluralism and Structural Change," *Rélations Industrielles* 26 (December 1971), pp. 801–28.

1972

Book review of *Regional Problems and Policies in Italy and France*, by Allen Kevin and M. C. MacLennan, *Annals of the American Academy of Political and Social Science* 402 (July 1972), pp. 196–97.
Book review of *Wage Restraint: A Study of Income Policies in Western Europe*, by Lloyd Ulman and Robert J. Flanagan, *Annals of the American Academy of Political and Social Science* 403 (September 1972), pp. 228–30.
Manpower Policy in Norway: Reviews of Manpower and Social Policies (Paris: OECD, 1972).
"The Social Industrial State," address before National Council for the Social Studies, November 24, 1972.
"Wages, Prices and Inflation," address before ILGWU Educational Conference, March 10–12, 1972.

1973

"A Rounded Cost-Benefit Approach to World Trade" (unpublished manuscript).

Book review of *Industrial Relations in the Common Market*, by Campbell Balfour, and *Labor Movements in the Common Market Countries and Growth of a European Pressure Group*, by Marguerite Bouvard, *Monthly Labor Review* 96 (April 1973) pp. 87–89.

Book review of *Welfare and Strikes: The Use of Public Funds to Support Strikers*, by A. J. Theiblot Jr. and Ronald M. Cowin, *Journal of Business* 46 (October 1973), pp. 644–45.

Book review of *Worker's Control: A Reader in Labor and Social Change*, by Gerry Hunnus, David Garson, and John Case, *Labor History* 14 (Fall 1973), pp. 653–55.

"Changing Profile of European Manpower Policies," in Gerald Somers, ed., *The Next Twenty-Five Years of Industrial Relations* (Madison, WI: Industrial Relations Research Association, 1973), pp. 83–100.

"State Manpower Office Responsibilities," *Labor Law Journal* 24 (January 1973), pp. 12–23.

"Trade Unionism and Consumerism," *Journal of Economic Issues* 7 (June 1973), pp. 317–21.

1974

Book review of *Trade Unions and National Economic Policy,*, by Jack Barbash, *Industrial and Labor Relations Review* 27 (January 1974), pp. 313–15.

1975

Book review of *Import of Labor: The Case of the Netherlands*, by Adriana Marshall, *Labor History* 6 (Summer 1975), pp. 439–42.

Industrial Relations Chronologies: No. 1 United Kingdom (Amherst, MA: University of Massachusetts Labor Relation Research Center, 1975).

Worker Militancy and Its Consequences, 1965–75: New Directions in Western Industrial Relations (New York: Praeger Publishers, 1975), p. 408, ed. and contributor.

1976

Book review of *Trade Unionism*, by J. A. Banks, *Industrial and Labor Relations Review* 29 (January 1976), pp. 313–14.

Book review of *White Collar Union: The Story of the OPEIU and Its People*, by John E. Finley, *Labor History* (Summer 1976), pp. 445–50.

"Diversity of Industrial Relations Patterns," *Labor Law Journal* 27 (November 1976), pp. 678–85.

Industrial Relations Chronologies: No. 2 Sweden (Amherst, MA: University of Massachusetts Labor Relations Research Center, 1976).

Industrial Relations Chronologies: No. 4 West Germany (Amherst, MA: University of Massachusetts Labor Relations Research Center, 1976).

"The American and Trade Union Credos," *Labor Center News*, Fall 1976.

1977

Book review of *Providing Adequate Retirement Income: Pension Reform in the United States and Abroad*, by James Schulz et al., *Journal of Economic Issues* 11 (March 1977), pp. 165–68.

"European Union Agreements Provide Framework for Public Policy," *Monthly Labor Review* 59 (January 1977), pp. 62–64.

Industrial Relations Chronologies: No. 5 Italy (Amherst, MA: University of Massachusetts Labor Relations Research Center, 1977).

Industrial Relations Chronologies: No. 3 The Netherlands, (Amherst, MA: University of Massachusetts Labor Relations Research Center, 1977).

"Labor Participation: A Way to Industrial Democracy," *Industrial Relations* (Canada) 33:3 (1977), pp. 391–405.

Papers and lecture outlines, Erasmus University, Rotterdam, Netherlands.

Swedish Active Manpower Policy: Its Evolution and Chronological Development (Amherst, MA: University of Massachusetts Labor Relations Research Center, 1977).

"The Social Contract Becomes the Bargaining Tool in Europe," *World of Work Review* (July 1977), pp. 81–83.

"The Social Contract in Europe," *Free Labor World* (May-June 1977), pp. 6–9.

"The Total Labor Package: From Wage Bargain to Social Contract," *Journal of Economic Issues* 11 (June 1977), pp. 339–51.

1978

Report to the International Labor Activities Division of the U.S. Department of Labor, Labor Market Adaptation Programs to International Trade in Two Western European Countries and the European Economic Community (the Netherlands, Iron and Steel Community, and France), unpublished, 1978.

"The Road to Industrial Democracy," *Free Labor World* (March-April 1978), pp. 16–17.

"The United States Collective Bargaining System," Derek Torrington, ed., *Comparative Industrial Relations in Europe* (Westport, CT: Greenwood Press, 1978), pp. 234–52.

1979

"Generating Opinion," *Business Week*, February 12, 1979.

1980

Book review of *Industrial Democracy in Western Europe: A North American Perspective*, by John Crispo, *Industrial and Labor Relations Review* 33 (April 1980), pp. 415–26.

"European Industrial Relations: A Resource for the Reconstruction of the American System," *Rélations Industrielles* 35:3 (1980), pp. 436–449.

1981

Book review of *Manpower Research and Labor Economics* George I. Swanson and Jan Michaelson, eds., *Journal of Economic Issues* XV (March 1981), pp. 249–52.

"Diversity and Common Challenges on the Western Collective Bargaining Scene," Occasional Papers in Industrial Relations no. 29, Industrial Relations Centre, Victoria University of Wellington, Wellington, New Zealand, 1981.

"Emerging Unemployment Problem in the Western World," proceedings of a seminar: "Challenge or Disaster? Industrial Relations in the 1980s," June 23, 1981, Hawkes Bay Community College, Wellington, New Zealand, pp. 23–38.

"Management and Ownership in the New England Cotton Textile Industry," *Journal of Economic Issues* XV (June 1981), pp. 463–75.

"Manpower Policy: An Instrument and Independent Policy System," Occasional Papers in Industrial Relations no. 30, Industrial Relations Centre, Victoria University of Wellington, Wellington, New Zealand, 1981.

"Productivity Measures in Collective Bargaining," *Rélations Industrielles* 36 (1981), pp. 361–70.

1982

Book review of *Making America Work: Productivity and Responsibility*, by James A. O'Toole, *Journal of Economic Issues* XVI (September 1982), pp. 894–98.

1983

Book review of *National Industrial Strategies and the World Economy* John Pinder, ed., *Journal of Economic Issues* XVII (September 1983), pp. 819–23.

"Troubled Workers Militancy: Challenges Confronting Western Industrial Systems," *Rélations Industrielles* 38, no. 3 (1983), pp. 713–72.

Worker Militancy and Its Consequences: The Changing Climate of Western Industrial Relations, 2nd ed. (New York: Praeger Publishers, 1983), p. 440.

1984

Book review of *The Economics of Work Reorganization*, by Marvin E. Rozen, *Journal of Economic Issues* XVIII (September 1984), pp. 958–62.

Interview: Helen M. Wise, "The Trade Union Movement: Studying the Past to Account for the Present" (contact: the University of Massachusetts at Amherst), IX (March-April 1984), pp. 32–34.

Statement: Memorandum on Conference Commemorating the 1934 Textile Strike and the First Years of the Textile Workers Organizing Committee, 1937–39, November 12, 1984.

1985

"An Agenda for the Revision of the American Industrial Relations System," *Labor Law Journal* 36 (November 1985), pp. 857–60.

Book review of *Women and Trade Unions in Eleven Industrial Countries*, Alice H. Cook, Val R. Lorwin, and Arlene Kapan Daniels, eds., *Journal of Economic Issues* XIX (June 1985), pp. 577–81.

Book review of *Years of Poverty and Years of Plenty*, by Greg J. Duncan et al., *Journal of Economic Issues* XIX (September 1985), pp. 876–80.

1986

Book review of *Industrial Relations in Europe: The Imperative of Change*, by B. C. Roberts, *Rélations Industrielles* 41 (October 1986) pp. 417–22.

Book review of *Inside the Circle: A Union Guide to QWL*, by Mike Parker, *Workplace Democracy* (Spring 1986).

Book review of *New Patterns of Work*, David Clutterback, ed., *Journal of Economic Issues* XX (December 1986), pp. 1164–67.

Book review of *Shifting Gears: Changing Labor Relations in the U.S. Automobile Industry*, by Harry C. Katz, *Journal of Economic Issues* XX (September 1986), pp. 875–80.

"Selected Aspects of the CIO Experience," *Proceedings of the Thirty-eighth Annual Meeting of the Industrial Relations Research Association,* 1986, pp. 187–94.
"The Current Unilateralist Counterattack on Unionism and Collective Bargaining," *Rélations Industrielles* 41:1 (1986) pp. 3–36.

1987

"The Flexibility Debate in Western Europe: The Current Drive to Restore Management's Rights over Personnel and Wages," *Rélations Industrielles* 42:1 (1987), pp. 12–43.

1988

Book review of *The Skeptical Economist,* by Eli Ginzburg, *Journal of Economic Issues* XXII (September 1988), pp. 911–14.
"Institutional Economics and the American Trade Union Movement," *Rélations Industrielles* 43:3 (1988) pp. 491–508.

1989

Book review of *The State of the Art in Industrial Relations,* by Gerard Hebert, Hem C. Jaim, and Noah M. Meltz, *Rélations Industrielles* 44:4 (1989), pp. 905–14.
"Human Resources Management Examines Itself and Its Limitations," *Rélations Industrielles* 44:3 (1988), pp. 691–700.

1990

"A New Environment Confronts Trade Unions in Advanced Industrial Countries: A Comparative Institutional Analysis," *U.S. Labor Relations 1945–1989: Accommodation and Conflict,* Bruce Nissen, ed. (New York: Garland Publishing, 1990), pp. 209–41.
Book review of *The Crisis of American Labor: Operation Dixie and the Defeat of the CIO,* by Barbara S. Griffiths, *Labor History* 31 (1990), pp. 378–85.

1992

Book review of *Hanging by a Thread: Social Change in Southern Textiles,* by Michael D. Schulman and Rhonda Zingraff, eds., *Labor History* 33 (January 1992), pp. 397–99.
Letter on Labor's Future in the United States, *Dissent* (Winter 1992).
"Organizing for the '90s," Labor Research Association's *Economic Notes* (January-February 1992), p. 12.
"Pure and Simple Unionism: An Adequate Base for Union Growth?" in George Strauss, Daniel G. Gallagher, and Jack Fiorito, eds., *The State of the Unions* (Madison, WI: Industrial Relations Research Association, 1992), pp. 353–60.

Other Works Cited

AFL-CIO Committee on the Evolution of Work, "The Changing Situation of Workers and Their Unions" (February 1985).

AFL-CIO, "Excessive Executive Pay," *AFL-CIO Reviews the Issues,* Report No. 42 (June 1990).

AFL-CIO, *The Pocketbook Issues* (Washington, DC: AFL-CIO, 1989).

Atleson, James B., *Values and Assumptions in American Labor-Law* (Amherst, MA: University of Massachusetts Press, 1983).

Baker, Richard, *Clockwork: Life Inside and Outside an American Factory* (Garden City, NY: Doubleday, 1976).

Bakke, E. Wright, "Some Basic Characteristics of Unions," *see* Bakke, Kerr, and Anrod (1967).

———, "To Join or Not to Join," *see* Bakke, Kerr and Anrod (1967).

———, "Why Workers Join Unions," *Personnel* 22 (July 1945), *see* Bakke, Kerr, and Anrod.

Bakke, E. Wright, Clark Kerr, and Charles W. Anrod, eds., *Unions, Management and the Public,* 3rd ed. (New York: Harcourt, Brace and World, Inc., 1967).

Bellante, Don, and Mark Jackson, *Labor Economics* (New York: McGraw-Hill Book Co., 1979).

Belous, Richard S., and Rebecca S. Hartley, "Regional Trading Blocs and International Trade: Challenges in the 1990s," *Looking Ahead* XI, no. 4 (1990).

Bernstein, Aaron, "In Search of the Vanishing Nest Egg," *Business Week,* July 30, 1990.

Bernstein, Irving, "Review of *The Decline of the Labor Movement and What Can Be Done About It?,*" *Industrial and Labor Relations Review* 15 (January 1963).

———, *The Turbulent Years* (Boston: Houghton Mifflin Co., 1970).

Blauner, Robert, *Alienation and Freedom* (Chicago: University of Chicago Press, 1964).

Bloom, Gordon F., and Herbert R. Northrup, *Economics of Labor Relations* (Homewood, IL: Richard D. Irwin, Inc., 1969).

Bluestone, Barry, and Bennett Harrison, *The Deindustrialization of America* (New York: Basic Books, 1982).

Bok, Derek C., and John T. Dunlop, *Labor and the American Community* (New York: Simon & Schuster, 1970).

Brody, David, "Labor History, Industrial Relations and the Crisis of American Labor," *Industrial and Labor Relations Review* 43 (October 1989).

———, *Workers in Industrial America* (New York: Oxford University Press, 1980).

Cary, Lorin Lee, "Middle-Echelon Labor Leaders and the Union-Building Process," Merl E. Reed, Leslie S. Hough, and Gary M. Fink, eds., *Southern Workers and Their Unions* (Westport, CT: Greenwood Press, 1981).

Chaison, Gary N., and Joseph B. Rose, "New Directions and Divergent Paths: The North American Labor Movements in Troubled Times," *Industrial Relations Research Association, Proceedings of the 1990 Spring Meeting,* May 2–4, 1990.

Chamberlain, Neil W., *The Union Challenge to Management Control* (New York: Archon Books, 1967).

Chase, Nan, "North Carolina's Beauty Masks a Bleak Social Reality," *Washington Post,* March 20, 1990, p. A4.

Clark, John Maurice, *Studies in the Economics of Overhead Costs* (Chicago: University of Chicago Press, 1923).

Columbia University Seminar on Labor, Minutes of Seventh Meeting, 1957–58.

Columbia University Seminar on Labor, Minutes of Third Meeting, 1957–58.

Columbia University Seminar on Labor, Minutes to Meeting, December 12, 1956.

Columbia University Seminar on Labor, Minutes to Meeting, December 18, 1957.

Columbia University Seminar on Labor, Minutes to Meeting, March 5, 1958.

Cornfield, David B., ed., *Workers, Managers and Technological Change* (New York: Plenum Press, 1987).

Dubofsky, Melvyn, and Warren Van Tine, eds., *Labor Leaders in America*, (Urbana and Chicago, IL: University of Illinois Press, 1987).

Dunlop, John, "Consensus and National Labor Policy," *see* Lester (1965).

Dunlop, John T., and James J. Healy, "The Grievance Procedure," Bakke, Kerr, and Anrod (1967).

Eatwell, John, *Whatever Happened to Britain?* (New York: Oxford University Press, 1982).

Edsall, Thomas Byrne, *The New Politics of Inequality* (New York: W. W. Norton and Co., 1984).

Edwards, Richard, Paolo Garonna, and Franz Todtling, *Unions in Crisis and Beyond: Perspectives from Six Countries* (Dover, MA: Auburn House Publishing Co., 1986).

"Eggheads Are Leaving Unions," *Nation's Business* (September 1963).

Fraser, Steven, "Sidney Hillman: Labor's Machievelli," *see* Dubofsky and Van Tine (1987).

————, "The 'Labor Question,' " *see* Fraser and Gerstle (1989).

Fraser, Steven, and Gary Gerstle, eds., *The Rise and Fall of the New Deal Order, 1930–1980* (Princeton, NJ: Princeton University Press, 1989).

Freeman, Richard B., "Does the New Generation of Labor Economists Know More Than the Old Generation?" *see* Kaufman (1988).

————, "Effects of Unions on the Economy," *see* Lipsett (1986).

Freeman, Richard B., and James L. Medhoff, *What Do Unions Do?* (New York: Basic Books, Inc., 1984).

"Free Trade with Mexico? Set a Safety Net," *Business Week*, November 12, 1990, p. 166.

Galbraith, John Kenneth, *American Capitalism: The Concept of Countervailing Power* (Boston: Houghton Mifflin Co., 1952).

Galenson, Walter, *The CIO Challenge to the AFL* (Cambridge, MA: Harvard University Press, 1960).

Garland, Susan B., "The Protector of Pensions Develops Its Biceps," *Business Week*, March 11, 1991, p. 80.

Gehan, Shaun, "Bargaining '90," *AFL-CIO Reviews the Issues*, 1990.

Goldberg, Arthur J., "Fallacies of the 'Labor Monopoly' Issue," *see* Bakke, Kerr, and Anrod (1967).

Goldfield, Michael, *The Decline of Organized Labor in the United States* (Chicago: University of Chicago Press, 1987).

Griffith, Barbara S., *The Crisis of American Labor: Operation Dixie and the Defeat of the CIO* (Philadelphia: Temple University Press, 1988).

Groshen, Erica L., "How Are Wages Determined?" *Economic Commentary*, Federal Reserve Bank of Cleveland, February 15, 1990.

Hamilton, Lee, "Tax Fairness," *Washington Post*, August 5, 1990.

Harris, Howell John, *The Right to Manage* (Madison, WI: University of Wisconsin Press, 1982).

Hartford, William F., "Unions, Labor Markets, and Deindustrialization," Kenneth Fones-Wolf and Martin Kaufman, eds., *Labor in Massachusetts: Selected Essays* (Westfield, MA: Institute for Massachusetts Studies, 1990).

Hoerr, John, "Business Shares the Blame for Workers' Low Skills," *Business Week*, June 25, 1990.

———, "With Job Training, a Little Dab Won't Do Ya," *Business Week*, September 24, 1990.

Hoxie, Robert F., *Trade Unionism in the United States* (New York: Appleton, Century, Crofts, Inc., 1921).

Josephson, Matthew, *Sidney Hillman: Statesman of American Labor* (New York: Double-day and Company, Inc., 1952).

Kaboolian, Linda, "Auto Workers Assess 'Employee Involvement,' " *Proceedings of the Forty-second Meeting, Industrial Relations Research Association*, December 1989.

Kapp, K. William, *Social Costs, Economic Development and Environmental Disruption*, J. E. Ullman, ed., (Washington, DC: University Press of America, 1983).

———, *Social Costs of Private Enterprise* (New York: Schocken Books, 1971).

Kassalow, Everett, Frederick Myers, and Charles Myers, eds., *International Labor* (New York: Harper and Row, 1968).

Kaufman, Bruce E., ed., *How Labor Markets Work* (Lexington, MA: Lexington Books, 1988).

———, "The Postwar View of Labor Markets and Wage Determination," *see* Kaufman (1988).

Kerr, Clark, "Economic Analysis and the Study of Industrial Relations," Clark Kerr, ed., *Labor Markets and Wage Determination: The Balkanization of Labor Markets and Other Essays* (Berkeley, CA: University of California Press, 1977).

———, Foreword to Solomon Barkin, *The Decline of the Labor Movement and What Can Be Done About It* (Santa Barbara, CA: Center for the Study of Democratic Institutions, 1961).

———, "Labor's Income Share and the Labor Movement," in Clark Kerr, ed., *Labor Markets and Wage Determination*.

———, "Labor's Share," *see* Bakke, Kerr, and Anrod.

———, *Marshall, Marx and Modern Times* (Cambridge, England: Cambridge University Press, 1969).

———, "The Balkanization of Labor Markets," *see* Bakke, Kerr, and Anrod.

———, "The Neoclassical Revisionists in Labor Economics (1940–1960)—R.I.P.," *see* Kaufman (1988).

Keynes, John Maynard, *The General Theory of Employment, Interest, and Money* (New York: Harcourt, Brace and World, 1965).

Kochan, Thomas A., Harry C. Katz, and Robert B. McKersie, *The Transformation of American Industrial Relations* (New York: Basic Books, Inc., 1986).

Labor-Management Cooperation: Recent Efforts and Results (Washington, DC: U.S. Bureau of Labor Statistics, 1982).

Laurie, Bruce, *Artisans into Workers* (New York: Noonday Press, 1989).

Lebergott, Stanley, *The Americans: An Economic Record* (New York: W. W. Norton and Co., 1984).

Lester, Richard A., *As Unions Mature: An Analysis of the Evolution of American Unionism* (Princeton, NJ: Princeton University Press, 1958).

———, "Labor Markets: Their Character and Consequences," *see* Lester (1965).

———, ed., *Labor: Readings on Major Issues* (New York: Random House, 1965).

Levitan, Sar, *Federal Aid to Depressed Areas: An Evaluation of the Area Redevelopment Administration* (Baltimore: Johns Hopkins University Press, 1964).

Levitan, Sar A., and Joyce K. Zickler, *The Quest for a Federal Manpower Partnership* (Cambridge, MA: Harvard University Press, 1974).

Lichtenstein, Nelson, "From Corporatism to Collective Bargaining: Organized Labor and the Eclipse of Social Democracy in the Postwar Era," see Fraser and Gerstle (1989).

———, "Walter Reuther and the Rise of Labor-Liberalism," Dubofsky and Van Tine (1987).

Lipsett, Seymour Martin, "In the Public Mind," *see* Lipsett (1986).

———, "The Historical Role of American Trade Unionism," *see* Lipsett (1986).

———, ed., *Unions in Transition* (San Francisco: ICS Press, 1986).

Marshall, F. Ray, *Labor in the South* (Cambridge, MA: Harvard University Press, 1967).

Mason, Edward S., "Labor Monopoly and All That," *see* Bakke, Kerr, and Anrod (1967).

McGregor, Douglas, *The Human Side of Enterprise* (New York: McGraw-Hill, 1960).

McNulty, Paul J., *The Origins and Development of Labor Economics* (Cambridge, MA: Massachusetts Institute of Technology Press, 1980).

Mitchell, Broadus, *Depression Decade* (New York: Harper Torchbooks, 1947).

Moody, Kim, *An Injury to All: The Decline of American Unionism* (London and New York: Verso, 1988).

Morin, Richard, "The Curious Politics of Greed and Envy," *Washington Post*, October 21, 1990.

Murray, Philip, "The Gap Between Wages and Prices," *Atlantic Monthly* (July 1948), reprinted in Arleigh P. Hess Jr., Robert H. Gallman, John P. Rice, and Carl Stern, *Outside Readings in Economics* (New York: Thomas Y. Crowell Co., 1951).

National Academy of Science–National Research Council, *Current Needs in Research Relevant to the Interests of the U.S. Textile Industry*, by Ad Hoc Textile Research Committee, March 1962.

Nelson-Horchler, Joani, "What's Your Boss Worth?" *Washington Post*, August 5, 1990.

Parker, Mike, *Inside the Circle: A Union Guide to QWL* (Boston: South End Press, 1985).

Perlman, Selig, "A Theory of the Labor Movement," Simon Larson and Bruce Nissen, eds., *Theories of the Labor Movement* (Detroit: Wayne State University Press, 1987).

Raskin, A. H., "Labor: A Movement in Search of a Mission," *see* Lipsett (1986).

Rayback, Joseph G., *A History of American Labor* (New York: Free Press, 1966).

"Reconversion in New England," *Monthly Labor Review* 63 (July 1946).

Rees, Albert, *The Economics of Trade Unions*, 3rd ed. (Chicago: University of Chicago Press, 1989).

Reynolds, Lloyd, "Competitive and Union Forces in the Labor Market," *see* Bakke, Kerr, and Anrod (1967).

Reynolds, Morgan, "The Case for Ending the Legal Privileges and Immunities of Trade Unions," *see* Lipsett (1986).

Rich, Spencer, "28% in U.S. Seen Lacking Steady Health Insurance," *Washington Post*, April 12, 1990.

Ross, Arthur M., "What Is Responsible Wage Policy," *see* Bakke, Kerr, and Anrod (1967).

Salvatore, Dominick, "The New Protectionism and the Threat to World Welfare: Editor's Introduction," *Journal of Policy Modeling* 7 (1985).

Schilling, George, "Less Hours, Increased Production—Greater Progress," *American Federationist* (October 1900).

Segal, Martin, "Post-Institutionalism in Labor Economics: The Forties and Fifties Revisited," *Industrial and Labor Relations Review* 39 (April 1986).

Siegel, Irving H., and Edgar Weinberg, *Labor-Management Cooperation: The American Experience* (Kalamazoo, MI: W. E. Upjohn Institute for Employment Research, 1982).

Seligman, Ben B., *Economics of Dissent* (Chicago: Quadrangle Books, 1968).

———, *Main Currents in Modern Economics* (New York: Free Press of Glencoe, 1962).

Shultz, George P., "Worker Participation on Productivity Problems," Frederick G. Leiseur, ed., *The Scanlon Plan: A Frontier in Labor-Management Cooperation* (Cambridge, MA: Massachusetts Institute of Technology Press, 1958).

Slichter, Sumner, *The American Economy: Its Problems and Prospects* (New York: Alfred A. Knopf, Inc., 1948).

———, *Union Policies and Industrial Management* (New York: Greenwood Press, 1968).

———, "Weakness on Individual Bargaining," *see* Bakke, Kerr, and Anrod (1967).

Slichter, Sumner H., James J. Healy, and E. Robert Livernash, *The Impact of Collective Bargaining on Management* (Washington: The Brookings Institution, 1960).

Smith, Adam, *An Inquiry into the Nature and Causes of the Wealth of Nations* (New York: Modern Library, 1937).

Soule, George, *Sidney Hillman* (New York: Macmillan Co., 1939).

Stabile, Donald R., "Herbert Hoover, the FAES and the AF of L," *Technology and Culture* 27 (October 1986).

———, *Prophets of Order: The Rise of the New Class, Technocracy and Socialism in America* (Boston: South End Press, 1984).

———, "The New Class and Capitalism: A Three-and-Three-Thirds-Class Model," *Review of Radical Political Economics* 15 (Winter 1983).

Staines, Gordon L., and Robert P. Quinn, "American Workers Evaluate the Quality of their Jobs," U.S. Bureau of Labor Statistics, *Labor-Management Cooperation*.

State Historical Society of Wisconsin, Textile Workers Union of America Oral History Project.

Staudohar, Paul D., *The Sports Industry and Collective Bargaining*, 2nd ed. (Ithaca, NY: ILR Press, 1989).

Sunstein, Cass R., *After the Rights Revolution: Reconceiving the Regulatory State* (Cambridge, MA: Harvard University Press, 1990).

Swaboda, Frank, "A Revised Manual for Keeping Out Unions," *Washington Post*, October 28, 1990.

"The Reminiscences of Solomon Barkin," Oral History Research Office, Columbia University, 1961.

"There's Nothing Universal About Plans for Universal Health Care," *Business Week*, January 22, 1990.

Tomlins, Christopher L., *The State and the Unions: Labor Relations, Law and the Organized Labor Movement in America 1880–1960* (Cambridge, England: Cambridge University Press, 1985).

Troy, Leo, "The Rise and Fall of American Trade Unions: The Labor Movement from FDR to RR," *see* Lipsett (1986).

"Union Self-Criticism," *New York Times*, December 6, 1961.

Vittoz, Stanley, *New Deal Labor Policy and the American Industrial Economy* (Chapel Hill, NC: The University of North Carolina Press, 1987).

Webb, Sidney and Beatrice, *Industrial Democracy* (London: Longmans, Green, 1920).

Wells, Donald M., *Empty Promises: Quality of Working Life Programs and the Labor Movement* (New York: Monthly Review Press, 1987).

Wilensky, Harold L., *Intellectuals in Labor Unions* (Glencoe, IL: Free Press, Publishers, 1956).

"Will Consumers Shop Away the Recession?" *Business Week*, March 19, 1990.

Witt, Matt, "Needed: A New Day for Labor," *Washington Post*, September 3, 1989.

Zaeger, Robert, "The Problem of Job Obsolescence: Working It out at River Works," U.S. Bureau of Labor Statistics, *Labor-Management Cooperation*.

Zeiger, Robert, *American Workers, American Unions, 1920–1985* (Baltimore: Johns Hopkins University Press, 1986).

Index

About the Author

Donald R. Stabile is professor of economics at St. Mary's College of Maryland. He holds a B.S. in business from the University of Florida and M.A. and Ph.D. degrees in economics from the University of Massachusetts at Amherst. Professor Stabile's scholarly work includes articles on the ideas of Thorstein Veblen, on scientific management and engineers, and on the public debt of the United States. He authored Prophets of Order: *The Rise of the New Class, Technocracy and Socialism in America* (1984) and coauthored *The Public Debt of the United States: An Historical Perspective, 1775–1990* (1991).